Siddika Berna Ors Yalcin (Ed.)

Radio Frequency Identification:

Security and Privacy Issues

6th International Workshop, RFIDSec 2010
Istanbul, Turkey, June 8-9, 2010
Revised Selected Papers

 Springer

Volume Editor

Siddika Berna Ors Yalcin
Istanbul Technical University
Faculty of Electrical and Electronics Engineering
Department of Electronics and Communication Engineering
34469 Maslak, Istanbul, Turkey
E-mail: siddika.ors@itu.edu.tr

Library of Congress Control Number: 2010937761

CR Subject Classification (1998): C.2, K.6.5, D.4.6, E.3, H.4, J.1

LNCS Sublibrary: SL 4 – Security and Cryptology

ISSN   0302-9743
ISBN-10   3-642-16821-3 Springer Berlin Heidelberg New York
ISBN-13   978-3-642-16821-5 Springer Berlin Heidelberg New York

springer.com

© Springer-Verlag Berlin Heidelberg 2010
Printed in Germany

Typesetting: Camera-ready by author, data conversion by Scientific Publishing Services, Chennai, India
Printed on acid-free paper   06/3180

Preface

RFIDSec 2010, the 6th workshop on RFID Security, was held in İstanbul, Turkey, June 8–9, 2010. The workshop was sponsored by the FP7 Project ICE (Grant Agreement No: 206546) of The Scientific and Technological Research Council of Turkey—National Research Institute of Electronics and Cryptology (TÜBİTAK-UEKAE).

The workshop attracted a record number of 47 submissions from 23 countries, of which the Program Committee selected 17 for publication in the workshop proceedings, resulting in an acceptance rate of 40%. The review process followed strict standards: each paper received at least three reviews. The Program Committee included 31 members representing 13 countries and 5 continents. These members were carefully selected to represent academia, industry, and government, as well as to include world-class experts in various research fields of interest to RFIDSec. The Program Committee was supported by 38 external reviewers.

Additionally, the workshop included three excellent invited talks. Ari Juels from RSA Laboratories discussed his vision of RFID security, in a talk entitled "The Physical Basis of RFID Security." Pim Tuyls from Intrinsic-ID described his experiences in a talk entitled "Hardware Intrinsic Security." Serge Vaudenay from EPFL discussed his vision of privacy in RFID systems in a talk entitled "Privacy Models for RFID Schemes."

I deeply thank A. Murat Apohan and Serhat Sağdıçoğlu, the General Chair and Co-chair of RFIDSec 2010, for their excellent and always timely work on managing the local organization and orchestrating conference logistics. I would like to deeply thank the Steering Committee of RFIDSec for their trust, constant support, guidance, and kind advice on many occasions. Special thanks go to Vincent Rijmen, Manfred Aigner, and Gildas Avoine, who were always first to respond to my questions and concerns, and often volunteered the advice and support needed to resolve a wide array of challenging issues associated with the fair, firm, and transparent management of the evaluation process.

Finally, I would like to profoundly thank and salute all the authors from all over the world who submitted their papers to this workshop, and entrusted us with a fair and objective evaluation of their work. I appreciate your creativity, hard work, and commitment to push forward the frontiers of science.

June 2010   Berna Örs

Organization

RFIDSec 2010 was organized by The Scientific and Technological Research Council of Turkey—National Research Institute of Electronics and Cryptology (TÜBİTAK-UEKAE).

Executive Committee

Conference Chair	A. Murat Apohan
	TÜBİTAK-UEKAE, Turkey
Conference Co-chair	Serhat Sağdıçoğlu
	TÜBİTAK-UEKAE, Turkey
Program Chair	Berna Örs
	İstanbul Technical University, Turkey
Local Organizations	Müzeyyen Gökçen Arslan
	TÜBİTAK-UEKAE, Turkey
	Hüseyin Demirci
	TÜBİTAK-UEKAE, Turkey

Program Committee

Manfred Aigner	TU Graz, Austria
Özgür B. Akan	Middle East Technical University, Turkey
Mete Akgün	TÜBİTAK-UEKAE, Turkey
Gildas Avoine	UCL, Louvain-la-Neuve, Belgium
Lejla Batina	Radboud University Nijmegen, The Netherlands and Katholieke Universiteit Leuven, Belgium
Mike Burmester	Florida State University, USA
Ufuk Çağlayan	Boğaziçi University, Turkey
Vanesa Daza	Universitat Pompeu Fabra, Catalonia, Spain
Stephan Engberg	Priway ApS, Denmark
Josep Domingo-Ferrer	Universitat Rovira i Virgili, Catalonia, Spain
Julio Cesar Hernandez-Castro	University of Portmouth, UK
Talha Işık	Middle East Technical University, Turkey
Christian Damsgaard Jensen	Technical Univerity of Denmark, Denmark
Yongki Lee	University of California, Los Angeles, USA
Kerstin Lemke-Rust	Ruhr Universitat Bochum, Germany
Antoni Martinez-Balleste	Universitat Rovira i Virgili, Catalonia, Spain
Florian Michahelles	ETHZ, Switzerland
David Molnar	Microsoft Research Redmond, USA

Axel Poschmann   Nanyang Technological University, Singapore
Damith Ranasinghe   University of Adelaide, Australia
Ahmad-Reza Sadeghi   Ruhr Universitat Bochum, Germany
Kazuo Sakiyama   The University of Electro Communications,
                                    Japan
Bernd Sieker   Universitat Bielefeld, Germany
Agusti Solanas   Rovira i Virgili University, Catalonia, Spain
Andrea Soppera   British Telecom, UK
Franois-Xavier Standaert   UC Louvain-la-Neuve, Belgium
Paul Syverson   Naval Research Laboratory, USA
Juan E. Tapiador   University of York, UK
Alp Üstündağ   İstanbul Technical University, Turkey
Avishai Wool   Tel Aviv University, Israel

Referees

Atakan Arslan   Selçuk Kavut   Pedro Peris-Lopez
Santoso Bagus   Yutaka Kawai   Thomas Plos
Selçuk Baktır   Chong-Hee Kim   Gökay Saldamlı
Muhammed Ali Bingöl   Mehmet Sabır Kiraz   Erkay Savaş
Sandra Dominikus   Miroslav Knezevic   Jorn Marc Schmidt
Özgür Ergül   Heiko Knospe   Ali Aydın Selçuk
Albert Fernndez-Mir   Benjamin Martin   Stefaan Seys
Flavio Garcia   Tania Martin   Dave Singelee
Yoshikazu Hanatani   Charlotte Miolane   Rolando Trujillo Rasua
Michael Hutter   Miyako Ohkubo   Pim Vullers
Orhun Kara   Yaman Özelçi   Christian Wachsmann
Süleyman Kardaş   Thomas Brochmann   Lei Wang
Timo Kasper   Pedersen   Erich Wenger

Sponsoring Institutions

The Scientific and Technological Research Council of Turkey—National Research Institute of Electronics and Cryptology (TÜBİTAK-UEKAE)
FP7 project ICE (Grant Agreement No: 206546)

Table of Contents

The Physical Basis of RFID Security

Ari Juels

RSA Laboratories, USA

Abstract. Data security is usually an exercise in crafting information flows. RFID tags' behavior, though, depends heavily on their physical environment. Because they are tiny, passive (i.e., battery-less) devices, issues such as power consumption, read range, and physical placement directly impact security and privacy for RFID tags. In this talk, I'll illustrate the physical basis of RFID security protocol design with a number of examples from recent research, namely: (1) Cloning of RFID-enabled travel documents, and how power calibration in readers can help prevent it; (2) How power-consumption characteristics of "computational" RFID tags inspire new trust models; (3) How physical tagging costs can act as an incentive for good behavior in supply chains; and (4) Why a physical view of RFID suggests that anti-tracking privacy, a mainstay of RFID security research, is probably futile.

S.B. Ors Yalcin (Ed.): RFIDSec 2010, LNCS 6370, p. 1, 2010.
© Springer-Verlag Berlin Heidelberg 2010

Still and Silent: Motion Detection for Enhanced RFID Security and Privacy without Changing the Usage Model

Nitesh Saxena and Jonathan Voris

Computer Science and Engineering
Polytechnic Institute of New York University

Abstract. Personal RFID devices – found, e.g., in access cards and contactless credit cards – are vulnerable to unauthorized reading, owner tracking and different types of relay attacks. We observe that accessing a personal RFID device fundamentally requires moving it in some manner (e.g., swiping an RFID access card in front of a reader). Determining whether or not the device is in motion can therefore provide enhanced security and privacy; the device will respond only when it is in motion, instead of doing so promiscuously. We investigate extending the concept of min-entropy from the realm of random number generation to achieve *motion detection* on an RFID device equipped with an accelerometer. Our approach is quite simple and well-suited for use on low-cost devices because the min-entropy of an accelerometer's distribution can be efficiently approximated. As opposed to alternative methods, our approach does not require any changes to the usage model expected of personal RFID devices.

Keywords: RFID; min-entropy; activity recognition; context recognition.

1 Introduction

The importance of inexpensive wireless devices, such as those utilizing Radio Frequency Identification (RFID) technology, continues to grow as their deployment in various applications and settings becomes increasingly common. These devices are primarily designed to be inexpensive and as such are equipped with minimalist hardware, often having just enough processing power and memory to achieve their primary function and perhaps also a few low-cost sensors, such as accelerometers and thermometers. Providing security and privacy services in systems consisting of such low cost appliances presents unique challenges due to their highly constrained nature. In order to keep hardware costs down, it is critical to use existing and inexpensive components for these devices as efficiently and in as many ways as possible.

RFID is a wireless technology designed primarily for computerized identification that has been growing in popularity as of late. An RFID infrastructure consists of two main components: tags and readers. Tags are small transponders that store data about their corresponding subject, such as a unique identifier.

S.B. Ors Yalcin (Ed.): RFIDSec 2010, LNCS 6370, pp. 2–21, 2010.

Readers are used to query these tags over a wireless radio channel. In most cases, tags are passive or semi-passive. This indicates that they derive the power to transmit data to a reader from the electromagnetic field generated when a reader issues a query to a tag. Additionally, tags typically have memory only in the range of 32 to 128 bits, perhaps just enough to store a unique identifier [15]. These ultra-low memory, computational, and power constraints are necessitated by the fact that RFID tags are designed to be placed ubiquitously in consumer products, appliances, and, in the case of implantable tokens, even users themselves.

RFID tags can already be found in a wide variety of personal devices, including access cards, contactless credit cards, passports, and driver's licenses. In many cases, RFID tags store sensitive personally identifiable information. For example, a US passport stores the name, nationality, date of birth, digital photograph, and (optionally) fingerprint of its user [12]. When stored on an RFID tag, such information can easily be subject to clandestine eavesdropping and unauthorized reading. This data can then be used in order to track the owner of the tag [11]. In addition, the information gleaned from an RFID enabled device may also be utilized to clone the tag, which provides adversaries with the capability to impersonate users [11].

Perhaps even more troubling is the fact that RFID tags are susceptible to "ghost-and-leech" relay attacks [17]. In this type of an attack, an adversary, called a "ghost," relays the information surreptitiously read from a legitimate RFID device to a colluding entity known as a "leech." The leech can then transmit the forwarded information to a corresponding legitimate reader and vice versa. Thus, a ghost and leech pair can succeed in impersonating a legitimate RFID device without actually possessing the device, which violates the security these devices are designed to provide. Although cryptography may be used to address the problem of promiscuous tag transmissions, ghost-and-leech attacks are more stubborn as all known reader-to-tag authentication protocols are vulnerable to this type of attack [7].

1.1   Research Challenges

The common thread among all of the threats to the security and privacy of RFID tags is that the owners of these devices are not in full control of when their tags transmit or which readers the tags transmit to. Techniques aiming to address this dilemma fall into three categories. First, tags could be equipped with a method of determining whether a given reader has been deemed safe to transmit to, which is called *reader-to-tag authentication. Tag-to-reader authentication*, on the other hand, can be used as a means to prevent tag cloning and impersonation. Of course, these overarching techniques are easier stated than achieved. Each comes with its own set of shortcomings and design challenges due to the minimalist capabilities of passive RFID tags. In particular, traditional cryptographic techniques may not be suitable for these tags. To this end, there has been a growing interest in designing novel lightweight cryptographic protocols [15,1,16,6].

Rather than having an RFID reader authenticate to the tags, tags can be programmed to detect what is occurring in their environment and only communicate when it makes sense to do so. This third strategy, which is the focus of this paper, is known as *context or activity recognition*. Context recognition can serve as a means of selective tag locking and unlocking and thus addresses the issues of tag privacy, unauthorized reading, and ghost-and-leech attacks. For example, a tag could be programmed to transmit only when it detects a valid context, such as when a user intends to enter his or her office building or make a payment. When not in a situation that is deemed to be relevant, the tag remains in a locked state. As with tag-to-reader and reader-to-tag authentication, activity recognition would be trivial to achieve if RFID tags were rich in computing resources. However, this is clearly not the case in practice. The resource constraints of RFID tags severely hamper the complexity of the algorithms that can be used to judge what activity a tag is undergoing. This process can be outsourced from the tag to the reader [2], but this only exacerbates the issue of reader trust.

Another obstacle confronting activity recognition is the lack of ways in which users can interact with their tags. RFID devices, in contrast to other personal devices, were designed to be as transparent as possible to their users, and as such do not possess any input or output interfaces, such as buttons, displays, or speakers. Furthermore, recall that these passive devices lack a power source of their own. Therefore, in terms of energy, they are wholly reliant on being activated by a reader. Having an intermittent power supply means that it is not possible for a tag to control precisely when it will be able to take readings using the few sensors it may have on board. This makes it very difficult for a tag to reliably receive data about its environment, in turn making activity recognition a challenging problem. Finally, it is very important that any form of context recognition must not alter the expected usage model of the devices they protect in any way. Even subtle changes may have an adverse effect on an RFID system's efficiency and usability, and may severely undermine the benefits the RFID technology was supposed to provide in the first place.

While the security and privacy challenges faced by RFID tags are not specific to this class of devices, their unique combination of minimalist hardware and an atypical usage model necessitates new solutions. In order to fully secure an RFID infrastructure, a combination of tag-to-reader authentication, reader-to-tag authentication, and context recognition might be necessary. The central research challenge presented by RFID tags is how to accomplish these objectives given their constraints and limitations. The focus of this paper is on developing a viable lightweight context recognition technique suitable for low cost RFID tags.

1.2   Overview of Contributions

RFID systems can generally be divided into two main categories in terms of mobility. In a *mobile reader system*, tags are immobilized by embedding them into stationary objects and a reader is carried around to read these tags at fixed locations. An example of this scenario is RFID tags that are encased in concrete at a construction site to monitor the substance's solidification progress [19]. In a *mobile tag environment*, on the other hand, tags are associated with free moving objects which are read when brought within the range of a fixed reading device. Personal RFID tags, found in contactless access cards and payment tokens, fall into this grouping. This paper focuses on providing improved security and privacy to RFID tags of the mobile variety.

We utilize a theoretical concept from the realm of random number generation, *min-entropy*, to address the issue of context recognition. Our proposal involves the estimation of the min-entropy of a sensor's sample distribution, specifically that of an accelerometer, as a way of performing a limited and simplistic kind of activity detection, which we dub *motion detection*. This approach hinges on the straightforward observation that accessing a personal mobile RFID device fundamentally involves moving it in some manner; the device needs to be brought close to the reader so that its contents can be read, which implies motion of some form. For example, an RFID access card is commonly swiped in front of an antenna in order for a reader to extract its contents. Thus, determining whether or not this type of device is in motion provides a means of controlled locking and unlocking, which in turn provides enhanced privacy as well as protection against ghost-and-leech relay attacks. Intuitively, when motion detection is in place, a device will only respond when it is mobile instead of doing so promiscuously. In other words, if the device is *still*, it remains *silent*. A working prototype implementation of this motion detection technique, on Intel's WISP tags [21,24], is provided and several associated experiments have been conducted as evidence of its applicability to low-cost RFID devices.

Motion detection, as a downside, is not capable of performing nearly as fine grained activity assessments as full fledged context recognition. However, we argue that this technique is sufficient for preventing some of the most common attacks on RFID devices. In fact, its simplicity is a boon in terms of the range of devices that are capable of supporting it. Moreover, and more importantly, as opposed to all recently proposed alternatives (we review these in Section 2), this approach does not require any changes to the usage model expected of typical RFID devices.

Although we demonstrate the viability of our motion detection method on low cost RFID devices, the method is not limited solely to RFID devices. It extends easily to more traditional mobile devices such as laptops, cell phones, personal fitness aids [18], MP3 players, and video game remote controls. Out of these, mobile phones, fitness aids, and video game controllers are the most likely to come pre-equipped with accelerometers.

Paper Organization: The rest of this paper is organized as follows. We first provide a comparison of our motion detection approach with other solutions in Section 2. We discuss the design of our motion detection approach, the associated experiments and implementation in Section 4. Finally, we discuss several salient features of our proposal and its other applications in Section 5.

2   Related Work: Motion Detection vs. Other Solutions

In this section, we discuss other solutions to the problem of selective unlocking of an RFID device. We provide a side-by-side comparison of motion detection with other relevant approaches in Figure 1.

Secret Handshakes: A recent approach, called "Secret Handshakes" [4] relates closely to our proposal. In order to authenticate to an accelerometer-equipped RFID device (such as a WISP [21,24]) using Secret Handshakes, a user must move or shake his or her device in a particular pattern. For example, a user might be required to move his or her tag parallel with the surface of an RFID reader's antenna in a circular manner. A number of these kinds of patterns were studied and shown to exhibit low error rates [4].

A central drawback to this method is that a special-purpose movement pattern is required for tags to be unlocked in this fashion. This requires subtle changes to the expected RFID usage model. While a standard, insecure RFID setup only requires users to bring their RFID tags within range of a reader, when tags are secured using "Secret Handshakes", users are required to consciously move their tag in a certain pattern. This may result in a degradation of usability and an increase in the time taken to authenticate to an RFID reader, due to the explicit manual involvement. A full usability study of this scheme has not yet been conducted and its user acceptability is unknown.

Unlocking Technique	Requires explicit user involvement?	Works while tag is stored in a wallet or other objects?	Affects tag form factor?	Auxiliary device needed?	False unlocking possible?
Motion Detection	No	Yes	No	No	Yes, when the tag is mobile
Secret Handshakes	Yes	Yes	No	No	Yes, when a pattern is accidentally executed
Onboard Button	Yes	No	Yes, in case of a physical button	No	No
NFC Phone	Yes	N/A	No (tags are virtual)	Yes, an NFC phone	No
Temperature Detection	Yes	No	No	No	Yes
Sound Detection	Yes	No	Somewhat	No	Yes
Light Detection	Yes	No	No	No	Yes

Fig. 1. Comparison of Motion Detection with Alternative Solutions (highlighted cells represent positive features)

In contrast, the main advantage of the motion detection approach presented in this paper is that it requires no conscious effort on behalf of users and no changes to the standard RFID usage model. Tags will simply detect whether or not they are in motion at the time at which they are read and respond accordingly. Our approach adheres more closely to a typical RFID usage model and as such is not at all demanding and is already psychologically acceptable. It is also a much simpler and more efficient scheme due to the fact that it only entails an analysis of the frequency of sensor values and not the values themselves. As a result, motion detection is better suited for use on inexpensive wireless devices. A detailed comparison of motion detection and Secret Handshakes, in terms of efficiency, usability and other factors, is provided later in Section 5.

A shortcoming of motion detection relative to the Secret Handshakes approach to context recognition is that the latter is more secure, as the patterns it detects can be somewhat unique and therefore less likely to be executed during the course of routine activities. While securing a tag via motion detection provides no protection against unauthorized reads while the tag is mobile, secret handshake patterns are also likely to be unknowingly exhibited in a user's daily activities as reported in [4]. Thus, a more full fledged form of context recognition such as Secret Handshakes does not rule out the possibility of unauthorized tag reading or ghost-and-leech attacks.

Onboard Button: A simple way to allow a user to selectively activate her tags is by making use of an on-board tag button. In fact, some vendors have started producing such tags for access card applications [3]. This approach, however, requires the user to take out the card from her wallet or purse whenever access is needed. Buttons may also impact the size and shape of the card containing the tag. Our proposal, on the other hand, addresses these drawbacks; the size, shape and bulk cost of an accelerometer might also compare favorably to that of a button. Some vendors have been selling low-power 3 axis accelerometers for around $1 [5]. Note that the mass manufacturing cost of a WISP tag equipped with an accelerometer is also expected to be close to $1 [2]. Instead of a physical button, it is possible to use a virtual button based on capacitive sensing, as proposed in [22]. However, this will still require explicit user involvement, as the tags need to be first removed from the objects (such as wallets) in which they are often stored and carried [4].

NFC Phones: NFC (Near Field Communication) technology is also relevant to the subject of this paper. NFC allows RFID tags to be integrated with a phone and to use the phone as tags. Unlocking of tags can be trivially achieved by having the user press a button on her phone. NFC technology relies on the assumption that mobile phones are almost constantly available to their users. Although emerging in some countries, NFC phones are not widespread today, however. Moreover, NFC is not compatible with other RFID standards, such as Electronic Product Code (EPC); this means that an NFC phone/tag may not work with an EPC reader. As pointed out in [25], deployment of NFC phones is still in early stages and it is likely that for some time to come, the user's tags and the phones will continue to remain as physically separate devices.

Alternative Sensors: It is logical to wonder whether sensors, other than accelerometers, can also be used for selective tag activation, in a similar or superior capacity. Unfortunately, unlike accelerometers, no other type of sensor seems capable of monitoring whether or not passive wireless equipment should be unlocked. In a system consisting of mobile RFID tags and stationary readers, the movement of a tag implies a context in which it is safe for the tag to transmit. As a motion sensor, accelerometers are exceptionally qualified to serve this function. Different sensors monitor different environmental factors, however, none of which are indicative of an unattacked state. For example, microphones can be quite sensitive to ambient noise, but an increase or decrease in volume level does not imply anything about whether or not it is safe for an RFID tag to transmit its data. Similarly, a thermometer could be used to record the temperature of a device's environment, but there is nothing unique about the temperature near a legitimate reader that would allow an appliance to discern it from a malicious piece of equipment.

Beyond this, the unique RFID usage model must also be taken into consideration when determining the usefulness of various sensors for detecting different contexts. One of the crucial benefits of using RFID tags is that they may be left stowed in a wallet, backpack, purse, or some combination thereof when in use. The ability of sensors to collect information about their surroundings may be severely curtailed when stored in this manner. For example, photometers will be obstructed from collecting ambient light, external sounds will be muffled for microphones, and thermometers will be insulated against external sources of heat. Unlike these forms of sensory equipment, accelerometers can operate unhindered in an enclosed environment. This characteristic also contributes to the unique suitability of accelerometers to the task of securing inexpensive mobile hardware.

Other Approaches: Other approaches to selective tag blocking are "blocker tag" [13], RFID Enhancer Proxy [14] and RFID Guardian [20]. All of these approaches, however, require the users to carry an auxiliary device (a blocker tag in [13] and PDA like special-purpose device in [14,20]); such an auxiliary device may not be available every time access to RFID tags is needed. A Faraday cage can also be used to prevent an RFID tag from responding promiscuously by shielding its transmission. However, a special-purpose cage (a foil, envelope or a wallet)[1] would be needed and the tag would need to be removed from the cage in order to be read, thus requiring explicit user involvement. Moreover, building a true Faraday Cage that shields all communication is known to be a challenge.

3   Background

3.1   WISP Tags

In order to investigate motion detection on inexpensive wireless devices, we utilized a special type of RFID tag designed by Intel Research known as a Wireless Identification and Sensing Platform (WISP) [21,24]. WISPs are passively-powered RFID tags that are compliant with the Electronic Product Code (EPC) protocol. Specifically, we utilized version 4.1 of the WISP hardware, which partially implements Class 1 Generation 2 of the EPC standard. By following this protocol and deriving power only from the transmissions of a commercial off-the-shelf RFID reader, WISPs closely model the type of RFID tag one might

---

[1] These products are available in the market. See, e.g., MobileCloak:
  http://www.mobilecloak.com/mobilecloak

expect to find in a typical contactless access token. Where the WISP differs from standard tags, however, is in its inclusion of an onboard Texas Instruments MSP430F2132 microcontroller and sensors such as the ADXL-330 three-axis $\pm 3g$ accelerometer. This 16-bit MCU features an 8 MHz clock rate, 8 kilobytes of flash memory, and 512 bytes of RAM. WISPs are the first programmable passive RFID devices. They have seen use in studies on a variety of topics, from energy harvesting experiments [10,9] to monitoring animal behavior [8,23]. Unlike standard RFID tags, which are fixed function and state machine based, the flexibility of WISP tags allowed us to implement novel security solutions on a live, passive RFID device. Recall that the manufacturing cost of a WISP tag is expected to be close to $1 [2].

3.2   Random Number Generation Theory

In this section, background information on the generation of random values is presented. This is necessary due to the fact that the motion detection system presented in this work is based on a concept from the domain of cryptographic random number generation. When designing cryptosystems, an infinite source of perfect randomness is often assumed to be present. This assumption raises several important questions. In practice, how can this ideal randomness be realized? And exactly what are the properties that the random output should possess?

Cryptographic applications demand "strongly" uniform numbers. The bits of the number must be independent and uniformly distributed, or as close to this as attainable. In other words, each bit should be the result of an idealized, unbiased coin toss where there is always an even chance that the outcome is a 0 or a 1. If this type of random value was naturally occurring, utilizing it would be a relatively simple matter of recording it and handing it to the cryptographic application. Unfortunately, such "strong" randomness is unlikely to be available in practice. While many naturally occurring phenomena are unpredictable, they necessarily contain some bias rather than being distributed uniformly. From the perspective of a cryptographic application expecting high quality randomness, this bias is unacceptable because it could potentially be exploited by an adversary to extract information about the cryptosystem's internal state.

Extraction functions have been created to bridge the gap between the expectations of cryptographic designers and the realities of entropy availability. An extractor is a function that takes a string of unpredictable but biased, or "weakly" random, bits as input and returns a string of close to uniform, or "strongly" random, bits as output. Because unpredictable bits derived from observations of natural phenomena are unlikely to have a known mathematical structure, extractors have been developed that can be used on forms of input that can have any structure, but are instead required to have a certain amount of min-entropy. Min-entropy, a mathematical property of a distribution, is defined as follows:

Definition 1. *The min-entropy of a given distribution X on $\{0,1\}^n$ is:*

$$min\text{-}entropy(X) = \min_{x \in \{0,1\}^n} \log_2 \frac{1}{Pr[X = x]} \qquad (1)$$

In words, the min-entropy of a distribution is equal to the probability of the most likely element in X being drawn from X. From a different perspective, if a distribution X has a min-entropy of k, the likelihood of drawing any single element x from X does not exceed $1/2^k$ for all $x \in X$.

Min-entropy is an important measurement of a distribution because it captures the amount of randomness a distribution is capable of supporting. Despite the fact that elements of X are n bits in length, due to the bias of the distribution, X may not contain enough entropy to actually support the extraction of n unbiased bits. Only k "strongly" random bits can be derived from a distribution that has a min-entropy of k regardless of the distribution's element length n.

4   Motion Detection

In this section, we describe the design of our motion detection technique and the associated experiments. Recall, from Section 1.2, that accessing a mobile RFID device always involves the device being moved. Thus, determining whether or not the device is in motion is sufficient to provide a reasonable level of security and privacy in the context of most common usage scenarios. This is because motion implies an unlocked state and stillness implies a locked state. The aim of these experiments was to create a lightweight mechanism that, while being unable to differentiate between many types of motions, would still be capable of detecting movement properties in a way that is simple enough to be implemented on low-cost wireless devices, irrespective of their hardware restrictions.

For such a mechanism, we turned to the measurement discussed in Section 3.2 to evaluate the amount of randomness contained within a distribution – min-entropy. Clearly, the min-entropy of a distribution of accelerometer readings is closely related to how the RFID tag housing the accelerometer is moving. Min-entropy estimation is a very simple measurement, however. While this simplicity is attractive from the perspective of what devices it can be estimated on, it remained to be seen whether this was also a hindrance in terms of whether or not the measurement would be of any use at all in terms of movement recognition accuracy. Thus, we set out to determine whether or not the measurement of min-entropy is sufficient to accomplish motion detection.

The equation for calculating min-entropy based on a sample distribution was shown in Definition 1. This is computationally simple enough that it can be performed on a wide range of wireless devices. Prior to performing any tests by implementing this on the WISP tags, however, we observed that in order to approximate the min-entropy of a sensor sample, the min-entropy value itself does not actually need to be computed. This is because with a fixed distribution size, min-entropy is a function with only one input, namely the number of occurrences of the most frequently occurring value within the distribution. Thus, rather than actually calculating min-entropy using the equation in Definition 1, the device can quickly develop a rough estimate of a sample distribution's relative min-entropy by instead keeping track of the frequency at which each value occurs and dividing the count of the most common value by the size of the distribution. (Pseudocode for the motion detection algorithm we employed is shown in Algorithm 1).

If acceleration samples could be taken over an extended time interval on a lightweight wireless device, it would ensure an accurate estimate of the sensor's min-entropy. Unfortunately, this is not possible. First, the limited memory capacity of this class of wireless devices renders storing these many samples implausible. Furthermore, processing a large number of samples would be taxing for a device with low computational and power resources. Finally, aside from hardware restrictions, gathering this many samples would simply take too much time to result in a usable security solution. For this reason, we settled on a sample size of 40 as a level that would be attainable on even the most minimalist hardware, such as a passive RFID tag.

4.1   Experiments

Accelerometer samples were taken from a wireless sensor while various types of motions were performed. These were necessary in order to determine the feasibility of differentiating between movement and stillness. Measurements were recorded over a 10 minute interval while a variety of different movements were performed with the tags. The sample with the least amount of motion involved was the *stationary test*, where the WISP tag was simply left sitting on a desk. This test was meant to model a scenario where a tag is placed in front of an (adversarial) RFID reader's antenna without actually being held by a user. The *overnight test* was identical to the stationary test, only the tag was left to be queried by the reader overnight rather than for just 10 minutes.

The *hand test* measured the min-entropy of the accelerometer readings while the WISP tag was held in the palm of a hand. This test was meant to model a scenario where a tag is presented in front of an RFID reader's antenna while being hand-held by a user. Along the same lines, the *hand wallet test* was performed with a tag placed inside a wallet while the wallet was being hand-held

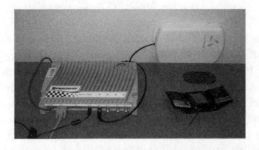

Fig. 2. WISP tag inside of a wallet in front an Impinj RFID Reader

(see Figure 2). The *arc swipe* sample involved moving the WISP tag in an arc like half circle pattern from the middle left hand side of the reader's antenna, to the center top of the antenna, then to the middle right hand side of the antenna, and then back again. This test was meant to model a scenario where a tag is swiped in front of an RFID reader's antenna in a certain manner while being held by a user.

For the *drop test*, the WISP tag was repeatedly picked up and vertically dropped in from the antenna. This test was meant to stimulate items being deposited in front of an RFID reader as they move down a conveyor belt in a factory or retail checkout, or simply when the device accidentally falls. Next on the list is the *triangle test*, for which the WISP tag was moved in a triangular pattern from the bottom left hand corner of the reader's antenna, to the top center of the reader's antenna, then to the bottom right hard corner, before being moved back to the bottom left. For the *alpha test*, the tag was moved in a loop resembling a lower-case Greek letter alpha. Both the alpha and triangle tests were also meant to model a scenario where a tag is swiped in front of an RFID reader's antenna in a certain manner while being held by a user.

Instead of moving the tag parallel to the reader surface, for the *key twist test*, the tag was held relative to the antenna but spun in circles around its central axis. This test represents the motion underwent by an RFID tag embedded in a key when opening a door. The *circle test* saw the WISP tag moved roughly in a circle in front of the antenna, once again to model a scenario where a tag is swiped in front of an RFID reader's antenna in a certain manner while being held by a user. The arc swipe, triangle, alpha, key twist, and circle motions were first suggested in the study of Secret Handshakes [4] and were included to provide a basis for comparison with this work.

For the *sitting still test*, a 10 minute sample was taken while sitting motionless on an office chair. The WISP tag was placed in a side pocket of the tester's pants while the RFID reader's antenna was placed alongside the tester's thigh. The setup for the *sitting shaking test* was similar, but instead of not moving while sitting, the tester rocked and shook back and forth on the chair. This test was meant to simulate the effect of sitting on a train, bus, or other form of mass transit as it moved along bumpy tracks or a poorly-maintained road. We also simulated the effect of *walking or running* on the tag by placing the tag in a side pants pocket and walking or jogging in place for 10 minutes while the reader's antenna was held alongside the leg where the tag was placed.

Personal Fitness Aids: We also considered other personal devices, such as the "Nike + iPod Sports Kit". The Nike Kit is a wireless appliance that works with Apple iPods and iPhones. It consists of a wireless sensor which users place in one of their shoes as well as a receiver that they attach to their iPod or iPhone. The sensor records information during a user's workout and transmits it over the wireless channel to the receiver, which then relays it to the user through audio output. The authors of [18] demonstrated that the information this device transmits, specifically, a unique identifier, is subject to eavesdropping and illicit user tracking, even while users are not working out. Although the sensor is

Fig. 3. WISP tag fastened to a shoe in front of an Alien Antenna connected to an off-camera Impinj RFID Reader

equipped with an On/Off button, once the sensor is placed inside the shoe, users no longer have access to this switch. Our motion detection technique can be used to address this problem.

Rather than purchasing and working directly with a Nike Kit, several supplemental measurements were taken with a powerless WISP tag and its onboard accelerometer to reproduce the expected usage scenario for this appliance. Each of these tests was performed with a WISP tag affixed to the tester's sneaker using inexpensive electrical tape. For the *shoe stationary test*, a 10 minute sample was taken with this RFID enhanced shoe left sitting still on the floor and the antenna of the RFID reader placed alongside it. See Figure 3 for a pictorial representation of this setup. The *shoe walking* and *shoe jogging* were, as one might anticipate, modifications of the walking or jogging samples where the WISP tag was mounted on the subject's shoe rather than placed in his or her pocket. In both instances, the antenna attached to the RFID reader was again shifted to the floor several inches away from the tag in order to be capable of reading it while the tester's foot was in motion.

Samples with Different Users: All of the samples taken thus far were performed by the same test subject. While little variation was anticipated in the non-interactive samples, such as the stationary ones where a tag was left sitting on a desk, we wanted to make sure our tests captured any differences that might exist between the motions when performed by different volunteers. We therefore repeated the hand held and arc swipe tests with four different volunteers.

4.2   Motion Detection Algorithm

Having obtained the samples from our different tests, it next had to be determined how to partition these into 40 unit pieces that could be analyzed for motion detection accuracy. Initially, we simply broke the n length samples into $n/40$ pieces and analyzed them separately. When it came time to implement our motion detection scheme on WISP tags, however, we realized this was a flawed approach. This is due to the fact that testing for motion in this manner meant that a judgment regarding motion could only be made every 40 samples. As an alternative, we adopted a "sliding window" technique. In this approach,

---

Algorithm 1. Motion Detection Pseudocode

```
sampleList[sampleIndex] = currentSample
sampleIndex = (sampleIndex + 1) mod sampleListSize
for sample1 in sampleList do
    for sample2 in sampleList do
        if sample1 = sample2 then
            occurrences = occurrences + 1
        end if
    end for
    if occurrences > maxOccurances then
        maxOccurances = occurrences
    end if
end for
if maxOccurrences < threshold then
    tag = moving
else
    tag = still
end if
```

---

40 samples are still initially buffered before the first decision is made regarding movement. After the next sample is obtained, however, the earliest sample is discarded and replaced with the new one. In this way, instantaneous snap judgments regarding motion are possible because only one additional sample is required after the initial sample buffering period. The pseudocode for our approach is depicted in Algorithm 1.

With the sample determination method settled upon, all that remained was to find suitable thresholds for each of the accelerometer axes. To achieve this, each of the movement samples was iterated over in the sliding window fashion described above. For each of these windows, the number of times each value repeated was counted, and the maximum number of repeated values was noted. Recall that min-entropy is a function of the number of times the most frequently occurring value in a distribution occurs. The minimum, average and maximum number of these maximum occurrences were recorded across all sliding windows for each sample.

These measurements were used to create a range of potential thresholds. This range of thresholds was searched until a suitable value was found. In order to measure the performance of threshold values relative to one another, a scoring metric was used where each time 90% or more of the windows analyzed in a sample were correctly identified as moving or still, the threshold values were awarded a point. The threshold value with the most points was selected as optimal.

4.3   Implementation Challenges

Our motion detection algorithm was designed to be readily used by wireless devices of all kinds, including those whose computing resource are severely lacking. As a result, there were few notable challenges encountered while implementing it on a WISP tag. Minimal changes were needed to port the motion detection code from a traditional computer to the computational RFID device. Rather than storing and comparing the accelerometer readings as binary strings, each axis was converted to a unsigned integer to reduce the amount of storage space required and improve the efficiency of value comparison. Along the same lines, rather than allocating memory for a new temporary sliding window array each time a new sample was introduced, a single array was used where the oldest accelerometer value was overwritten by the newest value each time one was recorded.

4.4   Results, Interpretation and WISP Implementation

The performance of our motion detection scheme with the best possible threshold value is provided in Table 1. For the volunteer hand tests, the average "still" recognition percentage was 98.388% and the mean percentage mistakenly labeled

Table 1. Accuracy of Motion Detection for Different Types of Movement

Type of Movement	% Still	% Moving
Overnight #1	100.000%	0.000%
Overnight #2	100.000%	0.000%
Stationary #1	100.000%	0.000%
Stationary #2	100.000%	0.000%
Sitting Still	99.786%	0.214%
Hand	94.091%	5.909%
Volunteer Hand #1	98.246%	1.754%
Volunteer Hand #2	100.000%	0.000%
Volunteer Hand #3	95.950%	4.050%
Volunteer Hand #4	99.354%	0.646%
Hand Wallet	99.663%	0.337%
Shoe Stationary	100.000%	0.000%
Arc Swipe	0.000%	100.000%
Volunteer Swipe #1	0.000%	100.000%
Volunteer Swipe #2	0.000%	100.000%
Volunteer Swipe #3	0.000%	100.000%
Volunteer Swipe #4	0.000%	100.000%
Drop	2.369%	97.631%
Triangle	0.000%	100.000%
Alpha	0.000%	100.000%
Key Twist	0.000%	100.000%
Circle	0.000%	100.000%
Sitting Shake	1.579%	98.421%
Walking	0.000%	100.000%
Jogging	0.000%	100.000%
Shoe Walking	4.318%	95.682%
Shoe Jogging	0.000%	100.000%

as "moving" came to 1.6125%. The standard deviation values for stillness and motion of the volunteer hand samples were equal to 1.541. For the volunteer swipe motion tests, the motion detection scheme correctly identified all windows as moving for all volunteers. The mean stillness and movement percentage were therefore 0.000%, and 100.000% with standard deviations of 0.

In all cases, this motion detection algorithm was able to correctly identify whether a WISP tag was in motion or at rest for at least 94.091% of the sample windows. This demonstrates the ability of this minimalist technique to correctly capture whether or not a wireless device is in motion at any given time. However, does this meet the desired goal of being applicable to enhancing the security of mobile devices? All the cases where the tag has been identified as still are situations where the tag should not be read. This approach therefore handles these cases without difficulty.

Some of the cases identified as being in motion are problematic, however. Rows colored in dark gray indicate a sample identified as stationary for which it is desirable to keep tags locked. Light gray rows are cases identified as moving for motions indicative of unlocking tags. Medium gray rows are the undesirable cases where tags are identified as moving but it would be beneficial from a security perspective to keep the tags locked. While all the swiping related motions indicate a willingness to unlock the tag, others do not. These troubling cases include Sitting Shake, Walking, Jogging, Shoe Walking, and Shoe Jogging. Thus, while this technique is useful for defending against unauthorized tag access while a tag is held in a motionless hand, pocket, or simply left on a surface, it leaves tags vulnerable while their user is undergoing intense motion such as running. So it would still be possible to perform a man-in-the-middle attack on a person who is walking with their tags or riding a train down turbulent tracks.

Finally, to demonstrate the ability of constrained low-cost wireless hardware to handle this motion detection technique, it was implemented on WISP tags. Rather than programming the tags to transmit only when moving as would be the case in a practical setting, for our tests we programmed the tag to transmit a static EPC identifier indicating three states: insufficient samples to make a judgment regarding motion, still, and moving. This was done because a non-transmitting tag is an ambiguous result; the tag may simply have insufficient power to perform the given computation, for example. Repeating the motions depicted in Table 1 with a tag programmed in this fashion verified that the motion detection technique was indeed functioning as well on the WISP tag as in the sample based simulations. That is, activities where the majority of windows were identified as moving in the threshold tests were also identified as moving by the tag-based movement detection code, and the same was true for movements identified as being still.

5   Discussion

5.1   Efficiency

In our experimental setup, the time between consecutive WISP reads over all 4,254,166 samples taken over the course of our study was 31.245 milliseconds. In terms of timing, our motion detection technique requires an initial 40 samples to draw the first conclusion regarding whether the tag is moving or not, which takes $40 * 31.245$ milliseconds $= 1.250$ seconds to collect. After this, a new conclusion can be drawn as to whether or not the tag is in motion with each sample that is collected approximately every 31.245 milliseconds. Thus, there is no reason why motion detection could not immediately be deployed into present RFID systems.

Please note that the alternative Secret Handshakes solution takes about a second to register a given gesture followed by two seconds of transmission over the device's wireless interface [4]. In contrast, motion detection takes 1.25 seconds on average to first notice whether or not a device is in motion and approximately 31 milliseconds for each subsequent judgment, inclusive of all necessary reader-to-tag and tag-to-reader transmission overhead. Motion detection therefore compares favorably to Secret Handshakes in terms of efficiency.

5.2   Usability

Both Secret Handshakes and motion detection were tested with a small group of three or four users and were found to be robust to variations caused by minute differences between the way different people performed different motions. It may be possible that Secret Handshakes suffers from usability issues that were not captured in this study, however. For example, prior to testing for false positives (i.e., the possibility of the tag remaining locked even when the user intends to unlock it) when using Secret Handshakes, users were allowed to practice the gesture in question for five minutes [4]. It may be the case that in practice, when trying to recall the precise pattern required to unlock a tag, it may take a user several attempts to perfect the gesture, leading to an increase in false positives and a decrease in usability as users are effectively denied the services of their access token or have to repeat the process. Since motion detection does not rely on the ability of users to recall a single gesture, it does not suffer from this drawback. Additionally, when faced with a device that is not operating as expected, a common user response is to jostle the device. In the unlikely event that a tag is not undergoing sufficient motion to be unlocked when presented to a reader, the intuitive user action of shaking or tapping the tag will automatically activate it. Thus, another usability benefit of motion detection is that it requires little to no training.

Furthermore, Secret Handshakes requires a registration phase in which a motion template is constructed that can infer user's movements. This is undesirable for several reasons. First, having to perform this registration step puts an unnecessary burden on the device's user. The authors of [4] suggest that it might be possible to construct a single generic motion template that would work for every user. However, it is unclear how this would be accomplished in practice and, perhaps more critically, what the implications of such a template would be for the level of false negatives (i.e., false unlocking) and false positives experienced by individual users. The motion template must also be stored on each user's RFID tag, using up some of the device's precious storage resources and leading to further complications. How would a tag receive a new template? If it is transmitted to the tag over its wireless interface, this leads to the possibility of a malicious entity replacing a user's desired template with one of their own design. An attacker could use this opportunity to craft a template that either never unlocks a users tag, thus launching a denial of service attack on the RFID infrastructure, or always unlocks a tag, undermining the level of protection which this scheme was designed to offer. Since motion detection does not hinge on an RFID tag's capacity to detect one individual's specific hand motion, it does not require any enrollment prior to use and is therefore exempt from having to address these challenges as well.

A final aspect in which the usability of motion detection and Secret Handshakes differs lies in the flexibility it offers to users in terms of where they may choose to keep their tags during the authentication process. One of the central benefits of Secret Handshakes is the fact that it provides increased security and privacy without requiring that users remove their tags from their wallets. Survey results presented in [4] show that this is by far the most popular way in which RFID tags are utilized, since it is preferred by 64.4% of contactless access card users. It is still far from the only way in which users have become accustomed to stowing their passive access tokens, however. The same study found that 13.6% of users held their wireless devices on a lanyard, either above or below their clothing. It is unclear how applicable Secret Handshakes is to this class of users, as the attachment of the tag to an object or themselves via a cord may severely hamper their ability to freely move the device in a specific Handshake pattern.

Along the same lines, performing a Secret Handshake seems even less plausible for the 5.2% of users who responded that they keep an access card stored loose in a purse. This is because moving a large bag containing an RFID tag, among its many contents, in a specific pattern does not imply that the tag will register the exact same movement as a tag on its own or in a smaller means of storage such as a wallet. The other objects in the bag, as well as the material of the bag itself, will surely have an impact on the motion the tag undergoes. The results of this study did not report preferred forms of contactless identification storage that are similar to tags being loosely placed in a purse, such as tags that are placed loosely in a backpack, tags in wallets that are placed in a purse, or tags in wallets that are placed in a backpack. Secret Handshakes seems similarly problematic for users who typically utilize these storage techniques, which means that the percentage of users to which this method does not apply may be higher in practice. Since motion detection is agnostic to the manner in which an RFID device is stored, it is applicable to a wider array of users and their varied access token usage habits. Thus, in several regards, motion detection demonstrates improvements in usability over Secret Handshakes.

5.3 Simplicity

Due to its uncomplicated design, motion detection is not capable of differentiating between motions of all kinds. It is not capable of discerning whether a wireless device is in motion due to a particular gesture or because its owner is in motion, for example. However, including this mechanism on wireless devices would raise the bar required for attacks to succeed by eliminating many of the most common attack scenarios, such as those where an unattended tag is read without its owner's consent or knowledge. Furthermore, motion detection has several advantages over more robust forms of activity recognition. One such asset is its ability to be implemented on all wireless devices, regardless of their hardware limitations. Secondly, including motion detection as a security measure requires absolutely no change in usage by end users, as opposed to the subtle changes required by alternative schemes such as Secret Handshakes.

5.4   Other Applications

In this paper, our focus was on personal RFID devices. However, our motion detection technique can in principle also be used to improve the security and privacy of impersonal tags carried by users, such as the ones on clothing products, books and other items. The only problem with using our approach on an impersonal tag is the increased cost due to the requirement of an onboard accelerometer. Note that such tags need to be very inexpensive due to their deployment in massive numbers. Motion detection can also be applied to secure vehicle toll payment tokens under the condition that a vehicle must always be accelerating or decelerating when the tag is to be authenticated, as an automobile moving at a constant velocity will obviously not cause an accelerometer to register any change in speed. Note that even with this restriction in place, recognizing motion is better suited to this scenario than more specialized forms of detecting activity, such as Secret Handshakes.

In addition, motion detection can be used to augment security in scenarios that do not involve mobile devices directly. One such application is providing physical security by affixing RFID tags to objects which need to be stationary such as safes, lock boxes, or other containers for storing valuables. If a thief were to try to steal an object with a motion recognizing tag embedded in it, the object will have to be moved. As a result, the tag would detect the motion and could take a precautionary measure such as activating an alarm.

5.5   Applicability to Other Devices

Throughout this work, we have illustrated the viability of our proposal by implementing it on WISP RFID tags. This does not imply that this approach is only applicable to these appliances, however. WISP tags were selected as our primary target because they represent the lowest common denominator of wireless devices. This is due to their ultra-low cost hardware and passive backscatter power source. Having shown that the technique of motion detection works by implementing it on these devices implies that it will also be capable of functioning on more full featured hardware. While this proposal may be most beneficial for hardware with constraints that rules out any alternative methods of activity recognition, it is applicable to all wireless devices.

6   Conclusions and Future Work

In this paper, motion detection, a novel approach to activity recognition, was described. By reducing the expectations of the precision of the detection procedure, the applicability and usability of the approach were actually increased. This is particularly beneficial for RFID systems with no tolerance for any usage model changes as well as where hardware constraints put standard activity recognition techniques out of reach. As future work, we intend to investigate several aspects of motion detection in greater detail. We will explore simple mechanisms which can detect the motion context more precisely and with a finer granularity, such as differentiating the tag swiping context from the one imposed on the tag due to the walking/running of the tag's owner. More accelerometer samples will be taken via a user study. Furthermore, while the samples in this work present strong evidence of the applicability of our approaches to different scenarios, the degree to which the motions performed in the lab may differ from those observed in real life remains an open question. Thus, field experiments can be conducted to compare the laboratory readings to those in the external world, such as while actually riding various forms of mass transit or running a distance.

Acknowledgments

We would like to thank RFIDSec'10 anonymous reviewers for their helpful feedback. This work was partially supported by the United States Department of Education GAANN grant P200A090157.

References

1. Bringer, J., Chabanne, H., Dottax, E.: HB++: a Lightweight Authentication Protocol Secure against Some Attacks. In: Security, Privacy and Trust in Pervasive and Ubiquitous Computing (2006)
2. Buettner, M., Prasad, R., Philipose, M., Wetherall, D.: Recognizing Daily Activities with RFID-Based Sensors. In: International Conference on Ubiquitous Computing (UbiComp) (2009)
3. Corporation, S.: SMARTCODE Solves the Privacy Issue Relating to Potential Unauthorized Reading of RFID Enabled Passports and ID Cards (2006)
4. Czeskis, A., Koscher, K., Smith, J., Kohno, T.: RFIDs and Secret Handshakes: Defending Against Ghost-and-Leech Attacks and Unauthorized Reads with Context-Aware Communications. In: ACM Conference on Computer and Communications Security (2008)
5. Electronics, M.: MMA7660FCR1 Freescale Semiconductor Board Mount Accelerometers (2009)
6. Gilbert, H., Robshaw, M., Seurin, Y.: HB#: Increasing the Security and Efficiency of HB+. In: Smart, N.P. (ed.) EUROCRYPT 2008. LNCS, vol. 4965, pp. 361–378. Springer, Heidelberg (2008)
7. Hancke, G.: Practical Attacks on Proximity Identification Systems (Short Paper). In: IEEE Symposium on Security and Privacy, S&P (2006)

8. Holleman, J., Yeager, D., Prasad, R., Smith, J., Otis, B.: NeuralWISP: An Energy-Harvesting Wireless Neural Interface with 1-m Range. IEEE Transactions on Biomedical Circuits and Systems, BioCAS (2008)
9. Jiang, B., Roy, S., Sundara-Rajan, K., Philipose, M., Smith, J., Mamishev, A.: Energy Scavenging for Inductively Coupled Passive RFID Systems. IEEE Instrumentation and Measurement Technology Conference (2005)
10. Jiang, B., Smith, J., Philipose, M., Roy, S., Sundara-Rajan, K., Mamishev, A.: Energy scavenging for inductively coupled passive RFID systems. IEEE Transactions on Instrumentation and Measurement (2007)
11. Juels, A.: RFID Security and Privacy: A Research Survey. IEEE Journal on Selected Areas in Communications (2006)
12. Juels, A., Molnar, D., Wagner, D.: Security and Privacy Issues in E-passports. Security and Privacy for Emerging Areas in Communications Networks, Securecomm (2005)
13. Juels, A., Rivest, R.L., Szydlo, M.: The blocker tag: selective blocking of rfid tags for consumer privacy. In: ACM Conference on Computer and Communications Security, CCS (2003)
14. Juels, A., Syverson, P.F., Bailey, D.V.: High-power proxies for enhancing rfid privacy and utility. In: Danezis, G., Martin, D. (eds.) PET 2005. LNCS, vol. 3856, pp. 210–226. Springer, Heidelberg (2006)
15. Juels, A., Weis, S.A.: Authenticating Pervasive Devices with Human Protocols. In: Shoup, V. (ed.) CRYPTO 2005. LNCS, vol. 3621, pp. 293–308. Springer, Heidelberg (2005)
16. Katz, J., Shin, J.S.: Parallel and Concurrent Security of the HB and HB+ Protocols. In: Vaudenay, S. (ed.) EUROCRYPT 2006. LNCS, vol. 4004, pp. 73–87. Springer, Heidelberg (2006)
17. Kfir, Z., Wool, A.: Picking Virtual Pockets using Relay Attacks on Contactless Smartcard. In: Security and Privacy for Emerging Areas in Communications Networks, Securecomm (2005)
18. Lester, T.S.J., Hartung, C., Agarwal, S., Kohno, T.: Devices That tell on You: Privacy Trends in Consumer Ubiquitous Computing. In: USENIX Security Symposium (2007)
19. O'Connor, M.: RFID Cures Concrete (2006)
20. Rieback, M.R., Crispo, B., Tanenbaum, A.S.: Rfid guardian: A battery-powered mobile device for rfid privacy management. In: Boyd, C., González Nieto, J.M. (eds.) ACISP 2005. LNCS, vol. 3574, pp. 184–194. Springer, Heidelberg (2005)
21. Sample, A., Yeager, D., Powledge, P., Smith, J.: Design of a Passively-Powered, Programmable Sensing Platform for UHF RFID Systems. In: IEEE International Conference on RFID (2007)
22. Sample, A., Yeager, D., Smith, J.: A capacitive touch interface for passive RFID tags. In: Proceedings of the 2009 IEEE RFID Conference (2009)
23. Segawa, N.: Behavior Evaluation of Sika Deer (Cervus Nippon) by RFID System. In: WISP Summit (2009)
24. Smith, J., Sample, A., Powledge, P., Mamishev, A., Roy, S.: A Wirelessly-Powered Platform for Sensing and Computation. In: Dourish, P., Friday, A. (eds.) UbiComp 2006. LNCS, vol. 4206, pp. 495–506. Springer, Heidelberg (2006)
25. Sutter, J.: CNN Article: Wallet of the future? Your mobile phone(2009), http://www.cnn.com/2009/TECH/08/13/cell.phone.wallet/index.html?eref=igoogle_cnn

Cryptanalysis of the David-Prasad RFID Ultralightweight Authentication Protocol

Julio Cesar Hernandez-Castro[1], Pedro Peris-Lopez[2], Raphael C.-W. Phan[3], and Juan M.E. Tapiador[4]

[1] School of Computing, University of Portsmouth
[2] Security Lab, Faculty of EEMCS, Delft University of Technology
[3] Department of Electronic and Electrical Engineering, Loughborough University
[4] Department of Computer Science, University of York

Abstract. In September 2009, David and Prasad proposed at MobiSec'09 an interesting new ultralightweight mutual authentication protocol for low-cost RFID tags. In this paper, we present a quite powerful cryptanalytic attack against their proposal: we start with a traceability attack, then describe how it can be extended to leak long-term stored secrets, and finally present a full disclosure attack (named Tango attack) where all the secrets that the protocol is designed to conceal are shown to be retrievable, even by a passive attacker after eavesdropping only a small number of authentication sessions. These results imply that very realistic attack scenarios are completely possible. The Tango attack constitutes a new, simple, yet powerful technique of cryptanalysis which is based on the computation and full exploitation of multiple approximations to the secret values, using Hamming distances and the representation of variables in an n-dimensional space.

1 Introduction

Authentication protocols for Radio Frequency IDentification (RFID) systems allow an RFID reader and a tag to mutually authenticate each other. Numerous protocols have been recently proposed in the literature, and the field is challenging since RFID tags can only work in very confined environments with scarce resources, so protocols should ensure that the underlying computations are not resource intensive. Along this line, a class of ultralightweight authentication protocols have been proposed, notably [7,8,9]. These protocols use only triangular operations, e.g. exclusive OR (XOR), bitwise AND, bitwise NOT, which are very lightweight but, on the other hand, only offer very limited diffusion properties.

One of the critical requirements for RFID authentication protocols is that they should be untraceable, i.e. it should not be possible for a tag's movements to be traced; this is especially relevant when considered that tags are to be embedded within objects (e.g. clothing), and thus inherently ubiquitous. Aside from mounting traceability attacks, stronger attacks can be performed by passive adversaries, including the recovery of all the long-term secrets stored on tags, which implies that the tag is not only traceable but also fully identifiable and clonable. Anonymity would be thus entirely broken.

S.B. Ors Yalcin (Ed.): RFIDSec 2010, LNCS 6370, pp. 22–34, 2010.

This paper presents cryptanalytic results both in terms of traceability attacks and attacks that recover long-term stored secrets, including the keys and the static identifier. These only require the adversary to be passive (i.e. to eavesdrop), and thus are devastating attacks with huge security implications for the protocol under scrutiny.

In mounting these attacks, we demonstrate the full power of recent cryptanalytic developments, notably the traceability attack based on truth table differences with respect to an untraceability game [10], and the Tango cryptanalysis which is based on the computation of multiple approximations, and is a novel technique firstly introduced in this paper.

In the following we apply these cryptanalytic techniques to a recent RFID protocol proposed by David and Prasad at MobiSec '09 [2], and show and analyze the results in some depth.

2   The David-Prasad Protocol

In September 2009, David and Prasad proposed at MobiSec'09 a new ultralightweight authentication protocol inspired by previous approaches such as the UMAP family of protocols [7,8,9], and the SASI [1] and Gossamer [6] schemes. Their proposal aims to provide a strong authentication mechanism and, at the same time, to offer a significant reduction in the computational load of the tag, without compromising security.

The tag and the server (also called back-end database) share four values: The old and the potential new pseudonym $\{P_{ID}, P_{ID2}\}$, respectively, and two secret keys $\{K_1, K_2\}$. Furthermore, the tag stores a static identifier ID which facilitates its unequivocal identification. The authors assume that the ID and all the remaining variables have the same bit length (i.e. $\{P_{ID}, P_{ID2}, K_1, K_2, ID\} \in Z_2^{96}$). The common communication model is assumed, so communications between the reader and the server – both arguably powerful devices – are considered to be secure as these entities can afford to use classical security solutions (e.g., TLS or SSL). On the other hand, the forward (reader-to-tag) and backward (tag-to-reader) channels are considered to be insecure and open to all sorts of attacks.

We now describe the protocol, which is divided into six steps. The operands $\{\oplus, \wedge\}$ symbolize the bitwise exclusive OR (XOR) and the bitwise AND, respectively, while $\overline{x}$ denotes the bitwise NOT of x.

Step 1: The reader sends a request message $C_{request}$ to the server. If it proves to be an authorized reader, the server sends a one-day authorization access certificate C. If the reader has already a valid certificate, it jumps directly to Step 2.

Step 2: The reader sends a request message $ID_{request}$ to the tag, which replies with its pseudonym P_{ID2}.

Step 3: The reader sends the tuple $\{P_{ID2}, C\}$ to the server in order to acquire the private information linked to the tag. If the certificate is valid and P_{ID2} matches one of the entries in the database, the server sends $\{K_1, K_2\}$ back to the reader. Otherwise, the server informs the reader that P_{ID2} does not correspond to any entry in its database. In that case, the reader repeats Step 2 in order to get access to the old pseudonym P_{ID} of the tag. Then, Step 3 is executed with the tuple $\{P_{ID}, C\}$.

Step 4: The reader generates two random numbers n_1 and n_2. Then, it computes messages $\{A, B, D\}$ as follows and sends them to the tag:

$$A = (P_{ID2} \wedge K_1 \wedge K_2) \oplus n_1 \tag{1}$$

$$B = (\overline{P_{ID2}} \wedge K_2 \wedge K_1) \oplus n_2 \tag{2}$$

$$D = (K_1 \wedge n_2) \oplus (K_2 \wedge n_1) \tag{3}$$

Step 5: From messages $\{A, B\}$, the tag can easily infer the value of the nonces $\{n_1, n_2\}$ associated to the current session. Using these values, it computes its local version of message D (let's call it D') and checks if it is identical to the received value. If they coincide, then the reader is authenticated. Otherwise, the protocol is aborted. After a successful reader authentication, the tag computes messages $\{E, F\}$ as follows and sends them back to the reader:

$$E = (K_1 \oplus n_1 \oplus ID) \oplus (K_2 \wedge n_2) \tag{4}$$

$$F = (K_1 \wedge n_1) \oplus (K_2 \wedge n_2) \tag{5}$$

Finally, the tag updates its pseudonyms values using the session nonces:

$$P_{ID} = P_{ID2} \tag{6}$$

$$P_{ID2} = P_{ID2} \oplus n_1 \oplus n_2 \tag{7}$$

Step 6: Upon receiving messages E and F, the reader computes a local version, F', and checks if it is identical to the received value. If both coincide, the tag is authenticated and the reader can obtain the static identifier ID of the tag by using message E and the now known values $\{K_1, K_2, n_1, n_2\}$ (i.e., $ID = E \oplus (K_2 \wedge n2) \oplus K_1 \oplus n_1$). It then updates the pseudonyms linked to the tag in the same way:

$$P_{ID} = P_{ID2} \tag{8}$$

$$P_{ID2} = P_{ID2} \oplus n_1 \oplus n_2 \tag{9}$$

Finally, the reader sends an updated version of the pair $\{P_{ID}, P_{ID2}\}$ and its certificate C to the server. If the certificate is valid, the server updates the information (pseudonyms) associated to the tag.

3   Traceability Attack

Traceability is one of the most important security threats in RFID environments. Nevertheless, numerous RFID protocols put it at risk by designing schemes where tags answer readers' queries with static values, thus making traceability attacks not only possible but trivial. For these and other reasons (notably the privacy implications due to tags' mobility), the traceability problem has recently attracted a lot of interesting research. In [4], Juels and Weis gave a formal definition of traceability, that was later reformulated, in a style more similar to that used for security protocols, in [10]. We use the latter approach to analyze the David-Prasad protocol. For completeness and readability, we will first present the model, and later we will detail our proposed attack.

In RFID schemes, tags ($\mathcal{T}$) and readers ($\mathcal{R}$) interact in protocol sessions. In general terms, the adversary ($\mathcal{A}$) controls the communications between all the participants and interacts passively or actively with them. Specifically, $\mathcal{A}$ can run the following queries:

- Execute($\mathcal{R}$, $\mathcal{T}$, i) query. This models a passive attacker. $\mathcal{A}$ eavesdrops on the channel, and gets read access to the exchanged messages between $\mathcal{R}$ and $\mathcal{T}$ in session i of a genuine protocol execution.
- Test(i, $\mathcal{T}_0$, $\mathcal{T}_1$) query. This does not model any ability of $\mathcal{A}$, but it is necessary to define the untraceability test. When this query is invoked for session i, a random bit is generated $b \in \{0, 1\}$. Then, a pseudonym $P_{ID2}^{\mathcal{T}_b}(i)$ and a new set of exchanged messages $\{A^{\mathcal{T}_b}, B^{\mathcal{T}_b}, D^{\mathcal{T}_b}, E^{\mathcal{T}_b}, F^{\mathcal{T}_b}\}$ from the set $\{P_{ID2}^{\mathcal{T}_0}(i), P_{ID2}^{\mathcal{T}_1}(i)\}$ and $\{\{A^{\mathcal{T}_0}, B^{\mathcal{T}_0}, D^{\mathcal{T}_0}, E^{\mathcal{T}_0}, F^{\mathcal{T}_0}\}, \{A^{\mathcal{T}_1}, B^{\mathcal{T}_1}, D^{\mathcal{T}_1}, E^{\mathcal{T}_1}, F^{\mathcal{T}_1}\}\}$, respectively, and corresponding to tags $\{\mathcal{T}_0, \mathcal{T}_1\}$ is given to $\mathcal{A}$.

Upon definition of the adversary's abilities, the untraceability problem can be defined as a game $\mathcal{G}$ divided into three phases:

Phase 1 (Learning): $\mathcal{A}$ can make any number of Execute queries, which facilitate the eavesdropping of exchanged messages – modeling a passive attack – over the insecure radio channel.

Phase 2 (Challenge): $\mathcal{A}$ chooses two current tags whose associated identifiers are $ID^{\mathcal{T}_0}$ and $ID^{\mathcal{T}_1}$. He then sends a Test(i, $\mathcal{T}_0$, $\mathcal{T}_1$) query. As a result, $\mathcal{A}$ is given a pseudonym $P_{ID2}^{\mathcal{T}_b}(i)$ and a new set of exchanged messages $\{A^{\mathcal{T}_b}, B^{\mathcal{T}_b}, D^{\mathcal{T}_b}, E^{\mathcal{T}_b}, F^{\mathcal{T}_b}\}$ from the set $\{P_{ID2}^{\mathcal{T}_0}(i), P_{ID2}^{\mathcal{T}_1}(i)\}$ and $\{\{A^{\mathcal{T}_0}, B^{\mathcal{T}_0}, D^{\mathcal{T}_0}, E^{\mathcal{T}_0}, F^{\mathcal{T}_0}\}, \{A^{\mathcal{T}_1}, B^{\mathcal{T}_1}, D^{\mathcal{T}_1}, E^{\mathcal{T}_1}, F^{\mathcal{T}_1}\}\}$, respectively, which depend on a chosen random bit $b \in \{0, 1\}$.

Phase 3 (Guessing): $\mathcal{A}$ ends the game and outputs a bit d ($d \in \{0, 1\}$) as its conjecture of the value of b.

$\mathcal{A}$'s success in winning $\mathcal{G}$ is equivalent to the success of breaking the untraceability property offered by the protocol. So the advantage of $\mathcal{A}$ in distinguishing whether the messages correspond to $\mathcal{T}_0$ or $\mathcal{T}_1$ is defined below, where t is a security parameter (e.g. the bit length of the key shared by the tag and the reader) and r is the number of times $\mathcal{A}$ runs an Execute query.

$$Adv_{\mathcal{A}}^{\mathsf{UNT}}(t, r) = |Pr[d = b] - \frac{1}{2}|.$$

So, an RFID protocol offers resistance against traceability, i.e. it is said to be untraceable (UNT), if $Adv_{\mathcal{A}}^{\mathsf{UNT}}(t, r) < \varepsilon(t, r)$, where $\varepsilon(\cdot, \cdot)$ symbolizes some negligible function.

In essence, this untraceability (UNT) notion is analogous to the conventional notion of ciphertext indistinguishability (IND) for encryption or key indistinguishability for key establishement protocols. In similar vein, the UNT notion captures the fact that no adversary can distinguish between two tags even if s/he can choose what they are to be. Indeed, if the adversary cannot do this, then clearly s/he cannot track a tag's movements.

We will show in the following how the David-Prasad scheme does not satisfy the above mentioned condition, thus putting at risk the privacy location of tags holders. More precisely, an adversary $\mathcal{A}$ conducts the procedure described below:

Phase 1 (Learning): $\mathcal{A}$ makes the query Execute($\mathcal{R}, \mathcal{T}_0, i$), and thus obtains the pseudonym $P_{ID2}^{\mathcal{T}_0}(i)$ and messages $\{A, B, D, E, F\}$. By computing the XOR between E and F, we get

$$
\begin{aligned}
E \oplus F &= (K_1 \oplus n_1 \oplus ID) \oplus (K_2 \wedge n_2) \oplus (K_1 \wedge n_1) \oplus (K_2 \wedge n_2) \\
&= (K_1 \oplus n_1 \oplus ID) \oplus (K_1 \wedge n_1) \\
&= (K_1 \oplus n_1) \oplus (K_1 \wedge n_1) \oplus ID.
\end{aligned}
$$

If we analyze bit by bit the truth tables provided below

a	b	$a \oplus b$	$a \wedge b$
0	0	0	0
0	1	1	0
1	0	1	0
1	1	0	1

it is easy to see that XOR and AND are complements of each other with probability $\frac{3}{4}$. Therefore, for any bit position, the bit value of $(K_1 \oplus n_1)$ is the opposite of that of $(K_1 \wedge n_1)$ with probability $\frac{3}{4}$, so their XOR is 1. Thus we have that $E \oplus F = \overline{ID}$ for each bit with probability $\frac{3}{4}$.

Phase 2 (Challenge): $\mathcal{A}$ chooses two new tags whose associated identifiers are $ID^{\mathcal{T}_0}$ and $ID^{\mathcal{T}_1}$. He then sends a Test($i', \mathcal{T}_0, \mathcal{T}_1$) query. As a result, $\mathcal{A}$ is given a new pseudonym $P_{ID2}^{\mathcal{T}_b}(i')$ and a new set of exchanged messages $\{A^{\mathcal{T}_b}, B^{\mathcal{T}_b}, D^{\mathcal{T}_b}, E^{\mathcal{T}_b}, F^{\mathcal{T}_b}\}$ from the set $\{P_{ID2}^{\mathcal{T}_0}(i'), P_{ID2}^{\mathcal{T}_1}(i')\}$ and $\{\{A^{\mathcal{T}_0}, B^{\mathcal{T}_0}, D^{\mathcal{T}_0}, E^{\mathcal{T}_0}, F^{\mathcal{T}_0}\}, \{A^{\mathcal{T}_1}, B^{\mathcal{T}_1}, D^{\mathcal{T}_1}, E^{\mathcal{T}_1}, F^{\mathcal{T}_1}\}\}$, respectively, which depend on a chosen random bit $b \in \{0, 1\}$.

Phase 3 (Guessing): $\mathcal{A}$ ends $\mathcal{G}$ and outputs a bit $d = \overline{\mathsf{lsb}(E \oplus F)} \oplus \overline{\mathsf{lsb}(E^{\mathcal{T}_b} \oplus F^{\mathcal{T}_b})}$ as its conjecture of the value b, where $\mathsf{lsb}(\cdot)$ denotes the least significant bit. Thus we have,

$$
Adv_{\mathcal{A}}^{\mathsf{UNT}}(t, 1) = |Pr[d = b] - \frac{1}{2}| = \frac{5}{8} - \frac{1}{2} = \frac{1}{8} > \varepsilon.
$$

Thus, the David-Prasad protocol in an RFID system (S= $\{R_i, \mathcal{T}_0, \mathcal{T}_1, \ldots\}$) in which a passive adversary $\mathcal{A}$ only eavesdrops a single run of the protocol (modeled by one Execute query in the game $\mathcal{G}$), is vulnerable to the most simple and effective traceability attack conceivable.

4   Leakage of Stored Secrets

Aside from traceability problems, the David-Prasad protocol also leaks out its long-term stored secrets, notably the static identifier ID and secret keys K_1, K_2. Generalizing our above analysis, specifically the Phase 1 of the traceability attack, if we denote by k the bitlength[1] of ID, then the full static identifier ID can be recovered with probability $\left(\frac{3}{4}\right)^{-k}$. This leaks out too many bits of ID, and seriously threatens the anonymity of the tag.

An attack to leak out information on the stored secret keys works as follows. The adversary can make the queries Execute($\mathcal{R}$, $\mathcal{T}_0$, $i-1$), Execute($\mathcal{R}$, $\mathcal{T}_0$, i) for two consecutive sessions, to obtain the pseudonyms $X^{i-1} = P_{ID2}^{\mathcal{T}_0}(i-1)$, $X^i = P_{ID2}^{\mathcal{T}_0}(i)$ and messages $\{A_{i-1}, B_{i-1}, D_{i-1}, E_{i-1}, F_{i-1}\}$, $\{A_i, B_i, D_i, E_i, F_i\}$, respectively. From equation (7), we see that X^{i-1}, X^i allows us to compute the XOR between the two nonces $\{n_1, n_2\}$ of the ith session:

$$Y = X^{i-1} \oplus X^i$$
$$= n_1 \oplus n_2.$$

Furthermore, the adversary can compute the XOR of A_i and B_i:

$$Z = A_i \oplus B_i$$
$$= ((P_{ID2}^{\mathcal{T}_0}(i) \wedge K_1 \wedge K_2) \oplus n_1) \oplus ((\overline{P_{ID2}^{\mathcal{T}_0}(i)} \wedge K_2 \wedge K_1) \oplus n_2)$$
$$= (K_1 \wedge K_2) \oplus n_1 \oplus n_2.$$

Thus, the adversary obtains

$$Y \oplus Z = K_1 \wedge K_2$$

Note that for those bits where $K_1 \wedge K_2$ is 1, this implies that both key bits are 1. Consequently, on average $(\frac{k}{4})$ bits of both keys will be retrieved after two sessions. These observations have great security implications, and can be further explored and refined to disclose even more information, but this is no longer necessary in view of the following full disclosure attack.

5   A Passive Tango Cryptanalysis

In this section we present a novel passive (i.e. completely realistic in the underlying security model) and extremely efficient attack to fully recover both the secret key values $\{K_1, K_2\}$ and the static identifier of the tag ID, which are indeed all the secret information the protocol is designed to conceal. The attack is divided into two main phases: 1) Selection of good approximations; and 2) Combination of the thus obtained good approximations for disclosing K_i or ID. We describe each of these phases below.

---

[1] David and Prasard assume that the bitlength of all variables is set to 96.

Phase 1: The attack exploits the leakage of secret information over the insecure radio channel due to fact that exchanged messages are derived from secret values by using triangular functions [5] only. Triangular operations and their composition (which is also triangular) are well known to have very poor diffusion properties. This is why the attacker can check and succeed in using multiple simple combinations of the exchanged public messages $\{A, B, D, E, F\}$ as Good Approximations (GA) for the secrets K_i or ID. Public exchanged messages do not hide well enough these secret values. From all the set of approximations, the adversary is interested on those that are systematically closer (on average) to the target secret value $X \in \{K_1, K_2, ID\}$. That is, those for which the Hamming distance between an approximation Z and the value X deviates from the expected value $\frac{96}{2}$, so either $hw(Z, X) < 48$ or $hw(\overline{Z}, X) < 48$.[2] In Appendix A, we list the average Hamming distance $dist(X, \cdot)$ of all possible combinations of the exchanged messages to the secrets. We present in the following table the best approximations for each of the three secret values we want to retrieve, which are the ones we employ in our attack:

Target	Good Approximations
K_1	$GA\text{-}K_1 = \{D, F, (A \oplus D), (\overline{A \oplus F}), (B \oplus D), (B \oplus F),$ $(A \oplus B \oplus D), (A \oplus B \oplus F)\}$
K_2	$GA\text{-}K_2 = \{D, F, (A \oplus D), (A \oplus F), (B \oplus D), (\overline{B \oplus F}),$ $(A \oplus B \oplus D), (A \oplus B \oplus F)\}$
ID	$GA\text{-}ID = \{(\overline{E \oplus F}), (A \oplus B \oplus E), (A \oplus D \oplus E),$ $(A \oplus E \oplus F), (B \oplus D \oplus E), (D \oplus E \oplus F), (\overline{A \oplus B \oplus D \oplus E}),$ $(A \oplus D \oplus E \oplus F), (\overline{B \oplus D \oplus E \oplus F})\}$

Phase 2: The basic idea in this phase of the attack is to combine multiple approximations (i.e. $Z \in \{GA\text{-}K_1, GA\text{-}K_2, GA\text{-}ID\}$)) obtained in different sessions, to construct a global one which is highly correlated with the secret values (i.e. keys $\{K_1, K_2\}$, and static identifier ID). This can be done in a number of different ways and forms, but in the case of the David-Prasad protocol a very simplistic approach works quite nicely. The way we proceed is the following: For each authentication session eavesdropped, we compute a number of good approximations to the secret values, and then store them as rows of three different matrices (one for each of K_1, K_2 and ID). After eavesdropping a given number of sessions, we compute the global values just by repeatedly adding each of the columns of the matrices, and returning a **0** if the total number of ones in the said column is below a given threshold γ, or a **1** in any other case. In Figure 1, we provide a simple numerical example to further describe the attack, where the bitlength of the involved variables has been set to only 8 bits. The procedure to retrieve $\{K_1, K_2\}$ is very similar. The adversary has to provide a conjecture of the static identifier ID or the key K_i after the eavesdropping of some sessions. In each of them, multiple

---

[2] We assume a bitlength of 96 for each of K_i, ID [3].

$$\boxed{ID = 0\text{x}52} \qquad\qquad [0,1,0,1,0,0,1,0]$$

Session i	$(E \oplus F)$	$[0,0,0,1,0,1,1,0]$
$PID2 = 0\text{xE6}$	$(A \oplus B \oplus E)$	$0,1,0,1,0,1,1,1$
$A \quad = 0\text{xA8}$	$(A \oplus D \oplus E)$	$0,1,1,1,0,0,0,1$
$B \quad = 0\text{x94}$	$(A \oplus E \oplus F)$	$0,1,0,0,0,0,0,1$
$D \quad = 0\text{xB2}$	$(B \oplus D \oplus E)$	$0,1,0,0,1,1,0,1$
$E \quad = 0\text{x6B}$	$(D \oplus E \oplus F)$	$0,1,0,1,1,0,1,1$
$F \quad = 0\text{x82}$	$(A \oplus B \oplus D \oplus E)$	$0.0,0,1,1,0,1,0$
	$(A \oplus D \oplus E \oplus F)$	$1,1,1,1,0,0,1,1$
	$(B \oplus D \oplus E \oplus F)$	$0,0,1,1,0,0,0,0$
Session $i+1$	$(E \oplus F)$	$0,1,0,1,0,0,1,0$
$PID2 = 0\text{xD0}$	$(A \oplus B \oplus E)$	$0,1,0,0,0,0,1,0$
$A \quad = 0\text{x7F}$	$(A \oplus D \oplus E)$	$0,1,0,0,0,0,1,0$
$B \quad = 0\text{xE3}$	$(A \oplus E \oplus F)$	$1,1,0,1,0,0,1,0$
$D \quad = 0\text{xE3}$	$(B \oplus D \oplus E)$	$1,1,1,1,1,1,1,0$
$E \quad = 0\text{xDE}$	$(D \oplus E \oplus F)$	$0,1,0,0,1,1,1,0$
$F \quad = 0\text{x73}$	$(A \oplus B \oplus D \oplus E)$	$0,1,0,1,1,1,1,0$
	$(A \oplus D \oplus E \oplus F)$	$0,0,0,1,1,0,0,1$
	$(B \oplus D \oplus E \oplus F)$	$0,1,0,1,0,0,1,0$

$$\boxed{ID_{approx} =} \qquad\qquad [3,14,4,13,6,6,13,7]$$

$$\boxed{\gamma * N_s = 4.5 * 2 = 9}$$

$$\begin{cases} \text{if } (id_i^{approx} \geq \gamma) & id_i^{conjecture} = 1 \\ \text{if } (id_i^{approx} < \gamma) & id_i^{conjecture} = 0 \end{cases}$$

$$\boxed{ID_{conjecture} =} \qquad\qquad [0,1,0,1,0,0,1,0]$$

$$\boxed{ID = ID_{conjecture} = 0\text{x}52}$$

Fig. 1. An scaled-down example (using 8-bit rather than 96-bit variables) of how Tango cryptanalysis works

approximations of the pursued value are obtained – each of these approximations represent a row in the corresponding matrix. The simplest way to obtain a final value is to select the majority value in each column of this matrix. We can quickly sum all the rows to obtain a final vector. Then, if the value in a column of this vector is greater than half of the number of approximations N_A times the number of eavesdropped sessions N_S, we conjecture a **1** in that column. Otherwise, we conjecture a **0**. We can define that in a more formal way: Let be X and Y two vectors and x_i and y_i the value in each column of these vectors respectively. If the vector X is the input of the threshold function $th(X)$, the resulting vector is defined by:

$$th(X) = \begin{cases} \text{if } (X_i \geq \gamma) & Y_i = 1 \\ \text{if } (X_i < \gamma) & Y_i = 0 \end{cases} \quad \text{where } \gamma = 0.5 * N_A * N_S$$

This extremely easy and efficient way of combining approximations works surprisingly well for producing very accurate global approximations to all three secret values after eavesdropping a relatively small number of authentication sessions. The results are presented in the following figures.

We have simulated our attack to evaluate its feasibility and effectiveness. First, we randomly initialize the secret values (i.e. $\{P_{ID}, P_{ID2}, K_1, K_2, ID\}$). Then, we simulate N_S legitimate sessions of the protocol – the attacker eavesdrops N_S sessions – and we run the adversary's strategy (Phase 2) to obtain a conjecture of the keys $\{K_1, K_2\}$ and the static identifier ID. Finally, we compare the global conjecture value $X_{conjecture} \in \{K_{1_{conjecture}}, K_{2_{conjecture}}, ID_{conjecture}\}$ with the real value $X \in \{K_1, K_2, ID\}$ to measure the adversary's success. The mean and standard deviation of the number of bits successfully recovered, for various values of eavesdropped sessions (N_S), are summarized in Figures 2, 3 and 4. In our simulations, the bitlength of variables is set to 96 and for each value of N_S we repeated the experiment 10.000 times. For $\{K_{1_{conjecture}}, K_{2_{conjecture}}, ID_{conjecture}\}$, the threshold is set to $\{0.5 * 8 * N_S, 0.5 * 8 * N_S, 0.5 * 9 * N_S\}$ respectively, which means that in all cases we are guessing the majority value between those observed.

As we are using the same number of approximations (8 for every eavesdropped session) for K_1 and K_2, and they are similarly powerful, the results obtained are quite close. In both cases, the number of required eavesdropped sessions by an attacker to disclose the full secret key K_i is less than or equal to 65. The effectiveness of this attack in disclosing the static identifier ID is slightly superior in comparison, partly due to the fact that in this case 9 approximations – instead of 8 – are used. For the ID, the adversary needs only around 50 sessions to completely disclose the full 96 bits of the static identifier. Even though these figures are more than enough to consider the protocol completely broken, we also note that a more constrained attacker is not forced to evasdrop such a number of sessions to fully recover the 96 bits: After only 5 or 10 sessions, more than 90 bits are correctly guessed, and the remaining can be easily identified by an offline brute force search.

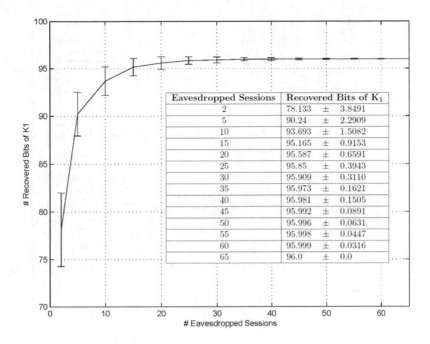

Fig. 2. K_1 bit recovery, against the # of eavesdropped sessions

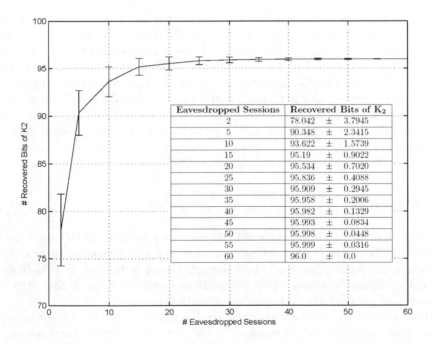

Fig. 3. K_2 bit recovery, against the # of eavesdropped sessions

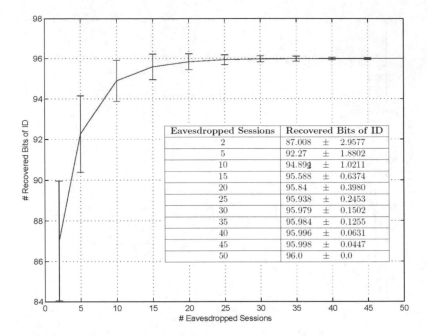

Fig. 4. ID bit recovery, against the # of eavesdropped sessions

The attacks just presented have serious consequences for the overall security of the protocol. In fact, they utterly ruin all the security properties claimed by their authors. After conducting the attack, the adversary is able to retrieve all the secret information shared between the tag and the server, so he can trivially bypass any authentication mechanisms (i.e. tag and reader authentication) and impersonate the tag in the future, or just clone it. Confidential information is put at risk and tag's answers can be tracked even though two random numbers are used in each session in a failed attempt to stop this from happening. A desynchronization attack against the tag (or the sever) is also quite straightforward, since the adversary can generate any desired valid synchronization messages.

6   Conclusions

The design of ultralightweight security protocols for low cost RFID tags is a stimulating challenge due to the severe computational restrictions of these devices. Although interesting proposals have recently been published in this research area, the design of secure schemes is still an open question. If fact, the vast majority of the published schemes are already broken.

Triangular functions are very attractive because they can be efficiently implemented in hardware, but a cryptanalyst can take advantage of their use due to their very poor diffusion properties. So they can and probably should be used, but not alone, as the composition of triangular functions is still triangular. They should be combined with non-triangular functions – as proposed in SASI [1] – to hinder the task of breaking the scheme. Rotation operations are a quite interesting possibility as they are not triangular, allow to amplify diffusion, and are also very efficient to implement in hardware. If we had to single out the main reason for the weaknesses found in the David-Prasad protocol, apart from the design of some messages, this would definitely be the non inclusion of any kind of rotations (Hamming based or modular) in the set of operations used. The inclusion of nonces is very likely a necessary condition to guarantee anonymity, but by itself does not ensure this desirable property, or any protection against traceability attacks.

We do not claim that the attacks and techniques presented here are optimal in any way, and can conceivably design more subtle and maybe slightly more powerful attacks, but we believe that in the light of the results offered here there is no need for that. However, possibly a mixture of the approximation to the ID obtained in Section 4, combined with the approximations used in the Tango attack might lead to a slightly more efficient approach.

The cryptanalytic technique introduced in this paper, named Tango attack, could also be seen as a new tool to analyze lightweight protocols, and thus helpful in the design of more secure future proposals. We believe it will prove successful against other lightweight protocols and algorithms because, almost by definition, they do not have in many cases the computational resources needed to allow for an adequate (i.e. highly nonlinear) mixture of the internal secret values as to avoid leaking some bits in every session.

References

1. Chien, H.-Y.: SASI: A New Ultralightweight RFID Authentication Protocol Providing Strong Authentication and Strong Integrity. IEEE Trans. Dependable Secur. Comput. 4(4), 337–340 (2007)
2. David, M., Prasad, N.R.: Providing Strong Security and High Privacy in Low-Cost RFID Networks. In: Proc. of Security and Privacy in Mobile Information and Communication Systems, MobiSec 2009, pp. 172–179. Springer, Heidelberg (2009)
3. EPCglobal: Class-1 Generation 2 UHF Air Interface Protocol Standard Version 1.2.0: Gen 2. (2008), http://www.epcglobalinc.org/standards/
4. Juels, A., Weis, S.: Defining strong privacy for RFID. In: Proc. of PerCom 2007, pp. 342–347. IEEE Computer Society Press, Los Alamitos (2007)
5. Klimov, A., Shamir, A.: New Applications of T-Functions in Block Ciphers and Hash Functions. In: Gilbert, H., Handschuh, H. (eds.) FSE 2005. LNCS, vol. 3557, pp. 18–31. Springer, Heidelberg (2005)
6. Peris-Lopez, P., Hernandez-Castro, J.C., Estevez-Tapiador, J.M., Ribagorda, A.: Advances in ultralightweight cryptography for low-cost RFID tags: Gossamer protocol. In: Chung, K.-I., Sohn, K., Yung, M. (eds.) WISA 2008. LNCS, vol. 5379, pp. 56–68. Springer, Heidelberg (2009)
7. Peris-Lopez, P., Hernandez-Castro, J.C., Estevez-Tapiador, J., Ribagorda, A.: LMAP: A Real Lightweight Mutual Authentication Protocol for Low-cost RFID tags. In: Hand. of RFIDSec (2006)

8. Peris-Lopez, P., Hernandez-Castro, J.C., Estevez-Tapiador, J., Ribagorda, A.:
   M2AP: A Minimalist Mutual-Authentication Protocol for Low-cost RFID Tags.
   In: Ma, J., Jin, H., Yang, L.T., Tsai, J.J.-P. (eds.) UIC 2006. LNCS, vol. 4159, pp.
   912–923. Springer, Heidelberg (2006)
9. Peris-Lopez, P., Hernandez-Castro, J.C., Estevez-Tapiador, J.M., Ribagorda, A.:
   EMAP: An efficient mutual-authentication protocol for low-cost RFID tags. In:
   Meersman, R., Tari, Z., Herrero, P. (eds.) OTM 2006 Workshops. LNCS, vol. 4277,
   pp. 352–361. Springer, Heidelberg (2006)
10. Phan, R.: Cryptanalysis of a new ultralightweight RFID authentication protocol
    - SASI. IEEE Transactions on Dependable and Secure Computing (2008), doi:
    10.1109/TDSC.2008.33

Appendix

A   Approximations to K_1, K_2, and ID (10.000 Tests)

X	$dist(\mathbf{X}, \mathbf{K_1})$	$dist(\mathbf{X}, \mathbf{K_2})$	$dist(\mathbf{X}, \mathbf{ID})$
A	49.4 ± 1.8547	48.3 ± 4.3829	49.3 ± 5.1196
B	49.4 ± 5.0990	48.3 ± 6.2578	49.3 ± 3.9560
D	$\mathbf{34.0 \pm 1.9493}$	$\mathbf{35.1 \pm 3.8587}$	52.4 ± 3.8000
E	47.8 ± 4.284	46.2 ± 4.6861	49.3 ± 4.1485
F	$\mathbf{36.1 \pm 3.3600}$	$\mathbf{35.6 \pm 3.1686}$	50.8 ± 5.0160
$A \oplus B$	48.6 ± 4.055	47.9 ± 5.1662	49.0 ± 3.7148
$A \oplus D$	$\mathbf{37.2 \pm 3.4293}$	$\mathbf{61.6 \pm 2.2000}$	48.7 ± 2.9343
$A \oplus E$	42.8 ± 3.628	48.3 ± 2.052	50.6 ± 4.3174
$A \oplus F$	$\mathbf{61.3 \pm 3.769}$	$\mathbf{37.7 \pm 4.6054}$	48.9 ± 3.0806
$B \oplus D$	$\mathbf{61.8 \pm 4.3543}$	$\mathbf{36.9 \pm 4.2532}$	47.1 ± 3.4771
$B \oplus E$	47.6 ± 3.8262	47.8 ± 3.1874	47.6 ± 7.1722
$B \oplus F$	$\mathbf{37.7 \pm 2.6851}$	$\mathbf{60.8 \pm 4.5343}$	46.9 ± 2.3000
$D \oplus E$	42.6 ± 2.9732	45.7 ± 3.5228	52.3 ± 5.3675
$D \oplus F$	47.1 ± 1.9723	46.7 ± 4.0509	51.6 ± 2.8355
$E \oplus F$	41.9 ± 4.5705	56.2 ± 4.1665	$\mathbf{67.7 \pm 5.4598}$
$A \oplus B \oplus D$	$\mathbf{37.6 \pm 5.8173}$	$\mathbf{36.8 \pm 2.4000}$	48.2 ± 5.8617
$A \oplus B \oplus E$	56.0 ± 2.1448	44.5 ± 3.4132	$\mathbf{24.5 \pm 3.6946}$
$A \oplus B \oplus F$	$\mathbf{35.5 \pm 3.2939}$	$\mathbf{36.3 \pm 3.0348}$	49.8 ± 3.6824
$A \oplus D \oplus E$	47.2 ± 3.1875	38.4 ± 3.9294	$\mathbf{35.8 \pm 4.9759}$
$A \oplus D \oplus F$	47.5 ± 3.5284	47.0 ± 5.0398	50.3 ± 6.4195
$A \oplus E \oplus F$	48.5 ± 3.3838	48.1 ± 2.6627	$\mathbf{22.2 \pm 1.7205}$
$B \oplus D \oplus E$	51.2 ± 4.7286	45.7 ± 3.1953	$\mathbf{34.0 \pm 3.7947}$
$B \oplus D \oplus F$	49.9 ± 4.5706	47.5 ± 4.7802	47.5 ± 3.4424
$B \oplus E \oplus F$	49.9 ± 5.1662	45.6 ± 4.200	47.6 ± 6.9022
$D \oplus E \oplus F$	50.3 ± 3.9762	45.3 ± 4.5177	$\mathbf{31.1 \pm 3.5903}$
$A \oplus B \oplus D \oplus E$	47.6 ± 4.5211	55.4 ± 4.8208	$\mathbf{61.1 \pm 4.3920}$
$A \oplus B \oplus D \oplus F$	44.5 ± 3.9812	49.2 ± 3.3106	49.4 ± 3.555
$A \oplus B \oplus E \oplus F$	48.3 ± 5.2354	44.9 ± 5.6648	45.7 ± 5.0408
$A \oplus D \oplus E \oplus F$	44.9 ± 3.8066	40.6 ± 2.7276	$\mathbf{35.8 \pm 6.1449}$
$B \oplus D \oplus E \oplus F$	45.5 ± 1.8028	55.5 ± 4.7592	$\mathbf{62.4 \pm 2.7276}$
$A \oplus B \oplus D \oplus E \oplus F$	53.5 ± 5.0843	45.4 ± 5.5534	42.7 ± 3.06757

Practical NFC Peer-to-Peer Relay Attack Using Mobile Phones

Lishoy Francis, Gerhard Hancke, Keith Mayes,
and Konstantinos Markantonakis

Information Security Group, Smart Card Centre,
Royal Holloway University of London,
Egham Hill, TW20 0EX, Surrey, United Kingdom
{L.Francis,Gerhard.Hancke,Keith.Mayes,K.Markantonakis}@rhul.ac.uk,
http://www.scc.rhul.ac.uk/

Abstract. NFC is a standardised technology providing short-range RFID communication channels for mobile devices. Peer-to-peer applications for mobile devices are receiving increased interest and in some cases these services are relying on NFC communication. It has been suggested that NFC systems are particularly vulnerable to relay attacks, and that the attacker's proxy devices could even be implemented using off-the-shelf NFC-enabled devices. This paper describes how a relay attack can be implemented against systems using legitimate peer-to-peer NFC communication by developing and installing suitable MIDlets on the attacker's own NFC-enabled mobile phones. The attack does not need to access secure program memory nor use any code signing, and can use publicly available APIs. We go on to discuss how relay attack countermeasures using device location could be used in the mobile environment. These countermeasures could also be applied to prevent relay attacks on contactless applications using 'passive' NFC on mobile phones.

Keywords: relay, security, attack, p2p, peer-to-peer, NFC, NFC-enabled-mobile-phones, transactions, countermeasure, location, practical-implementation.

1 Introduction

Near Field Communication (NFC) [1] is intended as a short-range standardised technology for providing contactless communications for mobile devices. NFC is intended to be an intuitive method of establishing ad-hoc connections, simply requiring that two NFC-enabled devices are brought in close physical proximity to each other. NFC also allows for devices to interact with existing contactless/RFID (Radio Frequency Identification) systems. In 'passive' communication mode NFC allows devices to emulate passive contactless smart cards, while 'active' mode allows for devices to act as contactless smart card readers or to communicate with each other. Although the use of NFC-enabled devices in contactless systems has received much publicity, the use of NFC to support peer-to-peer services is less well covered.

S.B. Ors Yalcin (Ed.): RFIDSec 2010, LNCS 6370, pp. 35–49, 2010.
© Springer-Verlag Berlin Heidelberg 2010

One of the earliest specified uses of active NFC was to pair Bluetooth devices by facilitating the exchange of information needed to setup the Bluetooth communication channel [2]. NFC can also be used for sharing data and content between mobile devices, such as digital business cards and social networking details, although the data rates are currently not best suited to high-bandwidth transfers. Mobile payments are becoming increasingly popular and there are a variety of schemes using a range of data bearers. NFC is seen as an ideal technology in this area with its ability to interact with existing contactless systems and facilitate peer-to-peer transactions between mobile phones [3].

In short range communication systems, it is usually assumed that the devices are actually in close physical proximity when successfully communicating. However, in a relay attack the communication between two devices are relayed over an extended distance by placing a proxy device within communication range of each legitimate participant and then forwarding the communication using another communication channel. The two legitimate participants receive valid transmissions from each other and therefore assume that they are in close physical proximity. In some systems, especially in smart token environment, this could lead to serious security vulnerabilities [4]. The risk posed to near-field channels by relay attacks and the possibility of using NFC-enabled mobile phones as a relay attack platform have been discussed [5] [6], but a practical relay attack using this platform has not been demonstrated.

In this paper, we describe how a relay attack against peer-to-peer NFC system could be practically implemented. The novelty of this attack is that it also uses available NFC-enabled mobile phones as attack platforms, providing the attacker with off-the-shelf proxy device. The attacker's mobile phones are of acceptable (non-suspicious) form factor, unlike custom built emulators used in other relay attacks. The attack functionality can also be implemented using only software via publicly available APIs in a standard MIDlet (Mobile Information Device Profile or MIDP application) using JSR 118 API [7]. The resources and technical skill required of the attacker are therefore greatly reduced. In Section 2 we provide a brief introduction to NFC communication and relay attacks. We describe the attack implementation in Section 3 and discuss current countermeasures that could be used to mitigate relay attacks in Section 4.

2   Background

NFC technology allows for the integration of contactless technology into active devices, such as mobile phones. NFC operates within the 13.56 MHz Radio Frequency (RF) band and has an operating distance up to 10cm. A NFC-enabled device can act as both a "contactless card" and a "contactless reader". NFC-enabled devices, as specified in ISO-18092/ECMA-340 [1] and ISO-21481/ECMA-352 [8], are compatible with existing contactless systems adhering to ISO 14443 [9], ISO 15693 [10] and FeliCa [11]. The NFC standards also define a communication mode for peer-to-peer (P2P) or 'active' communication, with the purpose of facilitating communication between two NFC-enabled devices.

In 'active' NFC, the participants communicate in a "client-server" model. The device that starts the data exchange is known as the Initiator and the recipient is known as the Target. In 'active' mode, the Initiator and Target uses their own generated RF field to communicate with each other. First the Initiator transmits an RF carrier, which it uses to send data to the Target. Once an acknowledgment for the data sent has been received from Target (by modulating the existing field), the Initiator switches the carrier off. The original Target then reprises the role of Initiator, switching on its carrier, and transmits a response to the original Initiator. For the purposes of reader's clarity, we call the NFC enabled mobile phone configured as the Initiator to be in "writing" mode and the phone configured as the Target to be in "reading" mode.

On NFC-enabled mobile phones the Secure Element (SE) provides the security means to establish trust between service provider and the device. The SE also provides a secure environment for hosting sensitive applications and storing cryptographic keys. Currently there are three main architectures for NFC. The first involves an SE that exists as an 'independent' embedded hardware module, i.e. a stand-alone IC (Integrated Chip) is built into the phone. In the second option, the SE is implemented within the UICC (Universal Integrated Circuit Card) [12]. Of the existing Subscriber Identity Application (SIA) modules such as the Subscriber Identity Module (SIM) [13], Universal Subscriber Identity Module ((U)SIM)[14] and Removable User Identity Module ((R)UIM) [15]. The third option implements the SE on a removable memory component such as a Secure Multi-Media Card (Secure MMC) or Secure Digital card (Secure SD) [16]. The discussion comparing the advantages and disadvantages of the above mentioned architectures is beyond the scope of this paper. It is important to note that the NFC standards does not specify any security services apart from the Signature Record Type Definition [17], leaving the security design to the application developer. The Signature RTD specifies how data is to be signed to ensure data integrity and provide data authentication. This standard is currently being reviewed by the NFC Forum [18].

The handsets that were used in our practical experiments implemented independent SEs, which supported Java Card 2.2.1 [19] (Java Card Open Platform [20]), Global Platform 2.1.1 [21] and Mifare Classic [22] emulation. To implement 'passive' emulation of a contactless token an application must be installed in the secure program memory of the SE. Currently, it is possible to unlock the SE in 'independent' architectures and to install custom applications [23]. However, this would be controlled when the UICC is used as the SE, as access to the UICC is strictly managed by the mobile operator [24]. When implementing 'active' NFC communication the functionality can be entirely controlled via a MIDlet installed in the non-secured application memory of the mobile phone. A developer using the mobile phone as a platform for 'active' communication does therefore not need to gain access to any secure parts of the NFC architecture. The MIDlet can implement the 'active' NFC functionality using standard functions available within the extensions of the public JSR 257 Contactless Communication API [25].

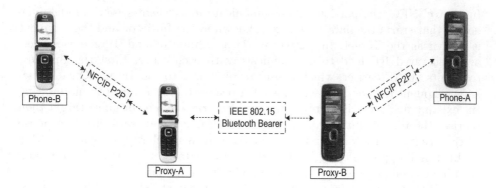

Fig. 1. P2P Relay Setup using Bluetooth

2.1   Relay Attack Theory

The Grand Master Chess problem as discussed in [26] provides a classic example of relay attack. In this scenario a player who does not know the rules of Chess can simultaneously play against two grand masters. The player starts a postal game of Chess with each grand master and subsequently forwards the moves originating from one grand master to the other. Although each grand master thinks that they are engaging the player they are essentially playing against each other. The application of this scenario to security protocols was first discussed in [27] as 'mafia fraud'. Subsequently this attack has also been referred to as a 'wormhole attack' [28] or as a 'relay attack' [29]. Using this attack an attacker is able to bypass security protocols by only relaying challenges and responses between two legitimate entities. As the attacker is always in the position to provide the correct reply, which he/she learned from the other party by forwarding the original message and recording the response, the security protocol is executed successfully and both parties will consider the attacker to be a legitimate participant in the protocol. In this scenario the attacker never needs to know any detail of the information he/she relays, i.e. he/she does not need to know the structure of the protocol, the algorithms used, the plain text data sent or any secret key material. The attacker must only be in a position where he/she can continue to relay the communication for the entire duration of the protocol. Earlier practical examples of relay attack in the contactless environment using custom-built hardware or using NFC-enabled contactless readers can be found in [30], [31] and [32].

3   Relay Implementation

We implemented the relay attack against two NFC enabled mobile phones operating in peer-to-peer mode and participating in a legitimate transaction. As illustrated in the Figure 1, Phone-A intends to interact with Phone-B to perform a legitimate peer-to-peer transaction. The attacker introduces two additional mobile phones into the transaction setup, namely Proxy-A and Proxy-B, to relay

Fig. 2. Devices used in the relay attack – Device B (Nokia 6131 NFC), Proxy A (Nokia 6131 NFC), Proxy B (Nokia 6212 Classic NFC) and Device A (Nokia 6212 Classic NFC)

the communications between Phone-A and Phone-B. In our proof-of-concept attack experiment, we practically implemented the relay attack using four NFC enabled mobile phones, as shown in Figure 2.

3.1   Phone-A and Proxy-B

The role of Proxy-B, as the name suggests, is to represent Phone-B and to relay communications to and from Phone-A. To realise both Phone-A and Proxy-B we used two Nokia 6212 Classic NFC mobile phones which are based on S40 5th Edition FP1 platform. On Phone-A, a MIDlet (MIDP 2.1 application [7]) was implemented (3 kilobytes in size) that utilised the JSR 257 extensions API to realise NFC peer-to-peer communications. Phone-A is designed to switch between "reading" and "writing" modes as required.

On Proxy-B, a MIDlet (MIDP 2.1 application) implemented (14 kilobytes in size) the JSR 257 extensions for NFC peer-to-peer and JSR 82 API [33] for IEEE 802.15 (Bluetooth) communications. By default, Proxy-B was configured in "reading" mode and also supports "writing" mode. The NFC platform of Phone-A and Proxy-B supported the active peer-to-peer mode of operations for both Target and Initiator. Hence these devices performed "reading" and "writing" in active mode.

3.2   Phone-B and Proxy-A

Phone-B and Proxy-A were realised on two Nokia 6131 NFC mobile phones, based on S40 3rd Edition FP1 platform. Proxy-A represented Phone-A in the transactions and relayed messages with Proxy-B. Similar to Phone-A, on Phone-B a MIDlet (MIDP 2.0 application [7]) was implemented (3 kilobytes in size) that utilised JSR 257 extensions API to realise NFC peer-to-peer communications. Phone-B is designed to switch between "reading" and "writing" modes as required.

On Proxy-A, a MIDlet (MIDP 2.0 application) implemented (14 kilobytes in size) the JSR 257 extensions API [25] for NFC peer-to-peer and JSR 82 API [33] for IEEE 802.15 (Bluetooth) communications. By default, Proxy-A was configured in "writing" mode and also supported "reading" mode. The NFC platform of Phone-B and Proxy-A supported active peer-to-peer mode of operation for Initiator, but only passive for Target. Hence these devices performed "reading" in passive mode and "writing" in active mode. Using JSR 257 extensions API, the connection open and receiving data in "reading" mode were made as follows,

```
private static final String TARGET_URL
= "nfc:rf;type=nfcip;mode=target";
NFCIPConnection conn = (NFCIPConnection) Connector.open(TARGET_URL);
byte[] data = conn.receive();
byte[] ack = {(byte) 0xFF,(byte) 0xFF};
conn.send(ack);
```

Similarly, the connection open and sending data in "writing" mode were made as follows,

```
private static final String INITIATOR_URL
= "nfc:rf;type=nfcip;mode=initiator";
NFCIPConnection conn = (NFCIPConnection) Connector.open(INITIATOR_URL);
byte[] cmd = {(byte) 0x9A,(byte) 0xED};
conn.send(cmd);
conn.receive();
```

3.3   Relay Bearer

Proxy-A and Proxy-B established the relay channel using Bluetooth, where Proxy-B acted as the "server" and Proxy-A act as the "client". Bluetooth is a short range radio technology developed by Bluetooth Special Interest Group (SIG) and utilises unlicensed radio in the frequency band of 2.45GHz. The supported data speed is approximately 720Kbps. Bluetooth communication range from 10 metres to 100 metres. The MIDlets implemented the Bluetooth communication on Proxy-A and Proxy-B using JSR 82 API. We used L2CAP (Logical Link Control and Adaption Protocol) available within the host stack of the Bluetooth protocol. L2CAP is layered over the Baseband Protocol and operates at the data link layer in the OSI (Open System Interconnection) Reference Model. It supports data packets of up to 64 kilobytes in length with 672 bytes as the default MTU (Maximum Transmission Unit) and 48 bytes as the minimum mandatory MTU. For creating an L2CAP server connection, a btl2cap scheme (url), a 16 byte service UUID (Universally Unique Identifier), a friendly name (device name) and other parameters were provided as follows,

```
String service_UUID = "00000000000010008000006057028A06";
String url = "btl2cap://localhost:" + service_UUID + ";ReceiveMTU
=672;TransmitMTU=672;name=" + deviceName;
L2CAPConnectionNotifier notifier =
```

```
(L2CAPConnectionNotifier) Connector.open(url);
conn = notifier.acceptAndOpen();
```

For creating an L2CAP client connection, a btl2cap scheme, unique Bluetooth MAC address (6 bytes) of the server device, protocol service multiplexer (port) for the remote device and other parameters were provided as follows,

```
String url = "btl2cap://00226567009C:6001;authenticate=false;
encrypt=false;master=false;ReceiveMTU=672;TransmitMTU=672";
conn = (L2CAPConnection) Connector.open(url);
```

The MIDlets used the DiscoveryAgent class to perform Bluetooth device and service discovery. The DiscoveryListener interface was implemented to handle the notifications of devices and services. When devices and services are discovered, the DiscoveryAgent notifies the MIDlet by invoking callback methods such as deviceDiscovered() and serviceDiscovered(). The methods such as retreivedDevices() and searchServices() caches the previously discovered devices and services, in order to reduce the time needed for discovery. The client MIDlet on Proxy-B listened for the registered service and when available, connected to the server. The sending and receiving of data were achieved by using an L2CAPConnection.

We note that the MIDlets implementing the Bluetooth bearer did not require any code signing [34] and executed in the untrusted 3rd party security domain. More information on Java security domains can be found in [35]. Currently the attacker just needs to enable the application access privilege [36] [37] for connectivity to be set as "always allowed" and enable Bluetooth to be used on the mobile phone. The device specific API access rights can be found in [38] for a Nokia 6131 and in [39] for a Nokia 6212.

Alternatively, Bluetooth can be replaced with SMS (Short Messaging Service) or mobile Internet [using intermediate server(s) via HTTP (Hyper Text Transfer Protocol) over GPRS/E–GPRS (Enhanced General Packet Radio Service)] as the data bearer in order to increase the relay range. These options were only briefly considered, but we found that these bearers introduced additional overheads. In SMS, the user interaction (key press to confirm the message sending) was required even when the MIDlet was signed in the trusted 3rd party security domain. Additionally, SMS is considered to be not so reliable due to its inherent nature such as low bandwidth and variable latency. The additional key presses would also introduce suspicion on the attacker by the victim. Even though, the mobile Internet bearer does not have user interaction overhead similar to SMS, it does need signed code operating within trusted 3rd party security domain.

3.4   Relay Experiment

To demonstrate a proof-of-concept attack, against peer-to-peer NFC transactions using NFC enabled mobile phones, we implemented a simple application in a controlled laboratory environment. Phone-A would act as the Initiator and 'write' a 2-byte message to Phone-B, who would then become the Initiator and answer by "writing" a different 2-byte message back to Phone-A. Our goal was simply to demonstrate that it is possible to relay this exchange or transaction with the mobile-based proxy platforms.

To start the relay experiment, Proxy-A and Proxy-B negotiates and establishes the Bluetooth channel. In order to simplify the experiment, a 2-byte command message was input by the user in Phone-A configured in "writing" mode. The Phone-A exchanged the command with Proxy-B which then relayed to Proxy-A over the Bluetooth data bearer. Proxy-A being in "writing" mode transferred the payload onto Phone-B. The response for the command message was transferred by Phone-B to Proxy-A in "writing" mode and then relayed over to Proxy-B. The Proxy-B switched to "writing" mode and transfered the response message to Phone-A completing the relay process. In effect, Phone-A was made to believe that the response message to the sent command message was originating from Proxy-B. Similarly, Phone-B was made to believe that command message was originating from Proxy-A, which was actually originating from Phone-A via Proxy-B. Therefore it is reasonable to conclude that, in the real world the security of applications using NFC peer-to-peer communication can be potentially be

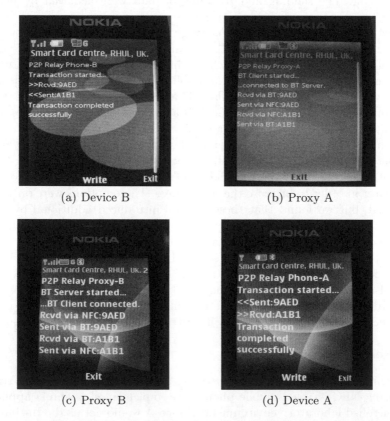

(a) Device B   (b) Proxy A

(c) Proxy B   (d) Device A

Fig. 3. Relay attack data flow on each device involved

bypassed using the method presented. The data flow of the relay, as processed by each device, is shown in Figure 3.

4   Using Location Information as Relay Attack Countermeasure

Protecting a system against a relay attack is difficult because this attack circumvents conventional application layer cryptography. Additional security measures are therefore needed to supplement existing authentication or encryption mechanisms. Several countermeasures to relay, or wormhole, attacks have been proposed. These countermeasures are intended for wireless sensor network and smart token environments. Although there are differences between these environments and mobile peer-to-peer services, there are aspects of these countermeasures that could be applied. This section provides a short overview of methods proposed for detecting relay attacks and we refer to an entity verifying the proximity of another entity as the "verifier" and the entity proving its proximity as the "prover".

One way of detecting relay attacks is to monitor any additional delay in the propagation time, which could be caused by the attacker when forwarding the data over a longer distance. Simply placing a time-out constraint on the round-trip time of a challenge-response exchange is not practical as the processing time of the prover can vary and a small error in the expected processing time could have a large influence on the round-trip time [4]. Distance-bounding protocols are designed to enable the verifier to accurately determine the round-trip time of a chosen cryptographic challenge-response [40], thereby eliminating the variability in the time taken to calculate the response. The security of distance-bounding protocols, however, are dependent on the underlying communication channel [41] and conventional channels similar to those used in NFC have been shown to be unsuitable for distance bounding [42]. Furthermore, more computationally advanced devices such as mobile phones can outperform legacy tokens and therefore circumvent systems implementing timing-based countermeasures that allow for processing time of legacy tokens.

The verifier could authenticate the prover based on physical characteristics of the communication channel. Using RF 'fingerprints' has been proposed as a method for source authentication in sensor networks [43] and for smart tokens [44]. An attacker would not be able to relay the communication as his proxy will not have the same RF fingerprint as the prover. This method requires that each device is 'fingerprinted', which is likely to be difficult in practice, especially for a large number of legitimate devices of varying ages (different versions of hardware platform) that are owned, managed or manufactured by multiple entities.

Relay attack could also be mitigated by asking the user to perform additional verification of the transaction. The user could be shown additional details of the underlying transaction by a trusted component to check that the transaction was executed faithfully [45], although this would place a significant responsibility on the user, reduce transaction throughput, and require that he/she has sufficient knowledge of how the transaction should be concluded. Another approach involving the user is multi-channel communication, where the user also verifies additional audio or visual channels [46]. This complicates the relay process, and the attacker must relay multiple channels, some of which might require high bandwidth. This approach is promising although it might increase the transaction time and reduce simplicity of operation, which are aspects of NFC that are attractive to both users and service providers.

A popular approach in wireless sensor networks is to verify proximity by comparing the location of the nodes [47]. A network-wide localization algorithm is used to determine the relative or absolute location of the nodes. Nodes participating in relay attacks will cause anomalies in the network topology and the attempted attack will be detected. This method usually requires multiple nodes to collaborate in the localization process and constructing a topology, and in the mobile environment a transaction only involved two entities. Location services are, however, becoming prominent in mobile environment providing a basis for implementing a countermeasure that is practical, effective and remains transparent to the end user.

4.1   Integrating Location into NFC Transactions

There are a number of robust Location Based Services (LBS) already deployed in the mobile environment. These services are based on the fact that the location of the handset can be accurately determined, either by the network operator, a third-party or the handset itself. It is therefore feasible that location information could be incorporated into peer-to-peer transactions in order to provide relay-resistant communication. This section briefly discusses two methods for determining handset location that are currently used in LBS.

A simple, and widespread, method of retrieving and handling location information starts with obtaining the information of the cell broadcast tower (or sector) identifier or the Cell-ID, and attaching it with other parameters in the network broadcast such as Mobile Country Code (MCC), Mobile Network Code (MNC) and Location Area Code (LAC). For instance, one can compute a Location Code (LC) as follows,

```
LC=''23415431824422847'', where MCC=234 | MNC=15 | LAC=43182 | Cell-ID=4422847
```

This information forms the basis for a simple/crude location of the user device, i.e. calculating the position based on the above mentioned location parameters; primarily the tower (or sector) identifier or Cell-ID which the device last accessed. This is applicable to most traditional handsets (e.g. GSM/UMTS). The advanced information obtained from the device can be shown on commercial mapping services, e.g. Google Maps [48]. An important point to note is that the accuracy of this form of deriving the location of a mobile device is very limited and dependent on the radius of the cell coverage, which can range from tens of metres to tens of kilometres. Global Positioning System (GPS) technology is becoming available in an increasing number of mobile handsets and it is a more accurate method of deriving the location information from the mobile phone itself. Providing the handset can detect the satellite signals (which is not always the case), the GPS-enabled handsets supply the application with the location co-ordinates giving a precise position for the device. The co-ordinates consist of Latitude (LAT) and longitude (LNG) information. For example,

```
LAT=51.42869568, LNG=-0.56286722
```

The location information maybe generated by the participants or generated and attested by a trusted 3rd party. An example of XML representation of location proof for mobile phones similar to that presented in [49] is given below.

```
<location proof>
<issuer>Issuer's Public Key</issuer>
<recipient>Recipient's Public Key</recipient>
<location information>
<gps>
<lat>51.42869568</lat>
<lng>-0.56286722</lng>
</gps>
<mcc>234</mcc>
<mnc>15</mnc>
<lac>43182</lac>
<cellid>4422847</cellid>
</location information>
</signature></signature>
</location proof>
```

4.2   Preventing Relay Attacks with Location

Examples of enabling mobile applications with 'location proofs' can be found in [49] and in [50]. Assuming that location information is available within mobile phones, the transaction data could be modified to enable the entities involved to verify their proximity. Hu et. al. [51] proposed a simple method using location information to prevent wormhole attacks in wireless sensor networks. This method required that the verifier and prover know their locations and that they have loosely synchronised clocks. The prover would basically add its location and a timestamp to the transmitted data. An additional authentication mechanism, such as a digital signature, is then used to verify that the packet was constructed by the prover. The verifier compares the prover's location to its own and confirms that the prover is in close proximity. If an attacker relays the data then the prover's location should in theory be further away from the verifier's location and the attack would be detected. The attacker cannot modify the data, or construct a new data packet as it does not know the prover's key material. The timestamp prevents an attacker recording a valid transaction and using it at a later stage at the same location. A simple application of this principle is shown in Figure 4. Implementing such a security mechanism in mobile environment is practically feasible and the success of the protocol would simply rely on the

A(Prover)   B(Verifier)

$$\underrightarrow{\{\{m, Loc_A, t\}Sign_{Priv_{K\_A}}\}Enc_{Pub_{K\_B}}}$$

Decrypt signature using $Priv_{K\_B}$
Verify signature using $Cert_A$
Check that $Loc_A \approx Loc_B$

where $m = message$, $t = timestamp$,
and $Loc_X = location\ proof\ of\ X$.

Fig. 4. An example of using location proof for preventing relay attacks in P2P NFC Transactions

accuracy and reliability of the location information available. Using a digital signature scheme, for the required cryptographic data authentication mechanism, is also feasible as mobile phones have sufficient processing resources. The use of digital signatures in NFC applications is also in the process of being standardised in the Signature RTD candidate specification currently being reviewed by the NFC Forum. Also, current work by the authors discusses a secure authentication method for proximity communication channels based on location information. The idea is to attest physical proximity of devices by using location information as an additional security metric. With the identity of the device or subscriber or token bound to the location information it is possible to restrict potential security threats to geographic areas or proximity zones. The method provides a means to test relative and absolute location, and to determine the proximity as well as provide non-repudiation for the devices involved in the transaction.

4.3   Limitations of Location Based Security

In this paper, we do not attempt to provide a comprehensive discussion on the issues surrounding the security of location based services, and it should be noted that some location based services have been shown to be insecure, e.g.[52]. However, we do wish to briefly discuss the practical issues in implementing a location-based countermeasure related to the work presented. The limitations of a location-based countermeasure depends upon how the location information is obtained and used within the application. There are external factors, such as host network policy, governing the availability of location information. Some operators may not be prepared to share this information nor to confirm its accuracy unless for legal or investigative reasons. As a result, the application designers would need to consider how the accuracy and detail of available location information could best be exploited. The application design should also take into account the differences in handsets owned by the legitimate participants. The two parties involved in the transaction might subscribe to two different networks. Hence, care needs to be taken in design of the application that generates the location information and its verification, as CellIDs and LACs will vary for different network operator. GPS provides more "independent" access to location information as the mobile phone could determine its own location and not depend on information from the network operator. The downside of this is that the devices would need to support GPS functionality and may not be able to derive GPS co-ordinates indoors. In practice, any application relying on location information to provide security would need to use a combination of location services to best suit the operational environment when a transaction takes place.

5   Conclusion

Peer-to-peer transactions in NFC is being considered for a range of applications including payments. Relay attacks are a threat in contactless and networked environments, and may bypass the security measures employing temporal contracts and cryptography. Our contribution in this paper included a practical demonstration of a first relay attack implementation using NFC-enabled mobile phone platform. We showed that with NFC an attacker can create and introduce proxies by software development (no hardware modification) of suitable MIDlets for the mobile device. The attack did not require any code signing, and did not need software to be installed in secure program areas such as the SE. It also used standard, easily available APIs such as JSR 257 and JSR 82. The need for countermeasures should therefore be taken seriously, and as discussed the use of location based solution to verify proximity is seen as a promising approach.

References

1. ISO/IEC 18092 (ECMA-340), Information technology Telecommunications and information exchange between systems Near Field Communication Interface and Protocol (NFCIP-1) (2004), http://www.iso.org/ (cited March 31, 2010)
2. Bluetooth Core Specification Version 2.1. + EDR. Vol. 2 (July 2007)
3. Lin, G., Mikhak, A.A., Nakajima, L.T., Mayo, S.A., Rosenblatt, M.: Peer-to-peer Financial Transaction Devices and Methods. Apple Inc. Patent Application WO/2010/039337 (April 2010)
4. Hancke, G.P., Mayes, K.E., Markantonakis, K.: Confidence in Smart Token Proximity: Relay Attacks Revisited. Elsevier Computers & Security 28(7), 615–627 (2009)
5. Anderson, R.: RFID and the Middleman. In: Conference on Financial Cryptography and Data Security, pp. 46–49 (December 2007)
6. Kfir, Z., Wool, A.: Picking Virtual Pockets using Relay Attacks on Contactless Smartcard Systems. In: Proceedings of IEEE/CreateNet SecureComm, pp. 47–58 (2005)
7. Sun Microsystems, JSR-000118 Mobile Information Device Profile 2.0, http://jcp.org/aboutJava/communityprocess/final/jsr118/index.html.
8. ISO/IEC 21481 (ECMA-352), Information technology Telecommunications and information exchange between systems Near Field Communication Interface and Protocol (NFCIP-2) (2005), http://www.iso.org/ (cited March 31, 2010)
9. ISO/IEC 14443, Identification cards Contactless integrated circuit cards Proximity cards, http://www.iso.org/ (cited March 31, 2010)
10. ISO/IEC 15693, Identification cards – Contactless integrated circuit cards – Vicinity cards, http://www.iso.org/ (cited March 31, 2010)
11. FeliCa, http://www.sony.net/Products/felica/ (cited March 31, 2010)

12. European Technical Standards Institute (ETSI), Smart Cards; UICC-Terminal interface; Physical and logical characteristics (Release 7), TS 102 221 V7.9.0 (2007-07), http://www.etsi.org/ (cited March 31,2010)
13. Third Generation Partnership Project, Specification of the Subscriber Identity Module-Mobile Equipment (SIM - ME) interface (Release 1999), TS 11.11 V8.14.0 (2007-06), http://www.3gpp.org/
14. Third Generation Partnership Project, Characteristics of the Universal Subscriber Identity Module (USIM) application (Release 7), TS 31.102 V7.10.0 (2007-09), http://www.3gpp.org/
15. Third Generation Partnership Project 2 (3GPP2), Removable User Identity Module (RUIM) for Spread Spectrum Systems, 3GPP2 C.S0023-C V1.0 (May 26, 2006), http://www.3gpp2.org/
16. SD Card Association, http://www.sdcard.org/ (cited March 31, 2010)
17. Candidate Technical Specification: Signature Record Type Definition. NFC Forum (October 2009)
18. Near Field Communication (NFC) Forum, http://www.nfc-forum.org (cited March 31, 2010)
19. Sun Microsystems, Java Card Platform Specification v2.2.1, http://java.sun.com/products/javacard/specs.html (cited March 31, 2010)
20. NXP, Java Card Open Platform, http://www.nxp.com/ (cited March 31, 2010)
21. Global Platform, Card Specification v2.1.1, http://www.globalplatform.org (cited March 31, 2010)
22. NXP Semiconductor: Mifare Standard Specification, http://www.nxp.com/acrobat_download/other/identification/ (cited March 31, 2010)
23. Francis, L., Hancke, G.P., Mayes, K.E., Markantonakis, K.: Potential Misuse of NFC Enabled Mobile Handsets with Embedded Security Elements as Contactless Attack Platforms. In: Proceedings of the 1st Workshop on RFID Security and Cryptography (RISC 2009), in conjunction with the International Conference for Internet Technology and Secured Transactions (ICITST 2009), , pp. 1–8 (November 2009)
24. Mayes, K.E., Markantonakis, K. (eds.): Smart Cards, Tokens, Security and Applications. Springer, Heidelberg (2008), ISBN: 978-0-387-72197-2
25. Sun Microsystems: JSR-000257 Contactless Communication API 1.0, http://jcp.org/aboutJava/communityprocess/final/jsr257/index.html
26. Conway, J.H.: On Numbers and Games. Academic Press, London (1976)
27. Desmedt, Y., Goutier, C., Bengio, S.: Special Uses and Abuses of the Fiat-Shamir Passport Protocol. In: Pomerance, C. (ed.) CRYPTO 1987. LNCS, vol. 293, p. 21. Springer, Heidelberg (1988)
28. Hu, Y.C., Perrig, A., Johnson, D.B.: Wormhole Attacks in Wireless Networks. IEEE Journal on Selected Areas in Communications (JSAC), 370–380 (2006)
29. Hancke, G.P., Kuhn, M.G.: An RFID Distance Bounding Protocol. In: Proceedings of IEEE/CreateNet SecureComm, pp. 67–73 (September 2005)
30. Hancke, G.P.: Practical Attacks on Proximity Identification Systems. In: Proceedings of IEEE Symposium on Security and Privacy, pp. 328–333 (May 2006) (short paper)
31. Libnfc.org, Public Platform Independent Near Field Communication (NFC) Library, http://www.libnfc.org/documentation/examples/nfc-relay (cited March 31, 2010)
32. RFID IO Tools, rfidiot.org (cited March 31, 2010)
33. Sun Microsystems: JSR-000082 Java API for Bluetooth 2.1, http://jcp.org/aboutJava/communityprocess/final/jsr082/index.html (cited March 31, 2010)

34. Sun Microsystems: Java Code Signing for J2ME, http://java.sun.com/ (cited March 31, 2010)
35. Nokia Forum, Java Security Domains, http://wiki.forum.nokia.com/index.php/Java_Security_Domains (cited March 31, 2010)
36. Nokia Forum, MIDP 2.0 API Access Rights, http://wiki.forum.nokia.com/index.php/MIDP_2.0_API_access_rights (cited March 31, 2010)
37. Nokia Forum, MIDP 2.1 API Access Rights, http://wiki.forum.nokia.com/index.php/MIDP_2.1_API_access_rights (cited March 31, 2010)
38. Nokia Forum, Nokia 6131 API Access Rights, http://wiki.forum.nokia.com/index.php/API_access_rights_on_phones,_Series_40_3rd_FP1 (cited March 31, 2010)
39. Nokia Forum, Nokia 6212 API Access Rights, http://wiki.forum.nokia.com/index.php/API_access_rights_on_phones,_Series_40_5th_FP1 (cited March 31, 2010)
40. Brands, S., Chaum, D.: Distance Bounding Protocols. Advances in Cryptology. In: Helleseth, T. (ed.) EUROCRYPT 1993. LNCS, vol. 765, pp. 344–359. Springer, Heidelberg (1994)
41. Clulow, J., Hancke, G.P., Kuhn, M.G., Moore, T.: So Near and Yet So Far: Distance-Bounding Attacks in Wireless Networks. In: Buttyán, L., Gligor, V.D., Westhoff, D. (eds.) ESAS 2006. LNCS, vol. 4357, pp. 83–97. Springer, Heidelberg (2006)
42. Hancke, G.P., Kuhn, M.G.: Attacks on Time-of-Flight Distance Bounding Channels. In: Proceedings of the First ACM Conference on Wireless Network Security (WISEC 2008), pp. 194–202 (March 2008)
43. Rasmussen, K.B., Čapkun, S.: Implications of Radio Fingerprinting on the Security of Sensor Networks. In: Proceedings of IEEE SecureComm. (2007)
44. Danev, B., Heydt-Benjamin, T.S., Čapkun, S.: Physical-layer Identification of RFID Devices. In: Proceedings of USENIX Security Symposium (2009)
45. Anderson, R.J., Bond, M.: The Man-in-the-Middle Defense. Presented at Security Protocols Workshop (March 2006), http://www.cl.cam.ac.uk/~rja14/Papers/Man-in-the-Middle-Defence.pdf
46. Stajano, F., Wong, F.L., Christianson, B.: Multichannel Protocols to Prevent Relay Attacks. In: Conference on Financial Cryptography and Data Security (January 2010)
47. Boukerche, A., Oliveira, H.A.B., Nakamura, E.F., Loureiro, A.A.F.: Secure Localization Algorithms for Wireless Sensor Networks. IEEE Communications Magazine 46(4), 96–101 (2008)
48. Google Maps: Google Inc., http://www.googlemaps.com/ (cited March 31, 2010)
49. Saroiu, S., Wolman, A.: Enabling New Mobile Applications with Location Proofs. In: Proceedings of the 10th Workshop on Mobile Computing Systems and Applications, HotMobile 2009, Santa Cruz, California, February 23 - 24, pp. 1–6. ACM, New York (2009)
50. Luo, W., Hengartner, U.: Proving your Location without giving up your Privacy. In: Proceedings of the Eleventh Workshop on Mobile Computing Systems & Applications, HotMobile 2010, Annapolis, Maryland, February 22 - 23, pp. 7–12. ACM, New York (2010)
51. Hu, Y.C., Perrig, A., Johnson, D.B.: Packet leashes: A Defense Against Wormhole Attacks in Wireless Networks. In: Proceedings of INFOCOM, pp. 1976–1986 (April 2003)
52. Tippenhauer, N.O., Rasmussen, K.B., Pöpper, C., Capkun, S.: Attacks on Public WLAN-based Positioning. In: Proceedings of the ACM/Usenix International Conference on Mobile Systems, Applications and Services, MobiSys (2009)

Strong Authentication and Strong Integrity (SASI) Is Not That Strong

Gildas Avoine, Xavier Carpent, and Benjamin Martin

Université catholique de Louvain
Information Security Group
B-1348 Louvain-La-Neuve, Belgium

Abstract. In this work, we present a practical passive attack on SASI, an ultra-lightweight mutual authentication protocol for RFID. This attack can be used to reveal with overwhelming probability the secret ID of the prover by eavesdropping about 2^{17} authentications. The result dismantles SASI and, more generally, provides a new approach that threatens ultra-lightweight authentication protocols.

Keywords: RFID, authentication, lightweight cryptography, privacy, passive attack.

1 Introduction

The recent ubiquitous deployment of RFID systems raised many concerns about privacy. There is a growing need of lightweight authentication protocols to be implemented on low-cost tags that ensure privacy protection. Some existing solutions involve expensive building blocks, such as hash functions and pseudorandom number generators and do not scale well [12,19]. More recent proposals focus on extremely lightweight protocols that rely on bitwise operations, additions, or bit rotations. The UMAP family of protocols, by Peris-Lopez, Hernandez-Castro, Estevez-Tapiador and Ribagorda [13,14,16], paved the way to this new trend but suffers from teething problems [1,2,3,6,9,10,11]. In [5], Chien proposed another very lightweight authentication protocol providing Strong Authentication and Strong Integrity, so-called SASI. Security analyses have later highlighted weaknesses in its design, and various attacks have been published. In [7] and [18], the authors present active desynchronization and full-disclosure attacks. In [4], the authors proposed a traceability attack on a compromised tag by linking it with past actions performed on this tag. In [17], the author proposed a traceability attack allowing a passive attacker to guess the least significant bit on the static identifier, roughly one out of four times. Finally in [8], the authors proposed a passive full-disclosure attack against a variant of SASI when the rotation is defined as *modular*, whereas in the original paper, the rotation was defined as *Hamming weight*-based. Moreover, the attack presented in [8] is of theoretical interest because it roughly needs a number of observed runs exponential in the number of unveiled bits of the ID.

S.B. Ors Yalcin (Ed.): RFIDSec 2010, LNCS 6370, pp. 50–64, 2010.

In the following, we propose a *passive* full-disclosure attack on SASI which is more efficient than the one in [8] and that works with any definition of the rotation. It requires the attacker to eavesdrop 2^{17} (respectively 2^{19}) in the case of the Hamming-weight rotation (respectively modular rotation) in order to almost certainly disclose the full tag ID. Up to our knowledge, this is the first practical passive full-disclosure attack on SASI.

The rest of this paper is organized as follows. In Section 2, we describe the SASI protocol. In Section 3, we introduce some preliminary tools and solve two subproblems required in the attack. In Section 4, we present the attack itself. In Section 5, we present the efficiency analysis of the attack, as well as some optimizations and experimental results. We present our conclusions in Section 6.

2 The SASI Protocol

SASI [5] is a mutual authentication algorithm designed for ultra-lightweight RFID tags. In such tags, randomness must be provided by the reader, because no pseudorandom number generator (PRNG) is provided in the tag, nor is any cryptographic hash function.

Each tag has a secret static identifier ID, and two secret keys K_1 and K_2, as well as a public index-pseudonym IDS. The latter is used by the reader to identify an entry in its internal database, allowing it to retrieve the identifier and the keys related to this tag. Keys and index pseudonyms are updated after each authentication. All quantities involved, including the submessages exchanged are of fixed length $L = 96$ bits.

The SASI protocol relies on logical OR ($\vee$), logical XOR ($\oplus$), modular addition ($+$), and the rotation $Rot(x, y)$. This operation is defined as a circular left-shift of x of $r(y)$ bits, where:

$$ r : [0, 2^L - 1] \rightarrow [0, L - 1]. $$

Several rotations can be used with SASI, especially the *modular* rotation, that is $r(y) = y \bmod L$, and *Hamming weight* rotation, with $r(y) = \mathcal{H}(y) \bmod L$, where $\mathcal{H}$ is the Hamming weight function. In the latter, the modulus is there to fold the case where $\mathcal{H}(y) = L$ back to a number in $[0, L - 1]$ (a rotation of L bits is the same as a rotation of 0 bits).

Note that r was not precisely defined in [5], and it was pointed out in [18] that the rotation intended to be used in the original version of the protocol is the Hamming-weight one. The modular version was introduced in [8].

The protocol definition is as follows. The reader initiates the authentication by sending a *hello* message to the tag, which answers its current index-pseudonym IDS. The reader uses it to find an entry in its internal database with ID, K_1 and K_2. It then produces two nonces n_1 and n_2, and computes A, B, and C as detailed in Figure 1, and sends these three values to the tag.

From A and B, the tag extracts the nonces and uses them to compute C'. If C matches C', the tag authenticates the reader, and then sends D. The reader computes D' and if it matches the received D, it authenticates the tag.

Finally, each party updates the keys and the index pseudonym for further authentications. An overview of the protocol along with messages and update definitions can be found in Figure 1.

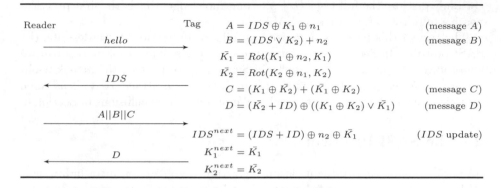

Fig. 1. The SASI protocol

3   Preliminary Tools

In this section we analyze in detail the mechanics of the addition, in order to have a better understanding of equations mixing additions and bitwise operations like logical OR and XOR. We then present two subproblems that are useful in the attack of SASI, but that might be used for other purposes as well.

3.1   Notations and Definitions

In the following, we denote by $[x]_i$ the bit at position i in x. In particular, $[x]_0$ is the least significant bit (LSB) of x, and $[x]_{L-1}$ its most significant bit (MSB). By convention, we say that $[x]_i = 0$ when $i > \lceil \log_2(x) \rceil$. When evoking the i-th bit of x, we refer to $[x]_i$.

We also introduce the following notation for the *carry* of the addition, and the *borrow* of the subtraction, respectively:

$\mathcal{C}(a, b, i)$ denotes the carry at bit i of the sum of a and b, and
$\mathcal{B}(a, b, i)$ denotes the borrow at bit i of the difference of a and b.

Using this notation, we write that the result of the addition of numbers a and b at bit i is:

$$[a + b]_i = [a]_i \oplus [b]_i \oplus \mathcal{C}(a, b, i - 1). \tag{1}$$

Likewise, we write the difference of two numbers a and b at bit i as:

$$[a - b]_i = [a]_i \oplus [b]_i \oplus \mathcal{B}(a, b, i - 1). \tag{2}$$

We compute the *carry* of two numbers a and b at bit index i as:

$$\mathcal{C}(a, b, i) = ([a]_i \wedge [b]_i) \vee \left[([a]_i \vee [b]_i) \wedge \mathcal{C}(a, b, i - 1) \right], \tag{3}$$

with the convention that $\mathcal{C}(x, y, i) = 0$ if $i < 0$, for any x and y. Indeed, there is a carry at bit i if either both operands' bits are 1, or if at least one of them is 1 while there is a carry at bit $i - 1$. This is no different of the way a computer performs addition.

Similarly, $\mathcal{B}(a, b, i)$ is the *borrow* of the subtraction of b to a at bit i, and is computed as:

$$\mathcal{B}(a, b, i) = ([\bar{a}]_i \wedge [b]_i) \vee \left[([\bar{a}]_i \oplus [b]_i) \wedge \mathcal{B}(a, b, i - 1) \right], \tag{4}$$

with the same convention, that is, $\mathcal{B}(x, y, i) = 0$ if $i < 0$, for any x and y. Again, there is a borrow at bit i if either a is 0 and b is 1, or if they are equal but there is a borrow at bit $i - 1$.

3.2   Modular Addition

If the $+$ operator is defined as *modular* addition, as often in cryptography, extra care is needed. Namely, when $a \equiv b \pmod{N}$, that does not necessarily mean that $[a]_i = [b]_i$. Indeed, even though $4 \equiv 1 \pmod{3}$, $[4]_0 = 0 \neq [1]_0 = 1$. Recall that $[4]_0$ denotes the bit at index 0 in its base two representation (its LSB). What is true, however, is that if $a \equiv b \pmod{N}$, then $a \bmod N = b \bmod N$, hence $[a \bmod N]_i = [b \bmod N]_i \ \forall i \geq 0$.

In the particular case of $N = 2^L$, then if $a \equiv b \pmod{N}$, we still have $[a]_i = [b]_i$ if $i < L$. Indeed, when N is a power of 2, computing the remainder is like dropping all the bits above L.

In the practical problems discussed below, we use addition modulo 2^L, and bit indices are smaller than L, so we will not refer to this issue later on.

3.3   First Subproblem

This first subproblem is stated as follows.

Problem 1. Given a and $[a + x]_i$, guess $[x]_i$.

To solve this problem, we use Equation (1), which yields:

$$[x]_i = [a]_i \oplus [a + x]_i \oplus \mathcal{C}(a, x, i - 1).$$

We know both $[a]_i$ and $[a + x]_i$, but the carry is unknown. Using Equation (3), we obtain the two following cases. When $[a]_k = 1$:

$$\begin{aligned}
\mathcal{C}(a, x, k) &= ([a]_k \wedge [x]_k) \vee \left[([a]_k \oplus [x]_k) \wedge \mathcal{C}(a, x, k - 1) \right] \\
&= [x]_k \vee \left([\bar{x}]_k \wedge \mathcal{C}(a, x, k - 1) \right) \\
&= [x]_k \vee \mathcal{C}(a, x, k - 1).
\end{aligned}$$

Likewise, when $[a]_k = 0$:

$$\begin{aligned}
\mathcal{C}(a, x, k) &= ([a]_k \wedge [x]_k) \vee \left[([a]_k \oplus [x]_k) \wedge \mathcal{C}(a, x, k - 1) \right] \\
&= [x]_k \wedge \mathcal{C}(a, x, k - 1).
\end{aligned}$$

If we know the distribution of x (usually uniform), we are able compute the probability of $[x]_k$ being 0 or 1, and thus the probability of $\mathcal{C}(a, x, i-1)$ being 0 or 1.

In the general case, we are not sure of the actual values taken by $[x]_i$, although we do have some information as we have seen. That information can be used to guess a possible value for it, which will be correct with a given computable probability. Assuming uniform distribution for x, the possible outputs and their probability of occurring are depicted in Table 1.

Table 1. Possible outputs of $\mathcal{C}(a, x, k)$ and their probability, given a

$[a]_k$	$\mathcal{C}(a, x, k)$	$\Pr(\mathcal{C}(a, x, k) = 1)$
0	$[x]_k \wedge \mathcal{C}(a, x, k-1)$	$\frac{1}{2} \cdot \Pr(\mathcal{C}(a, x, k-1) = 1)$
1	$[x]_k \vee \mathcal{C}(a, x, k-1)$	$1 - \frac{1}{2} \cdot \Pr(\mathcal{C}(a, x, k-1) = 0)$

We output $[x]_i = [a]_i \oplus [a+x]_i$ if we have probability of carry $\Pr(\mathcal{C}(a, x, i-1) = 1) < \frac{1}{2}$, and $[x]_i = [a]_i \oplus [a+x]_i \oplus 1$ otherwise. The probability of guessing right is computable given the distribution of x.

3.4 Second Subproblem

This second subproblem is stated as follows.

Problem 2. Given a, b, and the relation $a = (b \vee u) + x$, find $[x]_i$ for a given i (u is unknown).

We now see how to get as much information on x as possible. From Equation (2), we have:

$$[x]_i = [a - (b \vee u)]_i = [a]_i \oplus [b \vee u]_i \oplus \mathcal{B}(a, b \vee u, i-1),$$

in which we know $[a]_i$. We also know that, if $[b]_i = 1$, then $[b \vee u]_i = 1$, and if not, we have a 50% chance of guessing the right bit (assuming uniform distribution for u). As for the borrow $\mathcal{B}(a, b \vee u, i-1)$, we can use Equation (4) in the same fashion as we did for the previous subproblem. If $[b]_k = 1$, we have:

$$
\begin{aligned}
\mathcal{B}(a, b \vee u, k) &= ([\bar{a}]_k \wedge ([b]_k \vee [u]_k)) \vee \left[([\bar{a}]_k \oplus ([b]_k \vee [u]_k)) \wedge \mathcal{B}(a, b \vee u, k-1)\right] \\
&= [\bar{a}]_k \vee ([a]_k \wedge \mathcal{B}(a, b \vee u, k-1)) \\
&= [\bar{a}]_k \vee \mathcal{B}(a, b \vee u, k-1).
\end{aligned}
$$

However, if $[b]_k = 0$,

$$
\begin{aligned}
\mathcal{B}(a, b \vee u, k) &= ([\bar{a}]_k \wedge ([b]_k \vee [u]_k)) \vee \left[([\bar{a}]_k \oplus ([b]_k \vee [u]_k)) \wedge \mathcal{B}(a, b \vee u, k-1)\right] \\
&= ([\bar{a}]_k \wedge [u]_k) \vee \left[([\bar{a}]_k \oplus [u]_k) \wedge \mathcal{B}(a, b \vee u, k-1)\right].
\end{aligned}
$$

Again, we are not always sure of the actual values taken by $[x]_i$, although we can make a good guess with computable probability. Assuming uniform distribution for u, the possible outputs and their probability of occurring are depicted in Table 2.

Table 2. Possible outputs of $\mathcal{B}(a, b \vee u, k)$ and their probability, given a and b

$[a]_k$	$[b]_k$	$\mathcal{B}(a, b \vee u, k)$	$\Pr(\mathcal{B}(a, b \vee u, k) = 1)$
0	0	$[u]_k \vee \mathcal{B}(a, b \vee u, k - 1)$	$1 - \frac{1}{2} \cdot \Pr(\mathcal{B}(a, b \vee u, k - 1) = 0)$
0	1	1	1
1	0	$[u]_k \wedge \mathcal{B}(a, b \vee u, k - 1)$	$\frac{1}{2} \cdot \Pr(\mathcal{B}(a, b \vee u, k - 1) = 1)$
1	1	$\mathcal{B}(a, b \vee u, k - 1)$	$\Pr(\mathcal{B}(a, b \vee u, k - 1) = 1)$

4 Full-Disclosure Attack

4.1 Attack Outline

In this attack scenario, we consider a passive adversary who can only eavesdrop the communications between a reader and a tag, i.e. the submessages A, B, C and D, and IDS. We also assume that the channel between the reader and its database is secure.

The attack is a full-disclosure of the tag's secret ID. It is *probabilistic*, in the sense that the adversary is never 100% sure of the ID recovered. However she can be as close as she wants to this certainty, as long as she has more protocol runs to listen to. It is not dependent of the definition of the rotation, though its efficiency is.

The idea is to build a progressive knowledge on the ID with the information we compute from public quantities. Each information gain requires 3 consecutive successful authentications, but other successful authentications can exist between each information gain.

In order to carry out the attack, we first need to compute the least significant bit (LSB) of the ID, as described in Section 4.2. Once the LSB is retrieved, the attack described in Section 4.3 reveals the remaining bits of ID.

4.2 Attack Initialization

The aim here is to recover the LSB of ID. Therefore, we focus on the case $i = 0$, where the modular addition $(+)$ and bitwise XOR $(\oplus)$ are the same LSB-wise. Recall that we denoted by $[x]_i$ the i-th bit of x.

Lemma 1. *If $[IDS]_0 = 1$ and $[B]_0 \oplus [C]_0 \oplus [D]_0 \oplus [IDS^{next}]_0 = 1$, we have*

$$[ID]_0 = [B]_0 \oplus [IDS^{next}]_0 \oplus 1.$$

Proof. Let us first look at the submessage (message B) at the LSB:

$$[B]_0 = ([IDS]_0 \vee [K_2]_0) \oplus [n_2]_0.$$

Since $[IDS]_0 = 1$, we have $[n_2]_0 = [B]_0 \oplus 1$, no matter $[K_2]_0$. Moreover, from message definitions (message B), (message C), (message D), and (IDS update), we get the following equalities at the LSB:

$$[B]_0 = 1 \oplus [n_2]_0,$$
$$[C]_0 = [K_1]_0 \oplus [K_2]_0 \oplus [\bar{K}_1]_0 \oplus [\bar{K}_2]_0, \tag{5}$$
$$[D]_0 = [\bar{K}_2]_0 \oplus [ID]_0 \oplus (([K_1]_0 \oplus [K_2]_0) \vee [\bar{K}_1]_0), \tag{6}$$
$$[IDS^{next}]_0 = [IDS]_0 \oplus [ID]_0 \oplus [n_2]_0 \oplus [\bar{K}_1]_0.$$

Hence, we have:

$$[B]_0 \oplus [C]_0 \oplus [D]_0 \oplus [IDS^{next}]_0 = [K_1]_0 \oplus [K_2]_0 \oplus (([K_1]_0 \oplus [K_2]_0) \vee [\bar{K}_1]_0).$$

Since $[B]_0 \oplus [C]_0 \oplus [D]_0 \oplus [IDS^{next}]_0 = 1$, it is impossible that $[\bar{K}_1]_0 = 0$. We thus have:

$$[\bar{K}_1]_0 = 1,$$
$$[B]_0 \oplus [C]_0 \oplus [D]_0 \oplus [IDS^{next}]_0 = [K_1]_0 \oplus [K_2]_0 \oplus 1.$$

Now that we know those two quantities, we can get $[\bar{K}_2]_0$ using (5):

$$[\bar{K}_2]_0 = [B]_0 \oplus [D]_0 \oplus [IDS^{next}]_0, \tag{7}$$

that we then use in (6):

$$[D]_0 = [\bar{K}_2]_0 \oplus [ID]_0 \oplus (([K_1]_0 \oplus [K_2]_0) \vee [\bar{K}_1]_0),$$
$$= [B]_0 \oplus [D]_0 \oplus [IDS^{next}]_0 \oplus [ID]_0 \oplus 1,$$

which allows us to conclude.   □

We say that a quantity has a uniform distribution if every element of its domain is equally likely to be instantiated. It is quite easy to see that public quantities IDS, A, B, C, and D have uniform distribution, since their computation involve either a bitwise XOR, or a modular addition with a nonce or with a key (keys also have uniform distributions because they are also updated using a bitwise XOR with a nonce). The domain of these quantities is $[0, 2^L - 1]$, and hence we also have "bitwise" uniform distribution in the sense that every bit has an equal probability to be a zero or a one.

We have seen that getting the LSB of the ID requires two bits to be equal to 1. Since quantities taken into account for this observation have bitwise uniform distribution, the probability of occurrence is $\frac{1}{4}$. The number of runs needed for this observation has a geometric distribution of average 4. The result is quite similar as the one in [17], except here the adversary knows for sure when conditions are met, because they only involve public quantities.

In fact, we can generalize the attack to an arbitrary bit index, but this would need conditions of which probabilities of occurrence are negative exponential in the position of that bit index. Instead, we describe in Section 4.3 a much more efficient attack to retrieve $[ID]_i$ when $i > 0$.

4.3   Attack Details

Now that we have the required tools, we describe the core of the attack more thoroughly. We have seen in Section 4.2 that the adversary can easily recover the least significant bit of the ID of a tag, so we assume that this part of the attack has already been executed, and that we know $[ID]_0$.

At the LSB, (IDS update) becomes:

$$[IDS^{(n+1)}]_0 = [IDS^{(n)}]_0 \oplus [ID]_0 \oplus [n_2^{(n)}]_0 \oplus [\bar{K_1}^{(n)}]_0. \tag{8}$$

We have also seen in Section 4.2 that when $[IDS^{(n)}]_0 = 1$, $[n_2^{(n)}]_0$ is known by computing $[B^{(n)}]_0 \oplus [IDS^{(n)}]_0$. Thus, from Equation (8), we get:

$$[\bar{K_1}^{(n)}]_0 = [ID]_0 \oplus [B^{(n)}]_0 \oplus [IDS^{(n+1)}]_0.$$

The next round, according to the key updating process $K_1^{(n+1)} = \bar{K_1}^{(n)}$, we know $[K_1^{(n+1)}]_0$. Furthermore, if again $[IDS^{(n+1)}]_0 = 1$, we have $[n_2^{(n+1)}]_0 = [B^{(n+1)}]_0 \oplus [IDS^{(n+1)}]_0$. Thus, we know $[K_1^{(n+1)} \oplus n_2^{(n+1)}]_0$. So, since $\bar{K_1}^{(n+1)} = Rot(K_1^{(n+1)} \oplus n_2^{(n+1)}, K_1^{(n+1)})$, we have:

$$[K_1^{(n+1)} \oplus n_2^{(n+1)}]_0 = [\bar{K_1}^{(n+1)}]_{r(K_1^{(n+1)})}.$$

Recall from Section 2 that r denotes the function used in the rotation operation. In most cases, we do not know $r(K_1^{(n+1)})$, since we only know the LSB of $K_1^{(n+1)}$, but we can say that, assuming K_1 has a uniform statistical distribution,

$$\Pr(r(K_1^{(n+1)}) = i) = p_r(i) \qquad \forall\, i \in [0, L-1],$$

where p_r is the probability distribution function of r. For instance, in the case of modular rotation, $r(x) = x \bmod L$, and $p_r(x) = \frac{1}{L}$, and in the case of Hamming weight rotation, $r(x) = \mathcal{H}(x)$, and $p_r(x) = \frac{\binom{L}{x}}{2^L}$. So, with probability $p_r(i)$, we know $[\bar{K_1}^{(n+1)}]_i$. We then use this result in (IDS update):

$$[ID + IDS^{(n+1)}]_i = [IDS^{(n+2)}]_i \oplus [n_2^{(n+1)}]_i \oplus \underbrace{[\bar{K_1}^{(n+1)}]_i}_{[K_1^{(n+1)} \oplus n_2^{(n+1)}]_0} .$$

The computation of $[n_2^{(n+1)}]_i$ has already been discussed in Section 3.4. Finally, we have $[ID + IDS^{(n+1)}]_i$ and $IDS^{(n+1)}$, but this does not necessarily mean that we have $[ID]_i$. However, we can recover some information on $[ID]_i$ using what we know, as seen in Section 3.3. The result is that we obtain $[ID]_i$ with a *certain* probability, that will be quantified in the next section.

An outline of the attack can be seen in Figure 2.

In order to provide a more intuitive description of the attack, consider the following game. Having a slightly biased coin, we want to know what side of this

---

Execute the traceability attack to get $[ID]_0$
repeat
  if $[IDS]_0 = 1$ **then**
    if the previous $[K_1]_0$ was known (that is, previous $[IDS]_0$ was 1) **then**
      Compute n_2 probabilistically (2)
      Compute ID probabilistically given IDS and $IDS + ID$ (1)
      for all $i \in [1, L - 1]$ **do**
        Update the knowledge of $[ID]_i$ with the advantages of (1) and (2) and
        $p_r(i)$
      end for
    end if
    Compute $[K_1^{next}]_0 = [ID]_0 \oplus [B]_0 \oplus [IDS^{next}]_0$
  end if
until all the bits of ID are found with satisfactory probability

---

Fig. 2. Outline of the attack. (1) refers to the first subproblem discussed in Section 3.3, and (2) to the second one, which is discussed in Section 3.4. Note that the "computed" $[K_1^{next}]_0$ is on the attacker side, and that the actual $[K_1^{next}]_0$ is unknown. For clarity reasons, we did not make a difference of notation between computed (or guessed) values and real ones.

coin is biased. We can toss it as many times as we want, but we want to have a good probability of guessing the right side, while minimizing the number of tosses. The smaller the bias is, the harder it is to tell whether it is heads or tails that is the most favorable side. Indeed, if the bias is, for instance 75% for heads and 25% for tails, we already have a good information with 20 tosses. However, if the bias turns out to be 50.01% for heads, and 49.99% for tails, we would need a whole lot more of them.

This is exactly the idea of convergence of the attack, except that we are guessing the biased side of $L - 1$ independent coins, and that each toss has a different "weight". Indeed we have seen in the attack that we only get some information when $[IDS]_0 = 1$ for two consecutive runs. Moreover, each information gain has to be weighted with $p_r(i)$, the information we have on n_2, and the one we have on ID given $ID + IDS$. For instance, when $p_r(i)$ is small, the guessed rotation has a small probability of being right, thus we bring less valuable information than when $p_r(i)$ is big.

5   Efficiency Analysis and Experiments

5.1   Theoretical Analysis

We now analyze the efficiency of the attack, by showing what conclusion we can draw given the set of observations and by linking these observations with the probability of guessing the right ID.

Let us assume that we have at our disposal an oracle that has a secret bit b and a set of $0 \leq q_i \leq 1$ which, upon query, outputs a bit b_i and a value q_i such that $\Pr(b_i = b) = q_i$. We assume that $\Pr(b = 0) = \Pr(b = 1) = \frac{1}{2}$, that all the outputs are independent, and that $q_i \geq \frac{1}{2}$, without loss of generality. Indeed, if one guess is such that $q_i < \frac{1}{2}$, then it would be equivalent to output the opposite bit with complementary probability $1 - q_i > \frac{1}{2}$.

For convenience, let us denote by O the observations, that is the event corresponding to observing the set of bits b_i. Let us also define the sets:

$$S_0 = \{i \in [1, N] \mid b_i = 0\}, \text{ and}$$
$$S_1 = \{i \in [1, N] \mid b_i = 1\}.$$

If we observe $N = |S_0| + |S_1|$ outputs of the oracle, we have:

$$\Pr(O|b = 0) = \prod_{i \in S_0} q_i \prod_{i \in S_1} (1 - q_i), \qquad (9)$$

$$\Pr(O|b = 1) = \prod_{i \in S_0} (1 - q_i) \prod_{i \in S_1} q_i. \qquad (10)$$

Using Bayes' rule :

$$\Pr(b = 0|O) = \frac{\Pr(b = 0 \cap O)}{\Pr(O)}$$

$$= \frac{\Pr(O|b = 0) \cdot \Pr(b = 0)}{\Pr(O|b = 0) \cdot \Pr(b = 0) + \Pr(O|b = 1) \cdot \Pr(b = 1)}$$

$$= \frac{\Pr(O|b = 0)}{\Pr(O|b = 0) + \Pr(O|b = 1)},$$

since events $b = 0$ and $b = 1$ are equiprobable. Now we use Equations (9) and (10), and obtain:

$$\Pr(b = 0|O) = \frac{\prod_{i \in S_0} q_i \prod_{i \in S_1} (1 - q_i)}{\prod_{i \in S_0} q_i \prod_{i \in S_1} (1 - q_i) + \prod_{i \in S_0} (1 - q_i) \prod_{i \in S_1} q_i}$$

$$= \frac{1}{1 + \prod_{i \in S_0} \frac{1 - q_i}{q_i} \prod_{i \in S_1} \frac{q_i}{1 - q_i}}. \qquad (11)$$

An equivalent but more convenient way of seeing this is the following. Instead of outputting probabilities q_i, the oracle can output *advantages* a_i such that $|\Pr(b_i = b) - \Pr(b_i \neq b)| = a_i$. Put differently, we have $a_i = |2q_i - 1|$. In this scenario, Equation (11) becomes:

$$\Pr(b = 0|O) = \frac{1}{1 + \prod_{i \in S_0} \frac{1 - a_i}{1 + a_i} \prod_{i \in S_1} \frac{1 + a_i}{1 - a_i}}. \qquad (12)$$

Recall from Figure 2 that the information on each bit of the ID is weighted using:

- $p_r(i)$
- the level of trust on $[ID]_i$ given $[ID + IDS]_i$ (subproblem 1)
- the level of trust on $[n_2]_i$ (subproblem 2)

Indeed, each guess on the i-th bit of the ID is correct if:

- the guessed rotation is the correct one
- the guess of $[ID]_i$ given $[ID + IDS]_i$ is correct
- the guess at $[n_2]_i$ is correct

The probability of correctness for the rotation is simply $p_r(k)$, and the probability of correctness for the two subproblems (the level of trust or *advantage* on the quantities n_2 and ID) is computable, given public submessages, as seen in Sections 3.3 and 3.4. If we assume independence between these advantages, we just have to multiply them to obtain an advantage a_i related to the k-th bit on the i-th run. Using Equation (12), we can have a total probability on the value of a bit of the ID, given a certain amount of information materialized by the guesses and advantages on these guesses on that bit.

We have observed experimentally that the average advantages for the first and second subproblems are respectively roughly $\frac{1}{2}$ and $\frac{1}{3}$. This is particularly important for the second subproblem, because we see that simply knowing IDS and B, we can guess roughly one third of n_2.

Recall from Section 4.3 that to execute the inner part of the attack and thus bring information, we require $[IDS]_0 = 1$ for two consecutive runs. Since IDS has a uniform distribution, this will occurs with probability $\frac{1}{4}$. We thus need to multiply the number of runs needed by 4.

5.2   Optimizations and Experimentations

We introduce in this section some optimizations that improve in practice the efficiency of the attack presented in Section 4.3.

First of all, we raise that it is somewhat wasteful to only use $[ID]_0$ while more and more knowledge on ID is revealed along the attack. Progressive knowledge on the ID can not only help solving the first subproblem ($[ID]_i$ from IDS and $[ID + IDS]_i$), but it can also be used as a base, instead of $[ID]_0$ only.

This especially helps with the Hamming-weight rotations where the most and least significant bits are hard to guess using $[ID]_0$ only (because $p_r(i)$ is very small for small or big i).

We have carried out experiments with the two definitions of the rotation and have observed the number of *errors* (number of wrong guesses) on average. When this number is close to 0, it means that we manage to correctly recover the whole ID with good probability, and when it is close to $\frac{L}{2} = 48$, it means that the output guessed ID is not better than if we had guessed one at random. Table 3(a) and Table 3(b) contain the results respectively without and with optimizations (using other $[ID]_i$ as bases). Figure 3 shows the evolution of the quality of the ID recovered (when applying the optimization) with respect N, the number of observed runs.

Table 3. Average number of errors (number of wrong guesses on the ID) respectivelely without (a) and with (b) optimizations. These results were obtained on an average of roughly 500 experiments conducted with a simulated SASI initiated with random secrets. Recall that N is the total number of runs observed, and $L = 96$ is the length of the quantities involved in the protocol.

(a) No optimizations

N	$\mathcal{H}(x) \bmod L$	$x \bmod L$
2^{18}	-	16.230
2^{19}	-	8.011
2^{20}	-	2.973
2^{21}	-	1.375
2^{22}	-	0.628
2^{23}	-	0.154

(b) Optimization applied

N	$\mathcal{H}(x) \bmod L$	$x \bmod L$
2^{14}	22.985	38.741
2^{15}	9.944	33.81
2^{16}	2.908	19.45
2^{17}	0.620	5.436
2^{18}	0.159	1.294
2^{19}	0.041	0.436

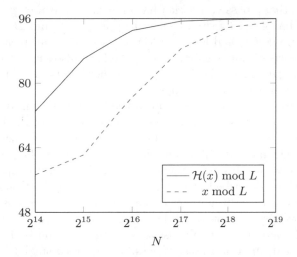

Fig. 3. Average number of bits correctly guessed in ID, for the two usual rotations (optimization applied)

Note that in Table 3(a), the results for Hamming-weight rotation are not shown since only the 40 or so middle bits are relevant, as explained above. However, when applying optimizations, we see that it becomes possible to solve it, with slightly better results than with modular rotation. We also see that optimizations reduce the average required number of observed runs, as expected.

Note also that using Equation (12), it is possible to have an idea of the trust on the guessed bits. Hence we can know if more runs are needed.

We can also imagine other optimizations such as the following. The adversary does not know K_1 in whole, but she does know $[K_1]_0$, and for instance in the case of modular rotation, she knows the parity of it, and thus she can reduce the possibilities from L down to $\frac{L}{2}$, which improves the advantage per sample quite a bit. She could also reuse old authentication sessions when she has better knowledge of ID. We did not take these into accout in the experiments for Table 3(b). The point is that we could further reduce the number of runs needed to achieve overwhelming probability, but the first optimization alone is enough to make the attack practical.

6   Conclusion

In this article we have presented a passive full-disclosure attack on SASI. We have shown that eavesdropping 2^{17} (respectively 2^{19}) in the case of the Hamming-weight rotation (respectively modular rotation) is enough to almost certainly disclose the full tag ID. Up to our knowledge, we provide the first practical full-disclosure attack against SASI with a passive adversary.

We have seen that the submessage B is weak and wraps n_2 quite poorly. We have indeed seen that a passive attacker has an average advantage of roughly one third over each bit of n_2, by simply eavesdropping IDS and B. It shows once more that logical OR ($\vee$) and logical AND ($\wedge$) should by all means be avoided in the external parts of public submessages. We have also seen how to deal with expressions mixing modular addition ($+$) with other bitwise operations, and that they are usually weaker than they appear.

Although rotations are a nice addition to the lightweight family of operations already used in previous similar protocols such as the ones of the UMAP family [16,14,13], we have seen that it is by itself not enough to ensure the security of the protocol. The inclusion of a non-triangular operation, however, has made the recovery process much more complex, and a "bottom-up" approach for an attack such as those described in [2,3] is no longer possible. Consequently, the average number of successful authentications needed to observe is much larger. The Hamming-weight rotation which has been praised in [8] did not prove any stronger than the modular one. The issue with the rotation is that the rotated bits are not changed, and that the set of possible outputs is small (L possibilities).

In conclusion, besides showing several weaknesses in the design of SASI, this attack also introduces a new way of cryptanalysis of ultralightweight authentication protocols, namely building progressive knowledge on a quantity given a series of observations of non-negligible advantage. Other protocols might suffer from the same weaknesses, and the same approach could be used to analyse their security. Gossamer, by Peris-Lopez et al. [15], was somewhat inspired by SASI and the protocols from the UMAP family, but is more mature and includes features such as double rotations and lightweight PRNG's. Determining whether this protocol is secure and if it can be analaysed using this novel technique remains an open question.

Acknowledgements. This work was partially funded by the Walloon Region Marshall plan through the SPW DG06 Project TRASILUX.

References

1. Alomair, B., Lazos, L., Poovendran, R.: Passive attacks on a class of authentication protocols for RFID. Information Security and Cryptology-ICISC 2007, 102–115 (2007)
2. Bárász, M., Boros, B., Ligeti, P., Lója, K., Nagy, D.: Breaking LMAP. Printed handout of Workshop on RFID Security RFIDSec (July 2007)
3. Bárász, M., Boros, B., Ligeti, P., Lója, K., Nagy, D.: Passive attack against the M2AP mutual authentication protocol for RFID tags. In: Proc. of First International EURASIP Workshop on RFID Technology (2007)
4. Cao, T., Bertino, E., Lei, H.: Security Analysis of the SASI Protocol. IEEE Transactions on Dependable and Secure Computing 6, 73–77 (2008)
5. Chien, H.-Y.: SASI: A New Ultralightweight RFID Authentication Protocol Providing Strong Authentication and Strong Integrity. IEEE Transactions on Dependable and Secure Computing 4, 337–340 (2007)
6. Chien, H.Y., Huang, C.W.: Security of ultra-lightweight RFID authentication protocols and its improvements. ACM SIGOPS Operating Systems Review 41(4), 86 (2007)
7. D'Arco, P., De Santis, A.: From Weaknesses to Secret Disclosure in a Recent Ultra-Lightweight RFID Authentication Protocol. Cryptology ePrint Archive, Report 2008/470 (2008), http://eprint.iacr.org/
8. Hernandez-Castro, J.C., Tapiador, J.M.E., Peris-Lopez, P., Quisquater, J.-J.: Cryptanalysis of the SASI Ultralightweight RFID Authentication Protocol with Modular Rotations. ArXiv e-prints (November 2008)
9. Li, T., Deng, R.: Vulnerability analysis of EMAP-an efficient RFID mutual authentication protocol. In: The Second International Conference on Availability, Reliability and Security, ARES 2007, pp. 238–245 (2007)
10. Li, T., Wang, G.: Security analysis of two ultra-lightweight RFID authentication protocols. New Approaches for Security, Privacy and Trust in Complex Environments, 109–120 (2007)
11. Li, T., Wang, G., Deng, R.H.: Security Analysis on a Family of Ultra-lightweight RFID Authentication Protocols. Journal of Software 3(3), 1 (2008)
12. Ohkubo, M., Suzuki, K., Kinoshita, S.: Cryptographic approach to privacy-friendly tags. In: RFID Privacy Workshop (2003)
13. Peris-Lopez, P., Hernandez-Castro, J., Estevez-Tapiador, J., Ribagorda, A.: EMAP: An efficient mutual-authentication protocol for low-cost RFID tags. In: Meersman, R., Tari, Z., Herrero, P. (eds.) OTM 2006 Workshops. LNCS, vol. 4277, pp. 352–361. Springer, Heidelberg (2006)
14. Peris-Lopez, P., Hernandez-Castro, J., Estevez-Tapiador, J., Ribagorda, A.: M^2AP: A minimalist mutual-authentication protocol for low-cost RFID tags. In: Ma, J., Jin, H., Yang, L.T., Tsai, J.J.-P. (eds.) UIC 2006. LNCS, vol. 4159, pp. 912–923. Springer, Heidelberg (2006)
15. Peris-Lopez, P., Hernandez-Castro, J., Tapiador, J., Ribagorda, A.: Advances in Ultralightweight Cryptography for Low-Cost RFID Tags: Gossamer Protocol. In: Information Security Applications, pp. 56–68 (2009)
16. Peris-Lopez, P., Hernandez-Castro, J.C., Estevez-Tapiador, J.M., Ribagorda, A.: LMAP: A real lightweight mutual authentication protocol for low-cost RFID tags. In: Proc. of 2nd Workshop on RFID Security, p. 6 Citeseer. (2006)

17. Phan, R.C.-W.: Cryptanalysis of a New Ultralightweight RFID Authentication Protocol - SASI. IEEE Transactions on Dependable and Secure Computing 6, 316–320 (2008)
18. Sun, H.-M., Ting, W.-C., Wang, K.-H.: On the Security of Chien's Ultra-Lightweight RFID Authentication Protocol. IEEE Transactions on Dependable and Secure Computing 99 (2009)(prePrints)
19. Van Le, T., Burmester, M., de Medeiros, B.: Forward-secure RFID authentication and key exchange. IACR ePrint (February 2007)

Privacy Models for RFID Schemes

Serge Vaudenay

EPFL, Switzerland

Abstract. We review several privacy models for RFID schemes, depending on the capabilities of the adversary. Namely, an adversary may access to the information about whether the identification succeeded or not. He may be able to corrupt tags or not. As for corruption, we may be interested in privacy of information prior to corruption or not. We review formal definition and discuss latest results about the stronger notion of privacy.

S.B. Ors Yalcin (Ed.): RFIDSec 2010, LNCS 6370, p. 65, 2010.
© Springer-Verlag Berlin Heidelberg 2010

On the Claimed Privacy of EC-RAC III*

Junfeng Fan, Jens Hermans**, and Frederik Vercauteren***

Department of Electrical Engineering - COSIC
K.U. Leuven and IBBT
Kasteelpark Arenberg 10, B-3001 Leuven-Heverlee, Belgium
firstname.lastname@esat.kuleuven.be

Abstract. In this paper we show how to break the most recent version of EC-RAC with respect to privacy. We show that both the ID-Transfer and ID&PWD-Transfer schemes from EC-RAC do not provide the claimed privacy levels by using a man-in-the-middle attack. The existence of these attacks voids the presented privacy proofs for EC-RAC.

Keywords: RFID, Protocols, EC-RAC, Privacy.

1 Introduction

Radio Frequency Identification (RFID) is a technology that has great potential. It can be used in supply chains, access control, product authentication and so on. The study on RFID has mainly two branches: design of RFID-specific protocols and implementation of security components. The former focuses on design and analysis of cryptographic schemes that can meet various requirements in terms of security and privacy. The latter focuses on low-cost and secure implementations of cryptographic primitives such as hash functions and Public Key Cryptography (PKC).

The EC-RAC (ECDLP Based Randomized Access Control) protocol is a cryptographic protocol designed for RFID systems. It was designed to offer anonymity, which is not offered by conventional ECDLP based protocols such as the Schnorr [6] and the Okamoto [5] protocol. It was also carefully designed to "minimize the computation workload of a tag" [3]. The first version of the EC-RAC protocol [3] was broken in [7] and [1], while the second version of EC-RAC [4] was broken in [8]. In this paper, we examine the third version of EC-RAC [2] (EC-RAC III) and we show that it does not provide the claimed privacy properties.

---

*   This work was supported in part by K.U. Leuven-BOF (OT/06/40), by the IAP Programme P6/26 BCRYPT of the Belgian State (Belgian Science Policy), by FWO project G.0300.07, by the European Commission through the ICT programme under contract ICT-2007-216676 ECRYPT II.
** Research assistant, sponsored by the Fund for Scientific Research - Flanders (FWO).
*** Postdoctoral Fellow of the Fund for Scientific Research - Flanders (FWO).

S.B. Ors Yalcin (Ed.): RFIDSec 2010, LNCS 6370, pp. 66–74, 2010.

The ID&Pwd-Transfer protocols (protocol 2,3) are broken by a (wide) man-in-the-middle attack, and a tag can be traced by the attacker. Since our attacks on the ID&Pwd-Transfer scheme do not require access to the tag's secrets, not even *wide-weak* privacy is provided by the protocols. *Narrow-weak* privacy might be provided by these protocols, but no formal proof for this is included. Also the ID-transfer protocol does not provide the claimed *wide-strong* privacy. An attacker that knows the identity of a certain tag, can always identify this tag using a man-in-the-middle attack. The highest privacy levels that could be provided by the ID-Transfer scheme are *narrow-strong* privacy or *wide-destructive*, although no formal proof for this exists.

The remainder of the paper is structured as follows: in Section 2 we introduce the different versions of EC-RAC in detail and discuss the vulnerabilities of EC-RAC I and EC-RAC II. Section 3 introduces the privacy model of Vaudenay, which is used throughout this paper. In Section 4 we present our attacks on the various schemes of EC-RAC III and discuss the impact on the claimed privacy properties of the protocol.

2 The EC-RAC Protocols

The basic setup considered in this paper is a world consisting of several tags and a single reader (or multiple connected to a central server). The reader/server is assumed trusted and the goal of the protocols is to authenticate the tag to the reader and, at the same time, protect the identity of the tag. Intuitively, it should be impossible for an adversary to impersonate a tag and it should be impossible for the adversary to derive any information on the identity of tags involved.

2.1 EC-RAC I/II and Related Attacks

The first version of the EC-RAC protocol was proposed in [3]. EC-RAC consists of several sub-protocols: ID-transfer, Pwd-Transfer and server authentication. The ID-transfer protocol allows the tag to identify itself to the server, the Pwd-Transfer protocol allows the tag to authenticate to the server. The two can be combined into the Id&Pwd-Transfer protocol. Figure 1 shows the ID&Pwd-Transfer protocol of EC-RAC I. Upper case symbols denote elliptic curve points, lower case symbols denote scalars.

This scheme was broken in [7] and [1], which show that a tag could be traced by an attacker using a quality-time attack [7]. If an attacker runs the protocol twice with the same r_2, collecting $\{v, T_1\}$ and $\{v', T_1'\}$, she can then derive

$$(v - v')^{-1}(T_1 - T_1') = x_1^{-1}P$$

which is a unique attribute of a tag. This unique attribute can then be used to identify the tag.

EC-RAC II [4] introduced three different sub-protocols: ID-transfer, Pwd-Transfer and server authentication. These sub-protocols were combined into several protocols. Figure 2 shows the ID transfer protocol.

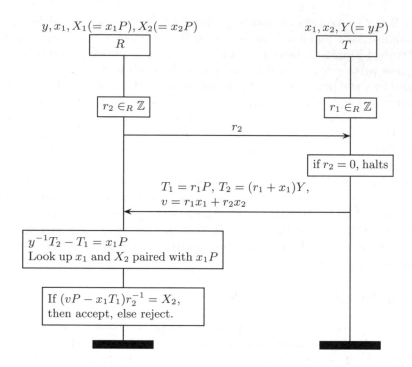

Fig. 1. ID&Pwd-Transfer protocol from EC-RAC I [3]

EC-RAC II was broken in [8]. The ID-transfer scheme was broken with respect to untraceability using a man-in-the-middle attack, in which the attacker uses a previous, valid execution of the protocol to modify the communication. If the reader accepts the modified values, the attacker can identify the previously eavesdropped tag.

One of the fundamental problems is that protocols, which in isolation are secure and/or untraceable, are not necessarily secure and/or privacy preserving when combined. The ID&Pwd-Transfer protocols were broken with respect to tag-to-server authentication, allowing the attacker to impersonate a tag. The main cause of this attack is the reuse of the same randomness for both the ID- and Pwd-Transfer sub-protocol.

2.2   EC-RAC III

In [2] Lee, Batina, Singelée and Verbauwhede present an improved version of EC-RAC. The paper [2] claims that the ID-transfer protocol (protocol 1 from [2]) and the ID&Pwd-Transfer protocol (protocol 3 from [2]) provide *wide-strong* privacy (see Section 3 for definition).

Let P be a generator of the elliptic curve group. Every tag has two private-public key pairs $x_1, X_1 = x_1P$ and $x_2, X_2 = x_2P$. In this case x_1 serves as the identity of the tag and is also known by the reader. The reader has a private-public key pair $y, Y = yP$.

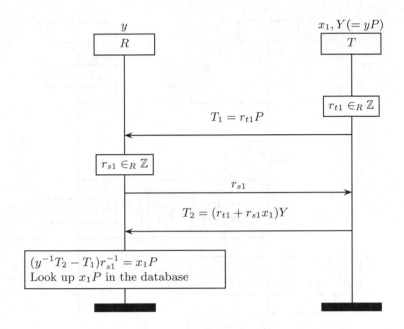

Fig. 2. ID Transfer protocol from EC-RAC II [4]

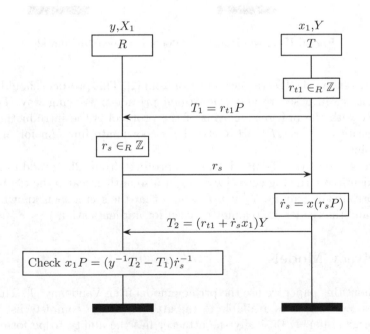

Fig. 3. ID-transfer protocol (Protocol 1) from [2]

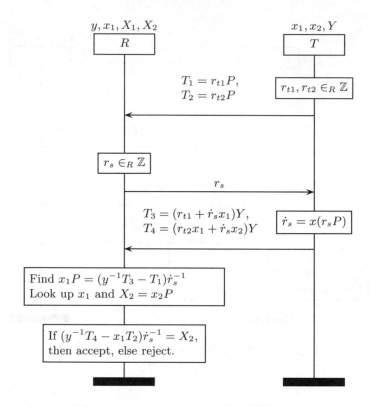

Fig. 4. ID&Pwd-Transfer protocol (Protocol 3) from [2]

Figure 3 shows the ID-transfer protocol from [2]. This protocol should identify the tag as x_1 in a secure and *wide-strong* privacy preserving way. The main difference with the previous versions of the protocol is the introduction of the non-linearity $\dot{r}_s = x(r_s P)$, with $x(\cdot)$ the x-coordinate function for an elliptic curve point.

Figure 4 shows the ID&Pwd-Transfer protocol from [2]. In addition to the reader identifying the tag correctly as x_1, it also authenticates the tag using the public-private key pair $x_2, X_2 = x_2 P$. (Note that the secret x_1 is known to both the tag and the reader and cannot be used for authentication.)

3　Privacy Models

Throughout this paper we use the privacy model from Vaudenay [9]. This model describes several oracles available to the attacker. For a complete list we refer to the original paper. Basically the attacker has the ability to perform a man-in-the-middle attack on any tag that is within its vincinity: it can influence all communication between tag and reader. The attacker also gets the result of the authentication of a tag, i.e. whether the reader accepts the tag or not. The attacker can also draw (at random) and free tags, moving them in and out of its range. During all of these interactions the attacker has to use a virtual identity to refer to the tags in its vincinity, i.e. it does not need to know the real identity to interact with a chosen tag. Finally the attacker can corrupt tags, reading out the entire internal state of the tag.

A *strong* attacker is allowed to use all the oracles available. A *destructive* attacker cannot use a tag anymore after it has been corrupted, i.e. corruption destroys the tag. In case of a *forward* attacker, the attacker can only do other corruptions after the first corruption. No protocol interactions are allowed after the first corrupt. A *weak* attacker does not have the ability to corrupt tags.

Orthogonal to these four attacker classes there is the notion of *wide* and *narrow* attackers. A *wide* attacker has access to the result of the verification by the server while a *narrow* attacker does not.

Definition 1. *(Simplified version of Definition 6 from [9]) Privacy - A protocol is called P-private, with P an adversary class from above (strong, destructive,...), if all adversaries belonging to the class P are trivial.*

Intuitively, an adversary is called trivial if it produces the same output, even when all protocol oracles are blinded (i.e. the attacker does not 'use' the communication captured during the protocol run to determine its output). Since the attacks presented in this paper allow tracing of tags, they clearly violate the privacy property, because the output of the attacker depends on information from the protocol runs that the attacker executes. As such, we do not require any detailed elements of the privacy definition used by Vaudenay.

The equations below show the most important relations between the privacy notions above:

$$\text{Wide Strong} \Rightarrow \text{Wide Destructive} \Rightarrow \text{Wide Forward} \Rightarrow \text{Wide Weak}$$
$$\Downarrow \qquad\qquad \Downarrow \qquad\qquad \Downarrow \qquad\qquad \Downarrow$$
$$\text{Narrow Strong} \Rightarrow \text{Narrow Destructive} \Rightarrow \text{Narrow Forward} \Rightarrow \text{Narrow Weak}$$

In this case $A \Rightarrow B$ means that if the protocol is A-private it implies that the protocol is B-private. It should be obvious that a protocol that is e.g. *Wide Strong* private will also belong to all other privacy classes above, that only allow weaker adversaries.

Besides privacy the protocol should also offer authentication of the tag. We refer to this property as the *security* of the protocol.

Definition 2. *(Simplified version of Definition 4 from [9]) Security - We consider any adversary in the class strong. The adversary wins if the reader identifies an uncorrupted legitimate tag, but the tag and the reader did not have a matching conversation. The RFID Scheme is called secure if the success probability of any such adversary is negligible.*

4   Attacks on the Protocols

The main flaw in the ID&Pwd-Transfer scheme is the fact that the "hash" of the challenge, i.e. $\dot{r}_s$ does not mask all of the secret keys x_1 and x_2. Indeed, in the response T_4, the x_1 part is only masked by the randomness r_{t2}.

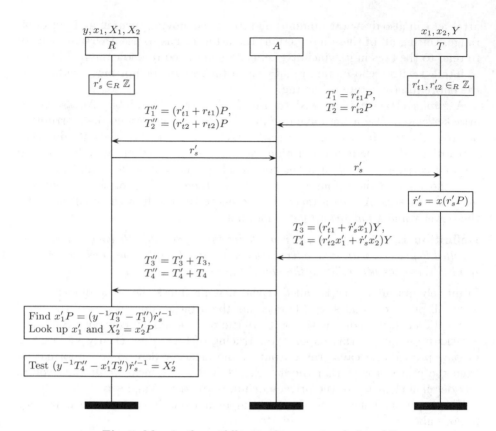

Fig. 5. Man-in-the-middle attack on protocols 2 and 3

4.1 First Attack

The first attack exploits the fact that it is possible to force $\dot{r}_s$ to become 0. Indeed, note that the protocol does not verify whether r_s is a multiple of the order of P. As such, it is possible for an attacker impersonating a reader to send $r_s = k \cdot \text{ord}(P)$ to the tag, who will then compute $\dot{r}_s = x(r_s P) = 0$ and therefore return $T_3 = r_{t1}Y$ and $T_4 = r_{t2}x_1Y$. Using the messages ($T_1 = r_{t1}P$, $T_2 = r_{t2}P$, $T_3 = r_{t1}Y$, $T_4 = r_{t2}x_1Y$), it is then possible to mount a man-in-the-middle attack on a second communication to test whether the same tag from the first run is present or not. This attack is described in Figure 5 where the tag's secret keys are now denoted by x'_1 and x'_2.

The adversary adds T_1 and T_2 to the messages T'_1 and T'_2 obtained from the unknown tag and forwards these to the reader. The reader responds with a nonce r'_s, which the attacker simply forwards to the tag. The tag responds with valid messages T'_3 and T'_4 which the attacker uses to obtain $T''_3 = T'_3 + T_3$ and $T''_4 = T'_4 + T_4$ and sends these to the reader. The reader then computes

$$(y^{-1}T''_3 - T''_1)\dot{r}'^{-1}_s = (r_{t1} + r'_{t1} + \dot{r}'_s x'_1 - r_{t1} - r'_{t1})\dot{r}'^{-1}_s P = x'_1 P,$$

and looks up x'_1 and $X'_2 = x'_2 P$. Note that this step always verifies. The reader then tests whether $(y^{-1} T''_4 - x'_1 T''_2)\dot{r}'^{-1}_s = X'_2$, which is equivalent with

$$(r'_{t2} x'_1 + \dot{r}'_s x'_2 + r_{t2} x_1 - x'_1 (r'_{t2} + r_{t2}))\dot{r}'^{-1}_s P = x'_2 P.$$

The test will succeed if and only if $x_1 = x'_1$, i.e. if the tag is the same as the one from the first run.

4.2   Second Attack

The second attack even works when the tag adds an extra verification that $\dot{r}_s \neq 0$. Note that the first attack worked because the attacker obtained $(T_1 = r_{t1} P$, $T_2 = r_{t2} P$, $T_3 = r_{t1} Y$, $T_4 = r_{t2} x_1 Y)$, so it suffices to explain how such a tuple can be obtained when the tag verifies whether $\dot{r}_s \neq 0$. In fact, obtaining such a tuple is trivial by querying the tag twice with the same r_s and subtracting the results, since the parts involving $\dot{r}_s$ will cancel out. As such we obtain a valid tuple $(T^*_1 = r^*_{t1} P, T^*_2 = r^*_{t2} P, T^*_3 = r^*_{t1} Y, T^*_4 = r^*_{t2} x_1 Y)$, which can then be used in the first attack.

4.3   Third Attack

The third attack shows that the ID-transfer scheme (protocol 1 from [2]) is not wide-strong. A *strong* attacker is able to read a tag's ID x_1 without destroying the tag. We will now show how a *strong* attacker can track a particular tag using a man-in-the-middle attack.

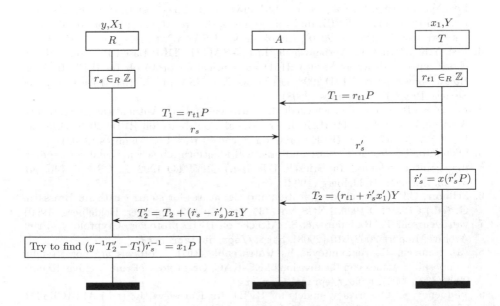

Fig. 6. Man-in-the-middle attack on protocol 1

This attack is described in Figure 6. By definition of *strong*, the attacker knows x_1 of a certain tag. In order to test if a random tag is the corrupted one, she plays a man-in-the-middle attack as follows. The attacker replaces the value r_s with another random value r'_s and replaces $T_2 = (r_{t1} + \dot{r}'_s x'_1)Y$ by

$$T'_2 = T_2 + (\dot{r}_s - \dot{r}'_s)x_1 Y = (r_{t1} + \dot{r}'_s(x'_1 - x_1) + \dot{r}_s x_1)Y$$

The reader will accept this only if $x_1 = x'_1$ (provided $\dot{r}'_s \neq 0$, which the attacker can assure). This allows the attacker to identify the tag x_1 upon acceptance by the reader. The ID-transfer protocol is thus not *wide-strong* private. Since our attacker is both *wide* and *strong*, the ID-transfer might be *narrow-strong* private or *wide-destructive* private, although no proof for this is given in the original paper.

5   Conclusions

In this paper we have shown three successful attacks on the latest version of EC-RAC [2]. We prove that the ID&PWD-Transfer scheme is not *wide-strong* private and is not even *wide-weak* private. The highest possible privacy level that might be achieved by the ID&PWD-Transfer scheme is *narrow-strong* privacy.

We also prove that the ID-transfer scheme is not *wide-strong* private as claimed and can be at most *wide-destructive* or *narrow-strong* private.

References

1. Bringer, J., Chabanne, H., Icart, T.: Cryptanalysis of EC-RAC, a RFID identification protocol. In: Franklin, M.K., Hui, L.C.K., Wong, D.S. (eds.) CANS 2008. LNCS, vol. 5339, pp. 149–161. Springer, Heidelberg (2008)
2. Lee, Y.K., Batina, L., Singelée, D., Verbauwhede, I.: Low-Cost Untraceable Authentication Protocols for RFID. In: Proceedings of the 3rd ACM conference on Wireless network security (WiSec 2010), Hoboken, NJ, USA, ACM Press, New York (2010)
3. Lee, Y.K., Batina, L., Verbauwhede, I.: EC-RAC (ECDLP Based Randomized Access Control): Provably Secure RFID authentication protocol. In: IEEE International Conference on RFID 2008, Las Vegas, NA, USA, pp. 97–104. IEEE Computer Society Press, Los Alamitos (2008)
4. Lee, Y.K., Batina, L., Verbauwhede, I.: Untraceable RFID Authentication Protocols: Revision of EC-RAC. In: IEEE International Conference on RFID 2009, Orlando, FL, USA, pp. 178–185. IEEE Computer Society Press, Los Alamitos (2009)
5. Okamoto, T.: Provably secure and practical identification schemes and corresponding signature schemes. In: Brickell, E.F. (ed.) CRYPTO 1992. LNCS, vol. 740, pp. 31–53. Springer, Heidelberg (1993)
6. Schnorr, C.P.: Efficient identification and signatures for smart cards. In: Brassard, G. (ed.) CRYPTO 1989. LNCS, vol. 435, pp. 239–252. Springer, Heidelberg (1990)
7. van Deursen, T., Radomirovic, S.: Attacks on RFID protocols. Cryptology ePrint Archive, Report 2008/310 (2008), http://eprint.iacr.org/
8. van Deursen, T., Radomirovic, S.: Untraceable RFID protocols are not trivially composable: Attacks on the revision of EC-RAC. Cryptology ePrint Archive, Report 2009/332 (2009), http://eprint.iacr.org/
9. Vaudenay, S.: On privacy models for RFID. In: Kurosawa, K. (ed.) ASIACRYPT 2007. LNCS, vol. 4833, pp. 68–87. Springer, Heidelberg (2007)

EC-RAC:
Enriching a Capacious RFID Attack Collection

Ton van Deursen* and Saša Radomirović

University of Luxembourg

Abstract. We demonstrate two classes of attacks on EC-RAC, a growing set of RFID protocols. Our first class of attacks concerns the compositional approach used to construct a particular revision of EC-RAC. We
invalidate the authentication and privacy claims made for that revision.

We discuss the significance of the fact that RFID privacy is not compositional in general.

Our second class of attacks applies to all versions of EC-RAC and
reveals hitherto unknown vulnerabilities in the latest version of EC-RAC.
It is a general man-in-the-middle attack executable by a weak adversary.

We show a general construction for improving narrow-weak private
protocols to wide-weak private protocols and indicate specific improvements for the flaws of EC-RAC exhibited in this document.

Keywords: RFID; attacks; privacy; authentication; compositionality.

1 Introduction

Secure communication protocols are essential for every networked application.
Yet, after more than thirty years of cryptographic protocol design, we appear to
be still struggling with the design of novel, secure three-message protocols. The
same applies to the *privacy* property of RFID protocols. Indeed, the design and
verification of privacy-preserving protocols is closely related to the much wider
studied classes of protocols aiming to achieve secrecy or authentication. While
it is true that the complexity of verification algorithms for any of these three
properties is exponential in the number of messages exchanged in a protocol,
it is frequently possible to find flaws "by hand" by simply considering a small
number of attack classes, most famously replay attacks or man-in-the-middle
attacks. Such an approach has led to a collection of attacks on RFID protocols
and to the discovery of RFID-specific attacks patterns, such as quality-time
attacks, algebraic replay attacks, and desynchronization attacks [1].

A simple strategy to decrease the design and verification complexity is to
construct protocols from smaller and simpler building blocks. It is then essential,
however, to prove that these building blocks do not break each others' security
properties. In fact, it is well known [2,3,4,5] that protocols satisfying a security

---

* Ton van Deursen was supported by a grant from the Fonds National de la Recherche
(Luxembourg).

property when executed in isolation do not necessarily satisfy the same security property when they are executed in an environment containing other protocols. In particular, it has been shown that composition of secrecy-preserving protocols may introduce attacks [6]. Similar results have been obtained for the composition of authentication protocols [7].

In the present paper, as a first contribution, we demonstrate that privacy is not compositional. The mechanism we use to show this is simple. Given two protocols P_1 and P_2, both satisfying privacy in isolation, we use protocol P_1 as an oracle to break protocol P_2.

Our second contribution is an analysis of EC-RAC II [8], a set of elliptic-curve based RFID protocols aiming to provide privacy and authentication. The protocols in the set are built from simple components which are individually claimed to provide privacy or authentication. We show that the EC-RAC II protocols nevertheless fail to satisfy privacy and authentication. This failure is exhibited by applying the mechanism outlined above to the simple components comprising the EC-RAC II protocols.

As a third contribution, we reiterate the difficulty of designing secure protocols by showing a man-in-the-middle attack on all versions of EC-RAC [8,9,10,11]. The attack can be executed by a weak adversary and breaks the privacy of all protocols in the set. This shows that the privacy claims made by the respective authors are incorrect.

Our final contribution is a demonstration of how to improve the privacy of a class of three-message RFID protocols to which the EC-RAC protocols belong.

Our paper is organized as follows. We briefly review Vaudenay's privacy model and the EC-RAC family in Section 2. We demonstrate non-compositionality of RFID privacy in Section 3 and apply the result to attack EC-RAC II in Section 4. We discuss wide-weak man-in-the-middle attacks on all revisions of EC-RAC in Section 5. We show a general construction for improving narrow-weak protocols to wide-weak protocol in Section 6 and suggest improvements specific to the EC-RAC protocols in Section 7. We present our conclusion in Section 8.

2   Preliminaries

We set the scene for our paper by briefly recalling Vaudenay's privacy model and then giving an overview of the different versions of EC-RAC.

2.1   The RFID Privacy Model of Vaudenay

Intuitively, an RFID protocol provides privacy (also referred to as location privacy or untraceability) if an adversary cannot recognize an RFID tag he previously observed or interacted with. The formalization of this intuition is, however, tricky and has been carried out in several different ways [12,13,14,15,16,17]. At present, the model by Vaudenay [14] can be considered to be the most comprehensive privacy model.

Vaudenay's model captures eight classes of adversary capabilities ranging over four different types of tag corruption and two modes of observation. Corrupting a tag means extracting the tag's cryptographic material as well as its state. An adversary is a probabilistic polynomial Turing Machine whose strength is defined by the set of oracles he is allowed to query. A *weak* adversary is not allowed to corrupt a tag. A *forward* private adversary may corrupt a tag at the end of the attack. A *destructive* adversary may corrupt a tag at any time, which leads to the destruction of the tag, that is, the adversary may no longer interact with the tag. A *strong* adversary may corrupt a tag at any time without destroying it. Corresponding to the two modes of observation, an adversary is called *wide* if he may observe whether the protocol ended successfully, and *narrow* else. Since the four types of corruption are orthogonal to the narrow/wide separation, eight different adversarial classes are considered.

Privacy is defined by comparing the adversary to a special adversary which makes no use of protocol messages, as follows. An adversary is called *blinded* if he is not allowed to communicate with tags and reader. An adversary is *trivial* if there exists a blinded adversary which essentially performs equally well at guessing a tag's identity. A protocol is *P private*, where *P* is one of the eight adversary classes, if all adversaries that belong to that class are trivial.

In this paper, we will primarily consider a wide-weak adversary, since this is the adversary against which the latest revision of EC-RAC [11] is claimed to be secure. The attacks related to compositionality flaws will be executable by a narrow-weak adversary.

2.2 EC-RAC

The EC-RAC protocols aim to provide private tag authentication. They are one of the first published and implemented asymmetric-key RFID protocols. The construction of such protocols is interesting for several reasons. Public-key-based protocols aim to maintain privacy against strong attackers. It has been shown that it is impossible to achieve narrow-strong privacy with symmetric key cryptography alone [14]. Asymmetric protocols also enable efficient tag lookup procedures on the reader's side. In fact, Damgård and Pedersen have shown that in a system relying on symmetric keys, either privacy, security, or efficiency has to be sacrificed [18].

To distinguish the various revisions of EC-RAC, we will call the original publication EC-RAC I [9], the first revision EC-RAC II [8], the second revision EC-RAC III [10], and the latest revision EC-RAC IV [11].

EC-RAC I is a challenge-response protocol on which several attacks have been published [19,1,20]. EC-RAC II introduced a commitment-challenge-response structure and four sub-protocols which were individually claimed to satisfy authentication or privacy properties. These sub-protocols were then composed into the six protocols shown in Figure 2. We will discuss EC-RAC II in Section 4. EC-RAC III consists of slightly modified versions of protocols 1, 2, and 3 of EC-RAC II. The modification only concerns the use of the RFID reader's challenge nonce in computations, but the protocol flow remains the same. Protocols 1 and 3 of EC-RAC III were claimed to be wide-strong private, protocol 2 to be wide-weak private. Fan et al. [21] showed that all these claims are false. In particular, they showed that protocols 2 and 3 are not wide-weak private and that protocol 1 is not wide-strong private. As a consequence, for EC-RAC IV weaker claims have been made about protocol 1 (now claimed wide-weak), protocol 2 was removed, and protocol 3 revised and claimed wide-weak [11].

Regarding EC-RAC III, it is worth noting that Vaudenay had already shown [14] that in his model there cannot be a correct[1] protocol that is wide-strong private. This explains the existence of the wide-*strong* man-in-the-middle attack of Fan et al. [21] on EC-RAC III. In Section 5, we will show that none of the EC-RAC IV protocols are even wide-*weak* private, thus invalidating the latest revisions [11]. The attacks we show are sufficiently general to be applicable to all protocols in the EC-RAC I through IV set.

2.3   Message Sequence Charts

We use message sequence charts, such as in Figure 1, for the description of protocols as well as attacks on protocols.

Every message sequence chart shows the role names, framed, near the top of the chart. Above the role names, the terms known to the role, but not known to the adversary, are shown. Actions, such as nonce generation, computation, verification of terms, and assignments are shown in boxes. Messages to be sent and expected to be received are specified above arrows connecting the roles. It is assumed that an agent continues the execution of its run only if it receives a message conforming to its role. Other conditions that need to be satisfied are shown in diamond boxes.

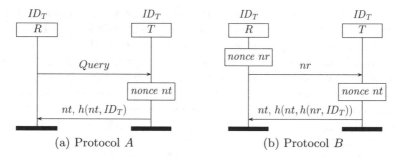

(a) Protocol A (b) Protocol B

Fig. 1. Protocols private in isolation, not in a common environment

For example, for protocol A in Figure 1, the role names are R and T, corresponding to the RFID reader and tag, respectively. Both reader and tag know the secret term ID_T. The picture represents the following execution flow. R sends a query to T. After receiving the query, T generates a random value nt, then sends the message $nt, h(nt, ID_T)$ to R.

We use primes to distinguish messages from different executions. For instance, $nt, h(nt, ID_T)$ and $nt', h(nt', ID_{T'})$ represent the second message of protocol A (Figure 1) for two different executions.

---

[1] A protocol is correct if it allows the RFID reader to infer a legitimate tag's identity from the communication with the tag.

3   RFID Privacy is Not Compositional

We first demonstrate that the composition of two private protocols may break the privacy of a tag. We then discuss the significance of this fact for RFID systems by showing two scenarios in which RFID privacy would be violated. In Section 4 we illustrate further implications of this result on the EC-RAC II protocols.

Consider the two protocols shown in Figure 1. The first protocol (A) is a tag identification protocol and the second protocol (B) is a tag authentication protocol. In both protocols we assume that a reader R and a tag T share a secret ID_T, not known to the adversary. The reader initiates the protocol by querying the tag. Then the tag generates a random number nt and sends its response to the reader.

If h is a cryptographically secure hash function, each of the protocols can be shown to be private in isolation. In a common environment, the protocols are not private.

Compositionality attack on protocols A and B. An attacker uses protocol A to build a database of tags he's interested in tracing. By querying a tag T, he obtains $nt, h(nt, ID_T)$ which he stores in the database. In order to test whether a random tag T' is equal to a particular tag T in his database, the attacker uses protocol B. He sends the challenge nt to the tag. In protocol B the tag answers with $nt', h(nt', h(nt, ID_{T'}))$. The attacker can then obviously determine whether $ID_T = ID_{T'}$ by computing $h(nt', h(nt, ID_T))$ and comparing it with $h(nt', h(nt, ID_{T'}))$.

There are at least two scenarios in which this type of attack can become a significant problem.

Chosen protocol attack. It is not uncommon for smart cards to implement a protocol suite in order to host several applications. Therefore it is plausible that in the future RFID tags will host an implementation of several protocols or even protocol versions. Additionally, in the RFID setting, ownership transfer systems [22,23,24] are frequently constructed by implementing several protocols on the RFID tag. In view of the compositionality attack, however, it is obvious that a tag which implements protocols A and B does not provide privacy, in spite of the fact that both protocol A and B are private in isolation.

Protocol revision attack. Consider an RFID-based system where a large number of RFID tags implementing protocol A have been deployed. Suppose the RFID tag's ID_T value is linked to a particular customer in any of several participating companies' databases. Since protocol A is private, the RFID tag identifies the customer to an authorized entity, such as a retailer, a transportation company, or the local post office, but not to any entity the customer has not signed up with.

At a certain point in time it is decided that for future applications the identification protocol's security does not suffice, since its messages can be replayed. Protocol B is thus developed for applications which need to authenticate an RFID tag. To avoid the chosen protocol attack, customers will be provided with new RFID tags implementing protocol B, but not protocol A, and their old tags will be destroyed. For convenience and in order not having to update all the customer entries in all distributed databases, the new tags will use the same credentials as the old tags. In particular, the tag identity communicated by a customer's RFID tag remains the same for each customer. This way, each retailer merely needs to update the firmware of its RFID readers to communicate using protocol B.

The compositionality attack described above, however, still applies. Anybody interested in tracing customers merely needs to be near a customer's tag once before the customer's RFID tag is replaced. This suffices to record the tag's protocol A message. Long after the transition to new tags has been completed and all protocol A tags are destroyed, the message recorded from protocol A can still be used to test whether a tag implementing protocol B belongs to the previously observed customer.

The protocols in Figure 1 are specially crafted protocols, designed to show that privacy is not a safely composable property and to illustrate the principle of using one protocol as an oracle to attack another protocol. In the following section the same principle will be used to show that the protocols comprising EC-RAC II [8] do not satisfy privacy nor security.

4   Compositionality Attacks on the EC-RAC II Protocols

4.1   Detailed Description of EC-RAC II

EC-RAC II consists of six protocols shown in Figure 2. Common to all protocols are the publicly known points P and $Y = yP$ on a fixed, system-wide elliptic curve. The point yP can be considered as the RFID reader's public key, y being a scalar only known to the RFID reader. In protocols 1 and 4, RFID tags store a secret x_1. The corresponding public key is $x_1 P$ and is used by the reader to identify a tag. In protocols 2, 3, 5, and 6, RFID tags have two secrets x_1, x_2 with the corresponding public keys $x_1 P$ and $x_2 P$ uniquely identifying a particular RFID tag. In these four protocols the RFID reader knows the scalar x_1 of each tag.

All protocols follow the same commitment-challenge-response structure. More precisely, in all protocols the tag sends out a random point on the elliptic curve which serves as a commitment. The RFID reader challenges the tag with a random integer upon which the tag answers with a point depending on the commitment and the challenge. The idea of such schemes is that anybody able to produce the correct response can also compute a particular secret. Thus successful completion of the protocol constitutes a proof of knowledge for the secret. A moment's thought shows that for the six protocols, knowledge of the points $x_1 Y$ and $x_2 Y$ allows an agent to authenticate itself as the tag whose public keys are $x_1 P$ and $x_2 P$. Thus the intractability of the computational Diffie–Hellman problem is necessary in order for the schemes to provide tag authentication.

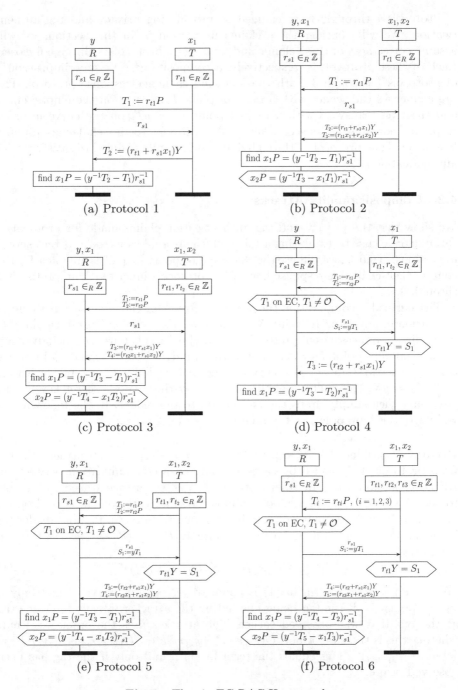

Fig. 2. The six EC-RAC II protocols

Protocols 1 through 3 are claimed to provide tag privacy and tag authentication. We will consider these claims in Section 5. In this section, we will assume correctness of these claims and investigate protocols 4 through 6 closer. Each of these protocols is, respectively, a composition[2] (or "superimposition") of protocols 1 through 3, with the following challenge-response protocol: The tag challenges the reader with a random point $T_1 = r_{t1}P$ on the elliptic curve and the reader answers with a related point $S_1 = yT_1$ on the curve in order to prove knowledge of its secret key y. We will refer to this challenge-response loop as O. Thus protocols 4 through 6 are additionally claimed to satisfy reader authentication.

4.2   Compositionality Attacks

We show that the privacy and tag authentication claims made for protocols 4 through 6 are false by exhibiting attacks which are analogous to the attack shown in Section 3. That is, we will use the challenge-response loop O as an oracle for the commitment-challenge-response flow of the protocols inherited from protocols 1 through 3.

The particular computation the oracle performs for the adversary is the multiplication of any nonzero point X by the reader's secret y. To use the loop O in the first two messages of protocols 4, 5, and 6 for this purpose, the adversary sends a nonzero point $T_1 = X$, along with a random point T_2 (and T_3 in protocol 6), on the system's elliptic curve to the reader. The reader replies with r_{s1} and $yT_1 = yX$, the multiple of the point X by the reader's secret key y. The adversary then simply drops the connection to the reader. In the following we will write this loop oracle as the function $X \to O(X) = yX$.

Privacy.   Consider the messages $r_{t2}P$, r_{s1}, $(r_{t2} + r_{s1}x_1)Y$ an attacker learns from protocols 4, 5, and 6 by eavesdropping on a communication between an RFID reader and a tag. In order to trace the tag, the attacker needs to be able to decide whether a tag presented to him is the same as the one he eavesdropped on earlier. By eavesdropping on another communication of a tag and reader (or by querying a tag himself) the attacker learns $r'_{t2}P$, r'_{s1}, $(r'_{t2} + r'_{s1}x'_1)Y$. He then computes

$$r_{s1}(r'_{t2} + r'_{s1}x'_1)Y - r'_{s1}(r_{t2} + r_{s1}x_1)Y \tag{1}$$

For $r_{s1}, r'_{s1} \neq 0$, the term in (1) is equal to $(r_{s1}r'_{t2} - r'_{s1}r_{t2})Y$ if and only if $x_1 = x'_1$, that is, if the tag being queried by the attacker later is the same tag as the one that was observed earlier. The attacker uses the oracle to decide whether this is the case or not: $O(r_{s1}r'_{t2}P - r'_{s1}r_{t2}P) = O((r_{s1}r'_{t2} - r'_{s1}r_{t2})P) = (r_{s1}r'_{t2} - r'_{s1}r_{t2})Y$. This equals the term in (1) if and only if the tag has been observed before.

---

[2] To prevent confusion, we have preserved the naming scheme of EC-RAC II. As a consequence, the term T_1 in protocols 1, 2, 3 corresponds to term T_2 in protocols 4, 5, 6, respectively.

Thus none of the protocols 4, 5, and 6 are narrow-weak private, which is the weakest privacy notion in Vaudenay's model. The attacker is narrow, since he is not relying on information related to the reader accepting or rejecting a tag. He is weak since he does not corrupt any tags.

Tag authentication. In order to break tag authentication in these protocols, an adversary needs to know the term x_1Y and in protocols 5 and 6 the adversary additionally needs to know the term x_2Y. The adversary learns these two terms from the tag's public keys x_1P, x_2P by computing $O(x_iP_1) = x_iY$, $(i = 1,2)$. According to the attacker model specified for these protocols [8], an attacker is initially only allowed to know Y, P, and the order of the system's elliptic curve, but not the tags' public keys. Under this restriction, only a rogue reader in the system is able to impersonate tags. Protocol 4, however, is even vulnerable if the adversary does not know the tag's public keys. In this case the adversary can learn x_1Y by eavesdropping on one protocol execution between a tag and a reader and performing the following computation.

By eavesdropping on one communication between a tag and a reader, an attacker obtains $r_{t2}P$, the challenge r_{s1}, and $(r_{t2} + r_{s1}x_1)Y$. He then computes $r_{s1}^{-1}r_{t2}P$ and $r_{s1}^{-1}(r_{t2} + r_{s1}x_1)Y = (r_{s1}^{-1}r_{t2} + x_1)Y$. Using the oracle, the attacker obtains $O(r_{s1}^{-1}r_{t2}P) = r_{s1}^{-1}r_{t2}Y$ and computes the difference $(r_{s1}^{-1}r_{t2} + x_1)Y - r_{s1}^{-1}r_{t2}Y = x_1Y$. After learning x_1Y and x_2Y by using the oracles as described above, an attacker can impersonate a tag as follows.

Protocol 4. The attacker chooses a random integer r_{t1}, submits $r_{t1}P$ to the reader, and is challenged by r_{s1}. To answer this challenge, the attacker computes $r_{s1}x_1Y$, and $r_{t2}Y$ and sends back the sum of these two points.

Protocol 5. The attacker chooses random integers r_{t1}, r_{t2}, submits T_1, T_2 to the reader, and is challenged by r_{s1}. To answer this challenge, the attacker computes T_3 from the sum of $r_{s1}x_1Y$, and $r_{t2}Y$. To compute T_4, the attacker multiplies x_1Y by r_{t2} and x_2Y by r_{s1} and computes the sum of these two points.

Protocol 6. The attacker chooses random integers r_{t1}, r_{t2}, r_{t3}, submits T_1, T_2, T_3 to the reader, and is challenged by r_{s1}. To answer this challenge, the attacker computes T_4 from the sum of $r_{s1}x_1Y$, and $r_{t2}Y$. To compute T_5, the attacker multiplies x_1Y by r_{t3} and x_2Y by r_{s1} and computes the sum of these two points.

5   Privacy Attacks on all EC-RAC Protocols

We demonstrate a man-in-the-middle attack that allows a wide-weak adversary to trace a tag in all of the six protocols of EC-RAC II, as well as in EC-RAC III and IV. Fan, Hermans, and Vercauteren have shown that EC-RAC III is vulnerable to a man-in-the-middle attack by a *wide-strong* attacker [21]. Our man-in-the-middle attack can be executed by *any* wide attacker, in particular a wide-*weak* one.

Consider protocol 1 of EC-RAC II (Figure 2a) which is called the *ID-transfer protocol* in [8]. The equally named protocol of EC-RAC III and EC-RAC IV is a revision of this protocol designed to mitigate man-in-the-middle attacks. The main difference is that in EC-RAC III and IV a non-linear operation is applied to the reader challenge before it is used in the computation of the response.

Consider now protocol π in Figure 3. By specifying the function h used in the protocol, the ID-transfer protocols of EC-RAC II, III, and IV can be obtained. For EC-RAC II, h is simply the identity function. The specification of the h function in EC-RAC III and IV will be discussed below. Our attacks do not depend on the choice of the function h used in the protocol and work even if h is a cryptographic hash function.

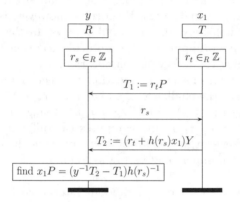

Fig. 3. Protocol π: A generalization of protocol 1

To attack privacy, a *wide-weak* adversary eavesdrops on two protocol executions between a tag and a reader. In these executions he observes $T_1 = r_t P$, r_s, $T_2 = (r_t + h(r_s)x_1)Y$ in the first execution and $T_1' = r_t'P$, r_s', $T_2' = (r_{t1}' + h(r_s')x_1')Y$ in the second execution. Then the adversary computes $T_Y = h(r_s')T_2 - h(r_s)T_2'$ which is equal to $(h(r_s')r_t - h(r_s)r_t')Y$ if and only if $x_1 = x_1'$.

To find out whether this is the case, i.e. whether the two executions were carried out by the same tag, the adversary uses a communication between *any legitimate tag* and a reader as an oracle, as shown in Figure 4. For brevity, in the MSC we have set $T_P = h(r_s')T_1 - h(r_s)T_1'$ and $T_Y = h(r_s')T_2 - h(r_s)T_2'$. Recall that a *wide* adversary can observe whether a tag was accepted by the reader or not, that is, whether the authentication protocol between the tag and reader was carried out successfully. If the reader accepts the legitimate tag, the adversary knows that $x_1 = x_1'$, otherwise $x_1 \neq x_1'$.

The attack can be applied to protocol 1 of EC-RAC II by taking the identity map for the function h. Since protocols 2 through 6 are extensions of protocol 1 they inherit the vulnerability and can be attacked in the same way. The attacker merely forwards all terms that have been additionally introduced in these protocols. To attack EC-RAC III and IV, the function h is instantiated

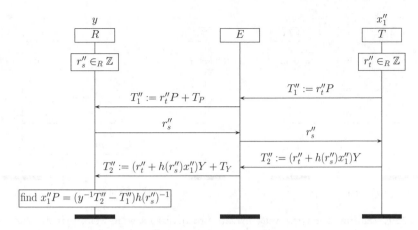

Fig. 4. Abusing any tag-reader communication of Protocol π as an oracle

by the following non-linear function introduced in EC-RAC III [10]. Let $x(P)$ denote the x-coordinate of a point P. Then $h(a) = x(aP)$. The attack can also be applied to the "Pwd-Transfer Scheme" of EC-RAC II and III. The only difference is that the adversary cannot use a communication between any tag and a reader as oracle, but only between the same tag and a reader. The combined "ID&Pwd-Transfer Scheme" of EC-RAC III and IV inherit the vulnerabilities of the ID-Transfer Scheme (and the Pwd-Transfer Scheme). The attack is applicable to EC-RAC I with a minor modification, since EC-RAC I does not follow a commitment-challenge-response structure.

6   Wide-Weak Privacy from Narrow-Weak Privacy

The man-in-the-middle attacks presented in the preceding section show that the EC-RAC family of protocols is not private against a *wide* attacker. Achieving narrow-weak privacy, however, appears to be significantly easier. In this section, we will show how to transform narrow-weak private protocols into wide-weak private protocols.

We consider three-message protocols such as protocol ρ_0 shown in Figure 5a. Note that protocol π shown in Figure 3 in Section 5 (and thus most EC-RAC protocols) as well as the Bringer et al. protocol [19], which has been formally shown to be narrow-weak private, follow this structure. Assuming that protocol ρ_0 is narrow-weak private, we show that protocol ρ, shown in Figure 5b is *wide*-weak private. Protocol ρ extends protocol ρ_0 by including a message authentication code in the third message. The message authentication code is a keyed hash $H_k(\cdot)$ computed over all previous messages (including the payload of the current message). The keyed hash depends on a secret k known only to reader and tag, unique to each tag.

Theorem 1. *If protocol ρ_0 is narrow-weak private then protocol ρ is wide-weak private in the random oracle model.*

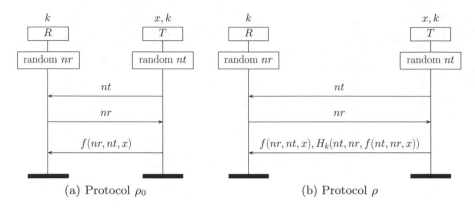

(a) Protocol ρ_0 (b) Protocol ρ

Fig. 5. Extending a narrow-weak private protocol to a wide-weak private protocol

Proof. We use the random oracle model and assume that the keyed hash function $H_k(m)$ is implemented as the random oracle $\mathcal{H}(k, m)$. We need to show that the addition of a hash preserves the narrow-weak privacy of protocol ρ_0 and that protocol ρ satisfies Vaudenay's definition of security [14]. The theorem then follows from Vaudenay's Lemma 8 [14].

Narrow-weak privacy of protocol ρ. Let ρ_0 be a narrow-weak private protocol. It follows that the probability of a tag generating the same bit string nt more than once in protocol ρ_0 is negligible, or else a narrow-weak adversary would have a non-negligible advantage in breaking a tag's privacy.

   We give now a step-wise transformation of protocol ρ_0 into protocol ρ. Concatenate with the last tag-to-reader message the keyed hash $H_c(nr, nt, f(nr, nt, x))$ of all preceding messages. Assuming that the adversary knows c and that all tags use the same keyed hash function H_c, this protocol is still narrow-weak private, since the adversary could have computed the hash himself. Now replace the key c of the hash function by a random key k_0, unknown to the adversary. Call this protocol ρ_1. This protocol is still narrow-weak private, because k_0 is independent of all tag identities.

   Given that $\mathcal{H}$ is a random oracle, $H_k(m)$ does not reveal any information about k. Furthermore, for two inputs $m \neq m'$, given $H_k(m)$ and $H_{k'}(m')$, it is impossible for the adversary to decide whether $k = k'$. Let ρ be equal to ρ_1, except that k_0 is replaced with a key k, unique to every tag and chosen independently at random. Thus, since the probability of a tag generating the same random bit string nt twice is negligible and k is never used outside of $H_k(m)$, protocol ρ is a narrow-weak private protocol.

Security of protocol ρ. We verify the security property of ρ by using that ρ satisfies Lowe's agreement property [25] in a Dolev-Yao model. Recall that a protocol guarantees to an RFID reader R *agreement* with a tag T on the exchanged messages m_1, m_2, m_3, if whenever R completes a protocol run, apparently with T, then T has previously been running the protocol, apparently with R, using the same values for the messages m_1, m_2, m_3 and there is a one-to-one relationship between the runs of R and T.

The agreement property of protocol ρ can be automatically verified with symbolic verification tools, such as Scyther [26] or Proverif [27]. We may then transfer the security property from the symbolic Dolev-Yao model to the random oracle model by using the fact that the Dolev-Yao model with hashes is sound in the random oracle model [28].

Security of ρ now follows by noticing that Lowe's agreement property implies Vaudenay's *matching conversation* definition for his security property (Definition 4 in [14]).   □

7   Repairing the Flaws

We indicate how to repair all the flaws discovered in the preceding sections. The primary purpose is to illustrate prudent design principles for composing protocol components in Section 7.1 and to give an application of Theorem 1 in Section 6 showing how to improve narrow-weak privacy to wide-weak privacy. The wide-weak privacy of the resulting protocols, thus, depends on the original protocols' narrow-weak privacy. It is known that EC-RAC I is not narrow-weak private [1,20,19] and it has already been improved upon in [19]. Since the protocol in [19] has been proven narrow-strong private (implying narrow-weak privacy) and since it is also more efficient than EC-RAC II, III, and IV, we do not attempt to prove narrow-weak privacy of these protocols.

7.1   Compositionality

In view of existing results on compositionality [2,3,4,5], the attacks shown in Section 3 are not surprising, because one secret key y is being used for two different purposes. Both the tag authentication and the reader authentication depend on y.

The security of the protocol compositions can be improved by using independent secrets for the two components. The independence of the secrets assures that one component in the composition cannot be used as an oracle for the other. This can be achieved without compromising efficiency of the scheme. We equip the reader with a second secret y_2, generated randomly and independently of y, and store the point y_2P in every tag. In the second message, the reader sends y_2T_1 instead of yT_1, to prove reader authenticity to the tag. This modification improves the authentication property of the protocols. With respect to privacy, the flaws shown in Section 5 still persist. Thus the improvements suggested in the following subsection need to be applied as well.

7.2   Man in the Middle

To defend against the man-in-the-middle attacks, message authentication seems to be unavoidable. In its current form, protocol 1 provides recent aliveness [25]:

the reader is guaranteed that the tag has recently produced a message. However, agreement [25] is clearly not satisfied as shown by the attack in Figure 4. At the end of the run, the reader believes the following messages were exchanged

$$r_t'' P + T_P, \quad r_s'', \quad (r_t'' + h(r_s'')x_1'')Y + T_Y,$$

while for the tag the transcript reads

$$r_t'' P, \quad r_s'', \quad (r_t'' + h(r_s'')x_1'')Y.$$

As shown in Section 5, the adversary abuses this discrepancy and the reader's reaction to trace tags. To foil the attack, we need to make sure that reader and tag agree on the contents of all messages.

The simplest solution is to use message authentication codes based on an independent, shared secret, as shown in Section 6. Let k denote a secret known only to reader and tag, unique to each tag. Assuming that protocol π satisfies narrow-weak privacy, the addition of the hash $H_k(r_t P, r_s, (r_t + h(r_s)x_1)Y)$ to the last message thus guarantees wide-weak privacy. The non-linear function introduced in EC-RAC III can be omitted, thus h can be chosen to be the identity function. Although our solution prevents the man-in-the-middle attacks described, it is more resource intensive, since it additionally requires a secure hash function to be computed by the tag.

8   Conclusion

We have shown that protocols that are private in isolation, are in general not private when executed in a common environment. This insight is of particular significance in systems which need to be upgraded to newer protocol versions and in systems which require more than one protocol to be implemented on the RFID tag, such as ownership transfer applications [22,23,24]. We have further demonstrated the implication of our result on EC-RAC II, a recently published family of RFID protocols. We have shown attacks whose existence is a direct consequence of the attempt to trivially compose private or authenticating components.

Our second class of contributions concerns wide-weak privacy. We have first proven that none of the EC-RAC protocols published to date is secure against any wide adversary, implying that all EC-RAC protocols are at most narrow-strong private. We have shown this by exhibiting a general man-in-the-middle attack, applicable to all versions of EC-RAC. We have then shown how to improve typical three-message narrow-strong private RFID protocols to wide-weak private protocols in the random oracle model. This improvement applies in particular to the provably narrow-weak private protocol proposed in [19]. We thus conclude EC-RAC noting that it does not improve upon more efficient nor provably narrow-strong private protocols.

References

1. van Deursen, T., Radomirović, S.: Attacks on RFID protocols (version 1.1). Cryptology ePrint Archive, Report 2008/310 (August 2009), http://eprint.iacr.org/2008/310
2. Heintze, N., Tygar, J.D.: A model for secure protocols and their compositions. IEEE Trans. Software Eng. 22(1), 16–30 (1996)
3. Kelsey, J., Schneier, B., Wagner, D.: Protocol interactions and the chosen protocol attack. In: Security Protocols Workshop, pp. 91–104 (1997)
4. Canetti, R.: Universally composable security: A new paradigm for cryptographic protocols. In: FOCS, pp. 136–145 (2001)
5. Andova, S., Cremers, C., Gjøsteen, K., Mauw, S., Mjølsnes, S., Radomirović, S.: A framework for compositional verification of security protocols. Information and Computation 206, 425–459 (2008)
6. Cremers, C.: Feasibility of multi-protocol attacks. In: Proc. of The First International Conference on Availability, Reliability and Security (ARES), pp. 287–294. IEEE Computer Society, Austria (April 2006)
7. Tzeng, W.G., Hu, C.M.: Inter-protocol interleaving attacks on some authentication and key distribution protocols. Inf. Process. Lett. 69(6), 297–302 (1999)
8. Lee, Y., Batina, L., Verbauwhede, I.: Untraceable RFID authentication protocols: Revision of EC-RAC. In: IEEE International Conference on RFID – RFID 2009, Orlando, Florida, USA, pp. 178–185 (April 2009)
9. Lee, Y.K., Batina, L., Verbauwhede, I.: EC-RAC (ECDLP based randomized access control): Provably secure RFID authentication protocol. In: Proceedings of the 2008 IEEE International Conference on RFID, pp. 97–104 (2008)
10. Lee, Y.K., Batina, L., Singelée, D., Verbauwhede, I.: Low-cost untraceable authentication protocols for RFID. In: 3rd ACM Conference on Wireless Network Security, WiSec 2010 (2010)
11. Lee, Y.K., Batina, L., Singelée, D., Verbauwhede, I.: Wide-weak privacy-preserving RFID authentication protocols. In: The 2nd International Conference on Mobile Lightweight Wireless Systems, Mobilight 2010. Springer, Heidelberg (2010)
12. Avoine, G.: Adversary model for radio frequency identification. Technical Report LASEC-REPORT-2005-001, Swiss Federal Institute of Technology (EPFL), Security and Cryptography Laboratory (LASEC), Lausanne, Switzerland (September 2005)
13. Juels, A., Weis, S.: Defining strong privacy for RFID. In: International Conference on Pervasive Computing and Communications, PerCom 2007, pp. 342–347. IEEE Computer Society Press, New York (March 2007)
14. Vaudenay, S.: On privacy models for RFID. In: Kurosawa, K. (ed.) ASIACRYPT 2007. LNCS, vol. 4833, pp. 68–87. Springer, Heidelberg (2007)
15. van Deursen, T., Mauw, S., Radomirović, S.: Untraceability of RFID protocols. In: Onieva, J.A., Sauveron, D., Chaumette, S., Gollmann, D., Markantonakis, K. (eds.) WISTP 2008. LNCS, vol. 5019, pp. 1–15. Springer, Heidelberg (2008)
16. Ha, J., Moon, S., Zhou, J., Ha, J.: A new formal proof model for RFID location privacy. In: Jajodia, S., Lopez, J. (eds.) ESORICS 2008. LNCS, vol. 5283, pp. 267–281. Springer, Heidelberg (2008)
17. Ma, C., Li, Y., Deng, R.H., Li, T.: RFID privacy: relation between two notions, minimal condition, and efficient construction. In: ACM Conference on Computer and Communications Security, pp. 54–65 (2009)

18. Damgård, I., Pedersen, M.Ø.: RFID security: Tradeoffs between security and efficiency. In: Malkin, T. (ed.) CT-RSA 2008. LNCS, vol. 4964, pp. 318–332. Springer, Heidelberg (2008)
19. Bringer, J., Chabanne, H., Icart, T.: Cryptanalysis of EC-RAC, a RFID identification protocol. In: Franklin, M.K., Hui, L.C.K., Wong, D.S. (eds.) CANS 2008. LNCS, vol. 5339, pp. 149–161. Springer, Heidelberg (2008)
20. van Deursen, T., Radomirović, S.: Algebraic attacks on RFID protocols. In: Markowitch, O., Bilas, A., Hoepman, J.-H., Mitchell, C.J., Quisquater, J.-J. (eds.) Information Security Theory and Practice. Smart Devices, Pervasive Systems, and Ubiquitous Networks. LNCS, vol. 5746, pp. 38–51. Springer, Heidelberg (2009)
21. Fan, J., Hermans, J., Vercauteren, F.: On the claimed privacy of EC-RAC III. Cryptology ePrint Archive, Report 2010/132 (2010), http://eprint.iacr.org/
22. Song, B.: RFID Tag Ownership Transfer. In: Workshop on RFID Security, RFIDSec 2008, Budapest, Hungary (July 2008)
23. Dimitriou, T.: rfidDOT: RFID delegation and ownership transfer made simple. In: Proc. 4th International Conference on Security and Privacy in Communication Networks, pp. 1–8. ACM, New York (September 2008)
24. van Deursen, T., Mauw, S., Radomirović, S., Vullers, P.: Secure ownership and ownership transfer in RFID systems. In: Backes, M., Ning, P. (eds.) ESORICS 2009. LNCS, vol. 5789, pp. 637–654. Springer, Heidelberg (2009)
25. Lowe, G.: A hierarchy of authentication specifications. In: 10th Computer Security Foundations Workshop (CSFW 1997), June 10-12, pp. 31–44. IEEE Computer Society, USA (1997)
26. Cremers, C.: Scyther - Semantics and Verification of Security Protocols. Ph.D. dissertation, Eindhoven University of Technology (2006)
27. Blanchet, B.: An efficient cryptographic protocol verifier based on prolog rules. In: 14th IEEE Computer Security Foundations Workshop (CSFW), pp. 82–96. IEEE Computer Society, Los Alamitos (2001)
28. Backes, M., Pfitzmann, B., Waidner, M.: Limits of the BRSIM/UC soundness of Dolev-Yao models with hashes. In: Gollmann, D., Meier, J., Sabelfeld, A. (eds.) ESORICS 2006. LNCS, vol. 4189, pp. 404–423. Springer, Heidelberg (2006)

Anonymous RFID Authentication Using Trusted Computing Technologies

Kurt Dietrich

Institute for Applied Information Processing and Communications
University of Technology Graz, Inffeldgasse 16a, 8010 Graz, Austria
{Kurt.Dietrich}@iaik.tugraz.at

Abstract. Anonymity protecting mechanisms are an important part of any Trusted Computing platform. They provide protection of a platform's anonymity and, consequently, protection of the privacy of the platform's owners. As Trusted Computing technologies have been introduced on mobile and embedded systems and more and more mobile devices are equipped with Near Field Communication (NFC) modules, the question arises whether the supported anonymization mechanisms can be used efficiently for anonymous authentication for NFC enabled applications. However, state-of-the-art technologies like the Direct Anonymous Attestation scheme require complex mathematical computations that put high requirements on the processing power of the signer's device which are typically not available on resource constrained devices like smart-cards. In this paper, we analyze how the Direct Anonymous Attestation protocol can be used for anonymous authentication in NFC scenarios and we propose an approach that allows a practical use of this technology in real-world scenarios.

Keywords: Mobile Trusted Computing, Secure Element, Direct Anonymous Attestation, NFC.

1 Introduction

Today, many desktop computers are equipped with Trusted Platform Modules (TPMs). They provide support for anonymity preserving technologies which have been a major topic in Trusted Computing since its beginnings. In order to achieve anonymity protection for trusted platforms, two different concepts have been introduced by the Trusted Computing Group (TCG): the *PrivacyCA* (PCA) scheme and the *Direct Anonymous Attestation* (DAA) scheme. Both allow a trusted platform to hide its identity when doing operations over the internet. Both schemes aim at preserving a platform's anonymity, however, with different methods. The first scheme is based on remote certification of public-keys on a regular basis, where the platform is required to create a temporary key-pair for each transaction prior to performing this transaction. The public part of the temporary key-pair has to be sent to the PCA which certifies it. A verifier who receives data that was signed with this temporary key is able to verify the

S.B. Ors Yalcin (Ed.): RFIDSec 2010, LNCS 6370, pp. 91–102, 2010.
© Springer-Verlag Berlin Heidelberg 2010

signature and the authenticity of the key with the certificate from the PCA. As each transaction requires a different key-pair and a new certificate, a verifier is not able to link the signature to the originating signer platform. However, this approach has some severe drawbacks. Every temporarily created key-pair has to be sent to the PCA, which consequently, has to be permanently available. Moreover, the PCA can operate in different modes. In the first mode, it does not record any certification requests. In the second mode, it records and stores all certification requests from the single platforms. Therefore, the PCA is able to link the issued certificates to the requesting platforms. This fact opens a security leak in case the PCA gets compromised. If an adversary gets hold of the recorded information, it could use this information to link transactions and signatures to the single platforms.

In order to overcome these problems, the TCG introduced another scheme: the Direct Anonymous Attestation scheme. It omits the requirement for a remote party to certify the temporary keys as the keys can be certified locally, on a platform, by a TPM. This scheme is based on a group signature scheme and Zero-Knowledge proofs of knowledge, allowing each platform to create signatures on behalf of a group which can be verified by a single group-public-key. The advantage of this scheme is that no on-line connection to a third party is required. Moreover, different signatures created by the same platform cannot be linked to this certain platform - not even by the group manager which is responsible for issuing group credentials to each platform in the group.

In case the issuer becomes compromised, an adversary only gets the knowledge that a certain platform is part of the group that is managed by this specific issuer. The adversary is not able to link any signature that has been created before the compromission or any signature that will be created afterwards, to a single platform.

However, this scheme requires complex computations, making it hard to use on resource constrained devices like smart-cards. Furthermore, the scheme requires a secure storage on the device for protection of the group and DAA credentials as they require authorized access for usage and must not be copied or moved to a different platform.

In contrast to the PCA approach, the DAA scheme allows local certification of public-keys, thereby omitting the requirement of certifying keys by a remote PCA. This fact makes the DAA scheme especially interesting for mobile devices, as it does not require the mobile to open remote connections. Moreover, with the raise of NFC technology, DAA like anonymous signature schemes become an interesting technology for preserving anonymity for NFC enabled applications. They can be used as a basic building block for providing anonymity in e-ticketing- and mobile-payment- scenarios. Furthermore, they may be used for anonymous access control in order to prevent tracking and profiling of user activities.

1.1   Related Work

Different approaches have been published to integrate DAA functionality on smart-cards: The basic idea of splitting the computations between a resource limited micro-controller and a powerful host has first been discussed by Brands in [3]. Bichsel et. al. [2] and Sterckx et. al. [15] analyzed implementations of variations of the DAA signature protocol on JavaCards. Both publications give performance results of their implementations which show that a practical use of the DAA scheme requires a powerful host to execute the host side computations of the protocol. This statement is supported by Balasch [9] who implemented a DAA scheme on an AVR micro controller. He concludes that the DAA scheme can only be practically used in combination with a resourceful host. As shown in [2], the computation of an entire signature takes about 16,55 seconds with a modulus length of 1984 bits on a JCOP v2.2/41 JavaCard. Balasch requires 133.5 seconds on an 8 bit micro-controller (with 1024 bit modulus) and Bichsel 450 seconds [2], however, Bichsel and Balasch only take the computations located inside the TPM into account.

Another publication concerning anonymous signatures on mobiles is [7]. Dietrich proposed to execute the DAA computations on a Java virtual machine which is executed in a protected environment on the mobile. This protection is achieved by the ARM TrustZone CPU extension [1] which supports the separated execution of trusted and un-trusted code in a *secure* and a *non-secure world*. This technique can be used as a building block for hosting TPM functionality [20] and for storing and using DAA credentials in a protected environment. The benefit of this approach is that the software running in the protected world can take advantage of the computing power of the main CPU so that anonymous signatures can be computed in sufficient and user acceptable time [7]. However, this special CPU extension is currently only available on some high-end smart phones using ARM 11 CPUs. For cheaper, low-cost phones, which typically employ ARM 9 or ARM 7 CPUs and which are the typical and, therefore, more widespread user devices, this technology is not available.

Furthermore, all of the publications mentioned before omit *rogue tagging*. Rogue tagging is a mechanism to detect malicious TPMs and is, therefore, an important feature when using anonymous credentials.

1.2 Our Contribution

In this paper, we discuss a design that allows the application of the DAA scheme for contactless, anonymous authentication in NFC enabled scenarios, with respect to secure storage, authorized access to the DAA credentials and sufficient performance. We show how the DAA protocol has to be extended in order to realize a system which is able to compute authentication information with a reasonable performance that can be applied in real-world scenarios. In addition, we use off-the-shelf devices to demonstrate our efforts in order to support this statement. Our approach can be used to enable privacy protecting technologies on low-cost devices which were previously only available on cost-intensive, high-end devices.

In our approach, we extend the idea of Dietrich [6] who proposes to place the TPM functionality into an on-board smart-card, also known as *Secure Element* (SE). A SE basically provides the same functionality as a common smart-card or SIM-card, thereby establishing two major requirements of Trusted Platform Modules, namely *shielded locations* and *protected capabilities* ([8], [18]).

The rest of this article is organized as follows: we provide background information on mobile Trusted Computing and the DAA scheme. We discuss our proposed approach and modifications and give experimental performance results followed by a discussion of our prototype implementation. Finally, we summarize our results and propose ideas for further research.

2   Background

2.1   Mobile Trusted Computing

The Trusted Computing Group has published a specification that defines requirements for mobile TPMs [17]. This specification allows the mobile TPM vendors a great amount of flexibility with regard to concrete implementations. A mobile TPM may be implemented as a dedicated micro-controller or as a software module, depending on the security features provided by the target platform. Such features may include isolation of the TPM functionality to establish shielded locations and protected capabilities as required by the TCG. Examples of such isolation techniques are the L4-micro-kernel operating system, the ARM Trust-Zone processor extension or, as in our approach, an on-board smart-card, the secure element.

2.2   Direct Anonymous Attestation

The DAA protocol is basically a group signature scheme based on Zero-Knowledge proofs [4]. Instead of showing a credential to a verifier like in common public-key infrastructures (PKIs), the creator of a DAA signature computes a proof that it is in possession of certain group credentials. A detailed discussion of the DAA protocol is out of scope of this document and we refer to [7] and [12] for further information. Hence, we focus on a high-level discussion of the basic protocols *DAA Join* and *DAA Sign*.

The DAA Join Protocol: Before a device can create anonymous signatures on behalf of a group, it has to *join* the group and obtain the group parameters $(S_0, S_1, n$ and $R)$ from the group manager. Moreover, the TPM creates the secret keys f and ν' that are created during the join phase. The key ν' is separated into two parts, ν'_1 and ν'_2 as the cryptographic co-processor of the JavaCard does not allow exponents (ν' is 2128 bits) to be larger than the modulus (2048 bits). During the join process, the client proves knowledge of f to the group manager. The group manager computes the credentials (A, e, ν'') where e is a random prime and ν'' a random integer and computes a proof that A was generated correctly. The client verifies the proof on A and verifies that e is a prime in a certain interval. After successful execution of the Join protocol, the client has obtained the credentials $(A, e, \nu = \nu' + \nu'')$ which represent a signature on the key f that is protected by the TPM. Moreover, the TPM has obtained a value ν

and the platform has obtained a value ν'' which allows the TPM together with the host to create a DAA signature σ on a message m.

The DAA Sign Protocol: After a device has obtained the required credentials from the group manager it may create signatures on behalf of this group. In the *DAA Sign protocol*, host and TPM compute a signature σ with the credentials obtained during the *Join protocol*.

Algorithm 1. DAA Signature Creation

Input: $R, S_0, S_1, Z, \nu_0, \nu_1, n, f, \Gamma, \rho$.
Output: $\sigma = (T, c, n_t, s_{\bar{\nu}}, s_e, s_f, s_{\nu_0}, s_{\nu_1})$

1. The *host* selects a random w and computes: $T = A * S^w$, note: $S = S_1 * S_2^{l_s}$ and $\nu = \nu_1 + \nu_2 * 2^{l_s}$ for $l_s = 1024$
2. *Host* and *TPM* compute the "signature of knowledge":
3. The *TPM* computes: $\tilde{T}_t = R^{r_f} S_1^{r_{\nu_1}} S_2^{r_{\nu_2}} \bmod n$ with random r_f and r_ν
4. The *host* computes: $\tilde{T} = \tilde{T}_t T^{r_e} S^{r_{\bar{\nu}}} \bmod n$
5. and: $c_h = H(n\|R\|S_1\|S_2\|Z\|T\|\tilde{T}\|\Gamma\|\rho\|n_\nu)$
6. The *TPM* selects a random n_t and computes computes $c = H(H(c_h\|n_t)\|m)$ and $s_f = r_f + c * f$, $s_{\nu_0} = r_{\nu_0} + c * \nu_0$, $s_{\nu_1} = r_{\nu_1} + c * \nu_1$,
7. The *host* computes $s_e = r_e + c * (e - 2^{l_e - 1})$ and $s_{\bar{\nu}} = s_\nu + r_{\bar{\nu}} - cwe$
8. Finally, the *host* assembles the signature $\sigma = (T, c, n_t, s_{\bar{\nu}}, s_e, s_f, s_{\nu_0}, s_{\nu_1})$

Algorithm 1 shows the basic steps for computing a DAA signature. n is an RSA modulus with $n = p * q$ an $p = 2p' + 1, q = 2q' + 1$. S_1 is a random quadratic residue   mod n that generates the bases $R, S_2, Z \in S_1$. For further details on the parameters we refer to [12].

Rogue Tagging: In order to identify malicious TPMs, the TCG has introduced the so-called *rogue tagging* mechanism. Algorithm 2 shows the basic steps for computing the rogue tagging pseudonym of the signer.

Algorithm 2. DAA Rogue Tagging

Input: $basename, \Gamma, \rho$.
Output: ζ.
1. The verifier selects a random $basename$ and sends it to the signer
2. The *TPM* computes $\zeta = H(basename)^{(\Gamma - 1)/\rho} \bmod \Gamma$

If a TPM is compromised and its private-key f becomes publicly known, a verifier can identify the compromised TPM via the pseudonym ζ [19]. The verifier holds a list with all known keys f, and computes the pseudonym values of these keys with respect to Algorithm 2 and the basename he provided. If ζ is on the computed list, the verifier knows that the signer was a malicious TPM.

3 Our Approach

All existing approaches ([2], [15], [9]) clearly show that current smart-cards do not provide sufficient performance for computing RSA based DAA signatures. Hence, it is inevitable to include a host that contributes the computation of such a signature. This can either be done by providing a host with adequate processing capabilities or by providing a host that controls and manages the pre-computation of such signatures. Idle phases of the device or the SE can be used to generate RSA key-pairs - which we address as ephemeral authentication keys (EAKs) from now on - which can then be certified by a DAA signature. Mobile phones, equipped with either SIM-cards or secure elements provide the ideal platform for such an approach.

We investigate two approaches how anonymous signatures can be used for authentication: in the first approach, the signature is computed entirely in the SE. In this case, the application on the host initiates the pre-computation of the keys and the signature creation. The algorithm listed in Algorithm 1 is executed entirely inside the TPM. The pre-computation of the certified EAK key-pairs can be executed on the card without further involvement of the host. In the second approach, the signature computation (see Algorithm 1) is partially computed inside the TPM and partially on the host. Details of the implementation and performance results can be found in Section 4.

However, in both approaches, the rogue tagging value cannot be computed in advance as it depends on a *basevalue* created by the verifier. Although a DAA signature, according to the specification [18], contains the actual signature and the computed rogue tagging value, both computations are rather independent cryptographic operations (only the computed hash c - see 1 contains the rogue parameters). Hence, they can be computed separately.

3.1 Anonymous Authentication Scenario

Figure 1 shows the application of our approach in a basic authentication scenario.

The mobile platform pre-computes a set of n EAK key-pairs (steps 1-3), certifies the public parts with DAA signatures[1] and stores the private parts of the keys either in the EEPROM of the SE or encrypts it and un-loads it to the host device. The public-keys and their credentials (i.e. the DAA signatures) are stored on the mobile platform. The same is true for the DAA credentials (f, ν_0 and ν_1, R_0, S_0, S_1). By loading different credentials, the TPM may create DAA signatures on behalf of different groups it has joined before.

A user can now use these keys and the NFC module on the phone to prove his authorization against an NFC terminal without revealing his identity. Before sending a request to the terminal, the mobile loads a certified EAK key into the TPM, either from the EEPROM or from the mobile device (steps 4-5). The terminal computes and sends a nonce r_n and *base* for rogue detection to the

---

[1] In Trusted Computing enabled application scenarios, the standard exponent 65537 is used. Hence, only the RSA modulus is signed and transmitted when required.

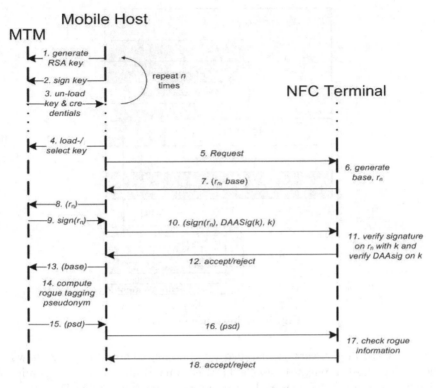

Fig. 1. Authentication Protocol Sequence

mobile (steps 6-7). The mobile forwards r_n to the TPM which signs r_n with the previously loaded EAK key. The mobile device forwards the signature $sign(r_n)$ on r_n, the public EAK key k and the DAA signature $DAASig(k)$ on this key to the terminal (step 10). The terminal verifies $DAASig(k)$ with the issuer's public-key (step 11) and continues the protocol if the verification succeeds. In steps 13-15, the TPM computes the pseudonym $psd = H(base)^{\Gamma-1/\rho} \bmod \Gamma$ which is verified by the terminal as discussed in [12].

If all verifications succeed, the terminal has the information that the requestor is a member of a certain group - namely the group represented by a certain issuer and its public-key - and that the used TPM is not on a list of compromised TPMs. However, the terminal has no information about the identity of the platform or its owner.

4   Implementation Aspects

For our experiments, we used a Nokia 6212 NFC mobile phone. This phone is equipped with a Giesecke & Devrient SmartCafe smart-card as SE. Our secure element based TPM uses this smart-card which provides a JCOP41 v2.2.1 run-time environment. The TPM commands and the DAA computations are handled

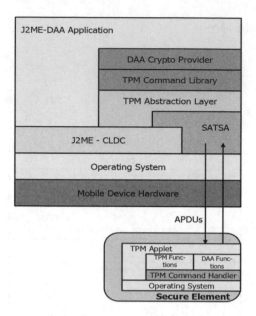

Fig. 2. Architecture Overview

by a JavaCard applet that is installed on the smart-card. Figure 2 shows our concept. The host application uses a TPM command library to issue commands which are sent to the SE via application protocol data units (APDUs).

The host part is implemented as a Java2MicroEdition (J2ME) [16] application that allows the installation of mobile applications on the phone. Moreover, we take advantage of the Security and Trust Service API (SATSA) [13] respectively of JSR 257 the *Contactless Communication API* [14] which allows our application to communicate with the card applet via APDUs. This approach, however, requires that the J22ME application is signed with a code signing certificate from Versign or Thawte.

For the DAA support in the TPM, we require several TPM commands and structures as defined in [18] as well as support for different algorithms. The JavaCard 2.2.1 environment does not provide support for implementing cryptographic protocols. We follow the ideas from [15] and [2] concerning algorithm implementations on JavaCard. For example, the modular exponentiation can be computed via the RSA cipher algorithm and modular multiplication via transformation into a binomial form, $((a*b) \bmod n = \frac{(a+b)^2 - a^2 - b^2}{2} \bmod n)$, the *hmac* algorithm has to be implemented in Java, reducing the overall performance when computing the integrity check of incoming TPM commands.

Our minimum implementation of the DAA scheme requires the following TPM commands and TPM structures on the host and TPM side:

1. a protocol for authorization: TPM_OIAP plus session handling,
2. the TPM_DAA_Join() command
3. the TPM_DAA_Sign() and TPM_DAA_Sign_Init() commands

4. TPM_FlushSpecific() and TPM_Terminate_handle commands for aborting the computation during one of the stages and freeing the resources inside the TPM.
5. TPM_DAA_Issuer_Struct. This structure holds the issuer parameters.
6. two containers for symmetric keys

For unloading the RSA key-pairs, the corresponding DAA signature and the DAA credentials, our TPM generates two symmetric keys k_0, k_1, one for encrypting the data and one for computing an integrity check on it. The TCG specification allows to use symmetric or asymmetric encryption for this purpose. In our approach, we use symmetric cryptography for encryption and - this is different to the TCG specification - a symmetric key for integrity protection to detect modifications of the encrypted authentication keys and DAA parameters when they are stored on the device.

4.1   The Pre-computation Step

The TCG specifies two commands *TPM_DAA_Join* and *TPM_DAA_Sign* which are executed repeatedly in different stages [18]. For simplicity reasons, we reduce these stages to a single stage.

Table 1 shows the measured performance values. The first row shows the values when the computation is split between host and TPM. The first column shows the required time for command handling which includes the computation and verification of *hmac* integrity checks on the command data and its transmission to the TPM. The second column shows the time consumed for computing the host part and the third column shows the time required for computing the TPM part inside the SE. The last column shows the overall result of all single operations.

Table 1 shows a slight performance advantage when computing the entire DAA signature in the TPM[2]. For the first approach, the JavaCard applet that includes the TPM command handler, the cryptographic algorithms and the DAA functionality, requires about 5284 bytes in the EEPROM of the card.

Table 1. Performance comparison of the DAA sign approaches

Command handling	Host	Secure Element	Total
1,1 s	23,8 s	4,8 s	29,7 s
1,4 s	-	26,0 s	27,4 s

A detailed performance analysis of the single cryptographic steps (i.e. random number generation, hash operations, modular exponentiation etc.) of the JavaCard applet and the Java application on the host can not be given in this

---

[2] For the interested reader, a DAA signature computation on an Infineon 1.2 TPM requires approximately 38 seconds.

version of the paper due to its length restrictions. Note that all performance measurements are average values that were estimated by 100 executions of the single operations.

4.2   The NFC Authentication Step

For the actual authentication over the NFC channel, we can use the certified EAK-keys from the pre-computation step. As shown in Figure 1, the terminal sends a nonce to the mobile/TPM which basically applies an RSA signature according to PKCS#1.5 [11] on the nonce which takes approximately 1 second.

Table 2. Performance of the authentication process

Command Handling	Nonce singing	Rogue Tagging	Total
1,0 s	1,3 s	1,1 s	3.4 s

Moreover, the TPM computes the rogue tagging parameter which is basically a single modular exponentiation which also takes approximately 1 second. Hence, the total time required for authentication requires 3,4 seconds.

Parameter lengths. In our prototype implementation, we use the following parameter lengths:

Table 3. Parameter lengths in number of bits

l_n	l_s	l_e	l_f	l_ν
2048 bits	1024 bits	368 bits	160 bits	2536 bits
l_ϕ	l_{r_w}	l_{r_ν}	l_{r_f}	l_Γ
80 bits	2128 bits	2228 bits	400 bits	2048 bits

5   Conclusion and Future Work

In this paper, we discuss how Trusted Computing based technologies can be used for anonymous authentication for NFC and RFID applications. Autonomous contactless smart cards are too constrained to achieve a satisfying performance, hence, we employ mobile phones equipped with NFC modules for our approach. We investigate two approaches, the first splitting the computation of such signatures between a resource constrained TPM and a more powerful host platform and the second, using solely the TPM to compute the entire DAA signature. Furthermore, we show how this approach can be used to circumvent the demanding computational requirements for computing the mathematical complex Direct Anonymous Attestation signatures in order to provide a feasible approach to show that our idea can be used in real-world scenarios. We achieve this by using the mobile phone for pre-computing and certifying authentication keys.

For generating experimental results, we use off-the-shelf mobile phones that are equipped with secure elements to host the TPM functionality and which are connected to NFC modules, allowing a practical implementation of our prototype.

We also propose modifications in the DAA protocol flow in order to speed-up the computations on the mobile platform.

Future investigations should include DAA schemes based on elliptic curve cryptography as discussed in ([10], [5]). ECC based schemes clearly show a performance advantage over the RSA based variant. Although support for ECC is provided by JavaCard vendors, adequate support for developing complex DAA protocols based on ECC is not yet available on current JavaCard platforms. Another interesting aspect for mobile devices is power consumption. How much power is drained from a device's battery depends strongly on the executed operations. Consequently, an analysis of the power consumption when computing DAA signatures is of great interest for future investigations.

Acknowledgements. This work has been supported by the European Commission through project FP7-2009.1.4(c)-SEPIA, Grant agreement number 257433.

References

1. ARM Ltd: TrustZone Technology Overview. Introduction, http://www.arm.com/products/esd/trustzone_home.html
2. Bichsel, P., Camenisch, J., Groß, T., Shoup, V.: Anonymous credentials on a standard java card. In: Proceedings of the 16th ACM conference on Computer and communications security, CCS 2009, Chicago, Illinois, USA, pp. 600–610. ACM, New York (2009)
3. Brands, S.A.: Rethinking Public Key Infrastructures and Digital Certificates: Building in Privacy. MIT Press, Cambridge (2000)
4. Brickell, E., Camenisch, J., Chen, L.: Direct Anonymous Attestation. In: Proceedings of the 11th ACM conference on Computer and communications security, CCS2004, Washington DC, USA, pp. 132–145. ACM, New York (2004)
5. Chen, L.: A daa scheme requiring less tpm resources. Cryptology ePrint Archive, Report 2010/008 (2010), http://eprint.iacr.org/
6. Dietrich, K.: An Integrated Architecture for Trusted Computing for Java Enabled Embedded Devices. In: Proceedings of the 2007 ACM workshop on Scalable trusted computing, STC 2007, pp. 2–6. ACM Press, New York (2007)
7. Dietrich, K.: Anonymous Credentials for Java Enabled Platforms. In: Chen, L., Yung, M. (eds.) INTRUST 2009. LNCS, vol. 6163, pp. 88–103. Springer, Heidelberg (2010)
8. Dietrich, K., Winter, J.: Implementation aspects of mobile and embedded trusted computing. In: Chen, L., Mitchell, C.J., Martin, A. (eds.) Trust 2009. LNCS, vol. 5471, pp. 29–44. Springer, Heidelberg (2009)
9. Balasch Masoliver, J.M.: Smart Card Implementation of Anonymous Credentials. Master's thesis, K.U.Leuven, Belgium (2008)
10. Page, D., Chen, L., Smart, N.P.: On the design and implementation of an efficient daa scheme. Cryptology ePrint Archive, Report 2009/598 (2009), http://eprint.iacr.org/

11. RSA Labs. PKCS1 v2.1: RSA Cryptography Standard (2001)
12. Mitchel, C.: Direct Anonymous Attestation in Context. In: Trusted Computing (Professional Applications of Computing), Piscataway, NJ, USA, pp. 143–174. IEEE Computer Society Press, Los Alamitos (2005)
13. SUN Community process: Java Specification Request (JSR-177): Security and Trust Services API. Specification (September 2004), http://jcp.org/en/jsr/detail?id=177
14. SUN Community process: Java Specification Request (JSR-257): Contactless Communication API. Specification (October 2004), http://jcp.org/en/jsr/detail?id=257
15. Sterckx, M., Gierlichs, B., Preneel, B., Verbauwhede, I.: Efficient Implementation of Anonymous Credentials on Java Card Smart Cards. In: 1st IEEE International Workshop on Information Forensics and Security (WIFS 2009), London,UK, pp. 106–110. IEEE Computer Society Press, Los Alamitos (2009)
16. SUN Community process JSR 139. J2ME(TM) Connected Limited Device Configuration (CLDC) Specification 1.1 Final Release. Specification (March 4, 2004), http://jcp.org/aboutJava/communityprocess/final/jsr139/index.html
17. Trusted Computing Group Mobile Phone Working Group. TCG Mobile Trusted Module Sepecification Version 1 rev. 1.0 Specification (June 12, 2007), https://www.trustedcomputinggroup.org/specs/mobilephone/tcg-mobile-trusted-module-1.0.pdf
18. Trusted Computing Group - TPM Working Group: TPM Main Part 3 Commands. Specification (October 26, 2006), http://www.trustedcomputinggroup.org/files/static_page_files/ACD28F6C-1D09-3519-AD210DC2597FE4C/mainP3Commandsrev103.pdf Specification version 1.2 Level 2 Revision 103
19. Trusted-Computing-Group-TSS-Working-Group. TCG Software Stack (TSS) Specification Version 1.2 Level 1. Specification (January 6, 2006), https://www.trustedcomputinggroup.org/specs/TSS/TSS_Version_1.2_Level_1_FINAL.pdf; Part1: Commands and Structures
20. Winter, J.: Trusted computing building blocks for embedded linux-based arm trustzone platforms. In: Proceedings of the 3rd ACM workshop on Scalable trusted computing, STC 2008, pp. 21–30. ACM, New York (2008)

Tree-Based RFID Authentication Protocols Are Definitively Not Privacy-Friendly

Gildas Avoine, Benjamin Martin, and Tania Martin

Université catholique de Louvain
Information Security Group
B-1348 Louvain-La-Neuve, Belgium
{gildas.avoine, benjamin.martin, tania.martin}@uclouvain.be

Abstract. Authentication for low-cost Radio-Frequency IDentification (RFID) is a booming research topic. The challenge is to develop secure protocols using lightweight cryptography, yet ensuring privacy. A current trend is to design such protocols upon the *Learning Parity from Noise* (LPN) problem. The first who introduced this solution were Hopper and Blum in 2001. Since then, many protocols have been designed, especially the protocol of Halevi, Saxena, and Halevi (HSH) [15] that combines LPN and the tree-based key infrastructure suggested by Molnar and Wagner [24]. In this paper, we introduce a new RFID authentication protocol that is less resource consuming than HSH, relying on the same adversary model and security level, though. Afterwards, we show that, if an adversary can tamper with some tags, the privacy claimed in HSH is defeated. In other words, either tags are tamper-resistant, then we suggest a protocol more efficient than HSH, or they are not, then we suggest a significative attack against the untraceability property of HSH.

Keywords: RFID, Security, Traceability, Authentication, HB, Tree-based, LPN.

1 Introduction

Radio Frequency IDentification (RFID) is a wireless technology that allows to identify/authenticate items without physical contact. An RFID interaction is proceeded between: (i) RFID tags, or transponders jointed with an antenna, embedded into objects such as access cards [33], books [24] or even electronic passports [27] and, (ii) RFID readers composed of a transreceiver securely connected to a back-end system.

RFID tags are divided into two categories, passive or active devices: active tags have their own power source (a battery), whereas passive tags draw their energy from the electromagnetic field of the reader. The latter tags so suffer from very limited resources, especially in terms of computation and memory. In secure applications where cryptography is required, tags (even passive) can embed a microprocessor. This solution being expensive, researchers got interested in building *lightweight* cryptographic building blocks that can be implemented

S.B. Ors Yalcin (Ed.): RFIDSec 2010, LNCS 6370, pp. 103–122, 2010.
© Springer-Verlag Berlin Heidelberg 2010

with wired logic only. Many such protocols have been published so far, but many attacks have been put forward as well. For many protocols [11,18,28,29,30], active and passive attacks were published [1,5,6,10,21,22,32,34] while for other protocols [19,31] only active attacks were found [7,12].

In 2000, Hopper and Blum [17,18] took benefit of the *Learning Parity from Noise* (LPN) problem to design a human-to-computer authentication protocol, today known as HB. Juels and Weis [19] then noticed the link between the human-to-computer and tag-to-reader authentication paradigms: the computation capabilities of the provers are quite restricted in both cases. They also stress that HB presents the noticeable particularity that it does not identify the prover who is involved in the protocol. This may be an interesting feature to protect the privacy of the prover, but this becomes a drawback when considering radio frequency *identification*. The idea of using the LPN problem to design lightweight authentication protocols was then taken up in several papers [13,15,19] leading to the HB-saga.

During RFIDSec 2009, Halevi, Saxena, and Halevi [15] presented a lightweight privacy-friendly authentication protocol that aims to reduce the reader computational load. The protocol consists of two phases. The first phase identifies the tag using a tree traversal, as suggested by Molnar and Wagner [24] at ACM CCS 2004. This technique allows the reader to retrieve in the database the key associated to the tag with a computation complexity $O(\log(n))$ instead of $O(n)$, where n is the number of tags in the system. In the second phase, the tag is authenticated using the HB+ protocol proposed by Juels and Weis [19] at Crypto 2005.

Our first contribution is a new LPN-based authentication protocol where the computation complexity of the reader is lower than those implied by HSH [15]. Nevertheless, our protocol complies with the privacy threat model considered in [15] and reaches the same security level. Another attractive property is that our protocol also reduces the memory requirement for the tag.

Our second contribution is related to the privacy model considered in [15]. This model considers that tags are tamper-resistant, which is quite a strong assumption. We demonstrate that if this assumption is relaxed, as it is commonly admitted in the literature [2,3], tampering with one or few tags threatens all the tags belonging to the system. Our attack generalizes the one presented by Avoine, Dysli, and Oechslin [4] at SAC 2005 against the protocol of Molnar and Wagner [24].

The paper is organized as follows: Section 2 provides the background and introduces HSH. Section 3 presents our protocol, and compares it with HSH. Section 4 points out a privacy attack against HSH. Finally, Section 5 concludes.

2   From LPN to HSH

2.1   The LPN Problem

The *Learn Parity with Noise* problem is one of the well-known problems in cryptography. Given that:

 − x is a secret k-bit vector,
 − a is a random known k-bit vector,
 − $\epsilon \in]0, \frac{1}{2}[$ is a noise parameter,
 − and η is a bit noise where $\Pr(\{\eta = 1\}) = \epsilon$,

then it is hard to recover x from the result $r = a \cdot x \oplus \eta$ (the scalar product of a and x, XORed with η).

Many attempts on identification and authentication protocols relying on the LPN problem have been proposed so far, such as all HB-family protocols [7,8,13,15,16,17,18,19,20,23,25,35], or the LPN-C protocol of Gilbert, Robshaw and Seurin [14]. During the sequel, we consider that the RFID systems are composed of n tags.

2.2   The HB+ Protocol

The HB+ protocol has been proposed by Juels and Weis in 2005 [19] to improve the original HB protocol [18] against active attacks.

At the system setup, each tag T has a unique pair of secret keys (x_T, y_T) known by every reader R, where $|x_T| = |y_T| = k$. T is also given a random noise parameter $\epsilon \in]0, \frac{1}{2}[$.

Then s rounds of challenge/response are required by the reader to authenticate the tag T (see Fig. 1), where s is a security parameter. For each round, R selects a random k-bit vector a and sends it to T. The latter also chooses a random k-bit vector b and noise bit η, and sends to R its answer $r = (a \cdot x_T) \oplus (b \cdot y_T) \oplus \eta$. R accepts the round if $(a \cdot x_T) \oplus (b \cdot y_T) = r$. Finally, the reader authenticates the tag T after s rounds if T's answers are correct in more than $s\epsilon$ rounds.

Reader R	**Tag T**
x_T, y_T, ϵ	x_T, y_T, ϵ
$a \in \{0,1\}^k$	$b \in \{0,1\}^k$
	$\eta \in \{0, 1 \mid \Pr(\eta = 1) = \epsilon\}$
$\xrightarrow{\quad a \quad}$	$r = (a \cdot x_T) \oplus (b \cdot y_T) \oplus \eta$
$\xleftarrow{\quad b,\, r \quad}$	
Accepts if $(a \cdot x_T) \oplus (b \cdot y_T) = r$	

Fig. 1. A single round of the HB+ protocol

2.3   The HSH Protocol

In this section, we present the authentication protocol proposed by Halevi, Saxena, and Halevi at RFIDSec 2009 [15] designed for radio-frequency applications. During the rest of the paper, it will be denoted by HSH. It is claimed to be light and fast, and to preserve tag privacy under the model provided below.

The heart of HSH is that all its design relies on the HB-family protocols combined with the tree-based key infrastructure proposed by Molnar and Wagner in [24] (called here MW). HSH is divided in two stages: the tree traversal and the authentication. The following table gives the notations and recommended values for HSH:

Notation	Meaning	Recommended Values [15]
d	depth of the tree	$d \in \{2,3\}$
β	tree branching factor	$\beta \in \{100, 1000\}$
k_x	length of the key x_T	$k_x = 80$
k_y	length of the key y_T	$k_y \in [224, 512]$
s	size of T's answer	$s \in [80, 212]$
ϵ	noise level	$\epsilon \in [\frac{1}{8}, \frac{1}{4}]$

The choice of HB-family comes from the fact that these kinds of protocols fit perfectly in low-cost RFID tags. Here we present HSH using HB+ (this choice is given by the HSH authors). Then the idea of MW is to consider the n tags of the system as leaves in a tree of branching factor β. Thus MW associates each edge in the tree with a secret key. The readers are assumed to know all the keys. Each tag stores the $\lceil \log n \rceil$ keys corresponding to its path from the root to the leaf. HSH builds the key infrastructure of the tree traversal stage on MW because it reduces significantly the complexity of the reader during the identification process: $\beta \lceil \log_\beta n \rceil$ operations in the worst case, instead of n. Thus the use of MW makes the protocol lighter on the reader side.

The HSH privacy threat model. Since all HB-like protocols are not resistant against active adversaries, [15] considers adversaries who can eavesdrop all the communications and who can interact with both R and T, but disregarding man-in-the-middle attacks. Also, since the MW key infrastructure does not resist to privacy traceability when several tags are compromised, [15] considers that the tags are tamper-resistant.

Initialization. Given a system with n tags, the parameters β and d are chosen at the system setup, such that they define a tree with $\beta^d \geq n$ leaves. Each leaf is associated randomly to a tag of the system. During the setup of the system, each tag T is assigned to a unique pair of secret keys (x_T, y_T), known by every reader R involved in the system.

Let $p_0, p_1, p_2, \ldots, p_d$ be the path in the tree from the root (denoted p_0) to the leaf that is associated to the tag T (denoted p_d). For each node p_i (except the root), T knows a corresponding k_y-bit key y_{p_i}. R knows the entire tree arrangement, and thus all the keys associated to the nodes.

Tree traversal stage. First of all, R must recover the right pair of secret keys to authenticate correctly the tag T. To do so, T chooses an $s \times k_y$ random binary matrix B and a s-bit random noise vector ν^i for every level i in the tree. Then T computes $z^i = B \cdot y_{p_i} \oplus \nu^i$; and it sends B and z^i for every level i of the tree to R.

Upon reception of these data, R goes down into the tree, node by node, using the z^i's. Clearly, R computes for every child c of the root: $z^c = B \cdot y_c$, where y_c is a child key. And R goes down to the child whose answer is the closest to the data z^1 sent by T. The same procedure is iterated for every level i in the tree.

At the end, R reaches one of the leaves of the tree, and uses the pair of corresponding secret keys (x, y) for the authentication stage.

Authentication. At the end of the tree traversal stage, R is convinced that the pair of keys found is the correct pair for the tag T.

Then R processes the HB+ protocol on this pair to confirm this result and to authenticate definitely T. Thus, the reader sends an $s \times k_x$ challenge binary matrix A to the tag T. The latter then chooses a s-bit random noise vector ν, and sends back the result $z = A \cdot x_T \oplus B \cdot y_T \oplus \nu$. R computes $z' = A \cdot x \oplus B \cdot y$ with the pair found at the end of the tree traversal stage, and computes the Hamming distance between z' and T's answer z. If this value is under the threshold $\tau = s\epsilon$, then R accepts T; otherwise it rejects it.

3   Our Protocol

In this section, we present an authentication protocol relying on the LPN problem. The goal of this protocol is to be as secure as HSH in the same threat model (see Section 2.3 for its definition). In such a case, we want to prove that, in the same weak threat model, it is possible to create a protocol with less needed tag memory and less computational complexity, especially on the reader side.

3.1   Problem Statement

As explained before, HSH is tree-based which leads to a $O(\log n)$ reader complexity, nevertheless better than a classical challenge/response protocol whose reader complexity is in $O(n)$. Since tags are tamper-resistant, we decide to put a unique pair of symmetric keys (x, y) shared between all readers and tags, in order to decrease R's complexity. Thus, having a common pair of keys for the whole system is better for R's computation search, rather than n pairs (one unique per tag in classical cryptography): R's complexity search will be in $O(1)$.

In a classical HB-family protocol, each tag T has a unique symmetric secret key (or pair of keys) to authenticate itself to the reader R. During the protocol execution, T adds some noise to its answer (with some probability). Then R tries every tags' secret key and, when it finds a result enough close to T's answer (with respect to the noise probability), the authentication succeeds. Basically, we consider that R scans its database of all tags' secret keys and stops when it finds such a match: it is a problem since R does not try all the secret keys to find the one whose computation will be the closest to T's answer, but the first one which is close to T's answer under the probability parameter ϵ. So the HB-family protocols provide tag authentication, but R will not be sure of the real tag's identity. That is the reason we associate a unique secret identifier Id_T

per tag, which is sent into the tag's answer to be identified by R. The latter knows all the tags' identifiers.

Thus, in order to merge all these properties, we present a variant of the LPN-C protocol proposed by Gilbert, Robshaw and Seurin in [14]. Actually, since the latter is vulnerable to replay attacks, our authentication protocol has to thwart such attacks. In our proposal, the tag's answer is built in the same way as for HB+ [19] (see Section 2.2). In comparison with LPN-C, we first decide to add a challenge sent by the reader to the tag: this is to avoid the problem of replay attacks that are inherent in LPN-C. Then in our protocol, the challenges are matrix whereas the secrets are vectors, and these latters are defined as in HB+, i.e. two secret keys instead of one: this choice is to store less information on the tag, to reduce the tag memory needed by the protocol and thus to reduce the potential price of the tag (*i.e.* less memory means lower costly tag). The final achievement of our protocol is to allow a reader to authenticate and identify a tag correctly, based on the following hypothesis :

- all tags and readers share a common pair of keys,
- every tag has a unique secret identifier.

3.2   The Protocol Description

Initialization. When the system is set up, every reader and tag share a pair (x, y) of secret keys. Each tag T is assigned with a unique secret identifier Id_T known by R. The notations and values that will be used in the protocol are given below:

Notation	Meaning	Usual choices
k_x	length of the key x	$k_x = 80$
k_y	length of the key y	$k_y \in [224, 512]$
s	length of T's identifier Id_T	$s \in [80, 212]$
ϵ	noise level	$\epsilon \in [\frac{1}{8}, \frac{1}{4}]$

We define C as the code of all the tags' identifiers of our system. For a given codeword $Id_T \in C$, we consider the ball $\mathcal{B}_{Id_T}$ of radius $t = \lceil s\epsilon \rceil$ around Id_T. Each ball represents all the codewords c such that $d_{\mathcal{H}}(Id_T, c) \leq t$, where $d_{\mathcal{H}}$ denotes the Hamming distance. The volume of $\mathcal{B}_{Id_T}$ is the number of all these codewords c, defined as: $\text{Vol}(\mathcal{B}_{Id_T}) = \sum_{i=0}^{t} \binom{s}{i}$. To make viable the tag identification, we distribute the identifiers such that all the balls are pairwise disjoint.

Authentication. The authentication protocol consists of three steps (see Fig. 2):

(1) The reader sends a random binary $s \times k_x$ matrix A.
(2) The tag chooses a random binary $s \times k_y$ matrix B, a s-bit random noise vector $\nu = (\nu_1, \nu_2, \ldots, \nu_s)$.
    $\forall i \in \{1, \ldots, s\} : \nu_i \in \{0, 1 | \Pr(\{\nu_i = 1\}) = \epsilon\}$.

Then it computes $r = (A \cdot x) \oplus (B \cdot y) \oplus Id_T \oplus \nu$, where $|r| = s$.
Finally, it sends B and r to R.

(3) The reader computes $r' = (A \cdot x) \oplus (B \cdot y)$, and recovers instantaneously $D = r \oplus r' = Id_T \oplus \nu$.

Then for each tag identifier I, R computes the Hamming distance between D and I. Since all the tags identifiers are well-distributed, when this distance is lower than t, that means D only belongs to $\mathcal{B}_I$. Thus R retrieves the real identifier $I = Id_T$.

Reader R	**Tag T**
x, y, Id_T, ϵ	x, y, Id_T, ϵ

$$(1) \quad \xrightarrow{\quad A \quad}$$
$$\xleftarrow{\quad B,\ r \quad} \quad (2)$$
$$(3)$$

Fig. 2. Authentication protocol

Remark 1. The step (3) of the authentication process can be improved. R must recover T's identifier from D. Clearly, D is the tag's identifier XORed with some noise vector ν, i.e. Id_T containing at most t error bits (t being the Hamming weight of ν). Instead of computing naively the Hamming distance between D and I, R can use an appropriate error-correcting code to recover Id_T without the t errors. This extension is out of the scope of this paper, though.

3.3   Analysis

Besides the assumption that all the balls $\mathcal{B}_{Id_T}$ are pairwise disjoint, we assume that (i) the identifiers space is large enough and, (ii) the tags' identifiers are uniformly distributed for security reasons. First, the distance between two identifiers must be at least two times the radius of a ball, i.e. $2t$. This will allow the reader to identify without mistakes every tag, since every D result will belong to a unique ball. But if the identifiers space is too small and if all the balls cover exactly the space, the security is nonexistent: an adversary can send a value at random and be sure to be identified by the reader. We thus want that the success probability of an adversary to send a random value that could match a result into a ball is negligible. That is why we choose an identifiers space large enough.

We compare our results to the ones given by the HSH protocol. If we take $n = 10^6$ tags, we have the following results when ϵ, d, β, k_x and k_y are fixed:

	FAR	s	Tag mem	Comm	$\mathbb{C}_T$	$\mathbb{C}_R$
HSH	$2^{-41.3}$	86	1400	44978	$2^{16.9}$	$2^{26.2}$
Our protocol	$2^{-41.5}$	128	648	66688	2^{16}	

- $n = \beta^d = 10^6$ = total number of tags in the system,
- $d = 2$ = tree depth for the HSH protocol,
- $\beta = 1000$ = tree branching factor for the HSH protocol,
- $\epsilon = 0.125$ = noise level,
- $k_x = 80$ = length of the key x,
- $k_y = 440$ = length of the key y,
- s = length of T's identifier/response,
- FAR = False Accept Rate = probability of guessing a tag authentication reply at random,
    - FAR $= n\dfrac{\mathrm{Vol}(\mathcal{B}(0,t))}{2^s}$ for our protocol,
    - FAR $= \dfrac{\mathrm{Vol}(\mathcal{B}(0,t))}{2^s}$ for HSH,
- Tag mem = the memory needed on the tag,
    - $k_x + k_y + s$ bits for our protocol,
    - $k_x + k_y(d+1)$ bits for HSH,
- Comm = total number of bits sent during the whole protocol,
    - $s(k_x + k_y + 1)$ bits for our protocol,
    - $s(k_x + k_y + d + 1)$ bits for HSH,
- $\mathbb{C}_T$ = tag computation complexity,
    - $s(k_x + k_y)$ bit operations for our protocol,
    - $sdk_y + s(k_x + k_y)$ bit operations for HSH,
- $\mathbb{C}_R$ = reader computation complexity,
    - $s(k_x + k_y)$ bit operations for our protocol (+ decoding $D = Id_T \oplus \nu$),
    - $\beta sdk_y + s(k_x + k_y)$ bit operations for HSH.

Here, we augment s to reach the same security level of HSH for our protocol (i.e. FAR $\approx 2^{-41}$). Thus we notice that our protocol needs less memory in the tag to achieve the same security level (around half less). The complexity for the reader and for the tag to process the protocol is also much lower than for HSH. This conclusion is further observable at the reader side: the tree traversal stage of HSH done by the reader to find the right pair of secret keys increases consequently the reader's time search.

4   Attack on HSH

In this section, we introduce an attack conducted on the HSH protocol to damage the tag privacy. First, let remind that HSH is a combination of HB+ and the tree-based key infrastructure of Molnar and Wagner (MW). Several attacks have already demonstrated that MW does not provide tag privacy: Avoine, Dysli, and Oechslin in [4] (called here ADO), then Buttyán, Holczer and Vajda in [9], and finally Nohl and Evans in [26]. HSH naturally inherits from MW's weaknesses. In what follows, we consider ADO being the first published attack on MW, and show that it can be adapted to break the untraceability of HSH.

In Section 3, we assumed that tags are tamper-resistant, and we provided a protocol better than HSH under this assumption. In this section, we consider that tags are not tamper-resistant, and we show that compromising a few tags smashes the whole system when based on HSH. The details of all the probabilities computations done in this section are given in the appendix.

4.1 Adversary Game

We explain here how the tree technique chosen in HSH is predisposed for tag tracing when the adversary $\mathcal{A}$ can tamper with one tag. We then show that the situation is still worse when $\mathcal{A}$ can tamper with several tags. Following ADO [4], we consider a *Challenger* that supplies two tags to the adversary, one of them being the target tag. The attack is done as follows:

1. $\mathcal{A}$ requests the *Challenger* and receives one tag T_0 (respectively several tags) that she can tamper with. Thus $\mathcal{A}$ can obtain all T_0 (respectively the tampered tags) keys. Since the number of tags in the system is large enough, we consider for the sake of simplicity that $\mathcal{A}$ is allowed to put T_0 (respectively all the tampered tags) back into circulation.
2. Then $\mathcal{A}$ requests the *Challenger* and receives a target tag T that she can query as much as she wants, but cannot tamper with it. Next $\mathcal{A}$ puts T back into circulation.
3. $\mathcal{A}$ requests the *Challenger* and receives two tags T_1 and T_2 such that $T \in \{T_1, T_2\}$. She can query T_1 and T_2 as much as she wants, without tampering with them.
4. Finally, $\mathcal{A}$ outputs $T = T_1$ or T_2.

$\mathcal{A}$ succeeds if she can guess correctly which one of T_1 and T_2 is the target tag T.

Notice that in our attack, $\mathcal{A}$ always provides an answer. The goal of our study is to compute $\mathcal{A}$'s advantage.

4.2 Tampering with One Tag

The purpose of this section is to evaluate the probability that the attack described above succeeds. To formalize the analysis, we denote the keys of T, T_0, T_1 and T_2 by $[y_1, \ldots, y_d]$, $[y_1^0, \ldots, y_d^0]$, $[y_1^1, \ldots, y_d^1]$ and $[y_1^2, \ldots, y_d^2]$ respectively. At a given level i in the tree ($1 \leq i \leq d$), the ADO attack considers four possibilities:

- $C_i^1 = \{y_i^0 = y_i^1\} \wedge \{y_i^0 \neq y_i^2\}$,
- $C_i^2 = \{y_i^0 \neq y_i^1\} \wedge \{y_i^0 = y_i^2\}$,
- $C_i^3 = \{y_i^0 \neq y_i^1\} \wedge \{y_i^0 \neq y_i^2\}$,
- $C_i^4 = \{y_i^0 = y_i^1 = y_i^2\}$.

MW is based on a classical challenge/response protocol using pseudo-random functions. But HSH is based on a challenge/response protocol using HB+. The noise inherent to HB+ does not allow to apply the ADO attack directly.

We first define $z_i^\ell = B^\ell y_i^\ell \oplus \nu_i^\ell$ being the answer of the tag T_ℓ at level i of the HSH tree traversal stage. Then, we define $\mathcal{B}_i^\ell$ being the ball of radius $t = \lceil s\epsilon \rceil$ (as defined in Section 3.3) around z_i^ℓ. A direct consequence of HSH is that the adversary can only evaluate the possibility that T_0's key y_i^0 was used to compute z_i^ℓ, i.e. $B^\ell y_i^0 \in \mathcal{B}_i^\ell$ or not. With these notations, we consider for our attack four possibilities related to the ADO ones :

- $A_i^1 = \{B^1 y_i^0 \in \mathcal{B}_i^1\} \wedge \{B^2 y_i^0 \notin \mathcal{B}_i^2\}$,
- $A_i^2 = \{B^1 y_i^0 \notin \mathcal{B}_i^1\} \wedge \{B^2 y_i^0 \in \mathcal{B}_i^2\}$,
- $A_i^3 = \{B^1 y_i^0 \notin \mathcal{B}_i^1\} \wedge \{B^2 y_i^0 \notin \mathcal{B}_i^2\}$,
- $A_i^4 = \{B^1 y_i^0 \in \mathcal{B}_i^1\} \wedge \{B^2 y_i^0 \in \mathcal{B}_i^2\}$.

Clearly here, the events that are taken into account for this attack are:

- $E_i^1 = C_i^1 \wedge A_i^1$ then the attack succeeds,
- $E_i^2 = C_i^2 \wedge A_i^2$ then the attack succeeds,
- $E_i^3 = C_i^3 \wedge A_i^3$ then the attack definitely fails,
- $E_i^4 = C_i^4 \wedge A_i^4$ then the attack fails at level i but can move to level $i+1$,

where all the E_i^j events are pairwise disjoint. The fact that the attack succeeds means that the adversary has been able to distinguish T_1 from T_2.

In order to simplify the notation in the following, we give and denote explicitly two probabilities to compare T_0's key y_i^0 and a given T_ℓ's key y_i^ℓ at level i:

- $\Pr(\{B^\ell y_i^0 \in \mathcal{B}_i^\ell\}|\{y_i^0 = y_i^\ell\}) = \sum_{j=0}^{t} \binom{s}{j} \epsilon^j (1-\epsilon)^{s-j} = S_t$,

- $\Pr(\{B^\ell y_i^0 \in \mathcal{B}_i^\ell\}|\{y_i^0 \neq y_i^\ell\}) = \Pr(d_{\mathcal{H}}(B^\ell y_i^0, z_i^\ell) \leq t) = \dfrac{\mathrm{Vol}(\mathcal{B}(0,t))}{2^s} = V_t$.

We compute the probabilities of the events E_i^1, E_i^2, E_i^3, and E_i^4. The final results are:

$$\Pr(E_i^1) = \Pr(E_i^2) = S_t(1 - V_t)\left(\frac{\beta - 1}{\beta^2}\right)$$

$$\Pr(E_i^3) = (1 - V_t)^2\left(\frac{\beta - 1}{\beta}\right)^2$$

$$\Pr(E_i^4) = \left(\frac{S_t}{\beta}\right)^2$$

Following ADO attack, the overall probability P_{succ} that the whole attack succeeds when the adversary tampers with one tag is:

$$P_{\mathrm{succ}} = 2S_t(1 - V_t)\left(\frac{\beta - 1}{\beta^2}\right)\left(\frac{1 - (\frac{S_t}{\beta})^{2d}}{1 - (\frac{S_t}{\beta})^2}\right)$$

4.3 Adversary Probability P_{succ} When Tampering with Several Tags

We now analyze the adversary success probability of tracing a tag when she tampers with c_0 tags ($c_0 \geq 1$). As before, we denote the keys of T, T_1 and T_2 by $[y_1, \ldots, y_d]$, $[y_1^1, \ldots, y_d^1]$ and $[y_1^2, \ldots, y_d^2]$ respectively. Then at a given level i of the tree, we consider $\mathcal{K}_i = \{k_{i,1}, k_{i,2}, \ldots, k_{i,c_i}\}$ the set of keys known by the adversary (with $\mathrm{Card}(\mathcal{K}_i) = c_i$). The ADO attack considers five possibilities:

- $C_i^1 = \{y_i^1 \in \mathcal{K}_i\} \wedge \{y_i^2 \notin \mathcal{K}_i\}$,
- $C_i^2 = \{y_i^1 \notin \mathcal{K}_i\} \wedge \{y_i^2 \in \mathcal{K}_i\}$,
- $C_i^3 = \{y_i^1 \in \mathcal{K}_i\} \wedge \{y_i^2 \in \mathcal{K}_i\} \wedge \{y_i^1 \neq y_i^2\}$,
- $C_i^4 = \{y_i^1 \notin \mathcal{K}_i\} \wedge \{y_i^2 \notin \mathcal{K}_i\}$,
- $C_i^5 = \{y_i^1 \in \mathcal{K}_i\} \wedge \{y_i^2 \in \mathcal{K}_i\} \wedge \{y_i^1 = y_i^2\}$.

In the same vein as the previous section, we define five possibilities related to ADO ones:

- $A_i^1 = \{\exists k_{i,m} \in \mathcal{K}_i : B^1 k_{i,m} \in \mathcal{B}_i^1\} \wedge \{\forall k_{i,m} \in \mathcal{K}_i : B^2 k_{i,m} \notin \mathcal{B}_i^2\}$,
- $A_i^2 = \{\forall k_{i,m} \in \mathcal{K}_i : B^1 k_{i,m} \notin \mathcal{B}_i^1\} \wedge \{\exists k_{i,m} \in \mathcal{K}_i : B^2 k_{i,m} \in \mathcal{B}_i^2\}$,
- $A_i^3 = \{\exists k_{i,m} \in \mathcal{K}_i : B^1 k_{i,m} \in \mathcal{B}_i^1\} \wedge \{\exists k_{i,m'} \in \mathcal{K}_i : B^2 k_{i,m'} \in \mathcal{B}_i^2\} \wedge \{k_{i,m} \neq k_{i,m'}\}$,
- $A_i^4 = \{\forall k_{i,m} \in \mathcal{K}_i : B^1 k_{i,m} \notin \mathcal{B}_i^1\} \wedge \{\forall k_{i,m} \in \mathcal{K}_i : B^2 k_{i,m} \notin \mathcal{B}_i^2\}$,
- $A_i^5 = \{\exists k_{i,m} \in \mathcal{K}_i : B^1 k_{i,m} \in \mathcal{B}_i^1\} \wedge \{\exists k_{i,m'} \in \mathcal{K}_i : B^2 k_{i,m'} \in \mathcal{B}_i^2\} \wedge \{k_{i,m} = k_{i,m'}\}$.

Then the events that are taken into account for this attack are:

- $E_i^1 = C_i^1 \wedge A_i^1$ then the attack succeeds,
- $E_i^2 = C_i^2 \wedge A_i^2$ then the attack succeeds,
- $E_i^3 = C_i^3 \wedge A_i^3$ then the attack succeeds,
- $E_i^4 = C_i^4 \wedge A_i^4$ then the attack definitely fails,
- $E_i^5 = C_i^5 \wedge A_i^5$ then the attack fails at level i but can move to level $i + 1$.

We compute the probabilities of the events $E_i^1, E_i^2, E_i^3, E_i^4$, and E_i^5 at level i:

$$\Pr(E_i^1) = \Pr(E_i^2) = \left(\frac{c_i(\beta - c_i)}{\beta^2}\right)\left(1 - (1 - S_t)^{c_i}\right)(1 - V_t)^{c_i}$$

$$\Pr(E_i^3) = \left(\frac{c_i(c_i - 1)}{\beta^2}\right)\left(1 - (1 - S_t)^{c_i}\right)^2$$

$$\Pr(E_i^4) = \left(\frac{\beta - c_i}{\beta}\right)^2 (1 - V_t)^{2c_i}$$

$$\Pr(E_i^5) = \left(\frac{c_i}{\beta^2}\right)\left(1 - (1 - S_t)^{c_i}\right)^2$$

Following ADO attack, the overall probability P_{succ} that the whole attack succeeds when the adversary tampers with c_0 tags is:

$$P_{\text{succ}} = \Pr(E_1^1 \vee E_1^2 \vee E_1^3) + \sum_{i=2}^{d}\left(\Pr(E_i^1 \vee E_i^2 \vee E_i^3) \times \prod_{j=1}^{i-1} \Pr(E_j^5)\right) \qquad (1)$$

where c_i, the number of different keys known by the adversary at level i, is given by the ADO attack:

$$c_1 = \beta\left(1 - \left(\frac{\beta-1}{\beta}\right)^{c_0}\right) \quad \text{and} \quad c_i = \beta\left(1 - \left(\frac{\beta-1}{\beta}\right)^{g(c_i)}\right) \quad \forall i,\ 2 \leq i \leq d$$

$$\text{where} \quad g(c_i) = c_0 \prod_{\ell=1}^{i-1} \frac{1}{c_\ell}$$

Remark 2. When $\epsilon = 0$, there is a perfect match between the ADO attack and ours. In such a case, there is not wanted noise added in the tag's answer, which influences the values of S_t and V_t ($S_t = 1$ and $V_t = 0$).

Table 1 gives numerical values of Eq. 1 when the parameters s and ϵ are fixed ($s = 86$ and $\epsilon = 0.125$).

Table 1. Numerical values of the probability P_{succ} of tracing tag T according to branching factor β when the adversary tampers with c_0 tags. The system contains 2^{20} tags, $s = 86$ and $\epsilon = 0.125$.

c_0 \ β	2	20	100	500	1000
1	33.7%	5.8%	1.2%	0.2%	0.1%
20	56.1%	84.3%	32.9%	7.7%	3.9%
50	56.3%	95.8%	63.0%	18.1%	9.5%
100	56.3%	96.9%	86.0%	33.0%	18.1%
200	56.3%	98.1%	97.4%	55.0%	33.0%

4.4 Adversary Probability P_{luck} When Tampering with Several Tags

Contrary to MW where the adversary can always determine with probability 1 that a given key has been used to generate a tag's answer, HSH does not provide such a deterministic verification procedure. In other words, the adversary can be unlucky, meaning that she checks the right key but concludes that the key is wrong due to the noise; but she can also be lucky, meaning that the noise makes her observe something wrong but, nevertheless, she provides the correct result.

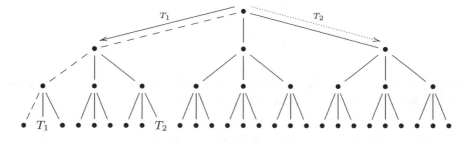

Fig. 3. An example of the event B

P_{luck} reflects the fact that an adversary $\mathcal{A}$ is lucky and finds the right answer even if she makes a mistake. It is divided in two events during the tree traversal:

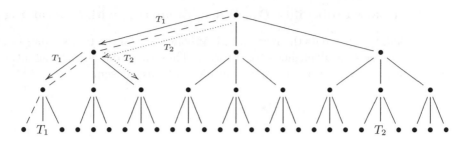

Fig. 4. An example of the event L

- B = {$\mathcal{A}$ separates too soon T_1 and T_2, while this can be done later},
- L = {$\mathcal{A}$ separates too late T_1 and T_2},

which define the adversary probability of luck as:

$$P_{\text{luck}} = \Pr(B) + \Pr(L) \qquad \text{where } B \wedge L = \emptyset \qquad (2)$$

Figures 3 and 4 are illustrations of the events B and L. As legend, the branches $-\ -\ -$ represent the paths compromised; $\xleftarrow{\ T_1\ }$ and $\xleftarrow{\ T_2\ }$ represent the paths supposed by $\mathcal{A}$ for T_1 and T_2, respectively.

Below are the formulas for $\Pr(B)$ and $\Pr(L)$. Notice that $\Pr(E_0^5) = 1$.

$$\Pr(B) = \sum_{i=1}^{d-2} \left(\Pr(\text{B-Separation}_i) \times \prod_{j=0}^{i-1} \Pr(E_j^5) \right)$$

$$\Pr(L) = \sum_{i=2}^{d} \left(\Pr(\text{L-Separation}_i) \times \sum_{k=1}^{i-1} \left(\prod_{j=0}^{k-1} \Pr(E_j^5) \times \prod_{\substack{\ell=i-1 \\ \ell=\ell-1}}^{k} \Pr(\text{L-Follow}_\ell) \right) \right)$$

Table 2 gives numerical values of Eq. 2 when the parameters s and ϵ are fixed ($s = 86$ and $\epsilon = 0.125$). We decide to only give values for $\beta = 2, 20$ and 100, because they are not significant for a larger β.

Table 2. Numerical values of the probability P_{luck} of tracing tag T according to branching factor β when the adversary tampers with c_0 tags. The system contains 2^{20} tags, $s = 86$ and $\epsilon = 0.125$.

c_0 \ β	2	20	100
1	13.10%	1.189%	0.238%
20	7.33%	0.023%	$1.2 * 10^{-10}\%$
50	7.25%	0.012%	$5.9 * 10^{-11}\%$
100	7.23%	$2.7 * 10^{-7}\%$	$3.9 * 10^{-11}\%$
200	7.22%	$1.0 * 10^{-7}\%$	$2.9 * 10^{-11}\%$

4.5   Adversary Probability P_{fail} When Tampering with Several Tags

This probability represents the fact that $\mathcal{A}$, at some level in the tree, cannot take any rational decision given her observations. Thus since our attack definition forces $\mathcal{A}$ to give an answer, the latter will be randomly chosen.

$$P_{\text{fail}} = \Pr(E_1^4) + \sum_{i=2}^{d-1}\left(\Pr(E_i^4) \times \Pr(\text{Continue}_{i-1})\right) \tag{3}$$

where Continue_i is the event that $\mathcal{A}$ continues the attack until level i.

Table 3 gives numerical values of Eq. 3 when the parameters s and ϵ are fixed ($s = 86$ and $\epsilon = 0.125$). Like with the table of P_{luck}, we decide to only give values for $\beta = 2, 20$ and 100, because they are not significant for a larger β.

Table 3. Numerical values of the probability P_{fail} of tracing tag T according to branching factor β when the adversary tampers with c_0 tags. The system contains 2^{20} tags, $s = 86$ and $\epsilon = 0.125$.

β / c_0	2	20	100
1	27.57%	90.33%	98.00%
20	0.31%	15.59%	66.89%
50	0.08%	4.11%	36.60%
100	0.02%	3.02%	13.39%
200	0.01%	1.88%	2.56%

4.6   The Adversary Advantage When Tampering with Several Tags

The advantage is defined as:

$$Adv_{\mathcal{A}} = 2\left(P_{\text{succ}} + P_{\text{luck}} + P_{\text{fail}} \cdot \frac{1}{2}\right) - 1 \tag{4}$$

Table 4 gives numerical values of Eq. 4 when the parameters s and ϵ are fixed ($s = 86$ and $\epsilon = 0.125$). The advantage $Adv_{\mathcal{A}}$ is plotted in Figure 5.

Table 4. Numerical values of the adversary advantage of tracing tag T according to branching factor β when the adversary tampers with c_0 tags. The system contains 2^{20} tags, $s = 86$ and $\epsilon = 0.125$.

β / c_0	2	20	100	500	1000
1	0.2122	0.0434	0.0091	0.0018	0.0004
20	0.2716	0.8422	0.3274	0.0768	0.0392
50	0.2712	0.9571	0.6262	0.1810	0.0951
100	0.2711	0.9692	0.8536	0.3292	0.1811
200	0.2711	0.9811	0.9654	0.5497	0.3294

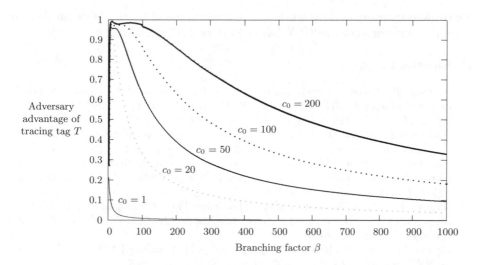

Fig. 5. Adversary advantage of tracing a tag T when she tampers with c_0 tags, $s = 86$, and $\epsilon = 0.125$

When c_0 is different from 1 and the branching factor β is less than 100, this advantage grows up to reach its maximum which is greater than 0.9. Then $Adv_{\mathcal{A}}$ reduces increasingly slower when c_0 augments. This outcome seams reasonable: clearly, the more tags an adversary $\mathcal{A}$ opens, the more secret keys she knows, which implies that the higher probability the attack success will be.

5   Conclusion

In this paper, we analyzed HSH which is an HB-like protocol using the MW tree-based key infrastructure.

First, we presented a new authentication protocol based on HB+ and on the LPN problem. We demonstrated that our proposal is as secure as HSH, in the same privacy threat model (i.e. the tags are considered tamper-resistant, and the adversaries are supposed active, but man-in-the-middle attacks are not allowed). We showed that it is possible to build an authentication protocol with better properties than HSH: tag memory, and reader computational complexity are reduced.

Second we proved that, in a more realistic threat model where the tags are not tamper-resistant, the HSH protocol is defeated by an attack based on the weaknesses of the tree-based key infrastructure. We redesigned the original attack given by Avoine, Dysli and Oechslin to strike the Molnar and Wagner protocol: the main difficulty of this adaptation was to take into account the LPN problem present in HSH, since it relies on the HB-family protocols. In this real-life privacy threat model, our results showed that the adversary has a significant advantage to trace a tag.

Acknowledgements. This work was partially funded by the Walloon Region Marshall plan through the SPW DG06 Project TRASILUX.

References

1. Alomair, B., Lazos, L., Poovendran, R.: Passive Attacks on a Class of Authentication Protocols for RFID. In: Nam, K.-H., Rhee, G. (eds.) ICISC 2007. LNCS, vol. 4817, pp. 102–115. Springer, Heidelberg (2007)
2. Anderson, R., Kuhn, M.: Tamper Resistance - a Cautionary Note. In: 2nd USENIX Workshop on Electronic Commerce, Oakland, CA, USA, pp. 1–11 (November 1996)
3. Anderson, R., Kuhn, M.: Low Cost Attacks on Tamper Resistant Devices. In: Christianson, B., Lomas, M. (eds.) Security Protocols 1997. LNCS, vol. 1361, pp. 125–136. Springer, Heidelberg (1998)
4. Avoine, G., Dysli, E., Oechslin, P.: Reducing Time Complexity in RFID Systems. In: Preneel, B., Tavares, S. (eds.) SAC 2005. LNCS, vol. 3897, pp. 291–306. Springer, Heidelberg (2006)
5. Barasz, M., Boros, B., Ligeti, P., Loja, K., Nagy, D.: Breaking LMAP. In: Workshop on RFID Security, RFIDSec 2007, Malaga, Spain (July 2007)
6. Bárász, M., Boros, B., Ligeti, P., Lója, K., Nagy, D.: Passive Attack Against the M2AP Mutual Authentication Protocol for RFID Tags. In : First International EURASIP Workshop on RFID Technology, Vienna, Austria (September 2007)
7. Bringer, J., Chabanne, H.: Trusted-HB: A Low-Cost Version of HB+ Secure Against Man-in-the-Middle Attacks. IEEE Transactions on Information Theory 54(9), 4339–4342 (2008)
8. Bringer, J., Chabanne, H., Emmanuelle, D.: HB++: a Lightweight Authentication Protocol Secure against Some Attacks. In: IEEE International Conference on Pervasive Services, Workshop on Security, Privacy and Trust in Pervasive and Ubiquitous Computing, SecPerU 2006, Lyon, France. IEEE, Los Alamitos (2006)
9. Buttyán, L., Holczer, T., Vajda, I.: Optimal Key-Trees for Tree-Based Private Authentication. In: Workshop on Privacy Enhancing Technologies, PET 2006, Cambridge, UK (June 2006)
10. Cao, T., Bertino, E., Lei, H.: Security analysis of the SASI protocol. IEEE Transactions on Dependable and Secure Computing 6, 73–77 (2008)
11. Chien, H.-Y.: SASI: A New Ultralightweight RFID Authentication Protocol Providing Strong Authentication and Strong Integrity. IEEE Transactions on Dependable and Secure Computing 4(4), 337–340 (2007)
12. Gilbert, H., Robshaw, M., Sibert, H.: An Active Attack Against HB+ - A provably Secure Lightweight Authentication Protocol (July 2005) (manuscript)
13. Gilbert, H., Robshaw, M.J., Seurin, Y.: HB#: Increasing the Security and Efficiency of HB+. In: Smart, N.P. (ed.) EUROCRYPT 2008. LNCS, vol. 4965, pp. 361–378. Springer, Heidelberg (2008)
14. Gilbert, H., Robshaw, M.J., Seurin, Y.: How to Encrypt with the LPN Problem. In: Aceto, L., Damgård, I., Goldberg, L.A., Halldórsson, M.M., Ingólfsdóttir, A., Walukiewicz, I. (eds.) ICALP 2008, Part II. LNCS, vol. 5126, pp. 679–690. Springer, Heidelberg (2008)
15. Halevi, T., Saxena, N., Halevi, S.: Using HB Family of Protocols for Privacy-Preserving Authentication of RFID Tags in a Population. In: Workshop on RFID Security, RFIDSec 2009, Leuven, Belgium (July 2009)
16. Hammouri, G., Sunar, B.: PUF-HB: A Tamper-Resilient HB Based Authentication Protocol. In: Bellovin, S.M., Gennaro, R., Keromytis, A.D., Yung, M. (eds.) ACNS 2008. LNCS, vol. 5037, pp. 346–365. Springer, Heidelberg (2008)

17. Hopper, N.J., Blum, M.: A Secure Human-Computer Authentication Scheme. Technical report, Computer Science Department, School of Computer Science, Carnegie Mellon University (May 2000)
18. Hopper, N.J., Blum, M.: Secure Human Identification Protocols. In: Boyd, C. (ed.) ASIACRYPT 2001. LNCS, vol. 2248, pp. 52–66. Springer, Heidelberg (2001)
19. Juels, A., Weis, S.A.: Authenticating Pervasive Devices with Human Protocols. In: Shoup, V. (ed.) CRYPTO 2005. LNCS, vol. 3621, pp. 293–308. Springer, Heidelberg (2005)
20. Leng, X., Mayes, K., Markantonakis, K.: HB-MP+ Protocol: An Improvement on the HB-MP Protocol. In: IEEE International Conference on RFID, pp. 118–124 (April 2008)
21. Li, T., Deng, R.H.: Vulnerability Analysis of EMAP - An Efficient RFID Mutual Authentication Protocol. In: Second International Conference on Availability, Reliability and Security, AReS 2007, Vienna, Austria (April 2007)
22. Li, T., Wang, G.: Security Analysis of Two Ultra-Lightweight RFID Authentication Protocols. In: IFIP SEC 2007, Sandton, Gauteng, South Africa (May 2007)
23. Madhavan, M., Thangaraj, A., Sankarasubramaniam, Y., Viswanathan, K.: NLHB: A Non-Linear Hopper Blum Protocol. arXiv.org (February 2010)
24. Molnar, D., Wagner, D.: Privacy and Security in Library RFID: Issues, Practices, and Architectures. In: ACM Conference on Computer and Communications Security, ACM CCS 2004, Washington, DC, USA, pp. 210–219. ACM, New York (October 2004)
25. Munilla, J., Peinado, A.: HB-MP: A Further Step in the HB-Family of Lightweight Authentication Protocols. Computer Networks 51(9), 2262–2267 (2007)
26. Nohl, K., Evans, D.: Quantifying Information Leakage in Tree-Based Hash Protocols. In: Ning, P., Qing, S., Li, N. (eds.) ICICS 2006. LNCS, vol. 4307, pp. 228–237. Springer, Heidelberg (2006)
27. Organization, I.C.A.: Machine Readable Travel Documents, Doc 9303, Part 1, Machine Readable Passports, 5 (edn.) (2003)
28. Peris-Lopez, P., Hernandez-Castro, J.C., Estevez-Tapiador, J., Ribagorda, A.: LMAP: A Real Lightweight Mutual Authentication Protocol for Low-cost RFID tags. In: Workshop on RFID Security, RFIDSec 2006, Graz, Austria (July 2006)
29. Peris-Lopez, P., Hernandez-Castro, J.C., Estevez-Tapiador, J., Ribagorda, A.: M2AP: A Minimalist Mutual-Authentication Protocol for Low-cost RFID Tags. In: Ma, J., Jin, H., Yang, L.T., Tsai, J.J.-P. (eds.) UIC 2006. LNCS, vol. 4159, pp. 912–923. Springer, Heidelberg (2006)
30. Peris-Lopez, P., Hernandez-Castro, J.C., Estevez-Tapiador, J.M., Ribagorda, A.: EMAP: An Efficient Mutual Authentication Protocol for Low-Cost RFID Tags. In: Meersman, R., Tari, Z., Herrero, P. (eds.) OTM 2006 Workshops. LNCS, vol. 4277, pp. 352–361. Springer, Heidelberg (2006)
31. Peris-Lopez, P., Hernandez-Castro, J.C., Estevez-Tapiador, J.M., Ribagorda, A.: Advances in Ultralightweight Cryptography for Low-cost RFID Tags: Gossamer Protocol. In: Chung, K.-I., Sohn, K., Yung, M. (eds.) WISA 2008. LNCS, vol. 5379, pp. 56–68. Springer, Heidelberg (2009)
32. Phan, R.C.-W.: Cryptanalysis of a New Ultralightweight RFID Authentication Protocol - SASI. IEEE Transactions on Dependable and Secure Computing 6, 316–320 (2008)

33. Semiconductors, N.: MIFARE Smartcards ICs,
    http://www.nxp.com/products/identification/card_ics/mifare
34. Sun, H.-M., Ting, W.-C., Wang, K.-H.: On the Security of Chien's Ultra-Lightweight RFID Authentication Protocol. IEEE Transactions on Dependable and Secure Computing 99 (2009)
35. Yoon, B.: HB-MP++ Protocol: An Ultra Light-weight Authentication Protocol for RFID System. In: IEEE International Conference on RFID, Orlando, FL, USA (April 2009)

A   The Details of Our Probabilities Computations

During the sequel, we compute the probability of $\Pr(E_i^1)$. Then $\Pr(E_i^2)$, $\Pr(E_i^3)$, $\Pr(E_i^4)$, $\Pr(E_i^5)$ are computed in the same way. We will also denote "$\exists!x$" as "there exists an *unique* x".

A.1   When the Adversary $\mathcal{A}$ Tampers with One Tag

The probability $\Pr(E_i^1)$ is computed as follows:

$$\begin{aligned}
\Pr(E_i^1) &= \Pr(C_i^1 \wedge A_i^1) \\
&= \Pr(\{y_i^0 = y_i^1\} \wedge \{B^1 y_i^0 \in \mathcal{B}_i^1\}) \times \Pr(\{y_i^0 \neq y_i^2\} \wedge \{B^2 y_i^0 \notin \mathcal{B}_i^2\}) \\
&= \frac{1}{\beta} \times S_t \times \frac{\beta-1}{\beta} \times (1 - V_t) \quad \text{(Bayes' law)}
\end{aligned}$$

The overall probability P_{succ} is:

$$\begin{aligned}
P_{\text{succ}} &= 2\Pr(E_1^1) + \sum_{i=2}^{d} \Big(2\Pr(E_i^1) \times \prod_{j=1}^{i-1} \Pr(E_j^4) \Big) \\
&= 2S_t(1 - V_t)\Big(\frac{\beta-1}{\beta^2} \Big)\left(\frac{1 - (\frac{S_t}{\beta})^{2d}}{1 - (\frac{S_t}{\beta})^2} \right)
\end{aligned}$$

A.2   When the Adversary $\mathcal{A}$ Tampers with c_0 Tags

P_{succ} computation. The probability $\Pr(E_i^1)$ is computed as follows:

$$\begin{aligned}
\Pr(E_i^1) &= \Pr(C_i^1 \wedge A_i^1) \\
&= \Pr(\{y_i^1 \in \mathcal{K}_i\} \wedge \{\exists k_{i,m} \in \mathcal{K}_i : B^1 k_{i,m} \in \mathcal{B}_i^1\}) \\
&\quad \times \Pr(\{y_i^2 \notin \mathcal{K}_i\} \wedge \{\forall k_{i,m} \in \mathcal{K}_i : B^2 k_{i,m} \notin \mathcal{B}_i^2\}) \\
&= \frac{c_i}{\beta} \times (1 - (1 - S_t)^{c_i}) \times \frac{\beta - c_i}{\beta} \\
&\quad \times (1 - \Pr(\{\exists! k_{i,m} \in \mathcal{K}_i : B^2 k_{i,m} \in \mathcal{B}_i^2\} | \{y_i^2 \notin \mathcal{K}_i\}))^{c_i} \\
&= \frac{c_i}{\beta} \times (1 - (1 - S_t)^{c_i}) \times \frac{\beta - c_i}{\beta} \times (1 - V_t)^{c_i}
\end{aligned}$$

P_{luck} **computation.** The event B-Separation$_i$ divided in four cases:

- $M_i^1 = \{T_1$ is identified by its real key $y_i^1 \in \mathcal{K}_i\} \wedge \{T_2$ is not identified at all (even if it should)$\} = \text{Normal}_{M_i}^{\oplus}(T_1) \wedge \text{False}_{M_i}(T_2)$,
- $M_i^2 = \{T_1$ is identified by its real key $y_i^1 \in \mathcal{K}_i\} \wedge \{T_2$ is identified by a wrong known key$\} = \text{Normal}_{M_i}^{\oplus}(T_1) \wedge \text{Normal}_{M_i^2}^{\ominus}(T_2)$,
- $M_i^3 = \{T_1$ is identified by a wrong known key$\} \wedge \{T_2$ is not identified at all (even if it should)$\} = \text{Normal}_{M_i}^{\ominus}(T_1) \wedge \text{False}_{M_i}(T_2)$,
- $M_i^4 = \{T_1$ is identified by a wrong known key$\} \wedge \{T_2$ is identified by a wrong known key$\} = \text{Normal}_{M_i}^{\ominus}(T_1) \wedge \text{Normal}_{M_i^4}^{\ominus}(T_2)$.

$$\Pr(\text{Normal}_{M_i}^{\oplus}(T_1)) = \Pr(\{\exists! k_{i,m} \in \mathcal{K}_i : B^1 k_{i,m} \in \mathcal{B}_i^1\} \wedge \{y_i^1 = k_{i,m} \in \mathcal{K}_i\}) = \frac{S_t}{c_i}$$

$$\Pr(\text{False}_{M_i}(T_2)) = \Pr(\{\nexists k_{i,m} \in \mathcal{K}_i : B^2 k_{i,m} \in \mathcal{B}_i^2\} \wedge \{y_i^2 \in \mathcal{K}_i\}) = \frac{c_i(1 - S_t)^{c_i}}{\beta}$$

$$\Pr(\text{Normal}_{M_i^2}^{\ominus}(T_2)) = \Pr(\{\exists! k_{i,m}' \in \mathcal{K}_i : B^2 k_{i,m} \in \mathcal{B}_i^2\} \wedge \{y_i^2 \in \mathcal{K}_i \setminus \{k_{i,m}', y_i^1\}\})$$
$$= \frac{(c_i - 2)V_t}{c_i}$$

$$\Pr(\text{Normal}_{M_i}^{\ominus}(T_1)) = \Pr(\{\exists! k_{i,m} \in \mathcal{K}_i : B^1 k_{i,m} \in \mathcal{B}_i^1\} \wedge \{y_i^1 \in \mathcal{K}_i \setminus \{k_{i,m}\}\})$$
$$= \frac{(c_i - 1)V_t}{c_i}$$

$$\Pr(\text{Normal}_{M_i^4}^{\ominus}(T_2)) = \Pr(\text{Normal}_{M_i}^{\ominus}(T_1)) + \Pr(\text{Normal}_{M_i^2}^{\ominus}(T_2)) = \frac{(2c_i - 3)V_t}{c_i}$$

$$\Pr(\text{B-Separation}_i) = \Pr(M_i^1) + \Pr(M_i^2) + \Pr(M_i^3) + \Pr(M_i^4)$$

The event L-Separation$_i$ is divided in four cases where T_2 is no longer part of the current sub-tree:

- $N_i^1 = \{T_1$ is identified by its real key $y_i^1 \in \mathcal{K}_i\} \wedge \{T_2$ is not identified at all$\} = \text{Normal}_{N_i}^{\oplus}(T_1) \wedge \text{False}_{N_i}(T_2)$,
- $N_i^2 = \{T_1$ is identified by its real key $y_i^1 \in \mathcal{K}_i\} \wedge \{T_2$ is identified by a wrong known key $k_{i,m}'\} = \text{Normal}_{N_i}^{\oplus}(T_1) \wedge \text{Normal}_{N_i}^{\ominus}(T_2) \wedge \{y_i^1 \neq k_{i,m}'\}$,
- $N_i^3 = \{T_1$ is identified by a wrong known key$\} \wedge \{T_2$ is not identified at all$\} = \text{Normal}_{N_i}^{\ominus}(T_1) \wedge \text{False}_{N_i}(T_2)$,
- $N_i^4 = \{T_1$ is identified by a wrong known key $k_{i,m}\} \wedge \{T_2$ is identified by a wrong known key $k_{i,m}'\} = \text{Normal}_{N_i}^{\ominus}(T_1) \wedge \text{Normal}_{N_i}^{\ominus}(T_2) \wedge \{k_{i,m} \neq k_{i,m}'\}$.

The event L-Follow$_\ell$ is defined as $\{T_1$ is identified by its real key $y_\ell^1 \in \mathcal{K}_\ell\} \wedge \{T_2$ follows the same branch as T_1 at level ℓ (which is a false branch for T_2)$\} = \text{Normal}_{N_\ell}^{\oplus}(T_1) \wedge \text{Fol}_\ell(T_2) \wedge \{y_i^1 - k_{\ell,m}'\}$. Thus we have:

$$\Pr(\text{L-Separation}_i) = \Pr(N_i^1) + \Pr(N_i^2) + \Pr(N_i^3) + \Pr(N_i^4)$$

$$\Pr(\text{Normal}_{N_i}^{\oplus}(T_1)) = \Pr(\text{Normal}_{M_i}^{\oplus}(T_1)) = \frac{S_t}{c_i}$$

$$\Pr(\text{Normal}_{N_i}^{\ominus}(T_2)) = \Pr(\{\exists! k'_{i,m} \in \mathcal{K}_i : B^2 k'_{i,m} \in \mathcal{B}_i^2\} \wedge \{y_i^2 \notin \mathcal{K}_i\}) = \frac{(\beta - c_i)V_t}{\beta}$$

$$\Pr(\text{Normal}_{N_i}^{\ominus}(T_1)) = \Pr(\text{Normal}_{M_i}^{\ominus}(T_1)) = \frac{(c_i - 1)V_t}{c_i}$$

$$\Pr(\text{False}_{N_i}(T_2)) = \Pr(\{\nexists k_{i,m} \in \mathcal{K}_i : B^2 k_{i,m} \in \mathcal{B}_i^2\} \wedge \{y_i^2 \notin \mathcal{K}_i\}) = \frac{(\beta - c_i)(1 - V_t)^{c_i}}{\beta}$$

$$\Pr(\text{Fol}_\ell(T_2)) = \Pr(\text{Normal}_{N_\ell}^{\ominus}(T_1)) + \Pr(\text{Normal}_{N_\ell}^{\ominus}(T_2)) = V_t\left(\frac{c_\ell - 1}{c_\ell} + \frac{\beta - c_\ell}{\beta}\right)$$

$$\Pr(\text{L-Follow}_\ell) = \frac{S_t V_t}{c_\ell^2}\left(\frac{c_\ell - 1}{c_\ell} + \frac{\beta - c_\ell}{\beta}\right)$$

P_{fail} **computation.** Continue$_i$ is composed of the following three main cases:

- for the i-th levels, T_1 and T_2 are identified by their real key: $\{y_i^1 \in \mathcal{K}_i\} \wedge \{y_i^2 \in \mathcal{K}_i\} \wedge \{y_i^1 = y_i^2\} = E_i^5$,
- for the i-th levels, T_1 and T_2 are identified by the same key, which is the real one only for T_1 = L-Follow$_i$,
- for the i-th levels, T_1 and T_2 are identified by the same wrong key = Q_i, $Q_i = \text{Fol}_i(T_1) \wedge \text{Fol}_i(T_2) \wedge \{k_{i,m} = k'_{i,m}\}$,

and of the ordered combinations of theses cases: for $1 \leq \ell < k < j \leq i$, $\{\text{L-Follow}_k\}$ can be only preceded by $\{E_\ell^5\}$, and $\{Q_j\}$ can be preceded by $\{\text{L-Follow}_k\}$ or $\{E_\ell^5\}$ or $\{\text{L-Follow}_k \text{ and } E_\ell^5\}$. Thus, we have:

$$\Pr(\text{Continue}_i) = \prod_{j=1}^{i}\left(\Pr(E_j^5) + \Pr(\text{L-Follow}_j) + \Pr(Q_j)\right)$$

$$+ \sum_{j=1}^{i-1}\left(\prod_{k=1}^{j}\Pr(\text{L-Follow}_k) \times \prod_{\ell=j+1}^{i}\Pr(Q_\ell)\right)$$

$$+ \sum_{j=1}^{i-1}\left(\prod_{k=1}^{j}\Pr(E_k^5) \times \prod_{\ell=j+1}^{i}\left(\Pr(\text{L-Follow}_\ell) + \Pr(Q_\ell)\right)\right)$$

$$+ \sum_{j=1}^{i-2}\left(\prod_{k=1}^{j}\Pr(E_k^5) \times \sum_{\ell=j+1}^{i-1}\left(\prod_{m=j+1}^{\ell}\Pr(\text{L-Follow}_m) \times \prod_{p=\ell+1}^{i}\Pr(Q_p)\right)\right)$$

Hardware Intrinsic Security

Pim Tuyls

Intrinsic-ID B.V., The Nederlands

Abstract. Counterfeiting of electronic goods and stealing of valuable and sensitive data has become a massive problem for companies, the economy and even the security of modern societies. In order to deal with these issues more and more security measures have to be put in place both at the system level as well as the device level. Since security solutions are only as strong as their weakest link, strong solutions can only build on strong foundations. It is widely accepted that secure hardware is a fundamental building block of a strong solution. In this talk we will introduce secure hardware technologies built on the intrinsic physical properties of the underlying device: Hardware Intrinsic Security. We will start by introducing the physical principles behind this concept. Next, we continue with the cryptographic primitives and the applications which can build upon these intrinsic hardware security foundations. These will be illustrated with some practical examples. Finally, we discuss existing challenges and new directions.

S.B. Ors Yalcin (Ed.): RFIDSec 2010, LNCS 6370, p. 123, 2010.
© Springer-Verlag Berlin Heidelberg 2010

Privacy-Preserving Pattern Matching for Anomaly Detection in RFID Anti-Counterfeiting

Florian Kerschbaum[1] and Nina Oertel[1,2]

[1] SAP Research, Karlsruhe, Germany
florian.kerschbaum@sap.com
nina.oertel@sap.com
[2] Chair of Business Administration and Information Systems,
University of Mannheim, Germany

Abstract. Traces of RFID-equipped item can be used to detect counterfeits. Nevertheless companies are reluctant to share the necessary traces, since it is unclear what can be inferred from them. In this paper we present a provably secure pattern matching algorithm that can be used for distributed anomaly detection. We improve performance and detection capabilities compared to competing approaches by storing partial, malleable information on the RFID tag.

1 Introduction

Counterfeit products lead to huge financial losses for legally run business. For example, European Customs seize up to one hundred million counterfeit articles per year [6]. It is well-known that RFID event traces can be used for anti-counterfeiting [15,24,19,26]. Yet companies are still reluctant to share the necessary data, since it is unclear what other information can be inferred from it [13,22].

Cryptography offers the ultimate solution: Secure Multi-Party Computation (SMC) [3,9,25]. In SMC a number of parties compute a joint function on their combined inputs without revealing any additional information except the result. Since general SMC allows the computation of any function, this function could be the correlation algorithm. Du and Atallah [5] have first proposed this setup.

SMC can be used for rather simple, infrequently used correlations [26], but it is still prohibitively slow for large-scale problems. The first measurements show a performance penalty compared to non-private computation on the order of tens of thousands [11,12] and even specialized protocols such as [26] only scale to a few clients. Implementations of privacy-preserving event correlation [14,16,17,20] therefore suggest alternative techniques. These techniques commonly rely on revealing the information necessary for the detection algorithm while revealing as little as possible additional information.

In this paper we use a different approach. We present a provably secure algorithm for a function with limited privacy. Our algorithm implements pattern matching which can be used as the building block for anomaly detection. We

S.B. Ors Yalcin (Ed.): RFIDSec 2010, LNCS 6370, pp. 124–137, 2010.
© Springer-Verlag Berlin Heidelberg 2010

complement the secure protocol by storing partial, malleable (by the attacker) information on the RFID tag. We experimentally evaluate the performance of our algorithm and it is acceptable for the intended use case.

In summary this paper contributes a privacy-preserving pattern matching algorithm that

- is *provably secure* and reveals no information if the pattern does not match.
- can be used to *implement anomaly detection*, e.g. for anti-counterfeiting.
- is *efficient* and can detect a counterfeit in less than 1 second using 20 KBytes of network communication in our use case example.

The remainder of the paper is structured as follows. Related work is reviewed in Section 2. The explanation of our anomaly detection algorithm for anti-counterfeiting follows in Section 3. We then continue by describing the privacy-preserving pattern matching algorithm in Section 4. We evaluate the computation and communication performance of this system in Section 5. Our conclusions are presented in Section 6.

2 Related Work

2.1 RFID for Anti-counterfeiting

The idea of our use case that RFID event data can be used for anti-counterfeiting has been first suggested in [24]. The first algorithm to detect changes in the owner (attached item in our case) has been presented in [18]. It is purely an anomaly-based detection approach and assumes a central repository of events. A refinement to deal with incomplete traces based on a stochastic detection approach is presented in [15]. The algorithm learns the transition probability from one event to another and identifies low probability transitions. The approach used in this paper based on an evaluation of complete traces was first presented in [19].

The first privacy-preserving RFID counterfeit detection algorithm is presented almost concurrently with this paper in [26]. We improve over this approach in two aspects: First, we enhance detection capabilities by the ability to detect more patterns. Instead of only two types of events – send and receive – we support an arbitrary number of events. Our detection algorithm has been independently evaluated in [19]. This enhanced capabilities make our algorithm also more general and applicable to related problems in distributed anomaly detection.

Second, we significantly improve performance. In particular, we do not use heavy weight secure computations in order to compute the ordering of events. Instead we store this information on the RFID tag, but ensure that in case the attacker maliciously modifies this information we are still able to detect the pattern (w.h.p.). Our numbers show better performance for a significantly increased case study.

2.2   Privacy in Distributed Intrusion Detection

This paragraph provides an overview on protecting privacy in distributed intrusion detection. The first proposal for a practical system was made in [16]. Its introduces the model with a central correlation agent also used in this paper. Privacy is achieved by cleverly pseudonymizing sensitive fields. Further pseudonymizing techniques are given in [14]. An implementation based on Bloom filters as pseudonymizing technique is described in [17,20].

In [1] key-word based aggregation using encryption and SMC has been implemented. They split the central correlation agent into two mutually distrustful ones. The first called proxy anonymizes the data and the second called database computes the correlation on the anonymized plaintext. This can only be done if the plaintext does not reveal sensitive information. We emphasize that their algorithms are not meant to be run on-line for each event.

In [4] SMC has been implemented for detecting frequent events using entropy and counters. They report running times on the order of minutes and communication on the order of several MBytes and claim an improvement of a factor of roughly 1000 over general frameworks, such as FairPlayMP [2]. No figures are given with respect to non-private computation, but we see a similarity in functionality and reported performance to [11,12]. Their algorithms use locally pre-aggregated events as input and are therefore also not run on-line for each event.

Efficient protocols for the two-party case of our pattern matching algorithm are given in [10]. The two-party case is significantly simpler, not only because of the limited number of participants, but also, since the pattern is not distributed, it does not need to be sorted. We extend that to the multi-party case and are significantly more efficient.

The advantages an attacker might have from a centralized detection system despite privacy protection are described in [21]. This corresponds to the common problem of privacy-preserving computation that the result may still reveal sensitive information. We recommend to treat detected events – counterfeits – with the necessary care and confidentiality.

3   Anomaly Detection for Anti-counterfeiting

Radio Frequency Identification (RFID) enables tracking individual products through the supply chain [23]. An RFID tag with an unique identifier (UID) is attached to each item and captured at distinct read points within companies handling the item. A suitable reading device is used to read the UID and a corresponding event is stored in a local database of the company. By default, each company has only access to RFID event data that was captured by readers belonging to the organization.

An event in our algorithm corresponds to reading an RFID tag. When a company X_k processes an item with attached tag with UID id it creates an event with $e.y_j = k$ (i.e. the event type is the organization's identity). Recall that X_k reads the event number j from the tag. As the item is forwarded along the supply chain, different companies create events for the same tag. Our pattern matching algorithm is applied to an event trace t for a specific tag with UID id. The correlation agent therefore initially sends id to the event sources.

We will now describe the different possibilities of counterfeiters to distribute fakes and the consequences of these actions on the event traces. Suppose all items of a certain type are equipped with UIDs. The first challenge for the counterfeiter is thus to obtain UIDs for the counterfeited goods. One option is to put no identifier at all on the item, but this strategy is easily detectable during authentication. For actually obtaining a UID, the options include guessing random numbers, transferring the UIDs of genuine products to counterfeits or copying the UIDs found on genuine products. For transferring UIDs, counterfeiters may remove (steal) RFID tags from genuine items and reapply them to counterfeits, or they may seek access to UIDs of disposed products and reuse the tags. As a consequence, the UID on a counterfeit product will be either duplicated (in case of copying) or truly unique (for transfer and most probably guessing). Furthermore, the UID will either be valid (for copying and transferring), meaning that a genuine item carrying the same UID exists, or invalid (for guessing). Any UID found on a counterfeit thus has at least one of these properties: it is invalid, has been transferred or is duplicated.

Besides obtaining UIDs, a counterfeiter must distribute the counterfeits and put them on the market, choosing a suitable location and time. Counterfeits can be distributed through illicit supply chains or injected in licit supply chains. Examples of illicit distribution are the smuggling of goods through customs and the sale on flea markets. Selling counterfeits in online shops is another increasingly popular distribution strategy. Counterfeiters also misuse the licit supply chain, sometimes mixing counterfeits with genuine products to better disguise them. For the resulting trace of items it is most relevant whether the chosen channels are visible, i.e. readers are deployed and item movements are captured, or invisible. Illicit distribution channels are likely to contain no read points and thus be invisible, while licit channels can be assumed to be visible.

In case a counterfeit carries a transferred UID (valid and unique), the events in the trace were triggered by the movements of two items: First by the genuine item until its UID was removed, then by the counterfeit carrying the stolen UID. Up to the transfer point, the trace will be that of a genuine item. When the counterfeit is re-injected in the licit supply chain, the sequence of events will only be valid if the counterfeit directly replaces a genuine item. If the injection takes place further upstream (Figure 1 part (a)), downstream (Figure 1 part (b)) or in another branch of the supply chain (Figure 1 part (c)), the trace will not conform to the traces of genuine items. The resulting traces contain transitions that are forbidden for genuine items, e.g., the transition $B \rightarrow B$ in Figure 1 part (a).

If counterfeits with duplicate UIDs are injected in the supply chain, the trace that is retrieved for the UID is a mix of all sub-traces created by the multiple items carrying the same UID (Figure 1 part (d)). If items with copied UIDs are injected in the supply chain, this will result in an invalid global trace that contains transitions between events created for different items, albeit they carry

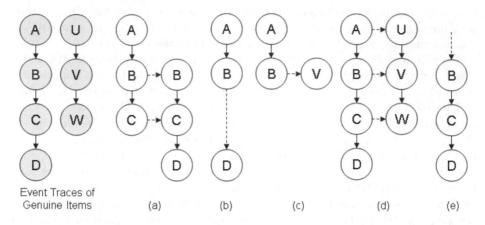

Fig. 1. Consequences of counterfeiter strategies on trace data

the same UID. For example, let event A be triggered by a genuine item, and let it be followed by event U, triggered by a counterfeit with a copied UID. The resulting transition from $A \rightarrow U$ is not allowed for genuine items as they would never travel on that path.

If counterfeits with guessed, i.e. invalid, but unique, UIDs are injected in the supply chain, the trace will be incomplete unless the counterfeiter manages to inject it at a licit producer. In all other cases, the trace starts with an invalid first event, e.g., B (Figure 1 part (e)) which is not allowed for genuine items, as they need to originate at an authorized producer.

Exploiting the impact of counterfeits on event traces, we model counterfeits as anomalies. We consider the set of all possible links between companies in the supply chain, i.e. pattern length $n = 2$. We then divide this set into "allowed" and "illegal" links. In order to detect a counterfeit the correlation agent S sends all patterns corresponding to "illegal" links (anomalies) to all event sources. If a match is detected, an investigation for counterfeits starts.

Note that our privacy guarantee only supports anomaly detection, i.e. detection of unwanted events, and not specification-based algorithms, i.e. detection of wanted behavior, since it reveals additional information in case of a match. This leakage is acceptable for anomalies, but in most cases not for compliant actions.

4   Privacy-Preserving Pattern Matching

4.1   Pattern Matching Function

An event trace t consists of a variable number of events e_j $(j = 1, \ldots, m)$. These events may be distributed across up to l parties X_k, i.e. each party X_k has a (usually but not necessarily consecutive) subset of the events e_j.

For now, we assume that each party is aware of the numbering of its events, i.e. each party knows j of its events e_j. We will revisit this assumption in Section 4.5

and show a method how to obtain the numbering without additional privacy-preserving computation.

Each event e_j has an event type $e_j.y$ from a finite set of types. A pattern p is a sequence of n event types $p.y_i$ $(i = 1, \ldots, n)$. It matches an event trace t, if there are n consecutive events e_j, such that $e_j.y = p.y_i$ $(j = \beta, \ldots, \beta + n - 1,$ $i = 1, \ldots, n)$. Loosely speaking, we slide the pattern over the event trace and if there is any position where event trace (completely) matches the pattern, the pattern matches the event trace.

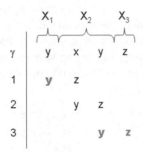

Fig. 2. Example of applying the basic mechanism

Consider the example of Figure 2. There are event types x, y, z and the event trace is y, x, y, z. It is distributed over the parties X_1, X_2, X_3. The pattern p is y, z. The pattern p is slid across the event trace and is depicted for positions $\gamma = 1, 2, 3$. A bold, gray font indicates a match.

4.2 Protocol

We show how to implement this pattern matching algorithm using a distributed privacy-preserving protocol. Our privacy goal is that no information about the events (i.e. their type) is revealed, if the pattern does not match. If the pattern matches, the sources of the events may be revealed. Their type is implicitly revealed by the match. Patterns are public and may be revealed to the data sources.

We use a pseudo-random function $PRF(\cdot, key)$ with a key key as the basis of our scheme. The secret key is known to all event sources X_k, but not the central correlation agent S. We assume that the output of the pseudo-random function cannot be distinguished from truely random numbers, i.e. given pairs $m_i, PRF(m_i, key)$ and a number r it is impossible to determine whether $r = PRF(m, key)$ for any $m \neq m_i$. In practice one uses a message authentication code (MAC) function which is resistant to MAC forgery.

Let n be the length of the pattern. The correlation agent S sends the pattern p to each event source X_k. Each party X_k looks up its events e_j. Let $\mathbb{J}_k$ be the set of numbers of found events at X_k.

X_k now considers each possible combination of positions $\gamma \in \{\min(j|j \in \mathbb{J}_k) - n + 1, \ldots, \max(j|j \in \mathbb{J}_k)\}$ in its events and corresponding positions $\delta \in$

$\{i | 0 \le i < n \wedge \gamma + i \in \mathbb{J}_k\}$ X_k in the pattern. For each pair γ, δ it computes a hashed value $x_{\gamma,\delta}$. The value $x_{\gamma,\delta}$ is the keyed hash of the concatentation of γ and δ, if there is a match of event and pattern at this pair of positions. Since the correlation agent S does not know the PRF key key, this maintains the privacy of the match towards it.

The key insight is that, since the PRF key key is known to all event sources, the hashes of other sources are known in case of a match. We therefore assign a special role to the event source matching the last pattern position ($\delta = n - 1$). It does not compute the keyed hash in case of a match, but computes the hashes of all other pairs (which may be at other sources) and then their negated sum, such that the subset of $x_{\gamma,\delta}$ for this pattern position in the event trace adds up to 0.

In case of mismatch, X_k chooses an uniform random number r from the domain of the pseudo-random function. If any source for a pattern position chooses a random number (i.e. there is a mismatch), the sum will be random as well.

The formula for $x_{\gamma,\delta}$ is

$$x_{\gamma,\delta} = \begin{cases} PRF(\gamma.\delta, key) & \text{if } e_{\gamma+\delta}.y = p.y_{\delta+1} \wedge \delta < n - 1 \\ -\sum_{i=0}^{n-2} PRF(\gamma.i, key) & \text{if } e_{\gamma+\delta}.y = p.y_{\delta+1} \wedge \delta = n - 1 \\ r & \text{if } e_{\gamma+\delta}.y \ne p.y_{\delta+1} \end{cases}$$

In order to not reveal information about the position of a match X_k permutes its set of $x_{\gamma,\delta}$. But, since there are n $x_{\gamma,\delta}$ for each γ with $\delta = 0, \ldots, n-1$, X_k may reveal the δ for each $x_{\gamma,\delta}$. So, X_k sends to S a randomly permuted set of pairs $\langle x_{\gamma,\delta}, \delta \rangle$.

Note that, if events at one party are consecutive, there are $n|\mathbb{J}_k|$ such pairs, i.e. we reveal the number of events an event source has. To conceal that an event source has no events it can send $r' \cdot n$ pairs with a random number for $x_{\gamma,\delta}$. To conceal the number of events all parties must agree on an upper bound u and always send $u \cdot n$ pairs (padded with random numbers).

After receiving the pairs the correlation agent S sorts all of them in ascending order of their second value δ in the pair. S computes the sum for each possible combination $\tau_1, \ldots, \tau_n$ of pairs $\langle x_{\tau_1}, 0 \rangle, \ldots, \langle x_{\tau_n}, n-1 \rangle$ that spans all values of δ. Due to the algorithm for computing $x_{\gamma,\delta}$ this $\sum_{i=1}^{n} x_{\tau_i} = 0$ will be equal to 0, if the pattern p matches the event trace t.

Consider party X_2 in the example from Figure 2: it has events at positions 2 and 3 and needs to compare for pattern positions $\gamma = 1, 2, 3$. It computes the pairs $\langle x_{1,1} = r, 1 \rangle$, $\langle x_{2,0} = r', 0 \rangle$, $\langle x_{2,1} = r'', 1 \rangle$ and $\langle x_{3,0} = PRF(3.0, key), 0 \rangle$. Since the length of the pattern is equal or below the number of its consecutive events and a match at positions inside its events can be determined by itself, but did not occur, X_2 can choose to omit the pairs for $\gamma = 2$. Party X_3 has an event at position 4 and computes $\langle x_{3,1} = -PRF(3.0, key), 1 \rangle$. It holds that $x_{3,0} + x_{3,1} = 0$, such that the correlation agent can detect the match.

4.3   Determining the Bit-Length of the PRF

Let κ be the bit-length of the PRF used above. We need to determine κ, such that false positives are unlikely. The correlation agent S receives nlu pairs using the algorithm above. It can then form $(lu)^n$ possible combinations of pairs, such that the following must hold

$$(lu)^n \ll 2^\kappa$$

for false positives to be negligible.

In our use case example given in Section 5 we have $l = 15$, $u = 1$ and $n = 2$, i.e. $\kappa \gg 7.81$. In this case we can save communication cost and even condense common PRF functions, such as HMAC based on SHA-1, by sending only the first 32 bits.

4.4   Security

As the event sources X_k do not share data with each other, but only with the correlation agent S, there is no risk of revealing information to other sources. We only need to prove privacy towards S. Assume the simplest attack where S tries to infer the event type of some victim $X_\star$. We argue that by using our algorithm it cannot do so and does not obtain any additional knowledge about the events at $X_\star$, i.e. our algorithm preserves the privacy of the events. We play the following game: S sends some pattern p of his choice to all X_k and receives the pairs $\langle x_{\gamma,\delta}, \delta \rangle$ in return including $\langle x_{\gamma^\star,\delta^\star}, \delta^\star \rangle$ from $X_\star$. We assume that the pattern p does not match the event trace beginning at position $\gamma^\star$, since that would reveal $X_\star$'s type from the result of the comparison. S is then asked to tell whether $x_{\gamma^\star,\delta^\star}$ is the PRF or a random number, i.e. whether $X_\star$ has a matching event type at pattern position $\delta^\star$.

Theorem 1. *Let m be the maximum number of events. If any adversary S wins the game above with probability $\frac{1}{2} + \epsilon$, then there is an algorithm $\mathcal{B}$ that successfully distinguishes PRF outputs with probability at least $\frac{\epsilon}{m}$.*

Proof. If S outputs random number, $\mathcal{B}$ outputs a random guess for the PRF pair. If S outputs PRF, $\mathcal{B}$ chooses a random starting position j ($j \in \{0, \dots, m-1\}$) for $\gamma^\star$. S knows $\delta^\star$ of $x_{\gamma^\star,\delta^\star}$ which is presumably $PRF(\gamma^\star.\delta^\star, key)$. So $\mathcal{B}$ outputs $j.\delta^\star$, $x_{\gamma^\star,\delta^\star}$ as its guess for the PRF pair. Its chances of success are $\frac{\epsilon}{m}$ (which is independent of the bit-length κ of the PRF).

Our security model could be translated into the semi-honest model for SMC [8]. Yet the ideal functionality is difficult to specify. Each event source's input are its events and their numbers. The correlation agent has no input, but the pattern is part of the (public) function to be computed. The output is whether there is a match and in case of a match the positions in the pattern of the sources' events comprising the match.

On the one hand, this is limited compared to other possible ideal SMC functionalities. E.g., SMC would allow implementing a function where the event sources input their events and correlation agent the pattern. The output would be a bit whether there is a match or not. This would clearly improve security by privacy for the pattern and privacy in the case of a match, but we remind the reader that we chose the function, such that its implementation can be efficient.

On the other hand, our security definition extends semi-honest security. No matter how the correlation agent behaves it is not able to infer information. This does not yet correspond to malicious or covert adversaries, since we do not protect the integrity of the computation, but confidentiality holds even against active adversaries.

4.5   Detection of Missing Events

So far we made the assumption that each party X_k is aware of the numbering of its events, i.e. each party knows the j of its events e_j. Since we are using RFID tags to generate the events, the simplest method to achieve this is to store j on the RFID tag. After reading the tag and storing the event in its database X_k updates j to $j + 1$ on the tag.

In order to raise the bar for a counterfeiter, the initial number should be randomized. Nevertheless a counterfeiter may interfere with the supply chain and alter the stored number of counterfeit goods. This may create overlapping event numbers which the pattern matching algorithm will still detect or missing event numbers which require additional consideration.

We extend our pattern matching algorithm to be able to detect missing events. The correlation agent sends a pattern p with event type $p.y_i = \star$ which matches an event trace t at position β, if no event source X_k has any event $e_{\beta+i-1}$.

The idea is very similar to the one for pattern matching. If no event source has an event, everyone knows the hashes of the other sources, such that we can control the sum. The difference is that this time the sum is computed for a specific pattern position $\delta = i$, such that this sum must be a summand $x_{\gamma,i} = PRF(\gamma.i, key)$ for the sum computed as above.

We assign the special role to event source X_l. Each party X_k $(1 \leq k < l)$, i.e. everybody except X_l computes

$$x^\star_{\gamma,i,k} = \begin{cases} PRF(\gamma.i.k, key) & \text{if } \gamma + i \notin \mathbb{J}_k \\ r & \text{if } \gamma + i \in \mathbb{J}_k \end{cases}$$

X_l computes

$$x^\star_{\gamma,i,l} = \begin{cases} -\sum_{k=1}^{l-1} PRF(\gamma.i.k, key) + PRF(\gamma.i, key) & \text{if } \gamma + i \notin \mathbb{J}_k \\ r & \text{if } \gamma + i \in \mathbb{J}_k \end{cases}$$

The detection algorithm at the correlation agent S is slightly different and actually has become simpler. Note that S knows i where $p.y_i = \star$. It computes the sum $x_{\gamma,i} = \sum_{k=1}^{l} x^\star_{\gamma,i,k}$ over all event sources and uses this one value $x_{\gamma,i}$ in the above detection algorithm (where there used to be l).

We omit the security proof for brevity, since it follows the same construction as before. Simply note that detection of a missing event without a complete pattern match implies PRF distinguishability.

5   Evaluation

We evaluate the performance and communication cost of our algorithm as used for anti-counterfeiting. We model the supply chain as a q stage process. The length m of a trace is then equal to q.

First, we estimate the number of necessary patterns ("illegal links"). Let $f(\chi)$ be the discrete probability density function of the number of companies in one stage of the supply chain and $F(\chi)$ be its cumulative distribution function. We assume all stages are independent identically distributed. Then the expected number of allowed links between two stages is

$$a = E(\chi^2) = E(\chi)E(\chi)$$

The expected number of all links is $qE(\chi)(qE(\chi) - 1)$ and the expected number of illegal links is

$$b = qE(\chi)(qE(\chi) - 1) - a(q - 1)$$

Thus we expect b patterns in the system.

Second, we estimate the necessary number of event traces that cover all "allowed" links called the clean set, since it may not contain any counterfeits. Between each two consecutive stages there are a allowed links and each needs to be present in at least one trace. We assume that the probability of links occurring at different stages is independent. We observe q stages in parallel and the number of necessary event traces is determined by the maximum number of links between any two stages. The probability density function of the maximum is given by

$$g(\chi^2) = \sum_{i=1}^{q-1} \binom{q-1}{i} f(\chi^2)^i F(\chi^2 - 1)^{q-1-i}$$

The expected value of the maximum is

$$c = \sum_{\chi^2} \chi^2 g(\chi^2)$$

If we assume that the probability of the occurrence of each link is uniform, then determining the expected number of traces, such that each link occurs at least once is an instance of the coupon collector's problem. The expected number of traces necessary can be then computed as

$$d = \lceil c \rceil \sum_{i=1}^{\lceil c \rceil} \frac{1}{i}$$

The formula for computing the expected number of traces necessary in case of a non-uniform distribution can be found in [7].

We will continue using numbers inspired by a real-world example. Assume a supply chain with $q = 5$ stages and let the number of parties at a stage be uniformly distributed between 1 and 5. The expected number of parties at a stage $E(\chi) = 3$ and the expected number of parties in the entire supply chain is $l = 15$.

Exceptional situations may significantly increase the necessary size of the clean set, such that in practice one can expect some false positives due to cases, such as a return delivery, and read errors, such as a failing RFID tag.

The expected number of allowed links between two stages is $a = 9$. The expected number of illegal links, i.e. patterns is $b = 174$. The expected value of the maximum number of links between any two stages is $c = 16.1$. The expected number of traces necessary in the clean set is then $d = 58.5$.

An inherent problem with our algorithm is that the detection of an anomaly is exponential in the length of the pattern. The algorithm has to exhaustively search $O((lu)^n)$ possible combinations. In our use case of counterfeit detection in supply chains this does not pose a problem, since $n = 2$ and the search algorithm can be further optimized using hash tables to $O(lu)$ expected time complexity.

We implemented the detection algorithm using 160-bit HMAC based SHA-1 on a 2.4 GHz Intel Xeon machine using Java 1.5 on Windows XP. We generated random patterns of a given length and matched them to randomly generated strings. We report the average of the spent wall clock time of 1000 runs of the matching algorithm. Figure 3 shows the results in milliseconds for a pattern length of 2 to 8 on a logarithmic scale. Even this non-optimized algorithm can perform counterfeit detection ($n = 2$) for a single pattern in less than 2 ms. Furthermore we see that detection times for pattern lengths up to 5 seem acceptable (< 1 s), but this assessment obviously depends on the rate of incoming events.

Computation of the detection input at the event sources scales linearly in the pattern length $O(n|\mathbb{J}_k|)$. On the test hardware we computed 1000 HMACs in 73 milliseconds and therefore this is not expected to be a performance bottleneck.

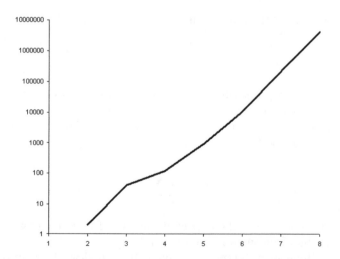

Fig. 3. Running time in ms over pattern length

For each tag we need to communicate one PRF value per event in the pattern (n), per event source (l), per match up to the limit (u) and per pattern to match (b). The communication complexity is consequently $O(nlub)$ per tag. Assuming the PRF length of 32 bits (4 bytes) from Section 4.3 we calculate 20 KBytes for our example.

We can estimate the communication cost when using secure multi-party computation with [2]. For this method we need a circuit implementing the pattern matching consisting of gates implementing any binary function. We construct this circuit from individual components from a library we have developed over a course of projects.

We start with a circuit that first sorts the events using a sorting network. Note that our algorithm does that implicitly. We continue our example and assume $l = 15$ parties which supply $u = 1$ event each. The event type corresponds to the party identifier and consists of 4 bits. The numbering of events consists of 8 bits. A sort-and-exchange operation in a sorting network can then be implement using 73 gates. Using Batcher's construction we need 80 such operations. The result must be compared to $b = 174$ at $l * u - n + 1 = 14$ positions with $n = 2$ events. The results of this comparison are condensed into the output bit – match or no match.

The entire circuit consists of 47252 gates. For each gate we need $4l = 60$ keys of 80 bits which results in 216 MByte which needs to be communicated by each computing party. This results in an overall communication of 3.2 GByte – compared to our 20 KByte a factor of more than $\cdot 10^6$. Our exponential computation complexity seems very reasonable compared with these absolute numbers.

6   Conclusion

We presented a privacy-preserving pattern matching algorithm. This algorithm is provably secure, but with limited privacy protection by its ideal functionality. We show how the matching algorithm and the privacy guarantee can be used to implement distributed anomaly detection. We show that computation and communication costs are acceptable for counterfeit detection in an example supply chain.

Our work extends the state-of-the-art with a novel protocol for practical privacy-preserving distributed event correlation. Therefore new detection algorithms, such as our anomaly detection, can be implemented with privacy for the event sources.

We differ from previous approaches by implementing provable security. We counterbalance the resulting performance penalty by limiting the privacy guaranteed by the ideal functionality. We anticipate that this strategy may lead to further practical and privacy-preserving protocols for different correlation algorithms.

Acknowledgements

The developments presented in this paper were partly funded by the European Commission through the ICT program under Framework 7 grant 213531 to the

SecureSCM project and by the German BMBF through the grant to the *Polytos* project.

References

1. Applebaum, B., Freedman, M., Ringberg, H., Caesar, M., Rexford J.: Collaborative, Privacy-Preserving Data Aggregation At Scale (2009),
   http://eprint.iacr.org/2009/180.pdf
2. Ben-David, A., Nisan, N., Pinkas, B.: FairplayMP: a system for secure multi-party
   computation. In: Proceesings of the 15th ACM Conference on Computer and Communications Security, CCS (2008)
3. Ben-Or, M., Goldwasser, S., Wigderson, A.: Completeness theorems for non-
   cryptographic fault-tolerant distributed computation. In: Proceedings of the 20th
   annual ACM symposium on Theory of computing (1988)
4. Burkhart, M., Strasser, M., Many, D., Dimitropoulos, X.: SEPIA: Security through
   Private Information Aggregation (2009),
   http://arxiv1.library.cornell.edu/abs/0903.4258
5. Du, W., Atallah, M.: Secure Multi-Party Computation Problems and Their Applications: A Review and Open Problems. In: Proceedings of the Workshop on New
   Security Paradigms (2001)
6. European Commission. Report on Community Customs Activities on Counterfeit
   and Piracy (2008)
7. Flajolet, P., Gardy, D., Thimonier, L.: Birthday paradox, coupon collectors, caching
   algorithms and self-organizing search. Discrete Applied Mathematics 39(3) (1992)
8. Goldreich, O.: Secure Multi-party Computation (2002),
   www.wisdom.weizmann.ac.il/~oded/pp.html
9. Goldreich, O., Micali, S., Wigderson, A.: How to play any mental game. In: Proceedings of the 19th ACM Symposium on Theory of Computing (1987)
10. Hazay, C., Lindell, Y.: Efficient Protocols for Set Intersection and Pattern Matching
    with Security Against Malicious and Covert Adversaries. In: Proceedings of the 5th
    Theory of Cryptography Conference (2008)
11. Kerschbaum, F.: Practical Privacy-Preserving Benchmarking. In: Proceedings of
    the 23rd IFIP International Information Security Conference (2008)
12. Kerschbaum, F., Dahlmeier, D., Schröpfer, A., Biswas, D.: On the Practical Impor-
    tance of Communication Complexity for Secure Multi-Party Computation Proto-
    cols. In: Proceedings of the 24th ACM Symposium on Applied Computing (2009)
13. Kuerschner, C., Thiesse, F., Fleisch, E.: An analysis of data-on-tag concepts in
    manufacturing. In: Proceedings of the 3rd Konferenz Ubiquitäre und Mobile Infor-
    mationssysteme (2008)
14. Lee, A., Tabriz, P., Borisov, N.: A Privacy-Preserving Interdomain Audit Frame-
    work. In: Proceedings of the ACM Workshop on Privacy in the Electronic Society
    (2006)
15. Lehtonen, M., Michahelles, F., Fleisch, E.: How to Detect Cloned Tags in a Reliable
    Way from Incomplete RFID Traces. In: Proceedings of the IEEE RFID Conference
    (2009)
16. Lincoln, P., Porras, P., Shmatikov, V.: Privacy-Preserving Sharing and Correlation
    of Security Alerts. In: Proceedings of the USENIX Security Symposium (2004)
17. Locasto, M., Parekh, J., Keromytis, A., Stolfo, S.: Towards Collaborative Secu-
    rity and P2P Intrusion Detection. In: Proceedings of the Information Assurance
    Workshop (2005)

18. Mirowski, L., Hartnett, J.: Deckard: A System to Detect Change of RFID Tag Ownership. International Journal of Computer Science and Network Security 7(7) (2007)
19. Oertel, N.: Tracking based product authentication: Catching intruders in the supply chain. In: Proceedings of the 17th European Conference on Information Systems (2008)
20. Parekh, J., Wang, K., Stolfo, S.: Privacy-Preserving Payload-Based Correlation for Accurate Malicious Traffic Detection. In: Proceedings of the SIGCOMM Workshop on Large-Scale Attack Defense (2006)
21. Porras, P., Shmatikov, V.: Large-Scale Collection and Sanitization of Network Security Data: Risks and Challenges. In: Proceedings of the Workshop on New Security Paradigms (2006)
22. Santos, B., Smith, L.: RFID in the Supply Chain: Panacea or Pandora's Box? Communications of the ACM 51(10) (2008)
23. Sarma, S., Brock, D., Engels, D.: Radio frequency identification and the electronic product code. IEEE Micro. 21(6) (2001)
24. Staake, T., Thiesse, F., Fleisch, E.: Extending the EPC Network – The Potential of RFID in Anti-Counterfeiting. In: Proceedings of the 20th ACM Symposium on Applied Computing (2005)
25. Yao, A.: Protocols for Secure Computations. In: Proceedings of the IEEE Symposium on Foundations of Computer Science (1982)
26. Zanetti, D., Fellmann, L., Capkun, S.: Privacy-preserving Clone Detection for RFID-enabled Supply Chains. In: Proceedings of the IEEE International Conference on RFID (2010)

Time Measurement Threatens Privacy-Friendly RFID Authentication Protocols

Gildas Avoine[*], Iwen Coisel[**], and Tania Martin

Université catholique de Louvain
B-1348 Louvain-La-Neuve, Belgium
{gildas.avoine,iwen.coisel,tania.martin}@uclouvain.be

Abstract. Privacy is one of the most important security concerns in radio frequency identification. The publication of hundred RFID-based authentication protocols during the last decade raised the need of designing a dedicated privacy model. An important step has been done with the model of Vaudenay that combines early models into a unified and powerful one. In particular, this model addresses the case where an adversary is able to know whether or not the protocol execution succeeded. This modelizes the fact that the adversary may get information from a side channel about the termination of the protocol, e.g., she notices that the access is granted to the RFID-tag holder. We go one step forward in this paper and stress that the adversary may also have access to a side channel that leaks the computational time of the reader. This modelizes an adversary who measures how long it takes to grant the access. Although this channel could be seen as an implementation flaw, we consider that it is always risky to require the implementation to solve what the design should deal with. This new channel enables to demonstrate that many key-reference protocols are not as privacy-friendly as they claim to be, e.g., WSRE, OSK, C^2, O-FRAP, O-FRAKE,... We then introduce the TIMEFUL oracle in the model of Vaudenay, which allows to analyze the resistance of the protocols to time-based attacks as soon as the design phase. Finally, we suggest some methods that make RFID-based authentication protocols immune to such attacks.

Keywords: RFID, Authentication, Privacy, Time-Attack.

1   Introduction

Radio Frequency IDentification (RFID) is a contactless technology used to identify and/or authenticate remote objects or persons, through a radio frequency channel using RFID *readers* and RFID *tags* (or transponders), the latters embedded into the items. RFID is becoming more and more widespread in daily-life

[*] This work was partially funded by the Walloon Region Marshall plan through the SPW DG06 Project TRASILUX.

[**] This work was partially funded by the Walloon Region Marshall plan through the 816922 Project SEE.

S.B. Ors Yalcin (Ed.): RFIDSec 2010, LNCS 6370, pp. 138–157, 2010.
© Springer-Verlag Berlin Heidelberg 2010

applications, from library management [17] or pet identification [14], to anti counterfeiting [26], access control [23] or even biometric passports [22]. The wide and fast deployment of RFID is mainly due to the diminution of the RFID tags price while their capacities steadily increase.

Moreover, the ubiquity of RFID raises new concerns about privacy. For instance in public transportation, a customer holding an RFID ticket might not want anybody else to be able to track his movings. One option to preempt such a worry is to build secure RFID authentication protocols, in order to ensure privacy for RFID users. Thus, an RFID system should provide *anonymity* (the identity of the tag should be kept secret) and *untraceability* (it should not be possible to link two different tag communications) for a user. Thereby, the design of secure and privacy-preserving RFID protocols requires an attentive and methodical analysis of its characteristics. Such an analysis is carried out with theoretical studies based on privacy models. In 2005, Avoine was the first to present such a framework in [2]. Since then, many attempts [11,15,16,24] have been done to propose a convenient and appropriate privacy model for RFID. But each one suffers from distinct shortcomings: generally, these models do not take into account some important adversary features, such that the information given by the result of a tag authentication (does the tag has been authenticated successfully or not?), or the behavior of a "corrupted" tag (can it still be used in the system?). Given all these proposals for privacy analysis, Vaudenay's model [25], presented at ASIACRYPT 2007, is known to be one of the most complete. Vaudenay defined eight privacy levels composed of:

- four notions related to the power of an adversary to compromise a tag (WEAK, FORWARD, DESTRUCTIVE and STRONG),
- and the notion related to the possible access by the adversary to the side-channel information given by the result of a tag authentication (NARROW),

and proved some feasible and some impossible privacy results for several well-known authentication protocols. The NARROW notion was introduced by Juels and Weis [15]. They clearly explain that an adversary may have a single bit information from the reader, i.e. whether or not the tag authentication succeeds. An example is an access card opening a building door. Vaudenay was the first to formalize this notion in his model. In the same way, we decide to formalize the time spent by the reader to open this door as an other side information. This crucial privacy notion related to *time* is missing in Vaudenay's model. To be precise, the *time* that a reader will take to authenticate a tag can also be a hint to recognize a tag from another. Actually, the reader database contains the keys of all the tags involved in the system. These keys are used by the readers to authenticate successfully every tag. Thus, this *time* notion is essentially related to the key infrastructure used by the readers database to organize and retrieve all this information.

The *time* notion in key infrastructures. An RFID scheme can use different key infrastructures. As RFID lives in a constrained environment, it seems that secret-key infrastructures are well-suited for this kind of applications. However, as some researches improve public-key techniques (*e.g.* efficient implementation of WIPR [20,21,28], or of GPS [13]), then an outstanding public-key infrastructure can be really interesting in this domain. It is possible to use a single key, shared between all the readers and tags of the system, or each tag can also hold its own secret key. In the latter situation, every reader has to know all the tags keys and carry on a search procedure during the protocol execution to guess which key it has to use to authenticate a particular tag.

It is quite obvious that the single secret-key infrastructure is not relevant. In fact, if we consider that RFID tags are not tamper-resistant, an adversary can compromise the whole system if she is able to corrupt a single tag.

This is not the case with a single public-key infrastructure as only the reader knows the private secret key and this device is not vulnerable against jeopardy. Some schemes already exist using a single public-key which is generally defined for a public-key encryption scheme (*e.g.* [10,20,25]). Although the time needed to authenticate a tag seems to be constant, and thus avoiding time-attacks, the requirements for the encryption scheme (*e.g.* IND-CCA2 in Vaudenay's model [25], or IND-CPA plus a MAC scheme in [10]) in order to ensure privacy implie a highest computation complexity from the tag's side. Consequently, these solutions seem still too expensive for RFID context.

In particular infrastructure cases (public or secret), in order to authenticate a tag, the reader has to retrieve the corresponding key(s). As the schemes we study in this paper manage to ensure, at least, the untraceability property, tags should not send a fixed information which allows the reader to immediately retrieve this key. Indeed, a fixed value allows an adversary to trivially link up several authentications of a same tag. As a consequence, this information should be given in an hidden way and the reader will perform a SEARCHID procedure to retrieve the corresponding key. An obvious method to do this is to perform an exhaustive search in the whole reader database. Following this example of exhaustive search, the reader might always scan its database in the same way. So clearly, for a given tag, the reader will always authenticate it at the same moment of its search. Thus the time that the reader will spend to authenticate this tag will be the same at every protocol execution. Consequently, an adversary can deduce which tag has been authenticated by the reader by only observing this time. Clearly, she can have access to this *time* information. In practice, this data is not given by the RFID system itself: the adversary will compute this time herself. Obviously, this is an important issue for tag privacy preservation. But this notion has not been yet included in any existing privacy model for RFID.

Our contributions. In this paper, we first modify Vaudenay's model in order to add this *time* notion into this model. To do so, we formalize this new privacy level. We call it TIMEFUL. This notion can therefore be combined with all the Vaudenay's levels. Then, we display the weaknesses of several existing protocols according to this *time* notion: we demonstrate that that OSK [19] is not TIMEFUL-NARROW-WEAK-private, and that neither WSRE [27], nor all the "undesynchronizable" protocols such as C^2 [9], O-FRAP or O-FRAKE [16] are TIMEFUL-WEAK-private. Finally, we propose various solutions to provide

TIMEFUL privacy. They consist in combining an appropriate choice for the reader database structure with a pertinent search procedure: our approaches are based on rainbow tables, hash tables, B-trees, and random search.

Structure of the paper. In Section 2, our modification of Vaudenay's model is detailed. The privacy analysis of some well-known existing protocols is done in Section 3. Section 4 introduces several solutions and improvements that can be conducted on the search procedure of the protocols to provide tag privacy. We conclude the paper in Section 5.

2 The Modified Vaudenay Privacy Model

In this section, we present a modification of the well-known Vaudenay privacy model [25] for authentication/identification schemes in RFID systems. Then we describe all the possible interactions of an adversary with this system.

A *tag* $\mathcal{T}$ is identified by a unique identifier ID, with limited memory and computational abilities, that can communicate with a *reader* $\mathcal{R}$ up to a limited distance. A reader is composed of (i) a transreceiver which communicates with possibly several tags and (ii) a back-end database containing all identifiers ID of valid tags and additional data such as secret keys. We assume that communications between the transreceiver and the database are secure. In terms of security, one main difference between a tag and a reader is that a tag cannot be considered as a tamper-resistant device (and thus an RFID tag can be corrupted by an adversary against the system). We also assume that the reader is more powerful than a tag.

2.1 Definition of the Procedures

A privacy-preserving RFID authentication scheme, denoted $\mathcal{S}$, is composed of the following procedures, where λ is a security parameter.

– SETUPREADER(1^λ) is a scheme which generates a private/public key pair $(\mathsf{K_S}, \mathsf{K_P})$ for the reader $\mathcal{R}$, depending on the security parameter λ. It also creates an empty database $\mathsf{DB}_\mathcal{R}$ which will later contain the identifiers and keys of all tags.
– SETUPTAG(ID, $\mathsf{K_P}$) is a probabilistic algorithm which returns a tag-dependent key set tk[ID]. (ID, tk[ID]) is added in the reader's database $\mathsf{DB}_\mathcal{R}$ when the tag is legitimate.
– IDENT is an interactive protocol between the reader $\mathcal{R}$ taking on inputs 1^λ, $\mathsf{K_S}$, $\mathsf{K_P}$ and $\mathsf{DB}_\mathcal{R}$, and a tag $\mathcal{T}$ with identifier ID taking on inputs 1^λ, tk[ID], $\mathsf{K_P}$ and possibly ID. At the end of the protocol, the reader either accepts the tag (if $\mathcal{T}$ is legitimate) and outputs its identifier ID, or rejects it (if not) and outputs $\perp$.

2.2   Definition of the Oracles

We now define the adversary $\mathcal{A}$ against such RFID systems. We consider that there is only one valid reader $\mathcal{R}$ in the system. However as we will see below, the adversary may play the role of dishonest readers to interact with a tag. In such a case, we assume that the tag does not know *a priori* if it is interacting with the valid reader $\mathcal{R}$ or the adversary $\mathcal{A}$. Then, the main features of an adversary are basically given by:

- the actions she is allowed to perform, which are represented by the *oracles* she can query,
- the goal of her attack and the way she will perform it, depicted by an *experiment* (or *game*) containing the rules she has to follow.

At the beginning of each experiment, we assume that the SETUPREADER procedure has already been executed by a challenger denoted $\mathcal{C}$ and thus that the values 1^{λ}, $\mathsf{K_S}$ and $\mathsf{K_P}$ already exist. We next assume that 1^{λ} and $\mathsf{K_P}$ are always given to $\mathcal{A}$, whereas $\mathsf{K_S}$ never (since the valid reader cannot be corrupted). At the beginning of one experiment, we consider that there is no tag in the system. We thus give to $\mathcal{A}$ the oracle $\mathcal{O}^{\textsc{CreateTag}}(\mathsf{ID}, b)$ to introduce new ones. As in the Vaudenay model [25], we consider that the adversary can only interact with tags that are sufficiently close to her without having access to other existing ones. We thus use Vaudenay's concept of *free* and *drawn* tags. Drawn tags are the ones within "visual contact" to the adversary so that she can communicate while being able to link communications. Free tags are the other tags with which the adversary cannot interact. At the creation of a new tag, that is after the call to $\mathcal{O}^{\textsc{CreateTag}}(\mathsf{ID}, b)$, the new tag has the status free and the adversary cannot interact with it.

- $\mathcal{O}^{\textsc{CreateTag}}(\mathsf{ID}, b)$: this oracle creates a free tag with a unique identifier ID, either legitimate ($b = 1$) or not ($b = 0$). This oracle uses the SETUPTAG algorithm with ID on input to set up the tag with $\mathsf{tk}[\mathsf{ID}]$. For $b = 1$ only, this oracle updates $\mathsf{DB_R}$, adding this new tag. By convention, b is implicitly 1 when omitted.

Next, the adversary can modify the status of the created tag by using the following oracles.

- $\mathcal{O}^{\textsc{DrawTag}}(\mathsf{distr}, k) \rightarrow (\mathsf{t}_1, b_1, \cdots, \mathsf{t}_k, b_k)$: with distribution probability distr, this oracle randomly selects k tags between all the existing (not already drawn) ones. For each chosen tag, the oracle gives it a new pseudonym denoted t_i and changes its status from free to drawn. Finally, the oracle outputs all the generated pseudonyms $(\mathsf{t}_1, \cdots, \mathsf{t}_k)$ in any order. If there is not enough free tags (*i.e.* less than k), then the oracle outputs $\bot$. We further assume that this oracle returns bits $(b_1, \ldots, b_k)$ telling whether the drawn tags are legitimate or not. All relations $(\mathsf{t}_i, \mathsf{ID})$ are kept in an *a priori* secret table denoted Tab.

- $\mathcal{O}^{\text{FREE}}(\mathsf{t})$: this oracle moves the tag with pseudonym t from the status drawn to the status free. This makes t unavailable from now on (in particular, $\mathcal{A}$ cannot interact with the tag t anymore).

Then, the adversary is only able to interact with tags by using the pseudonyms and only if the tag has the status drawn. To simplify notation, we denote by $\mathsf{tk}[\mathsf{t}]$ the secret key of the tag with pseudonym t, which is equal to the secret key $\mathsf{tk}[\mathsf{ID}]$ of the underlying identifier ID of this tag. Using a pseudonym, the adversary has now several ways to interact with tags.

First, $\mathcal{A}$ is able to corrupt drawn tags by using the following oracle.

- $\mathcal{O}^{\text{CORRUPT}}(\mathsf{t}) \to \mathsf{tk}[\mathsf{t}]$: returns the tag-dependent key $\mathsf{tk}[\mathsf{t}]$. The pseudonym t is now marked as "corrupted"[1]. If t is no longer used by $\mathcal{A}$ after this oracle call, we say that t is considered as "destroyed".

Next, the adversary can *passively* witness the whole protocol IDENT between a tag and the valid reader $\mathcal{R}$ by using the following oracle.

- $\mathcal{O}^{\text{EXECUTE}}(\mathsf{t}) \to (\pi, \text{transcript})$: executes an IDENT protocol between the reader and the tag with pseudonym t. This oracle outputs the transcript of the protocol instance π, that is the whole list of the successive messages of the protocol.

$\mathcal{A}$ can also *actively* participate in the IDENT protocol by playing the role of either a fake/corrupted tag, or an invalid reader. For this purpose, the following oracles are introduced, and they also allow $\mathcal{A}$ to stop at any step of a "standard" authentication protocol, delete or modify some messages.

- $\mathcal{O}^{\text{LAUNCH}}() \to \pi$: makes the legitimate reader $\mathcal{R}$ launch a new IDENT protocol instance, that is the first request to an unknown tag so as to authenticate and identify it. It outputs the identifier π for this protocol instance.
- $\mathcal{O}^{\text{SENDREADER}}(m, \pi) \to r$: sends a message m to the reader $\mathcal{R}$ in the protocol instance π. It outputs the response r from the reader.
- $\mathcal{O}^{\text{SENDTAG}}(m, \mathsf{t}) \to r$: sends a message m to the tag with pseudonym t. It outputs the response r from the tag.
- $\mathcal{O}^{\text{RETURN}}(\pi) \to x$: when π is completed, it outputs $x = 0$ if the output of the reader during the IDENT protocol instance π is $\perp$, and $x = 1$ otherwise.

Finally, the adversary is allowed to ask the time spent by the reader to compute all the operations and to perform its SEARCHID procedure, in order to authenticate the tag linked to a particular protocol instance.

- $\mathcal{O}^{\text{TIMER}}(\pi) \to \delta$: it outputs the time δ taken by the reader for its overall computations during the protocol instance π.

---

[1] Note that the underlying tag with identifier ID is also corrupted. However, a new pseudonym of this tag can also be corrupted. Thus, a pseudonym t can only be corrupted once while a tag ID may be corrupted several times.

2.3   The Security of an Authentication Scheme

We remind here the notions of *completeness*, *availability* and *soundness* that are the basis of the well functioning and the security level of an authentication protocol. First, it is necessary to prove that a valid tag is always authenticated successfully by a valid reader.

Definition 1 (Completeness). *For every legitimate tag* T *of an RFID system, the probability that the reader* R *returns the tag identifier* ID *at the end of the* IDENT *protocol is overwhelming.*

Because an adversary A is able to interact with a tag for an attack, it is also important to prove that a valid tag T is still authenticated successfully by a valid reader, even after that an adversary conducted an attack on T.

Definition 2 (Availability, Strong Completeness). *For every legitimate tag* T *of an RFID system that could have been subjected to an attack, the probability that the reader* R *returns the tag identifier* ID *at the end of the* IDENT *protocol is overwhelming.*

The previous notions ensure the authentication success of a legitimate tag T. But the security of a scheme is also based on the fact that an adversary must not be able to impersonate T. To prove it, A can use every oracle, except $\mathcal{O}^{\text{CORRUPT}}$ since this oracle makes the impersonation trivial.

Definition 3 (Soundness). *A scheme is said sound if the probability that an adversary impersonates a legitimate tag is negligible.*

2.4   Definition of the Adversary

We now define the different classes of adversaries who will play security experiments. We here give the classification given by Vaudenay in [25] with our modification which introduces the notion of *time*.

Definition 4 (Adversary Class). *An adversary* A *against the RFID system who has no access to the* $\mathcal{O}^{\text{TIMER}}$ *oracle is said to be:*

- STRONG *if* A *has no limit on all the others oracles;*
- DESTRUCTIVE *if* A *cannot use anymore a "corrupted" tag (*i.e. *the tag has been destroyed);*
- FORWARD *if* A *is committed to only use the* $\mathcal{O}^{\text{CORRUPT}}$ *oracle after her first call to the* $\mathcal{O}^{\text{CORRUPT}}$ *oracle;*
- WEAK *if* A *has no access to the* $\mathcal{O}^{\text{CORRUPT}}$ *oracle.*

A *is said* NARROW *if she has no access to* $\mathcal{O}^{\text{RETURN}}$.
A *is moreover said* TIMEFUL *if she has access to the* $\mathcal{O}^{\text{TIMER}}$ *oracle.*

According to the Vaudenay privacy model, a "blinded" adversary is defined as an entity which interacts with a simulated system, controlled by a simulator who does not know anything about secret values. Then, a scheme ensures the privacy property if, for a given experiment (see below), the success probability of an adversary which interacts with the system through oracles (as defined in section 2.2) is undistinguishable of a "blinded" adversary.

More formally, we define the following experiment with $\mathcal{A}_P$ being the adversary with power $P \in \{\emptyset, \text{TIMEFUL}\} \cup \{\emptyset, \text{NARROW}\} \cup \{\text{WEAK}, \text{FORWARD}, \text{DESTRUCTIVE}, \text{STRONG}\}$:

Experiment $Exp_{\mathcal{S},\mathcal{A}_P}^{\text{Vaud-priv}}$

1. The challenger $\mathcal{C}$ initializes the system and sends 1^λ, and $\mathsf{K_P}$ to $\mathcal{A}_P$.
2. $\mathcal{A}_P$ interacts with the whole system, limited by her class P.
3. $\mathcal{A}_P$ submits an hypothesis about the system and receives the hidden table Tab of the $\mathcal{O}^{\text{DRAWTAG}}$ oracle.
4. $\mathcal{A}_P$ returns 1 if her hypothesis is correct and 0 otherwise.

The adversary wins if she returns 1.

Definition 5 (Trivial Adversary). *An adversary $\mathcal{A}$ is said* trivial *if it is possible to define a simulator* Sim *who perfectly simulates the system, without knowing any secrets, for a "blinded" adversary denoted $\mathcal{A}^{Sim}$, such that $|Pr[\mathcal{A}\ wins] - Pr[\mathcal{A}^{Sim}\ wins]|$ is negligible.*

If those success probabilities are undistinguishable, it means that there is no privacy loss through the communication channel. In other words, the adversary makes no effective use of the messages as their simulation (without using the secret values) leads to the same probability of success. Thus the RFID authentication scheme $\mathcal{S}$ can be considered private.

Definition 6 (Privacy). *A scheme is said P-private if all the adversaries who belong to class P are trivial.*

For our modification of the Vaudenay model, it is essential to understand that the **TIMEFUL** adversary class formalizes the notion of *time* we want to introduce. Concretely, if $\mathcal{A}$ has access to the $\mathcal{O}^{\text{TIMER}}$ oracle, she knows the time that the reader has taken to authenticate a tag. With this information, if $\mathcal{A}$ cannot deduce anything about the tag identity, we will say that the protocol is **TIMEFUL**-private. We remind the following implications between Vaudenay privacy properties which are obvious.

STRONG	$\Rightarrow$	DESTRUCTIVE	$\Rightarrow$	FORWARD	$\Rightarrow$	WEAK
$\Downarrow$		$\Downarrow$		$\Downarrow$		$\Downarrow$
NARROW-STRONG	$\Rightarrow$	NARROW-DESTRUCTIVE	$\Rightarrow$	NARROW-FORWARD	$\Rightarrow$	NARROW-WEAK

With the introduction of the **TIMEFUL** adversary class, we now have new connections at each level (**STRONG, DESTRUCTIVE, FORWARD** and **WEAK**) of the previous diagram. For better clearness and understanding, we only give the new links for the **STRONG** level:

TIMEFUL-STRONG	$\Rightarrow$	STRONG
$\Downarrow$		$\Downarrow$
TIMEFUL-NARROW-STRONG	$\Rightarrow$	NARROW-STRONG

---

3   Existing Protocols

In this section, we analyze the authentication time of some existing schemes. We only get interested in protocols based on symmetric-key cryptography, since they are more suitable for lightweight RFID. In Vaudenay's model, all of the following schemes ensure at least the NARROW-WEAK privacy. Using our TIMEFUL adversary, we will prove that none of them reaches the TIMEFUL-WEAK privacy. Note that in the following, the only time difference appears in the SEARCHID procedure. We thus only focus on this part for our study. This is not always the case in practice, consequently, we define a more general model where the whole protocol execution is taken into account. For an example, the reader can look at the protocol O-FRAPv2 introduced by Burmester, de Medeiros and Motta in [6,7] and described in Appendix A.

3.1   A Trivial Example: WSRE

We first study the scheme introduced by Weis, Sarma, Rivest and Engels in [27]. This scheme is a simple challenge/response protocol. The reader sends an authentication request and the tag ID answers by $(f(\text{tk}[\text{ID}]||N_T), N_T)$, where N_T is a nonce and f a one-way function. To authenticate the tag, the reader performs a SEARCHID procedure where it computes for each possible key stored in the database the output of f using the received nonce. When there is a match, the reader outputs the associated identifier.

This scheme does not ensure the FORWARD privacy. Assume that an adversary has stored some transcripts of past authentications. Then when she corrupts a tag, she obtains its key, thereby she can recompute the output of f using this key and the nonce of a transcript to compare it with the sent output. If there is a match, that means the adversary has linked the identity of the tag with a previous authentication transcript.

In fact, we can also prove that a TIMEFUL adversary can trace a tag without corrupting it. Note that for the rest of the paper, we assume that the f function, but also hash functions, have the same execution time, whatever the input is.

Theorem 1. *The WSRE protocol does not ensure the* TIMEFUL-WEAK *privacy.*

Proof. To prove this result, we have to exhibit an adversary which has a success probability different than the one of whichever blinded adversary. This adversary, denoted $\mathcal{A}$, can be described as follows.

- $\mathcal{A}$ creates two legitimate tags using twice $\mathcal{O}^{\text{CREATETAG}}(\text{ID}, b)$ and affects them by a call to $\mathcal{O}^{\text{DRAWTAG}}(1/2, 2)$. $\mathcal{A}$ receives two pseudonyms t_1 and t_2.
- $\mathcal{A}$ calls $\mathcal{O}^{\text{EXECUTE}}(\text{t}_1)$ and $\mathcal{O}^{\text{EXECUTE}}(\text{t}_2)$. She receives $(\pi_1, \text{transcript}_1)$ and $(\pi_2, \text{transcript}_2)$. Then she asks the time for each of these authentication, thus she requests $\mathcal{O}^{\text{TIMER}}(\pi_1)$ and $\mathcal{O}^{\text{TIMER}}(\pi_2)$ to obtain δ_1 and δ_2.
- $\mathcal{A}$ frees both tags with the requests $\mathcal{O}^{\text{FREE}}(\text{t}_1)$ and $\mathcal{O}^{\text{FREE}}(\text{t}_2)$, and reaffects only one of them with $\mathcal{O}^{\text{DRAWTAG}}(1/2, 1)$. She obtains a new pseudonym t_3.

- Again $\mathcal{A}$ executes an instance protocol by requesting $\mathcal{O}^{\text{EXECUTE}}(\mathsf{t}_3)$ and asks for the time δ_3 of this authentication instance with $\mathcal{O}^{\text{TIMER}}(\pi_3)$.
- If $\delta_3 = \delta_1$, $\mathcal{A}$ claims that $\mathsf{t}_1 = \mathsf{t}_3$, else she claims that $\mathsf{t}_2 = \mathsf{t}_3$.

It is obvious that the success probability of this adversary is 1. Now we have to prove that any blinded adversary can have this probability. The simulator does not have any clue on which of the two tags has been drawn during the second call to the $\mathcal{O}^{\text{DRAWTAG}}$ oracle, but he can simulate perfectly the answer of the tags (as f is assumed to be pseudo-random). On the other hand, he has to make a choice between the two times δ_1 and δ_2. His only solution is to perform a random choice. In this way, the simulation stays perfect. But, the blinded adversary will only have a success probability of $1/2$ as her success is based on the correctness of the simulator's choice.

Consequently, the protocol is not **TIMEFUL-WEAK** private.

3.2 OSK Scheme

In order to ensure the **FORWARD**-privacy, Ohkubo, Suzuki, and Kinoshita have introduced the well-known OSK scheme in [19]. In the latter, they use a key-update mechanism in order to modify the internal state of a tag after each protocol execution (successful or not) in a one-way manner. The OSK scheme is presented in Figure 1, where H_1 and H_2 are cryptographic secure hash functions.

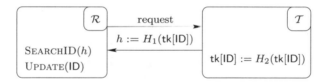

Fig. 1. OSK protocol

By updating the secret key of a tag after each authentication protocol, an adversary will not be able to recompute a previous answer of a tag after she had corrupted it (as the update is one-way). In the SEARCHID procedure, the reader computes for each tag the hash (using H_1) of its key. At any moment, if there is a match with the received value, the reader stops the procedure and outputs the corresponding identifier and updates the key, using H_2. After testing every key, if the reader did not find a match, it tries again with the updated key (computed on the fly), and so on.

Even so, it has been shown in [9,15] that the protocol is weakened by desynchronization attacks. Thus, this protocol does not ensure the **WEAK** privacy as it does not ensure the availability property. But it provides **NARROW-WEAK** privacy. See the original publications [9,15] for more details on this proof.

On the other hand, the time attack presented in the previous subsection is possible. Moreover, for any pair of tags, the difference of authentication times can be increased. Indeed, as the adversary can desynchronize a tag, she increases the authentication time of a tag at every desynchronization. Consequently, she can distinguish one tag among two easily, proving that the OSK scheme is not TIMEFUL-NARROW-WEAK private.

Remark 1. In the original article [19], the SEARCHID procedure was not described as presented here. In fact, the reader first performs all computations before comparing all these values with the one received. Thus, our time attack does not work with this procedure when tags are synchronized. Nevertheless, when a tag is desynchronized the authentication time will still be longer as the one of a synchronized tag. We present this SEARCHID procedure instead of the original one as it is generally how it is presented in many contributions.

3.3   Undesynchronizable Schemes

Some attempts have been done in order to define undesynchronizable schemes using key-update mechanisms. The objective of these schemes is to ensure the availability property and to reach the FORWARD privacy. To do so, mutual authentication schemes have been defined, where the tags update their key *if and only if* they authenticate the reader. Based on this fact, these schemes ensure that the key inside the tag and the one inside the reader database can be desynchronized at most one time. Thus to ensure the availability, it is sufficient to store in the database two keys per tag. As an example, we describe the C^2 scheme in Figure 2, introduced in [9].

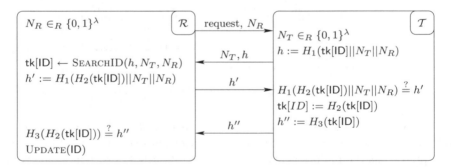

Fig. 2. C^2 protocol

As said previously, the database contains two keys per tag: the current one and the "next" one. As a consequence, the scheme is no longer vulnerable to traceability using desynchronization attacks. This technique was also present in the Dimitriou scheme [12], even if the WEAK privacy is not ensured by this scheme as proved in [9]. However, this scheme still does not reach the FORWARD privacy as the following attack is doable: if the tag is corrupted by an adversary just after the latter has blocked the last authentication of this tag after it sent N_T, h, then she is able to recompute h and thus to trace it. Consequently, this scheme only ensure the WEAK privacy property.

Although these schemes ensure the availability, an adversary is still capable to perform the previous time attack as the reader perform an exhaustive search. This implies at least one computation per tag. In the C^2 scheme, a tag can still be desynchronized one time which allows the adversary to distinguish any tag among two, as in the OSK scheme. As a result, C^2 is not TIMEFUL-WEAK private.

3.4   Overview

We have presented several schemes where a TIMEFUL adversary is able to break the privacy while some of them were assumed to ensure at least the WEAK privacy property. The different protocols that we have presented do not define an exhaustive list of those weakened by this new attack. For instance, the protocols O-FRAP and O-FRAKE, introduced by Le, Burmester and de Medeiros in [16], are also weakened by this attack as the SEARCHID procedure also implies a linear exhaustive search. This attack also works when the underlying architecture of the database is different. Namely, the tree-based protocol introduced by Molnar and Wagner in [17] suffers of a time-flaw when the SEARCHID procedure is defined as an exhaustive search at each tree level (see [17] for more details).

Moreover, one can think that this attack only affects protocols using symmetric cryptography architecture as we only present this kind of protocol. We have made this choice since most of them are affected by this attack. Nevertheless, some authentication schemes using public-key technique can be attacked by a TIMEFUL adversary. For example, this is the case of the protocol introduced by Bringer, Chabanne and Icart in [5].

4   Solutions and Improvements

Our attacks presented in the previous section always work in theory, but they require in practice a tight time measurement. For instance, we saw previously that WSRE involves a SEARCHID procedure done with an exhaustive search. Thus, if we consider two tags which data are very close in the reader database (*e.g.* one following the other), the time of the SEARCHID procedure will be almost the same for both: the time difference between the computation of one function f or two can be very small. Then in such a case, if the time measurement of the adversary is not precise enough, she will not be able to differentiate one of these two tags from the other. In our study, we consider that this adversarial issue mainly depends on the implementation of the function f, and thus that it is a programmer concern.

Here we want to propose theoretical solutions to this time problem that can be applied to these protocols. The most obvious one is to compute the worst case's time and that whatever happens, the reader waits[2] until it reaches this time to output the result. This has been mentioned by Burmester, Le, and de Medeiros

---

[2] During this time, it can also compute unused hash functions if the adversary has a look-up of its power consumption.

in [8]. This solution clearly repairs all the previous protocols against our time attack. However, the protocol efficiency can be highly decreased depending of the protocol. Our goal is to optimize the average authentication time while the protocol resists against a TIMEFUL adversary.

In our first study, we focus on protocols where the reader cannot predict the tag outputs (*i.e.* the tag inserts a nonce in its answer). Then we propose three solutions to improve OSK. Finally, we present a protocol which is claimed to be based on constant time.

4.1   The Random Search

In the case of C^2 or O-FRAP/O-FRAKE, the only solution for a reader to authenticate a tag is to compute for each key stored in its database the theoretical output of the corresponding tag, and to compare it with the received value. We have shown in the previous section (see Section 3.3) that, if this SEARCHID procedure is done linearly, then a TIMEFUL adversary can trace a tag with a non-negligible probability.

A simple solution is to randomize this search. The objective is to avoid the adversary to predict the time spent for a given tag authentication. To do so, the easiest way is to modify each time the "start-point" of the linear search in the database. If it is chosen uniformly in $[1, n]$, where n is the total number of tags, then the authentication time of a tag cannot be guessed in advance.

However, we have to take into account that a tag can be desynchronized once. In our solution, the reader first computes all the theoretical outputs using the current key. Then it only computes these outputs with the old key if it did not find a match before. Thus a "synchronized tag" will be authenticated in $\delta_h.n/2$ time in average, whereas a desynchronized tag is authenticated in $3\delta_h.n/2$ time in average, where δ_h denotes the execution time of the h function. So, by desynchronizing a tag, a TIMEFUL adversary is still able to trace a tag. Consequently, to ensure the TIMEFUL-WEAK privacy, the randomized SEARCHID procedure should indifferently test the current or the old key of tags. Thus, this procedure should consider a set of $2n$ keys and randomly tests one key after the other without considering if it is a current key or a future one.

Using this SEARCHID procedure, it is obvious that these kinds of protocols reach the TIMEFUL-WEAK privacy property. Unfortunately, the price to pay is that the system's efficiency is decreased. Indeed, the average time to authenticate a tag under a normal behavior (when the adversary does not desynchronize a tag) is $\delta_h.n$ instead of $\delta_h.n/2$. Yet we still improve the "wait" solution as this one requires a time of $2\delta_h.n$.

Remark 2. Considering the WSRE protocol (presented section 3.1) which does not use a key-update mechanism, this solution does not modify the average authentication time while it ensures the TIMEFUL-WEAK privacy property.

4.2   The OSK Scheme

Another situation is when it is possible to precompute the whole set of possible answers (or a part of it). Then it is possible to use some time/memory trade-off to enhance the complexity of the SEARCHID procedure and, in some cases, to obtain a constant look-up in the database. For example, in the OSK scheme (see Figure. 1) the tag answer does not include any nonce and thus the database can store all the tags answers. As said previously, this scheme is extremely desynchronizable. Consequently, instead of storing one answer per tag, the database should contain m successive answers for each tag. This highly increases the size of the database ($O(n.m)$ instead of $O(n)$), but depending of the database infrastructure, the SEARCHID procedure can be really efficient. We here present three infrastructure possibilities which ensure the TIMEFUL-NARROW-WEAK privacy property.

First, we shortly present an optimization called OSK-AO introduced by Avoine, Dysli and Oecshlin in [3,4] based on the well-known rainbow tables, introduced by Oecshlin in [18]. In a nutshell, all of the $n.m$ possible answers (*i.e.* the hash values of the m successive keys for each of the n tags) are distributed uniformly in a table (the table's size defines the time-memory trade-off). Each row of the database contains a succession of hash values. One value is obtained from the previous one by applying an arbitrary reduction function composed with the hash function. This reduction function takes in input a hash value and outputs an identifier in $[1, n]$ and the "update value" in $[1, m]$. Using these two values, the next hash value can be computed using the hash function. The database has to store the first and the final column of this table. Upon receiving a hash value, the reader will compose a chain of values (as done in the construction of the table) until a match is found with the last column of the table. When it happens, the reader reconstructs the corresponding row until it found the previous value, and thus obtains the identifier and the "update value". If the reduction function maps all the possible values in a uniformly manner in the database, an adversary will not be able to predict the authentication time for a given tag, and thus to trace it. Moreover, contrary to the next following solutions, this solution does not store the $n.m$ answers of tags. However, this structure is not dynamic and cannot be modified. Consequently, to introduce tags updates, the whole table must be recomputed.

Another solution is to compose the database as a hash table, where the entries are indexed by the hash values. In this kind of database, the SEARCHID procedure is quite instantaneous ($O(1)$ in average). However, to avoid collisions, the hash index used should be as long as the output of the hash function. This is quite impracticable when $n.m$ is large. Moreover, this solution is not adapted for dynamic system where the number of tags can increase during the life system. Indeed, as the number of inputs increases, so does the probability of a collision in the hash index. If this happens, then SEARCHID takes up to linear time (in $O(n)$).

Remark 3. Moreover, the database should keep in another table the current key (from the database point of view) of each tag. Indeed, if the tag is desynchronized, the use of the hash table allows the reader to authenticate the tag and to obtain the used key, but it will not be able to recompute the previous ones (as the hash function is one-way). Consequently, to delete the previous entries of the database (to keep it as small as possible), the reader should use this new table to recompute all the previous theoretical answers to delete them.

Finally, another possibility is to use a balanced binary search tree (called B-tree). This technique ensures a complexity in $O(\log n)$ for the SEARCHID procedure. The advantage of this structure is its dynamism. Contrary to the hash table, new entries can be added indefinitely in this structure without compromising its functioning. Moreover, in the worst case, the B-tree ensures a better complexity rather than the hash table where the complexity reach is in $O(n)$ in the worst case (*i.e.* when collisions happen on the hash indexes).

These three practical solutions avoid time attack for the OSK protocol, and thus ensure the TIMEFUL-NARROW-WEAK privacy. But, except for the OSK-AO solution, the database's size is $O(n.m)$ which becomes quickly infeasible, especially if the availability is highly recommended (and thus m must be large enough).

4.3   Constant-Time Identification

Not necessarily to solve the problem of time attack, but rather to reduce the complexity of the SEARCHID procedure, some protocols with a constant-time identification have been proposed (*e.g.* [1,6,7]). In this section, we present in detail the protocol proposed by Alomair, Clark, Cuellar and Poovendran in [1]. We give in appendix a description of the protocol of Burmester, de Medeiros and Motta [6,7] which unfortunately has some security flaws.

The protocol of Alomair, Clark, Cuellar and Poovendran is detailed in Figure 3. We give here a short description of it. For more details, see the original publication [1]. The important step in the tag authentication is the sent value $h(\Psi||m)$. Ψ represents a pseudonym associated to this tag and m is a counter value which is incremented after each (successful or not) tag authentication. In the database, all the possible hash values for all the possible pseudonyms and all the counter values are precomputed and stored. Based on a special infrastructure detailed later, the reader is able to retrieve quite instantaneously all the associated values to the corresponding pseudonym, *i.e.* the secret key of the tag and its identifier. The reader is then able to compute the last message of the protocol which is composed of three parts. The first one $(h(1||\Psi||\text{tk}[\text{ID}]||h_1))$ allows the tag to authenticate the reader. The second one $(h(2||\Psi||\text{tk}[\text{ID}]||h_1)\oplus\Psi')$ transmits to the tag securely a new pseudonym which has been selected among the available ones in the database. The last one $(h(3||\Psi'||\text{tk}[\text{ID}]||h_1))$ permits the tag to check the integrity of this new pseudonym.

As explained in [1], the database can be decomposed in three logical parts. The first one, denoted M-I, can be viewed as a hash table which allows to define a direct addressing to the hash values $h(\Psi||m)$. All these values are stored in the second part of the database, denoted M-II. Finally, each of these hash values points to one cell of the last part of the database, denoted M-III, which contains all the information related to the tag currently attached to the pseudonym Ψ.

Remark 4. There is a mistake in the description of this database in [1]. Indeed, in the cells of M-II, the authors said that this table only contains the hash value and a pointer to tag's data. However, this cell must contain the counter value m

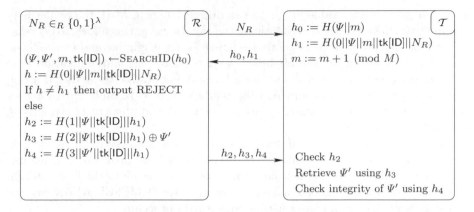

Fig. 3. Constant-Time Identification Protocol

and the pseudonym which are used in the hash value. These values are essential to check (by recomputing it) the message $h(0||\Psi||m||\mathsf{tk[ID]}||N_R)$ sent by the tag.

In their case study, the authors of [1] only consider the size of M-I as they claim that it is the only concern for the total size. We disagree with this fact and prove it by computing the size of the M-II part. We obviously use the same parameters as those of [1]. Namely the total number of pseudonyms is $N = 2.10^9$ and the counter m is majored by $M = 10^3$. Thus, the part M-II is composed of 2.10^{12} cells. Each of them contains the hash value $h(\Psi, m)$, the counter m and a pointer to the table M-III. Note that for addressing the 2.10^9 cells of the part M-III (one for each pseudonym), a pointer of 32 bits is enough. In [1], the authors said that the hash function's output must be at least of $\lfloor \log_2 NM \rfloor \approx 41$ bits. Then, each cell of M-II contains at least 83 bits (the counter is approximatively 10 bits long). We thus obtain a total of at least[3] 166.10^{12} bits, which is approximately equal to 19 terabytes. This is obviously not negligible compared to the 12 terabytes of M-I.

Although this is still feasible in practice, it is not so practicable. Furthermore, they neglect another fact yet highlighted in the paper. As a tag can be desynchronized once, each tag should be associated to two pseudonyms. Thus the total number of pseudonyms should not be twice the total number of tags, but more than this, for example three times this number. This again increases the database size (in this example from 31 to 40 terabytes).

We thus propose a modification of this database. The hash values should not be stored in M-II which then only contains the counter m and the pointer. In average this will not be a problem because, as presented in [1], in most cases, pointers of M-I are attached to only one cell. As the reader must check the correctness of $h(0||\Psi||m||\mathsf{tk[ID]}||N_R)$, it will be able to differentiate two tags which have the same address in M-I. We recognize that our optimization will increase the number of computations that the reader has to do to identify a tag.

---

[3] Recall that the hash function's output should be greater than 41 bits in practice.

For example, if a hash value points to two different tags in M-II, the reader may compute two hash values to authenticate the tag. However this allows to decrease the size of M-II from 28 to 14 terabytes which is not negligible and the collision event happens with a small probability. Note that now, the authentication time is no longer constant. Nevertheless, an adversary is not able to predict if a tag, and more precisely a pseudonym, will collide in the M-II table with another pseudonym with a given counter. Thus, she is not able at all to trace a tag using this difference of time.

Despite this huge amount of data, this protocol is however really efficient in terms of time and gives a solution to our time attack by providing a constant-time authentication. As a conclusion, this scheme is nowadays the best solution in terms of efficiency and security as it reaches the **TIMEFUL-WEAK** privacy property while having a constant-time SEARCHID procedure.

5   Conclusion

In this paper, we have exhibited and modeled a new attack based on the time required for a tag authentication. Lots of existing protocols are not resistant to this kind of attack, even when the adversary is not able to compromise the secret key of a tag (*i.e.* a **WEAK** adversary). However, we have also displayed some solutions to solve this problem. Some of them reduce the efficiency of the protocol, some others increase tremendously the data storage. To the best of our knowledge, there are nowadays no solutions (in secret-key infrastructure) which are at the same time efficient, **TIMEFUL** private and require a really small database. To our point of view, this problematic is really interesting and solutions to this problem should be found.

References

1. Alomair, B., Clark, A., Cuellar, J., Poovendran, R.: Scalable RFID Systems: a Privacy-Preserving Protocol with Constant-Time Identification. In: 40th Annual IEEE/IFIP International Conference on Dependable Systems and Network, DSN 2010, Chicago, IL, USA, 2010. IEEE Computer Society Press, Los Alamitos (2010)
2. Avoine, G.: Adversary Model for Radio Frequency Identification. Technical Report LASEC-REPORT-2005-001, Swiss Federal Institute of Technology (EPFL), Security and Cryptography Laboratory (LASEC), Lausanne, Switzerland (2005)
3. Avoine, G., Dysli, E., Oechslin, P.: Reducing Time Complexity in RFID Systems. In: Preneel, B., Tavares, S. (eds.) SAC 2005. LNCS, vol. 3897, pp. 291–306. Springer, Heidelberg (2006)
4. Avoine, G., Oechslin, P.: A Scalable and Provably Secure Hash Based RFID Protocol. In: International Workshop on Pervasive Computing and Communication Security, PerSec 2005, Kauai Island, HI, USA, pp. 110–114. IEEE Computer Society Press, Los Alamitos (2005)
5. Bringer, J., Chabanne, H., Icart, T.: Efficient Zero-Knowledge Identification Schemes which respect Privacy. In: ACM Symposium on Information, Computer and Communication Security, ASIACCS 2009, Sydney, Australia. ACM Press, New York (2009)

6. Burmester, M., de Medeiros, B., Motta, R.: Robust, Anonymous RFID Authentication with Constant Key-Lookup. Cryptology ePrint, Report 2007/402 (2007)
7. Burmester, M., de Medeiros, B., Motta, R.: Anonymous RFID authentication supporting constant-cost key-lookup against active adversaries. Journal of Applied Cryptography 1(2), 79–90 (2008)
8. Burmester, M., Van Le, T., De Medeiros, B.: Provably Secure Ubiquitous Systems: Universally Composable RFID Authentication Protocols. In: Conference on Security and Privacy for Emerging Areas in Communication Networks, SecureComm, Baltimore, MD, USA, 2006, IEEE Computer Society Press, Los Alamitos (2006)
9. Canard, S., Coisel, I.: Data Synchronization in Privacy-Preserving RFID Authentication Schemes. In: RFIDSec 2008, Budapest, Hungary (2008)
10. Canard, S., Coisel, I., Etrog, J.: Lighten Encryption Schemes for Secure and Private RFID Systems. In: Sion, R., Curtmola, R., Dietrich, S., Kiayias, A., Mitet, J.M., Sako, K., Sebé, F. (eds.) FC 2010 Workshops. LNCS, vol. 6054, pp. 19–33. IFCA/Springer, Heidelberg (2010)
11. Coisel, I.: Authentification et Anonymat à Bas-Coût: Modélisations et Protocoles, Thèse, Université de Caen (2009)
12. Dimitriou, T.: A Lightweight RFID Protocol to protect against Traceability and Cloning attacks. In: Conference on Security and Privacy for Emerging Areas in Communication Networks, SecureComm, Athens, Greece. IEEE Computer Society Press, Los Alamitos (2005)
13. Girault, M., Juniot, L., Robshaw, M.: The feasibility of on-the-tag public key cryptography. In: RFIDSec 2007, Malaga, Spain (2007)
14. Instruments, T.: Animal Tracking,
    http://www.ti.com/rfid/shtml/apps-anim-tracking.shtml
15. Juels, A., Weis, S.: Defining Strong Privacy for RFID. In: International Conference on Pervasive Computing and Communications, PerCom 2007, New York City, NY, USA, pp. 342–347. IEEE Computer Society Press, Los Alamitos (2007)
16. Le, T.V., Burmester, M., de Medeiros, B.: Universally Composable and Forward-secure RFID Authentication and Authenticated Key Exchange. In: ACM Symposium on Information, Computer and Communications Security, ASIACCS 2007, Singapore, pp. 242–252. ACM, New York (2007)
17. Molnar, D., Wagner, D.: Privacy and Security in Library RFID: Issues, Practices, and Architectures. In: Pfitzmann, B., Liu, P. (eds.) Conference on Computer and Communications Security, ACM CCS, Washington, DC, USA, 2004, pp. 210–219. ACM Press, New York (2004)
18. Oechslin, P.: Making a faster cryptanalytic time-memory trade-off. In: Boneh, D. (ed.) CRYPTO 2003. LNCS, vol. 2729, pp. 617–630. Springer, Heidelberg (2003)
19. Ohkubo, M., Suzuki, K., Kinoshita, S.: Cryptographic Approach to Privacy-Friendly Tags. In: RFID Privacy Workshop, MIT, MA, USA (2003)
20. Oren, Y., Feldhofer, M.: WIPR - a Public Key Implementation on Two Grains of Sand. In: RFIDSec 2008, Budapest, Hungary (2008)
21. Oren, Y., Feldhofer, M.: A Low-Resource Public-Key Identification Scheme for RFID Tags and Sensor Nodes. In: Second ACM Conference on Wireless Network Security, WiSec 2009, Zurich, Switzerland. ACM Press, New York (2009)
22. Organization, I.C.A.: Machine Readable Travel Documents, Doc 9303, Part1, Machine Readable Passports, 5 (edn.) (2003)
23. Semiconductors, N.: MIFARE Smartcards ICs,
    http://www.nxp.com/products/identification/card_ics/mifare

24. van Deursen, T., Mauw, S., Radomirović, S.: Untraceability of RFID Protocols. In: Onieva, J.A., Sauveron, D., Chaumette, S., Gollmann, D., Markantonakis, K. (eds.) WISTP 2008. LNCS, vol. 5019, pp. 1–15. Springer, Heidelberg (2008)
25. Vaudenay, S.: On Privacy Models for RFID. In: Kurosawa, K. (ed.) ASIACRYPT 2007. LNCS, vol. 4833, pp. 68–87. Springer, Heidelberg (2007)
26. Verayo. Anti-Counterfeiting Solution for Pharma, Liquor, Cigarettes, Food, Luxury Products, http://www.verayo.com/solution/anti-counterfeiting.html
27. Weis, S., Sarma, S., Rivest, R., Engels, D.: Security and Privacy Aspects of Low-Cost Radio Frequency Identification Systems. In: Hutter, D., Müller, G., Stephan, W., Ullmann, M. (eds.) Security in Pervasive Computing. LNCS, vol. 2802, pp. 454–469. Springer, Heidelberg (2004)
28. Wu, J., Stinson, D.: How to Improve Security and Reduce Hardware Demands of the WIPR RFID Protocol. In: IEEE International Conference on RFID – RFID 2009, Orlando, FL, USA (2009)

A   The Optimization for O-FRAP

Burmester, de Medeiros and Motta have introduced in [6,7] an improvement of the O-FRAP protocol, here denoted O-FRAP.v2, where the SEARCHID procedure is from now on in a constant-time. To obtain this result, they introduce in the O-FRAP protocol a new value for each tag which can be viewed as a pseudonym. During the protocol, the tag sends this value joined with an authentication value. As this scheme is build to ensure the unlinkability, this pseudonym must change between each (successful or not) authentication protocol. It happens in two different ways, depending if the tag suspects an attack or not. To prevent entrapment attacks, if the tag does not receive the confirmation that a reader authenticates itself, it will not update its pseudonym but a counter and compute on-the-fly a pseudonym based on the counter.

The database contains for each tag its identifier, its secret-key, and all its possible pseudonyms ($2M + 3$ values, where M is the highest value of the counter m). By storing this huge amount of data, a reader is able to perform a really fast SEARCHID procedure as all the possible tag answers are already precomputed in the database. The price to pay to obtain this result is a large database where the size is parametrized by M (and the number of tags). On the other hand, when the reader receives an answer from a tag, the SEARCHID procedure only verifies that the received value belongs to the database. If it is the case, the reader has authenticated the tag and the end of the protocol consists of an update procedure of the database keys and of the tag.

As presented in [6,7], the search procedure is in constant-time, but under certain conditions, the reader will spend more or less time to output its result. For example, if the tag uses an entrapment value for ps (*i.e.* $g(\mathsf{tk[ID]}; q||IV||M)$), the reader has to computes c values to replace each of the q^i_{cur}. On the other hand, if $ps = r$, the reader has no computation to realize. As a consequence, the time to output the result is different between these two cases and the adversary is thus able to distinguish if the reader has performed or not this computation. By stopping the protocol before the tag receives $conf$, the adversary forces the tag

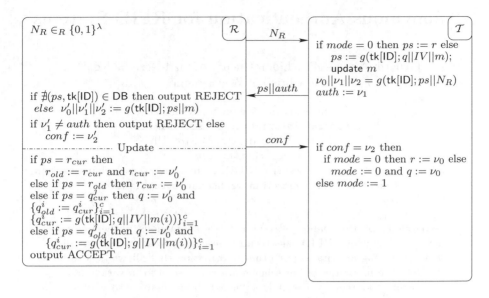

Fig. 4. Constant-Lookup Protocol Based on O-FRAP

to use an entrapment value and will consequently be able to distinguish this tag of a "synchronized" one (*i.e.* where $mode = 0$) during the next authentication protocol. A trivial solution to this attack is to output the result before processing to the values' update.

However, this protocol suffers of security flaws which allow a FORWARD adversary to trace all the previous authentications of a tag, and a WEAK adversary to rely two authentications of a tag.

For the first attack, it is sufficient to notice that an adversary who learns the secret key k of a tag is able to recompute all the previous values $auth$ of this tag, as she can recompute $g(k; ps||c)$ (because ps and c are sent in clear).

The second attack is based on the value ps sent by the tag. During a standard protocol, a tag sends $ps = r$. If the adversary blocks the last message, the tag updates nothing except its value $mode$ which is instantiated to 1. During the next protocol, the tag uses an entrapment value as $mode = 1$. When the protocol ends, the tag changes $mode$ to 0 and updates q to ν_0. Consequently, during the next protocol, the tag will send $ps = r$ where the value r is the same as in the first protocol because it has never been updated. Thus, the adversary can trivially recognize this tag.

Anonymous Authentication for RFID Systems

Frederik Armknecht[1], Liqun Chen[2], Ahmad-Reza Sadeghi[3],
and Christian Wachsmann[3]

[1] University of Mannheim, Germany
armknecht@informatik.uni-mannheim.de
[2] Hewlett Packard Labs, Bristol, UK
liqun.chen@hp.com
[3] Horst Görtz Institute for IT-Security (HGI), Ruhr-University Bochum, Germany
{ahmad.sadeghi,christian.wachsmann}@trust.rub.de

Abstract. In this paper, we present an anonymous authentication scheme that allows RFID tags to authenticate to readers without disclosing the tag identity or any other information that allows tags to be traced. The properties of our scheme are very useful for a variety of access control systems, where it is sufficient or mandatory to verify the authenticity of a tag without inferring its identity.

Our scheme is based on the recently proposed anoymizer-approach, where additional devices (called *anonymizers*) frequently interact with the tags to ensure anonymity and unlinkability of tags. This allows using cost-effective RFID tags that cannot perform public-key cryptography in an efficient and scalable way. Our solution provides (i) anonymity and untraceability of tags against readers, (ii) secure tag authentication even against collusions of malicious readers and anonymizers, and (iii) security against denial-of-service attacks.

Keywords: RFID, Privacy, Anonymity, Authentication.

1 Introduction

Radio Frequency Identification (RFID) enables RFID *readers* to perform fully automatic wireless identification of objects that are labeled with RFID *tags*, and is widely deployed to many applications (e.g., access control [1,2], electronic tickets [2,3], and e-passports [4]). As pointed out in previous publications (see, e.g., [5,6,7]), this prevalence of RFID technology introduces various risks, in particular concerning the privacy of its users and holders. The most deterrent privacy risk concerns the tracking of users, which allows the creation and misuse of detailed user profiles. Thus, it is desired that an RFID system provides *anonymity* (confidentiality of the tag identity) as well as *untraceability* (unlinkability of the communication of a tag), even in case the state (e.g., the secret) of a tag has been disclosed.

There is a vast amount of literature on privacy-preserving RFID systems and their formal treatment (see, e.g., [6,7,8,9]). Most existing approaches assume RFID readers to be fully trusted embedded devices, which often cannot be guaranteed in practice. Indeed, the entity that operates the readers may be interested

S.B. Ors Yalcin (Ed.): RFIDSec 2010, LNCS 6370, pp. 158–175, 2010.

in detailed user profiles and hence collect information on the users of the RFID system. Obviously, anonymity of tags cannot be preserved against readers in applications that require readers to identify tags. On the other hand, there are many applications (e.g., access control or electronic tickets) where it is sufficient to verify whether a tag is legitimate or not without determining its identity (see, e.g., [10,11,12]). Moreover, in practice RFID readers are embedded devices (which can be integrated to mobile phones or computers) that can easily be lost or stolen. The resulting complexity exposes them to sophisticated hard- and software attacks (e.g., viruses and Trojans). The problem of reader corruption and revocation of compromised readers has been considered only recently (see, e.g., [13,14,15]).

Related work. So far, fully anonymous authentication of RFID tags to readers has been discussed only in [10,11,12]. The schemes proposed in [10] and [12] both employ anonymous credential systems (see, e.g., [16,17,18]). The authors of [10] describe a generic anonymous payment system (which includes anonymous authentication) for RFID-powered public transport tickets based on anonymous credentials but do not give any implementation details. Moreover, [12] presents an implementation of a full fledged anonymous credential system on Java Cards, which are expensive contactless smartcards. Since the use of anonymous credentials implies high computational requirements (public-key cryptography) to all devices involved, these systems do not comply to the capabilities of most RFID systems in practice that require fast authentication of cost-effective tags (see, e.g., [19,3]). An alternative approach to anonymous RFID-based payment has been proposed in [11]. However, this approach is not scalable since the total number of tags in the system must be fixed during system initialization. Summing up, existing approaches to anonymous authentication of RFID tags are not applicable to most real-world RFID applications.

A promising approach to enhance privacy of RFID without lifting the computational requirements on tags are anonymizers (see, e.g., [20,21,22,23,24]). These are special devices that take off the computational workload (i.e., the public-key operations) from tags and enable privacy-preserving protocols with cost-efficient tags. Note that anonymizer-based RFID systems are *not* a straight-forward extension of a resource constrained RFID system to one with more capabilities. This is because an additional protocol is required between tags and anonymizers opening new attack surfaces that must be carefully considered. There are different ways to realize anonymizers: they can be devices installed at various places (e.g., railway stations) or a software running on the tag user's mobile phone or PDA, which allows operators of RFID systems to enable privacy for the concerned users with no or only minor extra costs.

Contribution. In this paper, we present an anonymous authentication scheme for RFID that adapts the scheme of [18] for our purposes. Our protocol employs anonymizers and has several appealing features that are important for practical applications:

Anonymity and untraceability of tags against readers. Our scheme allows tags to authenticate to readers without revealing any information that can be used to identify or trace a tag. Hence, even adversaries that can corrupt readers cannot identify or link the transactions of a tag. This is a major improvement to existing RFID systems that usually require the strong assumption of trusted readers (see, e.g.,[25,26,27,28]).

Tag authentication. Our protocol ensures that even adversaries that can corrupt anonymizers and readers cannot impersonate legitimate tags to honest readers. This an important advantage compared to existing RFID systems, where a compromised reader usually has a severe impact on the security (and privacy) of all tags in the system (see, e.g., [13,14,15]).

Availability. In our scheme, an adversary cannot manipulate (i.e., invalidate) legitimate tags without attacking an anonymizer. Availability is a crucial requirement in practice that is often not considered in the design of privacy-preserving RFID systems (see, e.g., [21,23,24]).

Efficiency for tags. Our protocol does *not* require tags to perform public-key cryptography. Hence, in contrast to existing solutions to anonymous tag authentication (see, e.g., [10,12]), our scheme matches the computational capabilities of standard RFID tags.

Outline. We present our anonymous authentication scheme for RFID in Section 2. In Section 3 we analyze the performance of our solution and prove its security in Section 4. Finally, we conclude in Section 5.

2   Our Anonymous RFID Authentication Scheme

Before presenting the details of our protocol, we give an informal description of the protocol, the underlying trust relations and assumptions, and introduce our notation. We formalize the relevant aspects in Section 4.

2.1   System Model

The players in our scheme are (at least) a trusted tag issuer I, a reader R, an anonymizer A and a tag T. We denote the adversary by $\mathcal{A}$. Our scheme consists of two protocols (see Figure 1): the tag authentication and the tag anonymization protocol. The former is executed by R and a tag T and allows R to check if T is legitimate. T is called *legitimate* if it has been initialized by I. The tag anonymization protocol ensures anonymity and untraceability of T by updating the authentication data (i.e., the anonymous credential) of T. Note that we do *not* assume that tags can perform public-key encryption since this exceeds the capabilities of most currently available RFID tags. However, T is assumed to be capable of performing basic cryptographic operations like random number generation, (lightweight) symmetric-key encryption and hashing.

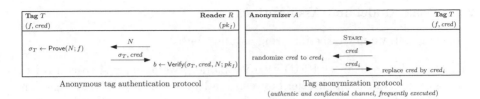

Anonymous tag authentication protocol

Tag anonymization protocol
(authentic and confidential channel, frequently executed)

Fig. 1. Protocol Overview

Each tag T is initialized by I with a tag-specific signing key f and a corresponding anonymous credential *cred*. In the tag authentication protocol, R challenges T to sign a random message N. T returns *cred* and a partial signature σ_T on N, which can be verified using the public key pk_I of I. If the verification succeeds, R has assurance that σ_T has been created by a tag that has been initialized by I. Hereby, the structure of *cred* and σ_T ensures that (i) only I can create a valid *cred* for any secret f, (ii) only a tag that has been initialized by I can create a valid σ_T that can be verified w.r.t. *cred* and pk_I, and (iii) R does not learn any information that allows R to deduce the identity of T.

Since *cred* is included in each partial signature issued by T, *cred* can be used as an identifier of T. This allows to link all partial signatures σ_T issued by T and to trace T. Hence, to provide untraceability of tags, it is crucial that each partial signature σ_T issued by T contains a different *cred*. The construction of *cred* allows to transform (*re-randomize*) *cred* into different anonymous credentials $cred_1, cred_2, \ldots$ for the same secret f without knowing the secret key of I. However, since this transformation requires public-key operations (i.e., exponentiations) it cannot be performed by T. Hence, T must frequently engage the tag anonymization protocol with A, which re-randomizes *cred* for T.

In our scheme we adapt the anonymous credential system proposed in [18]. The scheme of [18] is very promising w.r.t. to anonymizer-enabled RFID systems since it allows to split the signature generation between a constrained device and one with higher capabilities. However, due to the limited computational capabilities of RFID tags, the scheme of [18] cannot be applied directly. Hence, we removed the support for user-controlled anonymity. This means that, our protocol always ensures the unlinkability of all partial signatures issued by a user, whereas the scheme in [18] allows the user to decide to what extend partial signatures can be linked. Moreover, the signing protocol in [18] requires the signer to perform exponentiations, which exceeds the capabilities of most RFID tags in practice. Hence, we employ a similar time-memory tradeoff as used in [29]. This means that part of the exponentiation is precomputed by I and stored on the tag during tag initialization and instead of performing the exponentiation, the tag only needs to compute a few multiplications using the pre-computed values in its memory.

The main security objective of our protocol is anonymous tag authentication. More precisely, R should *only* accept legitimate tags *without* being able to link their transactions (anonymity and unlinkability of tags against readers).

2.2   Trust Model and Assumptions

Following [24], we make the following assumptions:

Adversary $\mathcal{A}$. As in most RFID security models, we assume $\mathcal{A}$ to control the wireless communication channel between readers, anonymizers, and tags. This means that $\mathcal{A}$ can eavesdrop, manipulate, delete and reroute all protocol messages sent by R, A, and T. Moreover, $\mathcal{A}$ can obtain useful information (e.g., by visual observation) on whether R accepted T as a legitimate tag [26,27].

Issuer I. We assume I to be trusted. Moreover, we assume that I initializes tags and readers in a secure environment.

Reader R. We assume that all readers have access to the same information and thus can be subsumed as one single reader entity R. Moreover, R can perform public-key cryptography and can handle multiple instances of the anonymous tag authentication protocol with different tags in parallel. In contrast to [24], we consider R to be untrusted.

Tags T. Each tag T is a passive device: it cannot initiate communication or participate in more then one protocol run at the same time, it has a narrow communication range (i.e., a few centimeters to meters) and erases its temporary state (i.e., all session-specific information and randomness) after it gets out of the reading range (i.e., the electromagnetic field) of R or A. As recently discussed in [28], protocols that preserve the privacy of corrupted tags are often very complex and inefficient and hence, not suitable for most practical RFID applications. Instead, [28] suggests to frequently revoke and to reissue tags at frequent intervals. In this way, the privacy loss of a tag whose secret has been disclosed is limited to only a small time period. Indeed, this is in line with many use cases like electronic tickets, where tags are expected to expire after some time. Moreover, in practice there are several moderately prized RFID tags that are protected against a variety of physical attacks (see, e.g., [30,31]). Further, emerging hardware-based security primitives like Physically Unclonable Funtions (PUFs) enable physical tamper-protection also for low-cost RFID tags (see, e.g., [32,33,34]). Hence, we assume T to be trusted, which means that $\mathcal{A}$ cannot obtain the secrets of T.

Anonymizers A. Anonymizers can perform public-key cryptography and can handle multiple parallel instances of the anonymization protocol with different tags. Similar to readers, we consider anonymizers to be untrusted. Hence, $\mathcal{A}$ can get full control over anonymizers and their secrets. Since a tag T does not posses the required computational resources to update its state, it can always be tracked between two anonymizations. Therefore, we assume that each tag T is frequently anonymized by an honest anonymizer (e.g., every few minutes). In practice, this can be achieved by a personal anonymizer that is trusted by its owner, i.e., the tag user. We stress that in order to eavesdrop on every interaction of a tag with an anonymizer, the adversary must always be within the reading range of the tag.

Due to the limited communication range of typical RFID systems this implies that the adversary is following the user of the tag, which obviously violates the user's privacy even if he does not carry an RFID tag. Hence, we assume that there are executions of the tag anonymization protocol in the absence of $\mathcal{A}$, i.e., where $\mathcal{A}$ cannot tamper with the protocol messages.

2.3 Notation and Preliminaries

For a finite set S, $|S|$ denotes the size of set S whereas for an integer (or a bitstring) n the term $|n|$ means the bit-length of n. The term $s \in_R S$ means the assignment of a uniformly chosen element of S to variable s. Let A be a probabilistic algorithm. Then $y \leftarrow A(x)$ means that on input x, algorithm A assigns its output to variable y. The term $[A(x)]$ denotes the set of all possible outputs of A on input x. $A_K(x)$ means that the output of A depends on x and some additional parameter K (e.g., a secret key). The term $\mathsf{Prot}[A : x_A; \ B : x_B; \ * : x_{pub}] \to [A : y_A; \ B : y_B]$ denotes an interactive protocol Prot between two algorithms A and B. Hereby, A (resp. B) gets a private input x_A (resp. x_B) and a public input x_{pub}. While A (resp. B) is operating, it can interact with B (resp. A). After the protocol terminates, A (resp. B) returns y_A (resp. y_B). Let E be some event (e.g., the result of a security experiment), then $\Pr[E]$ denotes the probability that E occurs. Probability $\epsilon(l)$ is called *negligible* if for all polynomials f it holds that $\epsilon(l) \leq 1/f(l)$ for all sufficiently large l. Probability $1 - \epsilon(l)$ is called *overwhelming* if $\epsilon(l)$ is negligible.

Definition 1 (Admissible Pairing). *Let* $\mathbb{G}_1, \mathbb{G}_2$ *and* $\mathbb{G}_T$ *be three groups of large prime exponent* $q \approx 2^{l_q}$ *for security parameter* $l_q \in \mathbb{N}$. *The groups* $\mathbb{G}_1, \mathbb{G}_2$ *are written additively with identity element* 0 *and the group* $\mathbb{G}_T$ *multiplicatively with identity element* 1. *A pairing is a mapping* $e : \mathbb{G}_1 \times \mathbb{G}_2 \to \mathbb{G}_T$ *that is*

– *bilinear, i.e., for all* $P, P' \in \mathbb{G}_1$ *and all* $Q, Q' \in \mathbb{G}_2$ *it holds that*

$$e(P + P', Q + Q') = e(P, Q) \cdot e(P, Q') \cdot e(P', Q) \cdot e(P', Q') \,.$$

– *non-degenerate, i.e., for all* $P \in \mathbb{G}_1^*$ *there is a* $Q \in \mathbb{G}_2^*$ *(and for all* $Q \in \mathbb{G}_2^*$ *there is a* $P \in \mathbb{G}_1^*$, *respectively) such that* $e(P, Q) \neq 1$.
– *computable, i.e., there is a probabilistic polynomial time (p.p.t.) algorithm that computes* $e(P, Q)$ *for all* $(P, Q) \in \mathbb{G}_1 \times \mathbb{G}_2$.

e is called admissible if $e(P_1, P_2) = g$ *such that* $\langle g \rangle = \mathbb{G}_T$.

We denote with $\mathsf{GenPair}(1^{l_q}) \to (q, \mathbb{G}_1, \mathbb{G}_2, \mathbb{G}_T, P_1, P_2, e)$ an algorithm that on input a security parameter $l_q \in \mathbb{N}$ generates three groups $\mathbb{G}_1$, $\mathbb{G}_2$ and $\mathbb{G}_T$ of large prime exponent q, two generators $\langle P_1 \rangle = \mathbb{G}_1$ and $\langle P_2 \rangle = \mathbb{G}_2$, and an admissible pairing $e : \mathbb{G}_1 \times \mathbb{G}_2 \to \mathbb{G}_T$.

2.4 Protocol Specification

There are three setup protocols where the reader R, anonymizer A and tag T are initialized and their system parameters (e.g., keys) are generated and defined. A protocol between T and A ensures anonymity and unlinkablity of tags whereas a second protocol between T and R covers anonymous tag-to-reader authentication. Moreover, there is an algorithm to revoke tags and anonymizers, respectively.

System initialization: $\mathsf{Init}(1^l) \rightarrow (sk_I, pk_I, \mathsf{RL})$. Given a security parameter $l = (l_q, l_h, l_e, l_n)$ with $l_q, l_h, l_e, l_n \in \mathbb{N}$, I generates the secret parameters sk_I of issuer I and the corresponding public system parameters (pk_I, RL), where DB is a database that contains the authentication secrets of all tags and anonymizers and RL is the revocation list. I generates $(q, \mathbb{G}_1, \mathbb{G}_2, \mathbb{G}_T, P_1, P_2, e) \leftarrow \mathsf{GenPair}(1^{l_q})$, chooses two secret parameters $x, y \in_R \mathbb{Z}_q$, and computes $X \leftarrow xP_2$ and $Y \leftarrow yP_2$ in $\mathbb{G}_2$. Then, I chooses a collision-resistant one-way hash function $\mathsf{Hash}: \{0,1\}^* \rightarrow \{0,1\}^{l_h}$ and initializes the secret database $\mathsf{DB} \leftarrow \emptyset$ and the revocation list $\mathsf{RL} \leftarrow \emptyset$. The secret key of I is $sk_I \leftarrow (x, y, \mathsf{DB})$ while the corresponding public system parameters are $pk_I \leftarrow (l, q, \mathbb{G}_1, \mathbb{G}_2, \mathbb{G}_T, P_1, P_2, e, X, Y, \mathsf{Hash})$ and RL.

Anonymizer setup: $\mathsf{SetupAnon}(A_i) \rightarrow K_i$. The issuer I checks if A_i has already been initialized, i.e., if there is a $(A_i, K_i) \in \mathsf{DB}$ for some K_i. If this is the case, I aborts. Otherwise I generates a symmetric encryption key $K_i \leftarrow \mathsf{GenKey}(1^{l_e})$, adds (A_i, K_i) to DB, and initializes A_i with K_i.

Tag setup: $\mathsf{SetupTag}(A_i, T_j, sk_I) \rightarrow \mathsf{S}_j$. The issuer I first checks that A_i has been initialized but has not been blacklisted. Moreover, I checks that T_j has not already been initialized, i.e., that there is no $(T_j, \mathsf{S}_j, A_i) \in \mathsf{DB}$ (for some S_j and some A_i). If one of these checks fails, then I aborts. Otherwise I generates a secret (signing) key f and a corresponding anonymous credential $cred = (D, E, F)$ for T. Moreover, I precomputes $\mathcal{G}$, t, and h that are used later by T_j in the tag authentication protocol to reduce the amount of computations to be performed by T_j. Therefore, I chooses $f, r \in_R \mathbb{Z}_q$ and computes $D \leftarrow rP_1$, $E \leftarrow yD$, $F \leftarrow (x + xyf)D$, $\beta \leftarrow e(E, X)$, $\mathcal{G} \leftarrow \{\beta_0, \dots, \beta_{l_q-1}\}$ where $\beta_k = \beta^{2^k}$, $t \leftarrow 1$, $h \leftarrow \mathsf{Hash}(D, E, F)$, and $\mathsf{S}_j \leftarrow (f, K_i, \mathcal{G}, D, E, F, t, h)$. Finally, I adds (T_j, S_j, A_i) to DB and initializes T_j with S_j.

Tag authentication: $\mathsf{AuthTag}(T_j : \mathsf{S}_j ; R : \mathsf{RL} ; * : pk_I) \rightarrow (T : - ; R : \mathsf{out}_R)$. The tag authentication protocol is shown in Figure 2. In this protocol, a tag T_j anonymously authenticates to R. Therefore, R challenges T_j to sign a random challenge N_r. Upon receipt of N_r, T_j computes a signature of knowledge $\sigma \leftarrow (D, E, F, v, s)$ (that includes the credential $cred = (D, E, F)$ of T_j) in a similar way as in [18]. However, in our case, T_j uses the time-memory tradeoff of [29] to compute $\tau \leftarrow \beta^{t \cdot z'}$ for $z' \in_R \mathbb{Z}_q$.[1] Hereby, t ensures that the precomputed

---

[1] Consider the square-and-multiply algorithm (SQM), which is a standard algorithm for fast modular exponentiation. Note that the set $\mathcal{G}$ contains the precomputed results of the squaring operations performed by the SQM. Hence, T_j only needs to perform the multiplications of the SQM, which significantly reduces the computational complexity of the exponentiation for T_j.

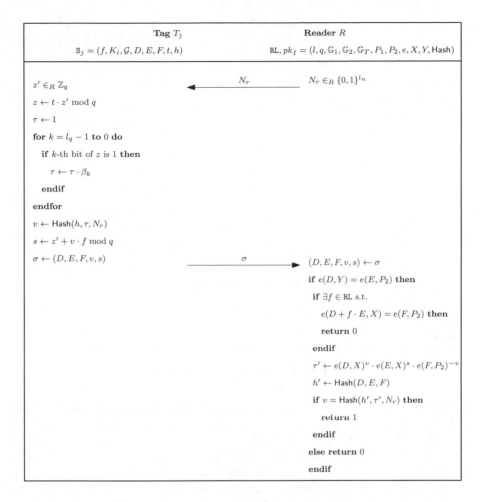

Fig. 2. Anonymous tag authentication protocol

set $\mathcal{G}$ is adjusted to the current randomization of the credential *cred* of T_j (see the tag anonymization protocol that is explained further below). Upon receipt of signature $\sigma = (D, E, F, v, s)$, R verifies that (i) (D, E, F) is a valid (randomized) credential *cred* w.r.t. pk_I, (ii) the secret f that corresponds to (D, E, F) has not been revoked (i.e., T_j has not been added to RL), and (iii) (v, s) is a valid signature of knowledge on N_r w.r.t. (D, E, F) and pk_I. If the verification is successful, then R accepts T_j as a legitimate tag and returns 1. Otherwise R returns 0.

Tag anonymization: $\mathsf{AnonTag}(T_j : \mathsf{S}_j \; ; A_i : K_i \; ; * : pk_I) \rightarrow (T_j : \mathsf{S}'_j \; ; A_i : -)$. In this protocol, an anonymizer A_i updates the credential *cred* $= (D, E, F)$ and the precomputed values (t, h) of T_j that are later used by T_j in the tag authentication protocol. Hereby, A_i and T_j communicate over an authentic and confidential channel based on symmetric encryption. Therefore, K_i, N_i and N_j are used to

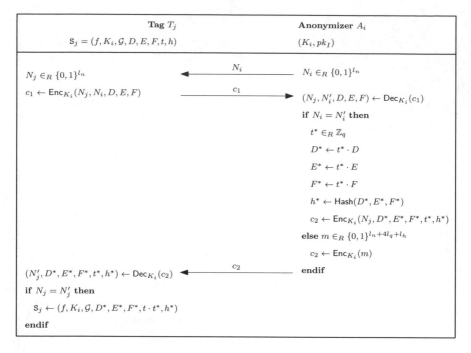

Fig. 3. Tag anonymization protocol

encrypt the communication between A_i and T_j and to mutually authenticate both parties. In the second protocol message, T_j sends its credential $cred = (D, E, F)$ for f to A_i, which re-randomizes it to another credential $cred^* = (D^*, E^*, F^*)$ for f that can still be verified by the public key pk_I of I. Finally, T_j replaces its old credential $cred$ by $cred^*$ and updates h and t such that in the tag authentication protocol T_j can adjust $\mathcal{G}$ to the new credential $cred^*$ (see the tag authentication protocol explained in the previous paragraph). The tag anonymization protocol is shown in Figure 3.

Tag revocation: $\mathsf{RevTag}(T_j, \mathsf{S}_j) \to \mathsf{RL}'$. To revoke a tag T_j, I first checks if there is a $(T_j, \mathsf{S}_j, A_i) \in \mathsf{DB}$ for some $\mathsf{S}_j = (f, K_i, \mathcal{G}, D, E, F, t, h)$ and some A_i. If this is the case, then I adds (T_j, f) to the revocation list RL, and sends RL to R using an authentic channel.

Anonymizer revocation: $\mathsf{RevAnon}(A_i)$. To revoke an anonymizer A_i, I first checks if there is a $(A_i, K_i) \in \mathsf{DB}$ for some K_i. If this is the case, then I blacklists A_i and removes (A_i, K_i) from DB.

3   Performance Evaluation

Note that the tag user does not notice the interaction between the anonymizer and a tag, whereas tag authentication usually requires the user to wait (e.g., at a door or gate) until the authentication protocol completes. Thus, most practical applications have strict time constraints on the identification protocol (see, e.g., [19,3]) while there are no critical constraints on the tag anonymization protocol. Moreover, compared to a tag, the reader possesses much more computing power. Hence, in this section, we only focus on the resources required by the tag to execute the tag authentication protocol. In particular, we consider the computational, communication and memory effort of the tag.

Computation. The tag authentication protocol requires the tag to generate l_q random bits, to perform two multiplications and one addition in $\mathbb{Z}_q$, $(l_q - 1)/2$ multiplications in $\mathbb{G}_T$ (on average), and one hash digest. Compared to a plain exponentiation, the time-memory tradeoff of [29] saves l_q squarings in $\mathbb{G}_T$, which are precomputed by the issuer I and stored in the memory of the tag when the tag is initialized. Note that these precomputed values can be reused in each tag authentication protocol run. To achieve a security level that is comparable to RSA 1024 bit, a reasonable choice for the security parameters is $l_q = 154$ [35], $l_e = l_n = 128$, and $l_h = 160$ [36].

Communication. The tag authentication protocol requires to send an l_n bit random value from R to T and three elements of $\mathbb{G}_1$, one l_h bit hash digest, and one element of $\mathbb{Z}_q$ from T to R. Hence, the total communication complexity of the tag authentication protocol is $l_n + 3l_{\mathbb{G}_1} + l_h + l_q$ bits, where $l_{\mathbb{G}_1}$ is the size (in bits) of an element of $\mathbb{G}_1$. For the choice of parameters discussed above $l_{\mathbb{G}_1} = 308$, which means that the total communication complexity of the tag authentication protocol is 1366 bits.

Memory. Each tag must store two elements of $\mathbb{Z}_q$, one l_e-bit key, l_q elements of $\mathbb{G}_T$, three elements of $\mathbb{G}_1$, and one l_h-bit hash digest. This means that each tag must store $2l_q + l_e + l_q \cdot l_{\mathbb{G}_T} + 3l_{\mathbb{G}_1} + l_h$ bits in total, where $l_{\mathbb{G}_T}$ is the size (in bits) of an element of $\mathbb{G}_T$. For the parameter choices discussed above $l_{\mathbb{G}_T} = 923$, which means that each tag must store about 17.6 kByte of data.

   Although we solved the problem of reducing the computational costs for the RFID tags to match the capabilities of existing tags, the memory requirements of our scheme still need further optimization.[2] To solve this memory issue, we are currently working on a memory-efficient solution where we hope that it fits the memory constraints of existing RFID tags.

4   Security Analysis

To prove the security of our scheme we need some intractability assumptions, which we introduce in the following.

---

[2] Most currently available RFID tags in practice (like MiFare Plus [2] that is used in electronic ticketing systems) can perform symmetric encryption (DES, 3DES, AES), keyed hashing based on encryption, generate random numbers, and provide up to 8 kByte of memory.

Definition 2 (Bilinear LRSW Assumption [18]). *Let $l \in \mathbb{N}$ be a security parameter, $pk_e \leftarrow \mathsf{GenPair}(1^l)$ where $pk_e = (q, \mathbb{G}_1, \mathbb{G}_2, \mathbb{G}_T, P_1, P_2, e)$, $x, y \in_R \mathbb{Z}_q$, $X \leftarrow xP_2$, and $Y \leftarrow yP_2$. Moreover, let $\mathcal{O}_{X,Y}$ be an oracle that on input $f \in \mathbb{Z}_q$ outputs a triple $\big(D, yD, (x + fxy)D\big)$ where $D \in_R \mathbb{G}_1$. Let Q be the set of oracle queries made to $\mathcal{O}_{X,Y}$. The Bilinear LRSW Assumption is that for every p.p.t. adversary $\mathcal{A}$ and every $(f, D, E, F) \in \big[\mathcal{A}^{\mathcal{O}_{X,Y}}(pk_e, X, Y)\big]$ it holds that*

$$\Pr\big[f \notin Q \wedge f \in \mathbb{Z}_q^* \wedge D \in \mathbb{G}_1 \wedge E = yD \wedge F = (x + fxy)D\big]$$

is negligible in l.

Definition 3 (DDH Assumption [18]). *Let $l \in \mathbb{N}$ be a security parameter, $pk_e \leftarrow \mathsf{GenPair}(1^l)$, where $pk_e = (q, \mathbb{G}_1, \mathbb{G}_2, \mathbb{G}_T, P_1, P_2, e)$, $x, y \in_R \mathbb{Z}_q$, $X \leftarrow xP_1$, $Y \leftarrow yP_1$, and $Z \in_R \mathbb{G}_1$. The Decisional Diffie-Hellman Assumption in $\mathbb{G}_1$ is that every p.p.t. adversary $\mathcal{A}$ has negligible (in l) advantage*

$$\mathbf{Adv}_{\mathcal{A}}^{\mathrm{DDH}} = \big| \Pr\big[1 \leftarrow \mathcal{A}(pk_e, X, Y, xyP_1)\big] - \Pr\big[1 \leftarrow \mathcal{A}(pk_e, X, Y, Z)\big]\big|.$$

Definition 4 (Real-or-Random Indistinguishability [38]). *Consider an encryption scheme $(\mathsf{GenKey}, \mathsf{Enc}, \mathsf{Dec})$, where GenKey is the key generation, Enc is the encryption, and Dec is the decryption algorithm. Moreover, let $K \leftarrow \mathsf{GenKey}(1^l)$ for a security parameter $l \in \mathbb{N}$. Further, let $\mathcal{O}_{\mathrm{RoR}}^b$ be an oracle that when queried with a message m returns either $\mathsf{Enc}_K(m)$ if $b = 0$ and $\mathsf{Enc}_K(m')$ for a randomly chosen message m' if $b = 1$. An encryption scheme is said to be real-or-random indistinguishable if every p.p.t. adversary $\mathcal{A}$ has at most negligible (in l) advantage*

$$\mathbf{Adv}_{\mathcal{A}}^{\mathrm{RoR}} = \big| \Pr\big[1 \leftarrow \mathcal{A}^{\mathcal{O}_{\mathrm{RoR}}^0}\big] - \Pr\big[1 \leftarrow \mathcal{A}^{\mathcal{O}_{\mathrm{RoR}}^1}\big]\big|$$

Now we formally define and prove tag authentication and unlinkability of tags for our protocol.

4.1   Tag Authentication

Tag authentication means that an adversary $\mathcal{A}$ should not be able to make an honest reader R to accept $\mathcal{A}$ as a legitimate tag. We formalize tag authentication by a security experiment $\mathbf{Exp}_{\mathcal{A}}^{\mathrm{aut}} = \mathsf{out}_R^\pi$, where a p.p.t. adversary $\mathcal{A}$ must make an honest R to authenticate $\mathcal{A}$ as some legitimate tag T_j by returning $\mathsf{out}_R^\pi = 1$ in some instance π of the tag authentication protocol $\mathsf{AuthTag}$. Hereby, $\mathcal{A}$ can arbitrarily interact with the RFID system. However, since in general it is not possible to prevent simple relay attacks, $\mathcal{A}$ is not allowed to just forward all messages from T_j to R in instance π.[3] This means that at least some of the protocol messages that made R to accept must have been (partly) computed by $\mathcal{A}$ without knowing the secrets of T_j.

---

[3] Note that simple relay attacks can be mitigated by distance bounding techniques. However, for simplicity we excluded relay attacks because the main focus of this paper is anonymous authentication against malicious readers.

Definition 5 (Tag Authentication). *An RFID system achieves tag authentication if for every p.p.t. adversary $\mathcal{A}$ $\Pr[\mathbf{Exp}_{\mathcal{A}}^{\text{aut}} = 1]$ is negligible in l.*

Theorem 1. *The RFID scheme described in Section 2.4 achieves tag authentication (Definition 5) in the random oracle model under the Bilinear LRSW Assumption (Definition 2).*

Proof (Theorem 1, Sketch). Assume by contradiction that $\mathcal{A}$ is an adversary such that $\Pr[\mathbf{Exp}_{\mathcal{A}}^{\text{aut}} = 1]$ is non-negligible. In the following, we show how to use $\mathcal{A}$ to construct an adversary that either violates the Bilinear LRSW Assumption (Definition 2) or the collision-resistance of the underlying hash function.

Note that $\mathbf{Exp}_{\mathcal{A}}^{\text{aut}} = 1$ implies that $\mathcal{A}$ computed some protocol message (D, E, F, v, s) for a given reader challenge N_r such that $e(D, Y) = e(E, P_2)$ and $v = \mathsf{Hash}(h, \tau, N_r)$, where $h = \mathsf{Hash}(D, E, F)$ and $\tau = e(D, X)^v \cdot e(E, X)^s \cdot e(F, P_2)^{-v}$. Hereby, $\mathcal{A}$ has two possibilities: (i) reuse a credential (D, E, F) from a previous tag authentication protocol run or (ii) create a new (forged) credential (D, E, F). In the following, we show that if $\mathcal{A}$ is successful in the first case, then $\mathcal{A}$ can be used to find a collision of Hash, which contradicts the assumption that Hash is a random oracle. Moreover, if $\mathcal{A}$ is successful in the second case, then $\mathcal{A}$ can be used to violate the Bilinear LRSW Assumption (Definition 2). Hence, the random oracle property of Hash and the Bilinear LRSW Assumption (Definition 2) ensure that $\Pr[\mathbf{Exp}_{\mathcal{A}}^{\text{aut}} = 1]$ is negligible.

CASE 1: $\mathcal{A}$ *reuses an old credential.* Assume by contradiction that $\mathcal{A}$ uses (a randomized version of) a credential (D', E', F') from a previous transcript $\left(N_r', (D', E', F', v', s')\right)$ of the tag authentication protocol to forge a signature (v, s) on a new reader challenge N_r. Note that $\Pr[N_r = N_r']$ is negligible since N_r is uniformly chosen at random in each execution of the tag authentication protocol. Hence, if R accepts an old signature (v', s') for a new challenge N_r, then with overwhelming probability $v' = \mathsf{Hash}(h', \tau', N_r') = \mathsf{Hash}(h', \tau', N_r)$ such that $N_r \neq N_r'$. This means that $\mathcal{A}$ found a collision of Hash. However, since Hash is assumed to be collision-resistant, this can only happen with negligible probability. Therefore, $\mathcal{A}$ must have computed a new signature of knowledge (v, s) such that $v = \mathsf{Hash}(h', \tau, N_r)$ and $s = z' + v \cdot f \bmod q$ where $\tau = e(E', X)^{z' \cdot t}$. Note that (v, s) includes a proof of knowledge of a value f such that $e(D' + f \cdot E', X) = e(F', P_2)$, which is a standard Σ-protocol for proving knowledge of a discrete logarithm. It follows from the proof-of-knowledge property that, if $\mathcal{A}$ can compute a valid (v, s), then there is a p.p.t. algorithm (knowledge extractor) that can extract f from $\mathcal{A}$. This implies that $\mathcal{A}$ knows f. However, $\mathcal{A}$ can guess f only with negligible probability. Hence, the proof-of-knowledge property ensures that $\mathcal{A}$ can forge a signature (v, s) on a message N_r for a given credential (D, E, F) only with negligible probability.

CASE 2: $\mathcal{A}$ *creates a new credential.* Assume that $\mathcal{A}$ can construct a tuple (D, E, F, v, s) where (D, E, F) is *not* (a randomized version of) a credential from a previous tag authentication protocol. In the following, we show that $\mathcal{A}$

can be used to construct an adversary $\mathcal{A}_{bLRSW}$ against the Bilinear LRSW Assumption (Definition 2). Given access to oracle $\mathcal{O}_{X,Y}$ and the public parameters $pk_{bLRSW} = (q, \mathbb{G}_1, \mathbb{G}_2, \mathbb{G}_T, P_1, P_2, e, X, Y)$, $\mathcal{A}_{bLRSW}$ simulates the initialization algorithm Init of the RFID system to $\mathcal{A}$ as specified in Section 2.4 but uses pk_{bLRSW} to construct pk_I. Note that $\mathcal{A}_{bLRSW}$ does *not* know the secret parameters (x, y) of the simulation of the RFID system, which are required for the simulation of the SetupTag algorithm. However, $\mathcal{A}_{bLRSW}$ can simulate SetupTag with the help of $\mathcal{O}_{X,Y}$. Instead of using (x, y) to compute the credential for the tag to be initialized, $\mathcal{A}_{bLRSW}$ chooses $f \in_R \mathbb{Z}_q$ and queries $\mathcal{O}_{X,Y}(f)$, which responds with a tuple $\big(D, yD, (x + fxy)D\big)$. Note that by definition of $\mathcal{O}_{X,Y}$ $D \in_R \mathbb{G}_1$, which means that D can be expressed as $D = rP_1$ where $r \in_R \mathbb{Z}_q$. Therefore, the output generated by $\mathcal{O}_{X,Y}$ is a valid credential and hence, the simulation of SetupTag is perfect. Moreover, $\mathcal{A}_{bLRSW}$ can perfectly simulate all other algorithms and protocols of the RFID system since they do not require knowledge of (x, y). Thus, after a polynomial number of queries to $\mathcal{A}_{bLRSW}$, $\mathcal{A}$ returns a protocol message (D, E, F, v, s) for a given N_r that makes R to return $\mathsf{out}_R = 1$. Since (v, s) includes a proof of knowledge of a value f such that $e(D + f \cdot E, X) = e(F, P_2)$, $\mathcal{A}_{bLRSW}$ can use the corresponding knowledge extractor to extract f from $\mathcal{A}$. Finally, $\mathcal{A}_{bLRSW}$ returns a tuple (f, D, E, F). Since (D, E, F) is not (a randomized version of) a credential from a previous tag authentication protocol, it holds that $\mathcal{O}_{X,Y}$ has never been queried for the corresponding secret f. Hence, (f, D, E, F) is a valid solution to the Bilinear LRSW problem, which is a contradiction to the Bilinear LRSW Assumption (Definition 2). Hence, $\mathcal{A}$ can generate a valid tuple (D, E, F, v, s) for a given message N_r that is not based on an existing credential only with negligible probability.

$\square$

4.2   Unlinkability of Tags

Unlinkability means that an adversary $\mathcal{A}$ cannot distinguish tags based on their communication.[4] This means that the protocol messages generated by tags should not leak any information to $\mathcal{A}$ that allows $\mathcal{A}$ to identify or trace them. We formalize tag authentication by a security experiment $\mathbf{Exp}_{\mathcal{A}}^{prv\text{-}b}$ for $b \in_R \{0, 1\}$, where a p.p.t. adversary $\mathcal{A}$ interacts with an oracle $\mathcal{O}_b$ that either represents two identical ($b = 0$) or two different ($b = 1$) legitimate tags T_0 and T_1. Hereby, $\mathcal{A}$ can arbitrarily interact with the RFID system and $\mathcal{O}_b$. However, to exclude trivial attacks (e.g., denial-of-service attacks), $\mathcal{A}$ is not allowed to corrupt an anonymizer nor to disturb the anonymization protocol (see Section 2.2). Finally $\mathcal{A}$ returns a bit b'.

Definition 6. *An RFID system achieves unlinkability if for every p.p.t. adversary $\mathcal{A}$ $\mathbf{Adv}_{\mathcal{A}}^{prv} = \big| \Pr\big[\mathbf{Exp}_{\mathcal{A}}^{prv\text{-}0} = 1\big] - \Pr\big[\mathbf{Exp}_{\mathcal{A}}^{prv\text{-}1} = 1\big]\big|$ is negligible in l.*

Theorem 2. *The RFID scheme described in Section 2.4 achieves unlikability (Definition 6) in the random oracle model under the Decisional Diffie-Hellman*

---

[4] Note that unlinkability implies anonymity since an adversary who can identify tags can also trace them.

Assumption in $\mathbb{G}_1$ *(Definition 3) if the underlying encryption scheme is real-or-random indistinguishable (Definition 4).*

Proof (Theorem 2, Sketch). Recall that unlinkability (Definition 6) requires that $\mathcal{A}$ cannot distinguish whether $\mathcal{O}_b$ represents two identical or two different tags. We show that if $\mathcal{A}$ has non-negligible advantage $\mathbf{Adv}_{\mathcal{A}}^{\mathrm{prv}}$, then $\mathcal{A}$ can be used to break the DDH-Assumption in $\mathbb{G}_1$ (Definition 3) or the real-or-random indistinguishability of the encryption scheme. For this purpose, we show that (i) the communication between tags and anonymizers does not leak any information that helps $\mathcal{A}$ to distinguish, and (ii) that executions of the tag authentication protocol cannot be linked.

For the first claim, we show that the advantage $\mathbf{Adv}_{\mathcal{A}}^{\mathrm{prv}}$ of $\mathcal{A}$ does not change whether $\mathcal{A}$ can eavesdrop executions of the tag anonymization protocol AnonTag or not. Here, we use the standard approach of game hopping. Let G_0 be the scenario, where $\mathcal{A}$ interacts with the real RFID system. More precisely, we consider a hypothetical simulator $\mathcal{S}_0$ that honestly simulates the whole RFID system to $\mathcal{A}$. Obviously, $\mathcal{A}$ has advantage $\mathbf{Adv}_{\mathcal{A}}^{\mathrm{prv}}$ in this case.

Next, we consider the game G_1 that is played by a simulator $\mathcal{S}_1$, which behaves exactly like $\mathcal{S}_0$ with the following difference: whenever a tag T_j runs the tag anonymization protocol with some anonymizer A_i, $\mathcal{S}_1$ replaces the ciphertexts c_1 and c_2 by dummy encryptions c_1' and c_2' that are constructed as explained further below. Observe that $\mathcal{S}_1$ ensures that T_j and A_i perform the same computations as if they received the correct ciphertexts c_1 and c_2. The encryptions c_1' and c_2' are generated as follows: in parallel to the execution of the anonymization protocol between T_j and A_i, a second instance of the tag anonymization protocol is honestly executed between some other tag $T_{j'}$ where $j' \neq j$ and an anonymizer $A_{i'}$ (which can be equal to A_i). The dummy encryptions c_1' and c_2' occurring in this second protocol-run are used as a replacement for c_1 and c_2. At the end of this second protocol-run, the involved tag is reset to its state before the protocol execution.[5] This ensures that encryptions of only well-formed plaintexts are transmitted. The only difference from an attacker's point of view is that in G_0 the correct (or real) plaintexts are encrypted, while in G_1 only randomly chosen (but well-formed) plaintexts are encrypted. If the advantage $\mathbf{Adv}_{\mathcal{A}}^{\mathrm{prv}}$ of $\mathcal{A}$ significantly differs in G_0 and G_1, then $\mathcal{A}$ can be turned into a real-or-random distinguisher for the underlying encryption scheme (see Definition 4). Thus, since the encryption scheme is assumed to be real-or-random indistinguishable, the difference of the advantage of $\mathcal{A}$ in G_0 and G_1 is negligible.

Finally, we define the game G_2 to be as G_1 with the only difference that an attacker $\mathcal{A}$ is not allowed to see the messages exchanged in any instance of the tag anonymization protocol. Since the dummy encryptions in G_1 are by definition *independent* of the computations and values used in the tag anonymization protocol and since the random value N_i is *not* used in the computations that update the tag state S_j, an attacker does not gain any useful information by

---

[5] Alternatively, we can consider a pair of tag and anonymizer that is created outside the system, i.e., that are never reported to $\mathcal{A}$, and that are only used for generating dummy ciphertexts.

eavesdropping the tag anonymization protocol. More precisely, any attacker in G_2 can be easily turned into an attacker in G_1 and vice versa by adding or removing dummy encryptions. Thus, the maximum possible advantage for linking is the same in G_1 and G_2. In particular, the communication between tags and anonymizers does not leak any useful information, which proves the first claim.

Now we show that executions of the anonymous tag authentication protocol AuthTag cannot be linked. With $\sigma[f, cred(f)]$ we denote a signature σ that has been generated by $\mathcal{O}_b$ using the secret signing key f and the credential $cred(f)$ on signing key f. Let f_0 be the signing key of T_0 and f_1 be the key of T_1. Note that both T_0 and T_1 are simulated by $\mathcal{O}_b$. In the following, we show that the distributions $\Delta = \langle \sigma_0[f_0, cred(f_0)], \sigma_1[f_0, cred(f_0)] \rangle$ and $\Delta' = \langle \sigma_2[f_0, cred(f_0)], \sigma_3[f_1, cred(f_1)] \rangle$ are computationally indistinguishable. More precisely, we show that if $\mathcal{A}$ can distinguish between Δ and Δ' with non-negligible advantage $\mathbf{Adv}_{\mathcal{A}}^{prv}$, then $\mathcal{A}$ can be used to construct an algorithm $\mathcal{A}_{DDH}$ that violates the DDH-Assumption in $\mathbb{G}_1$ (Definition 3).

Let (D_i, E_i, F_i) be the credential used to compute a signature σ_i. Note that all credentials (D_i, E_i, F_i) for $i \in \{0, 1, 2\}$ are randomizations of the credential $cred(f_0)$. Hence, $F_i = \alpha D_i$ for $i \in \{0, 1\}$ and $\alpha = x + xyf_0$. Moreover, for all signatures in Δ there is a $\gamma \in \mathbb{Z}$ such that $D_1 = \gamma D_0$. Similarly, all credentials (D_3, E_3, F_3) are randomized versions of $cred(f_1)$ and $F_3 = \alpha' D_3$ for $\alpha' = x + xyf_1$. Further, for all signatures in Δ' there is a $\gamma' \in \mathbb{Z}$ such that $D_3 = \gamma' D_2$. Note that for all signatures in Δ it holds that $(F_0, D_1, F_1) = (\alpha D_0, \gamma D_0, \alpha\gamma D_0)$ is a DDH-tuple, while this is *not* true for the signatures $(F_2, D_3, F_3) = (\alpha D_2, \gamma' D_2, \alpha'\gamma' D_2)$ in Δ'. However, the DDH-Assumption in $\mathbb{G}_1$ (Definition 3) ensures that both distributions Δ and Δ' are computationally indistinguishable. Hence, $\mathcal{A}$ cannot link tags based on their communication in the tag authentication protocol, which finishes the proof.   □

5   Conclusion

In this paper, we presented an RFID system that enables cost-effective anonymous authentication of RFID tags to readers. Our protocol enables RFID tags to authenticate to readers without disclosing any information that allows the identification or tracking of tags even to honest readers. This is often sufficient or even required by privacy regulations or laws for many RFID-based access control systems such as electronic tickets in practice. Our protocol is based on the anonymous credential system proposed in [18], which we adapted to the capabilities of current RFIDs in practice. For this purpose, we employ anonymizers and use a similar time-memory tradeoff as proposed in [29]. As a first step, we solved the problem of reducing the computational costs for the RFID tags to match the capabilities of current mid-range tags. However, the memory requirements of our scheme still need further optimization. We are currently working on a memory-efficient solution where we hope that it fits the memory constraints of existing RFID tags by adapting the recently presented anonymous authentication protocol in [37] to RFID. Moreover, our current solution does not capture availability and protection against cloning, which are interesting open problems for future research.

Acknowledgements. This work has been supported in part by the European Commission through the FP7 programme under contract 216646 ECRYPT II and 238811 UNIQUE.

References

1. Atmel Corporation: Innovative IDIC solutions (2007), http://www.atmel.com/dyn/resources/prod_documents/doc4602.pdf
2. NXP Semiconductors: MIFARE Smartcard ICs (September 2008), http://www.mifare.net/products/smartcardics/
3. Sadeghi, A.R., Visconti, I., Wachsmann, C.: User privacy in transport systems based on RFID e-tickets. International Workshop on Privacy in Location-Based Applications (PiLBA), Malaga, Spain (October 9, 2008)
4. Organization, I.C.A.: Machine Readable Travel Documents, Doc 9303, Part 1 Machine Readable Passports, 5 (edn.) (2003)
5. Weis, S.A., Sarma, S.E., Rivest, R.L., Engels, D.W.: Security and privacy aspects of low-cost radio frequency identification systems. In: Hutter, D., Müller, G., Stephan, W., Ullmann, M. (eds.) Security in Pervasive Computing. LNCS, vol. 2802, pp. 50–59. Springer, Heidelberg (2004)
6. Juels, A.: RFID security and privacy: A research survey. Journal of Selected Areas in Communication 24(2), 381–395 (2006)
7. Sadeghi, A.R., Visconti, I., Wachsmann, C.: Location privacy in RFID applications. In: Bettini, C., Jajodia, S., Samarati, P., Wang, X.S. (eds.) Privacy in Location-Based Applications. LNCS, vol. 5599, pp. 127–150. Springer, Heidelberg (2009)
8. Sadeghi, A.R., Visconti, I., Wachsmann, C.: On RFID privacy with mutual authentication and tag corruption. In: Zhou, J. (ed.) ACNS 2010. LNCS, vol. 6123, pp. 493–510. Springer, Heidelberg (2010)
9. Avoine, G.: RFID Lounge (April 2010), http://www.avoine.net/rfid/
10. Heydt-Benjamin, T.S., Chae, H.J., Defend, B., Fu, K.: Privacy for Public Transportation. In: Danezis, G., Golle, P. (eds.) PET 2006. LNCS, vol. 4258, pp. 1–19. Springer, Heidelberg (2006)
11. Blass, E.O., Kurmus, A., Molva, R., Strufe, T.: PSP: Private and secure payment with RFID. Cryptology ePrint Archive, Report 2009/181 (2009)
12. Bichsel, P., Camenisch, J., Groß, T., Shoup, V.: Anonymous credentials on a standard Java Card. In: Proceedings of the 11th ACM Conference on Computer and Communications Security, pp. 600–610. ACM Press, New York (2009)
13. Avoine, G., Lauradoux, C., Martin, T.: When compromised readers meet RFID. In: RFIDSec 2009 (2009)
14. Garcia, F.D., van Rossum, P.: Modeling privacy for off-line RFID systems. In: RFIDSec 2009 (2009)
15. Nithyanand, R., Tsudik, G., Uzun, E.: Readers behaving badly: Reader revocation in PKI-based RFID systems. Cryptology ePrint Archive, Report 2009/465 (2009)
16. Camenisch, J., Lysyanskaya, A.: A signature scheme with efficient protocols. In: Cimato, S., Galdi, C., Persiano, G. (eds.) SCN 2002. LNCS, vol. 2576, pp. 268–289. Springer, Heidelberg (2003)

17. Camenisch, J., Lysyanskaya, A.: Signature schemes and anonymous credentials from bilinear maps. In: Franklin, M. (ed.) CRYPTO 2004. LNCS, vol. 3152, pp. 56–72. Springer, Heidelberg (2004)
18. Chen, L., Morrissey, P., Smart, N.P.: DAA: Fixing the pairing based protocols. Cryptology ePrint Archive, Report 2009/198 (2009)
19. Spirtech: CALYPSO functional specification: Card application, version 1.3. (October 2005), http://calypso.spirtech.net/
20. Juels, A., Pappu, R.: Squealing Euros: Privacy protection in RFID-enabled banknotes. In: Wright, R.N. (ed.) FC 2003. LNCS, vol. 2742, pp. 103–121. Springer, Heidelberg (2003)
21. Golle, P., Jakobsson, M., Juels, A., Syverson, P.: Universal re-encryption for mixnets. In: Okamoto, T. (ed.) CT-RSA 2004. LNCS, vol. 2964, pp. 163–178. Springer, Heidelberg (2004)
22. Saito, J., Ryou, J.C., Sakurai, K.: Enhancing privacy of universal re-encryption scheme for RFID tags. In: Yang, L.T., Guo, M., Gao, G.R., Jha, N.K. (eds.) EUC 2004. LNCS, vol. 3207, pp. 879–890. Springer, Heidelberg (2004)
23. Ateniese, G., Camenisch, J., de Medeiros, B.: Untraceable RFID tags via insubvertible encryption. In: Proceedings of the 12th ACM Conference on Computer and Communications Security, pp. 92–101. ACM Press, New York (2005)
24. Sadeghi, A.R., Visconti, I., Wachsmann, C.: Anonymizer-enabled security and privacy for RFID. In: Garay, J.A., Miyaji, A., Otsuka, A. (eds.) CANS 2009. LNCS, vol. 5888, pp. 134–153. Springer, Heidelberg (2009)
25. Avoine, G.: Adversarial model for radio frequency identification. Cryptology ePrint Archive, Report 2005/049 (2005)
26. Juels, A., Weis, S.A.: Defining strong privacy for RFID. Cryptology ePrint Archive, Report 2006/137 (2006)
27. Vaudenay, S.: On privacy models for RFID. In: Kurosawa, K. (ed.) ASIACRYPT 2007. LNCS, vol. 4833, pp. 68–87. Springer, Heidelberg (2007)
28. Burmester, M., Le, T.V., Medeiros, B.D., Tsudik, G.: Universally composable RFID identification and authentication protocols. ACM Transactions on Information and System Security (TISSEC) 12(4) (2009)
29. Liu, J.K., Baek, J., Zhou, J., Yang, Y., Wong, J.W.: Efficient online/offline identity-based signature for wireless sensor network. Cryptology ePrint Archive, Report 2010/003 (2010)
30. Atmel Corporation: Secure RFID: CryptoRF (July 2009), http://www.atmel.com/products/SecureRF
31. NXP Semiconductors: MiFare SmartMX (July 2009), http://www.mifare.net/products/smartcardics/smartmx.asp
32. Tuyls, P., Batina, L.: RFID-tags for anti-counterfeiting. In: Pointcheval, D. (ed.) CT-RSA 2006. LNCS, vol. 3860, pp. 115–131. Springer, Heidelberg (2006)
33. Bolotnyy, L., Robins, G.: Physically unclonable function-based security and privacy in RFID systems. In: Proceedings of the Fifth IEEE International Conference on Pervasive Computing and Communications, pp. 211–220. IEEE Computer Society, Los Alamitos (2007)
34. Devadas, S., Suh, E., Paral, S., Sowell, R., Ziola, T., Khandelwal, V.: Design and implementation of PUF-based unclonable RFID ICs for anti-counterfeiting and security applications. In: IEEE International Conference on RFID 2008, Las Vegas, NV, USA, April 16–17, pp. 58–64. IEEE Computer Society, Los Alamitos (2008)

35. Boneh, D., Lynn, B., Shacham, H.: Short signatures from the Weil pairing. In: Boyd, C. (ed.) ASIACRYPT 2001. LNCS, vol. 2248, pp. 514–532. Springer, Heidelberg (2001)
36. Smart, N.: D.SPA.7 ECRYPT2 yearly report on algorithms and keysizes (2008-2009), http://www.ecrypt.eu.org/documents/D.SPA.7.pdf (August 2008)
37. Chen, L., Page, D., Smart, N.: On the design and implementation of an efficient DAA scheme. In: Gollmann, D., Lanet, J.-L., Iguchi-Cartigny, J. (eds.) CARDIS 2010. LNCS, vol. 6035, pp. 223–237. Springer, Heidelberg (2010)
38. Bellare, M., Desai, A., Jokipii, E., Rogawayy, P.: A concrete security treatment of symmetric encryption: Analysis of the DES modes of operation. In: Proceedings of the 38th Symposium on Foundations of Computer Science. IEEE, Los Alamitos (1997)

Leakage-Resilient RFID Authentication with Forward-Privacy

Shin'ichiro Matsuo[1], Le Trieu Phong[1], Miyako Ohkubo[1], and Moti Yung[2,3]

[1] National Institute of Information and Communications Technology (NICT), Japan
[2] Columbia University
[3] Google Inc.

Abstract. Low power devices, such as smart-card and RFID-tags, will be used around our life including in commercial and financial activities. A prime application of such devices is entity authentication in pervasive environment. The obvious concerns in this environment involves getting security against tag-forgery (even by adversary controlled readers) and, on the other hand, giving users privacy against linking of different authentication transcripts. Many cryptographic protocols have realizes such requirements. However, there is no scheme which realizes, both, forward-privacy and tag-forgery right after some leakage is occurred. Since some devices among the huge quantity of expected devices will surely be compromised, it seems highly important, from an engineering point of view, to deal with limited damage of such exposures. In this paper, we address the gap by proposing the first RFID scheme that realizes both requirements.

Keywords: RFID authentication, leakage-resilience and forward-privacy.

1 Introduction

1.1 Background

In coming years, more and more devices are going to be put at the hand of consumers, and are and will be used for authentication (smartcards, RFID-tags, etc.) for applications combining cyber as well as the physical world like point-of-sale authentication during shopping. This new technology poses increasingly important security and privacy issues. In these environments, cryptographic authentication protocols are used by users holding devices (e.g. mobile phones) with smart-cards and RFID-tags. They are also used for many services such as digital cash, transportation card and key-less entry system. As a consequence, these protocols become fundamentals of our activities and physical security.

In this integrated world, a typical inter-collaboration is performed between servers with huge computational power and a huge number of low-end devices. The weakest link in this environment is the low-end devices and it is crucial to provide security to the device and simultaneously privacy to its user, and mitigate properly security failure of some devices. Thus, main considerations

S.B. Ors Yalcin (Ed.): RFIDSec 2010, LNCS 6370, pp. 176–188, 2010.
© Springer-Verlag Berlin Heidelberg 2010

in RFID-tag authentication schemes are achieving tag-unforgeability as well as forward-privacy using modest computational resources. For authentication purpose, we must prevent forgery (where a forged tag is authenticated as valid). This requirement is general for authentication protocol.

Furthermore, a special requirement for RFID authentication, since it indicates location of the tag in the real world, is preserving privacy. In particular, two types of privacy are considered in previous researches. The first one is personal information disclosure. Namely, obtaining identifier from the tag (for example, we can obtain names of goods, amount of money a person posses and the name of a person, if the tag records and give them as answers for tag-reader). This privacy issue can be prevented by encrypting the data by using secure cryptographic algorithm. However, if we use deterministic algorithm for such encryption, the second type of privacy issue, that of tracing, occurs. If an adversary reads the same tag at two different times, he can trace activity of the owner of the tag by linking different protocol messages sent from the tag. Thus, "unlinkability" is also required for RFID-tag authentication protocol.

Let us elaborate on the intuition of unlinkability. Namely, it ensures past protocol messages are kept unlinkable *even when* the tag is corrupted and its internal state is given to the adversary. This is the standard "forward privacy" notion, first introduced by Ohkubo, Suzuki and Kinoshita in [20]. The OSK scheme was analysed in the random oracle model where hash functions are treated as truly random ones. We note that forward privacy is a stringent notion, so there are only a few schemes satisfying it, among which let us mention the works [4,3].

Another important concern is about the limited computational power of RFID tags. Generally, the tags have relatively limited capability of computation compared to personal computers and smart-phones. The limitation is inherent from their gate sizes and power supply, which is of greatly small amount. As a consequence, it is difficult for RFID-tags to perform public-key cryptography which requires modulo exponentiations. Also, it is not easy to execute cryptographic algorithms in RFID-tags. We therefore assume that allowed computations for the RFID-tags are XOR operations, small stream ciphers, small block ciphers and resulting hash functions (for example, Bogdanov et al [5] showed that 128-bit output hash functions can be implemented by 4,000 gates from the PRESENT block cipher).

1.2 Why Leakage-Resilient for RFID-World

As described above, in forward privacy, we allow the adversary to obtain the full internal state of the tag, denoted as "full leakage". Surely, we must consider this type of attack as the worst case. It is worth noting that, in the real usage of RFID-tags, it apparently takes quite much time and effort to conduct attacks leading to full leakage. (For example, the adversary steals the tag and brings it to his laboratory to obtain the internal state.) However, the adversary certainly has no chance to give the tag to the original owner again. Therefore, we can limit the number of full leakage to only one time.

In this paper, we additionally consider an attack scenario which we call "multi-time partial leakage". Namely, in the life time of a tag, its internal state may be partially leaked in a gradual way. It is obvious that partial leakage is more likely to occur than full leakage, because the adversary can conduct such attacks in a shorter time, with cheap and small-size devices. Furthermore, the adversary has enough time to bring back the tag to the original owner. Therefore, it is practical to consider the multi-time partial-leakage scenarios. However, despite many works on RFID in the literature, there is no scheme which is provably secure against general side channel attacks (see, e.g., [11] for an extensive list) which cause both partial leakage and full leakage of tags' state. Namely, there is not yet any work considering the situation where some information (say some bits, or the Hamming weight) of the tag state is leaked to the adversary. The goal of this work is to fill the gap by constructing a leakage-resilient RFID protocol.

The above discussion focused on forward privacy, and later on, we will formalize the notion of leakage-resilient forward privacy. We also do the same with tag unforgeability, a (known) notion ensuring that no-one except the tag can make the reader output OK. Namely, we formalize the notion of leakage-resilient tag unforgeability, assuring that even the internal state is partially leaked, no-one is able to make the reader output OK.

1.3   Our Contribution

In this paper, we propose the first leakage-resilient RFID authentication protocol, which fulfills rigorously both forward-privacy and security. Our security analysis is simple, and is in the standard model. Our proposal is also very modest in tag computation, in which the tag only needs to compute two PRFs (e.g., AES). We use the recent stream cipher of Pietrzak [21] as the main building block. We compare our proposal with some schemes with forward privacy in Table 1.

Table 1. A comparison of schemes with forward privacy

Schemes	Provable Security on Leakage Resiliency	Security model	Ingredient
OSK [20]	Only privacy against full-leakage	Random Oracle	2 random oracles
Berbain et al [3]	Only privacy against full-leakage	Standard	1 PRNG + 1 universal hash
Burmester et al [7]	Only privacy against full-leakage	Standard	5 PRNGs
Our proposal	Privacy against full-leakge and past partial-leakage Tag-unforgeability against partial-leakage	Standard	1 PRF + 1 wPRF

Above, PRNG = psuedo-random number generator, (w)PRF = (weak) psuedo-random function.

Organization of this paper is as follows. In Section 2, we define system model of RFID authentication protocol and present some definitions of leakage-resilient security and privacy suitable for RFID authentication. Then, we show our proposal in Section 3. We conclude this paper in Section 4.

1.4 Related Works

Since Juels et al pointed out privacy issue in RFID authentication protocol [14], many RFID authentication protocol studies have been conducted, such as [20,19,25,13,2]. Most protocols are based on hash functions, some scheme uses pseudo-random functions and pseudo-random number generator instead of hash functions [6,4,16,3]. There are three major RFID authentication schemes related to our result.

The first scheme which realizes "forward-privacy" against leakage of internal state was proposed by Ohkubo et al [20]. This protocol uses a hash-chain constructed by one-way hash function and random oracle for processing protocol message. The authenticity and indistinguishability can be proven in random oracle model. Forward privacy is mainly based on one-way function. Roughly speaking, the proof involves creating an adversary who breaks the one-wayness by using another adversary who breaches the forward privacy of this scheme.

The second scheme realizes forward-privacy in the standard model. Berbain et al in [3] proposed the first scheme in the standard model. The basic idea of the scheme is same as OSK protocol, however the chain for one-wayness is constructed by using pseudo-random number generator and the function for processing protocol message is realized by universal hash function and challenge-and-response protocols.

Let us also mention the recent work of Burmester and Munila [7]. They proposed a protocol, using pseudo-random functions, which has forward-privacy and tag unforgeability in the universally composable setting. However, the scheme assumes certain refresh operations *external* to the tag, which seems hard to be easily realized. Namely, the scheme security is based on periodically updating the random number generators with fresh randomness, which seems required some trusted device to handle the job.

This paper belongs to the so-called leakage-resilient cryptography, aiming at preventing side-channel attacks, and is a very current area of research. In ordinary cryptographic research, the security model does not consider leakage of secret information. In the symmetric world, Petit et al. [23] proposed a leakage-resilient pseudo-random generator from ideal ciphers. Dziembowski et al [10] proposed a leakage-resilient stream cipher based on pseudo-random generator in the standard model. Then Pietrzak [21] proposed simplified leakage-resilient stream cipher from wPRF. We will use the same model of leakage as [10,21] in this paper.

2   Model and Security Definitions

First, let us show the system model of RFID authentication. There exist three types of entities in this authentication protocol: a tag, a reader, and an authentication server. The functions and conditions for each entity are as follows:

Tag: We assume that the RFID tag T is a passive tag. It can operate only when interrogated by a reader and only for a short time. The most important limitation is computational power. Each tag can perform only basic cryptographic calculations: hash functions, pseudo-random number generation and symmetric encryption, as well as simple XOR calculations. It is not tamper-proofed. An adversary can obtain some of (or all) the information stored in the tag, for example via side channel attacks.

Reader: A reader communicates with each tag and the authentication server. The reader acts as an intermediary between the tag and the authentication server. It does not retain any secret information or execute any cryptographic operation.

Authentication server: An authentication server S is used to evaluate the correctness of T upon receiving protocol messages from T. The authentication server has huge computational power and storage and can be used to carry out any cryptographic computation. When the protocol message is valid for the tag, its output is 1; otherwise, its output is 0. An adversary cannot corrupt S.

Communication channel. The tag and the reader communicate over a wireless channel. Thus, an adversary can eavesdrop, modify, intercept, and insert any data in this channel. On the other hand, the reader and the authentication server communicate over a wired channel. We can easily establish a virtual private network between them. Thus, we assume that this channel is a secure channel, that is, both entities are authenticated and nobody can obtain plaintexts. For simplicity, we will think the reader and the server as one entity for the rest of this paper.

Now we consider leakage-resilient security and forward privacy of RFID tags. We follow the leakage-resilient model in [10,21] where the leakage-resilient property is captured by allowing the adversary to access to an oracle Leakage($\cdot$), by which the adversary can gain information on the tag internal state. Formally, as in [10,21], the adversary can submit a function f of its choice, and receives $f(\text{TState}^+)$ where TState^+ is the active part of the tag state. The adversary can repeat the submission many times, with different f's. One restriction is that for each f the length $|f(\text{TState}^+)|$ must be bounded away from $|\text{TState}^+|$ or otherwise no security is guaranteed. Our RFID proposal will tolerate the same type and amount of leakage as Pietrzak [21] stream cipher, which is briefly recalled Sect. 3.1. We will also describe the concrete type of leakage information in our RFID protocol later in the proofs.

We now adapt the (standard, no-leakage-resilient) security and forward privacy definitions (see, e.g. [3]) to leakage-resilient world. Below, we denote by

$A \leftrightarrow B$ interactions between the parties A and B; and by $\mathcal{A}^{\mathsf{Leakage}(\cdot)}$ we mean that $\mathcal{A}$ has access to the oracle $\mathsf{Leakage}(\cdot)$.

First, security of an RFID tag essentially means that no-one, except legitimate tags, can make the reader outputs OK.

Definition 1 (Leakage-resilient tag unforgeability). *The adversary $\mathcal{A}$ runs in two phases. In phase 1 (learning phase), it interacts with the tag and the reader in a man-in-the-middle way, and furthermore has access to a leakage oracle: Tag $\leftrightarrow \mathcal{A}^{\mathsf{Leakage}(\cdot)} \leftrightarrow$ Reader. In phase 2 (impersonation), $\mathcal{A}$ interacts only with the reader only once, and it wins if the reader outputs OK. An RFID protocol has leakage-resilient security iff the probability $\Pr[A \; wins]$ is negligible.*

Above, we assume that in phase 2, the adversary interacts with the reader only once. One may also let the adversary play polynomial times with the readers in the phase, but this case can be reduced to the above definition [3]. We will stick to the above for simplicity.

Second, forward privacy essentially means that no-one, even having the current state of a tag, can trace its past interactions, and is formalized in the definition below, which at the same time captures the intuition of unlinkability.

Definition 2 (Leakage resilient forward privacy). *The adversary $\mathcal{A}$ runs in two phases. In phase 1 (learning phase), it interacts with two tags: $Tag_0 \leftrightarrow \mathcal{A}^{\mathsf{Leakage}(\cdot)} \leftrightarrow$ Reader, and $Tag_1 \leftrightarrow \mathcal{A}^{\mathsf{Leakage}(\cdot)} \leftrightarrow$ Reader. (Recall that the $\mathsf{Leakage}(\cdot)$ oracle models the partial leakage gained by the adversary by side channel attacks.) In phase 2 (guessing phase), a bit d is chosen randomly, and now $\mathcal{A}$ interacts with tag d: $Tag_d \leftrightarrow \mathcal{A}^{\mathsf{Leakage}(\cdot)} \leftrightarrow$ Reader. At the end of phase 2, $\mathcal{A}$ is given the full internal state of tag d, and outputs a bit d' as a guess for d. The RFID protocol has leakage-resilient forward privacy iff the probability $\Pr[d' = d]$ is negligibly close to $1/2$.*

3   Our Proposal

3.1   Building Block

Recall the min-entropy of a random variable X is defined as

$$H_\infty(X) = -\log(\max_x \Pr[X = x]).$$

Below, $F : \{0,1\}^k \times \{0,1\}^n \to \{0,1\}^{k+n}$ is a weak PRF, which is intuitively a function returning a random output when the input is random. The difference between weak PRFs and normal PRFs is that, normal PRFs will output a random value on any (not just random) input. An adversary $\mathcal{A}$ against F will try to distinguish its outputs from random numbers. In particular, F is called (ϵ, q)-secure if the value

$$\left| \Pr[A(X_1 \ldots X_q, Y_1 \ldots Y_q) \to 1] - \Pr[A(X_1 \ldots X_q, R_1 \ldots R_q) \to 1] \right| \leq \epsilon$$

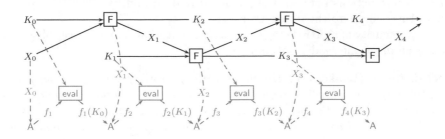

Fig. 1. Leakage resilient stream cipher in [21]. The gray, dashed lines show the leakage information the adversary gets in each round.

is negligible in the following experiment: $K \xleftarrow{\$} \{0,1\}^k$, $X_1, \ldots X_q \xleftarrow{\$} \{0,1\}^n$, $Y_i \leftarrow F(K, X_i)$, $R_i \xleftarrow{\$} \{0,1\}^{k+n}$ $(1 \leq i \leq q)$. When the value q can be set large and is not important in the context, we will omit to write it. The following theorem is an interesting fact on weak PRFs with *non-uniform* keys.

Theorem 1 (wPRF with non-uniform keys [21]). *A weak PRF, on random inputs, still returns random outputs if the key has high entropy (yet is non-uniform). More precisely, an ϵ-secure wPRF on random keys K, will become $(2^\lambda \cdot \epsilon)$-secure for keys K' with $H_\infty(K') \geq H_\infty(K) - \lambda$.*

We now consider the stream cipher of Pietrzak [21] based on any weak PRF $F$and is denoted as SC^F. In Fig. 1, the stream cipher is in black, while the related attack is in gray with dashed lines. The precise description is as follows.

Initialization: The initial state is $S_0 = [K_0, K_1, X_0]$, where $K_0, K_1 \xleftarrow{\$} \{0,1\}^k$
and $X_0 \xleftarrow{\$} \{0,1\}^n$. Only K_0, K_1 must be kept secret; X_0 can be public.
State: The state before the i-th round begins is $S_{i-1} = [K_{i-1}, K_i, X_{i-1}]$.
Computation: In the i-th round, the stream cipher SC^F on input of state S_{i-1},
computes

$$(K_{i+1}, X_i) := F(K_{i-1}, X_{i-1})$$

and outputs X_i. Then, the state $S_{i-1} = [K_{i-1}, K_i, X_{i-1}]$ is replaced with $S_i = [K_i, K_{i+1}, X_i]$.

Consider a side-channel adversary against the stream cipher; namely an adversary $\mathcal{A}$ who attacks SC^F by choosing an arbitrary function $f_i : \{0,1\}^k \rightarrow \{0,1\}^\lambda$ for fixed $\lambda < n$ before round i begins, and receives the output X_i of S^F and also leakage $\Lambda_i \overset{def}{=} f_i(K_{i-1})$ at the end of the round. Let $\mathsf{view}_l^{\mathsf{SC}}$ denote the view of the adversary after X_l has been computed, i.e.,

$$\mathsf{view}_l^{\mathsf{SC}} = [X_0, \ldots, X_l, \Lambda_1, \ldots, \Lambda_l].$$

The following theorem, which summarizes the results of [21], is the starting point of our work.

Theorem 2 ([21]). *Assume that* $F : \{0,1\}^k \times \{0,1\}^n \to \{0,1\}^{k+n}$ *is a secure weak PRF, the values* X_l, K_{l+1} *are indistinguishable from random, even when* $\mathsf{view}_{l-1}^{\mathsf{SC}}$ *is given to the adversary. Moreover, the value* X_l *still holds random even if the future states* $S_j = [K_j, K_{j+1}, X_j]$ *for* $j \geq l+1$ *are additionally given to the adversary.*

In addition to $\mathsf{view}_{l-1}^{\mathsf{SC}}$ *and* $S_j = [K_j, K_{j+1}, X_j]$ *for* $j \geq l+1$, *when the leakage* $\Lambda_l = f_l(K_{l-1})$ *(of* λ *bits) is given to the adversary, the value* X_l, *while not random anymore, still has high entropy (of about* $n - \lambda - 80$ *bits with probability* $1 - 2^{-80}$).

As estimated in [21], the leakage amount λ can reach $\Omega(|k|)$ if F is exponentially hard (like DES or AES).

3.2 Our Leakage-Resilient RFID Protocol

We provide in this section our RFID protocol secure against side chanel attacks with security proofs in the standard model. In essence, we build the scheme in a challenge-response manner, while utilizing Pietrzak mode of operation (Eurocrypt '09) as the main building block. The proposal is depicted in Fig. 2, and an imaginative illustration is in Fig. 3.

Let us mention some intuitions why the scheme is secure. The challenge-response construction helps the scheme resist against replay attack in which the adversary re-uses past transcripts. Security and forward privacy are ensured by the usage of Pietrzak mode in the tag, as well as an additional psuedo-random function F_2, which makes the responses look random.

Tag(ID, K_0, K_1, X_0)	Reader($\{\ldots, (ID, K_0, K_1, X_0), \ldots\}$)
Let TState $= (K_{i-1}, K_i, X_{i-1})$	$a \xleftarrow{\$} \{0,1\}^n$
	$\xleftarrow{\quad a \quad}$
$(K_{i+1}, X_i) \leftarrow F_1(K_{i-1}, X_{i-1})$	
$b \leftarrow F_2(X_i, a)$. Erase (K_{i-1}, X_{i-1})	
	$\xrightarrow{\quad b \quad}$
TState $= (K_i, K_{i+1}, X_i)$	For each (ID, K_0, K_1, X_0), compute
	$X_1, \ldots, X_L$ and check $b \overset{?}{=} F_2(X_i, a)$.
	Return OK soon after the first match.

Fig. 2. Our proposal in standard model. $F_1, F_2 : \{0,1\}^k \times \{0,1\}^n \to \{0,1\}^{k+n}$ (for $k = n$) are weak PRF, and PRF respectively. L is a big and fixed threshold. The notation $a \xleftarrow{\$} \{0,1\}^n$ stands for picking a randomly from the set. The tag runs Pietrzak mode of operation. For an imaginative illustration, see Fig. 3. The reader may be speeded-up as in Fig. 4, but for simplicity, we will stick to the above when proving securities.

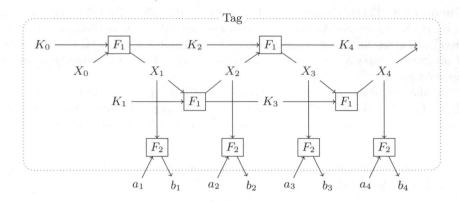

Fig. 3. An imaginative illustration of our leakage-resilient RFID protocol

Before stating security theorems, let us define the leakage to which our proposal is resilient. Mimicking the notation in Sect.3.1, denote

$$\mathsf{view}_l^{\mathsf{Tag}}(\mathcal{A}) = [g_0(X_0), \dots, g_l(X_l), f_1(K_0), \dots, f_l(K_{l-1})]$$

as the view in round l of an adversary $\mathcal{A}$ attacking our RFID scheme. The functions $g_0, \dots g_l, f_1, \dots, f_l : \{0,1\}^n \to \{0,1\}^\lambda$ are chosen by $\mathcal{A}$, representing the information $\mathcal{A}$ obtains from the tag's states up to the current round. Again, the value λ represents the leakage information on each value in the internal state of the tag, and is estimated as $\Omega(|k|)$ if F_1 is exponentially hard.

Theorem 3 (Tag unforgeability). *The RFID scheme has security even if for any round l in the learning phase (see Def.1), the adversary $\mathcal{A}$ is given* $\mathsf{view}_{l-1}^{\mathsf{Tag}}(\mathcal{A})$.

Proof. Recall that the adversary $\mathcal{A}$, playing actively between the tag and the reader for a while (learning phase), finally wants to impersonate the tag (impersonation phase). To impersonate the tag, the adversary has to create a value b satisfying $b = F_2(X_i, a)$ for random a (from the reader) and some X_i (unknown to the adversary). Note that the information on the value X_i may be partially leaked to $\mathcal{A}$, and since it is used just once, it may be leaked by at most λ bits, so its min-entropy is at least $n - \lambda$. Theorem 1 allows us to say that $F_2(X_i, a)$ is random-like for random a, so that the probability $\Pr[b = F_2(X_i, a)]$ is negligible since F_2 is a PRF.

Of course, before the above, we need to simulate the interaction (Tag $\leftrightarrow$ $\mathcal{A}^{\mathsf{Leakage}(\cdot)} \leftrightarrow$ Reader) in the learning phase of $\mathcal{A}$, where the adversary plays between the tag and the reader. However, the simulation is easy, since what sends from the reader is random, and what sends from the tag is random-like (F_2 is a PRF with random key), even if giving $\mathcal{A}$ the same leakage information as in Pietrzak [21]. More formal arguments are as follows. First, the simulator chooses X_0, K_0, K_1 randomly. In any subsequent round $l(\geq 1)$, the leakage

on internal states given to $\mathcal{A}$ is $\mathsf{view}_{l-1}^{\mathsf{Tag}}(\mathcal{A}) = [g_0(X_0), \ldots, g_{l-1}(X_{l-1}), f_1(K_0),$
$\ldots, f_{l-1}(K_{l-2})]$ for adversarily-chosen $g_0, \ldots, g_{l-1}, f_1, \ldots, f_{l-1}$ (which is adaptively submitted to the oracle $\mathsf{Leakage}(\cdot)$). It is ensured by Theorem 2 that given $\mathsf{view}_{l-1}^{\mathsf{Tag}}(\mathcal{A}) \subseteq \mathsf{view}_{l-1}^{\mathsf{SC}}$, the value X_l, K_{l+1} still looks random. Therefore, when receiving a challenge a'_l from $\mathcal{A}$ (who in turn has a_l from the reader), the simulator chooses $X_l = X \stackrel{\$}{\leftarrow} \{0,1\}^n$ and returns $b_l = F_2(X, a'_l)$ to $\mathcal{A}$. Since F_2 is a PRF and X is random, the value b_l looks random from the view of $\mathcal{A}$, and hence it gives the adversary essentially no information. The adversary then send b'_l to the reader, who returns OK iff $b'_l = F_2(X, a_l)$. (Certainly, if $\mathcal{A}$ did nothing, then $a'_l = a_l$ and $b'_l = b_l$, so OK will be returned.) The point here is in the random key X, which we can safely choose for simulation thanks to Theorem 2. $\square$

Remark. Our RFID tag, with a slight modification, can tolerate more leakage, of the form $\mathsf{view}'_{l-1}(\mathcal{A}) = [g_0(X_0), \ldots, g_{l-1}(X_{l-1}), f_1(K_0), \ldots, f_{l-1}(K_{l-2})] \cup [f_l(K_{l-1})]$. In this case, Theorem 2 ensures that X_l still has high entropy of $n - \lambda - 80$ bits with overwhelming probability. Now, in order to gain a random key for F_2, we can use a strong extractor [24] applied to X_l. The remark applies as well to the proof of forward privacy below. The trade-off for this bigger leakage amount is in the efficiency of the tag, since we need an extractor and additional randomness.

Theorem 4 (Forward privacy). *The RFID scheme has leakage-resilient forward privacy even if for any round l (before the exposure of the internal state), the adversary $\mathcal{A}$ is given $\mathsf{view}_{l-1}^{\mathsf{Tag}}(\mathcal{A})$.*

Proof. We first recall the definition of forward privacy for RFID tag. In the learning phase, the adversary $\mathcal{A}$ interacts with two tags and with the reader: $\mathsf{Tag}_0 \leftrightarrow \mathcal{A}^{\mathsf{Leakage}(\cdot)} \leftrightarrow \mathsf{Reader}$, $\mathsf{Tag}_1 \leftrightarrow \mathcal{A}^{\mathsf{Leakage}(\cdot)} \leftrightarrow \mathsf{Reader}$. And then a bit $d \stackrel{\$}{\leftarrow} \{0,1\}$, and $\mathcal{A}$ continues: $\mathsf{Tag}_d \leftrightarrow \mathcal{A}^{\mathsf{Leakage}(\cdot)} \leftrightarrow \mathsf{Reader}$. Finally in the guessing phase, the internal state of the tag d is given to $\mathcal{A}$, whose goal is to guess the bit d.

We now proceed to the proof. Note that, in the learning phase, the adversary obtain almost no information from our RFID system. Again, the reason is in the fact that the communication between the reader and the tag consists of random-like values. Formally, for each tag i ($= 0, 1$), the simulation goes as follows: at the beginning, random values X_0, K_0, K_1 are chosen randomly. For any subsequent round $l (\geq 1)$, the values X_l, K_{l+1} are also randomly picked to answer the query from $\mathcal{A}$ (with $\mathsf{view}_{l-1}^{\mathsf{Tag}_i}(\mathcal{A})$) in the round in the following manner: the adversary $\mathcal{A}$ (receiving a random a from the reader) sends its decided a', for which the adversary gets $b' = F_2(X_l, a')$ from the simulator. The adversary now decide the value b sent to the tag, and if $b = F_2(X_l, a)$, then OK will be returned to $\mathcal{A}$.

Furthermore, in some adversarily-chosen round l^* of the guessing phase, the simulator gives $\mathcal{A}$ randomly chosen values $[K_{l^*}, K_{l^*+1}, X_{l^*}]$ as the current internal state of Tag_d. The reason behind this simulation is that the current internal state of the tag is always random-like, even conditioned on the view so far of $\mathcal{A}$, which includes $\mathsf{view}_{l^*-1}^{\mathsf{Tag}_d}(\mathcal{A})$ (and the leakage $\mathcal{A}$ obtains from Tag_{1-d}, which is independent of $\mathrm{view}_{l^*-1}^{\mathrm{Tag}_d}(\mathcal{A})$). Also here, we make use of the fact that Pietrzak mode, as used in our proposal, is one-way: from the i-th state (K_i, K_{i+1}, X_i), no-one cannot compute the $(i-1)$-th state (K_{i-1}, K_i, X_{i-1}), because the key K_{i-1} have been deleted, and F_1 (a weak PRF) is one-way without the key K_{i-1}. (To see why one-wayness is needed, imagine the case $\mathcal{A}$ obtain the initial state (K_0, K_1, X_0) of one tag. It is then clear that $\mathcal{A}$ can easily trace back past action of that tag.)

Based on the above arguments, we conclude that the guess bit d' output by $\mathcal{A}$ is computationally independent of d and hence $\Pr[d' = d] \overset{c}{\approx} 1/2$, ending the proof.   □

Fig. 4 shows a speed-up version of our proposal, where the server begins its computation from the most recent tags' state (instead starting from the initial state). Both security and forward privacy are proven similarly as the original version.

Tag(ID, TState)   Reader(L, $\{\ldots, (ID, l(=1), K_0, K_1, X_0), \ldots\}$)

Retrieve TState $= (K_{i-1}, K_i, X_{i-1})$ $a \overset{\$}{\leftarrow} \{0,1\}^n$
$\qquad\qquad\qquad\qquad\qquad \overset{a}{\longleftarrow}$

$(K_{i+1}, X_i) \leftarrow F_1(K_{i-1}, X_{i-1})$
$b \leftarrow F_2(X_i, a)$. Erase (K_{i-1}, X_{i-1})
$\qquad\qquad\qquad\qquad\qquad \overset{b}{\longrightarrow}$

TState $\leftarrow (K_i, K_{i+1}, X_i)$ For each ID retrieve $(l, K_{l-1}, K_l, X_{l-1})$.
                                           Set $j \leftarrow l$.
                                           while ($j < L$)
                                               $(K_{j+1}, X_j) \leftarrow F_1(K_{j-1}, X_{j-1})$
                                               if $b = F_2(X_j, a)$ then
                                                   update ID's state to
                                                       $(ID, l \leftarrow j+1, K_j, K_{j+1}, X_j)$
                                                   return OK and halt
                                               else $j \leftarrow j+1$
                                           endwhile
                                           return NOK and halt

---

Fig. 4. Speed-up version for the reader, who keeps track of the most recent tag state (indexed by l), instead of starting from the initial (K_0, K_1, X_0) as in Fig. 2

3.3   Relation with Existing Schemes

Here, we show advantages of our proposal against existing schemes. Compared to Berbain et al. [3] scheme, our scheme has leakage-resiliency for security. Pietrzak's leakage-resilient stream cipher helps our scheme to realize this characteristic. Moreover, leakage model of our proposal for forward privacy is extended from existing schemes (OSK and Berbain et al.) In existing scheme, the adversary obtains full internal state at the end of the attack. However, he cannot obtain leakages on internal states of previous moments. On the other hand, our proposal is secure even if the adversary obtains partial internal states of previous protocol executions.

Security of our protocol is rigorously proven thanks to Pietrzak's work. Leakage-resiliency is involved in the protocol and we need no refresh operations, as compared to [7].

3.4 Using Other Leakage Resilient Stream Cipher

Recently, Yu et al. proposed leakage resilient stream cipher with less secret information [27]. We can also replace Pietrzak's leakage resilient stream cipher with this new stream cipher in the same manner as our proposed RFID authentication protocol.

4 Conclusion

In this paper, we propose a concept of leakage-resiliency suitable for RFID-authentication protocol. Then, we propose the first RFID authentication scheme with leakage resilience for security and forward privacy. Our protocol has an additional functionality, i.e., leakage resilience for both security and privacy in contrast to existing protocols [20,3,7] with forward privacy. The security of our protocol is proven based on Pietrzak's pseudo-random generator.

References

1. Alwen, J., Dodis, Y., Wichs, D.: Leakage-Resilient Public-Key Cryptography in the Bounded-Retrieval Model. In: Halevi, S. (ed.) Advances in Cryptology - CRYPTO 2009. LNCS, vol. 5677, pp. 36–54. Springer, Heidelberg (2009)
2. Avoine, G., Oechslin, P.: A Scalable and Provably Secure Hash Based RFID Protocol. In: Proc. of IEEE Int. Workshop on Pervasive Computing & Communication Security (PerSec 2005). IEEE Computer Society Press, Los Alamitos (2005)
3. Berbain, C., Billet, O., Etrog, J., Gilbert, H.: An efficient forward private RFID protocol. In: ACM Conference on Computer and Communications Security 2009 (ACM CCS 2009), pp. 43–53 (2009)
4. Burmester, M., van Le, T., De Medeiros, B.: Provably Secure Ubiquitous Systems: Universally Composable RFID Authentication Protocols. In: Proc. of 2nd IEEE Create Net Int. Conf. on Security and Privacy in Networks (SECURECOMM 2006). IEEE Press, Los Alamitos (2006)
5. Bogdanov, A., Leander, G., Paar, C., Posehmann, A., Robshaw, M.J.B., Seurin, Y.: Hash Functions and RFID Tags: Mind the Gap. In: Oswald, E., Rohatgi, P. (eds.) CHES 2008. LNCS, vol. 5154, pp. 283–299. Springer, Heidelberg (2008)
6. Burmester, M., De Medeiros, B.: The Security of EPC Gen2 Compliant RFID Protocols. In: Bellovin, S.M., Gennaro, R., Keromytis, A.D., Yung, M. (eds.) ACNS 2008. LNCS, vol. 5037, pp. 490–506. Springer, Heidelberg (2008)
7. Burmester, M., Munila, J.: A Flyweight RFID Authentication Protocol. In: Workshop on RFID Security, RFIDSec 2009, Leuven, Belgium (July 2009), http://eprint.iacr.org/2009/212.pdf

8. Cash, D., Ding, Y.Z., Dodis, Y., Lee, W., Lipton, R., Walfish, S.: Intrusion-Resilient Key Exchange in the Bounded Retrieval Model. In: Vadhan, S.P. (ed.) TCC 2007. LNCS, vol. 4392, pp. 479–498. Springer, Heidelberg (2007)

9. Di Crescenzo, G., Lipton, R., Walfish, S.: Perfectly Secure Password Protocols in the Bounded Retrieval Model. In: Halevi, S., Rabin, T. (eds.) TCC 2006. LNCS, vol. 3876, pp. 225–244. Springer, Heidelberg (2006)

10. Dziembowski, S., Pietrzak, K.: Leakage-resilient cryptography. In: Proc. In FOCS (2008), October 25-28, pp. 293–302 (2008)

11. European Network of Excellence (ECRYPT). The side channel cryptanalysis lounge, http://www.crypto.ruhr-uni-bochum.de/en_sclounge.html

12. Goldreich, O., Goldwasser, S., Micali, S.: How to construct pseudo-random functions. Journal of ACM 33(4) (1986)

13. Henrici, D., Muller, P.M.: Hash-based enhancement of location privacy for radio-frequency identification devices using varying identifiers. In: Proc. of IEEE Int. Conf. on Pervasive Computing and Communications, pp. 149–153 (2004)

14. Juels, A., Pappu, R.: Squealing Euros:Privacy-Protection in RFID-Enabled Banknotes. In: Wright, R.N. (ed.) FC 2003. LNCS, vol. 2742, pp. 103–121. Springer, Heidelberg (2003)

15. Juels, A., Weis, S.A.: Defining Strong Privacy for RFID, http://eprint.iacr.org/2006/137

16. Le, T.V., Burmester, M., de Medeiros, B.: Universally Composable and Forward-secure RFID Authentication and Authenticated Key Exchange. In: Proc. of ASI-ACCS 2007, pp. 242–252 (2007)

17. Naor, M., Segev, G.: Public-Key Cryptosystem Resilient to Key leakage. In: Halevi, S. (ed.) CRYPTO 2009. LNCS, vol. 5677, pp. 18–35. Springer, Heidelberg (2009)

18. Ng, C.Y., Susilo, W., Mu, Y., Safavi-Naini, R.: RFID Privacy Models Revisited. In: Jajodia, S., Lopez, J. (eds.) ESORICS 2008. LNCS, vol. 5283, pp. 251–266. Springer, Heidelberg (2008)

19. Ohkubo, M., Suzuki, K.: Forward Security RFID Privacy Protection Scheme with Restricted Traceability. In: Proc. of ACNS 2006 in Industrial Track, pp. 1–16 (2006)

20. Ohkubo, M., Suzuki, K., Kinoshita, S.: Cryptographic Approach to a Privacy Friendly Tags. Presented at the RFID Privacy Workshop, MIT, USA (2003)

21. Pietrzak, K.: A Leakage-Resilient Mode of Operation. In: Joux, A. (ed.) EURO-CRYPT 2009. LNCS, vol. 5479, pp. 462–482. Springer, Heidelberg (2010)

22. Pietrzak, K., Sjodin, J.: Range Extension for Weak PRFs; The Good, the Bad, and the Ugly. In: Naor, M. (ed.) EUROCRYPT 2007. LNCS, vol. 4515, pp. 517–533. Springer, Heidelberg (2007)

23. Petit, C., Standaert, F.-X., Pereira, O., Malkin, T., Yung, M.: A Block Cipher based Pseudo Random Number Generator Secure against Side-channel Key Recovery. In: Proc. of ASIACCS 2008, pp. 56–65 (2008)

24. Shaltiel, R.: Recent developments in explicit constructions of extractors. Bulletin of the EATCS 77, 67–95 (2002)

25. Sharma, S.E., Weiss, S.A., Engels, D.W.: RFID systems and security and privacy implications. In: Kaliski Jr., B.S., Koç, Ç.K., Paar, C. (eds.) CHES 2002. LNCS, vol. 2523, pp. 454–469. Springer, Heidelberg (2003)

26. Vaudenay, S.: On Privacy Models for RFID. In: Kurosawa, K. (ed.) ASIACRYPT 2007. LNCS, vol. 4833, pp. 68–87. Springer, Heidelberg (2007)

27. Yu, Y., Standaert, F.-X., Pereira, O., Yung, M.: Practical Leakage-Resilient Pseudorandom Generators. In: Proc. of ACM CCS 2010 (to appear, 2010)

An ECDSA Processor for RFID Authentication

Michael Hutter, Martin Feldhofer, and Thomas Plos

Institute for Applied Information Processing and Communications (IAIK),
Graz University of Technology, Inffeldgasse 16a, 8010 Graz, Austria
{Michael.Hutter,Martin.Feldhofer,Thomas.Plos}@iaik.tugraz.at

Abstract. In the last few years, a lot of research has been made to bring asymmetric cryptography on low-cost RFID tags. Many of the proposed implementations include elliptic-curve based coprocessors to provide entity-authentication services through for example identification schemes. This paper presents first results of an 192-bit Elliptic Curve Digital Signature Algorithm (ECDSA) processor that allows both entity and also message authentication by digitally signing challenges from a reader. The proposed architecture enhances the state-of-the-art in designing a low-resource ECDSA-enabled RFID hardware implementation. A tiny microcontroller is integrated to provide protocol scalability and re-use of common algorithms. The proposed processor signs a message within 859 188 clock cycles (127 ms at 6.78 MHz) and has a total chip size of 19 115 gate equivalents.

Keywords: Radio-Frequency Identification, VLSI Design, Elliptic Curves, ECDSA, Authentication, Digital Signatures.

1 Introduction

Radio-Frequency Identification (RFID) is a wireless communication technology that has gained a lot of importance in the last decade. Especially passively powered RFID tags are of major interest because they do not need a dedicated power supply. They simply draw their energy from an electromagnetic field of a reader. Furthermore, passive tags are produced in a large scale (over 3 billion tags were shipped worldwide in 2009) and can label products on the market with low costs. The hardware design of cryptographic algorithms for such RFID tags has to meet therefore low-resource requirements in terms of power and area.

One of the major challenges in the design of security-related RFID implementations is the integration of asymmetric cryptography into passive RFID tags. Asymmetric cryptography is considered to need more computational effort than symmetric cryptography but has the main advantage that no pairs of secret keys have to be maintained by tags and readers. Tags can be shipped along with a secretly kept private key whereas readers can use the corresponding public key to verify the authenticity of RFID tags. The integration of asymmetric cryptography into passive RFID tags seems therefore inevitable to allow tag authentication in open-loop systems. Indeed, the integration of public-key cryptography can effectively help to thwart the trade in counterfeiting goods of many products in the industry.

S.B. Ors Yalcin (Ed.): RFIDSec 2010, LNCS 6370, pp. 189–202, 2010.

There exist several implementation proposals for symmetric as well as asymmetric cryptography on passive RFID tags. Feldhofer et al. [7] presented a low-resource hardware implementation of the Advanced Encryption Standard (AES). They integrated AES in a challenge-response protocol to allow tag and reader authentication. Their 128-bit AES implementation needs 3 595 GE of area and is able to encrypt a challenge within 1 016 clock cycles. Many asymmetric primitives, in contrast, are based on elliptic curves due to the advantage of the smaller key sizes compared to other existing primitives like RSA. However, most of the elliptic-curve based implementations provide entity-authentication services through identification schemes and do not allow a transferable proof of the authenticity of an RFID tag. In particular, identification schemes do neither offer non-repudiation nor data-integrity services that would proof the origin of tag data. A reader that challenged a tag cannot be assured of the authenticity of the data received since identification schemes do not provide message authentication capabilities. Message authentication through digital signatures, in contrast, allows a proof of origin even at a later instant of time and thus enables many solutions for new RFID applications.

In this article, we present first results of a low-resource ECDSA hardware-implementation for RFID that provides both entity and also message authentication services. The processor is able to digitally sign the challenge of a reader by applying ECDSA using a standardized NIST $\mathbb{F}_{p192}$ elliptic curve. The design improves the state-of-the-art in implementing ECDSA for RFID applications by offering a scalable architecture using a tiny microcontroller. A digital signature can be generated within 859 188 clock cycles (i.e. 127 ms at 6.78 MHz). The total size of the ECDSA processor is 19 115 gate equivalents.

The paper is structured as follows. Section 2 gives related work on ECC processors and discusses most recent implementations. In Section 3, the tag-authentication protocol using ECDSA is described. In Section 4, the ECDSA processor is presented and details of the implemented microcontroller are given in Section 5. Results are shown in Section 6 and the conclusions are drawn in Section 7.

2   State-of-the-Art ECC Implementations

There exist many publications that present ECC hardware implementations. Only a few of them focus on low-resource ASIC designs for passive RFID devices. S. Kumar and C. Paar [18] presented a hardware implementation of an elliptic-curve coprocessor for RFID over binary fields. Also L. Batina et al. [1,2] made a lot of research on ECC implementations over binary fields and analyzed also higher-layer authentication protocols based on the Schnorr and Okamoto scheme. J. Wolkerstorfer [27] and F. Fürbass et al. [8] described an ECC processor over the recommended NIST $\mathbb{F}_{p192}$ elliptic curve that targets ECDSA signature generation for RFID tags. They reported results for point multiplication but they neither include random number generation (RNG) nor the hashing of messages to complete the signing process. An ECC processor over $\mathbb{F}_{2^{163}}$ has been proposed by Y. K. Lee et al. [19]. The processor includes a tiny microcontroller which is able to perform the Schnorr protocol for tag authentication. The same type of elliptic curve has been investigated by D. Hein et al. [11] who implemented an ECC coprocessor over $\mathbb{F}_{2^{163}}$ that is connected to an ISO 15693-compliant RFID front-end. Similar results have also been reported by H. Bock et al. [3]. They presented an ECC processor over $\mathbb{F}_{2^{163}}$ but included a Diffie-Hellman based authentication protocol. The chip is further equipped with an ISO 15693-compliant RFID front-end, random number generator, non-volatile memory, and provides countermeasures against implementation attacks.

3 Tag Authentication Using ECDSA

In the following, we give a short introduction to elliptic-curve cryptography (ECC). Afterwards, we will describe the tag authentication protocol using ECDSA.

3.1 Elliptic Curve Cryptography

Elliptic curves are algebraic structures that constitute a basic class of cryptographic primitives which rely on a mathematical hard problem. The elliptic curve discrete logarithm problem (ECDLP) is based on the intractability of deriving a large scalar after its multiplication with a given point on an elliptic curve. An elliptic curve E over a finite field $\mathbb{F}_p$ with characteristic $p > 3$ can be defined by the short Weierstrass equation $y^2 = x^3 + ax + b$, where $a, b \in \mathbb{F}_p$ are publicly-known curve parameters satisfying $4a^3 + 27b^2 \not\equiv 0 \pmod{p}$ and $x, y \in \mathbb{F}_p$ is a point on the elliptic curve. Let P be a fixed point on the curve $E(\mathbb{F}_p)$ with prime order n and k a large integer scalar in $[1, n - 1]$, then it is easy to compute the scalar multiplication $Q = kP$ but hard to find k by knowing only Q and P.

In practice, the scalar multiplication can be computed by iteratively applying group operations, i.e. addition and doubling of curve points. These operations use finite-field operations such as addition, subtraction, multiplication, squaring, and inversion. There exist several formulas for addition and doubling operations that try to reduce the number of finite-field operations. Especially formulas that represent elliptic curves in projective coordinates (the affine coordinates x and y are represented by the coordinates X, Y, and Z where $x = X/Z$ and $y = Y/Z$) are often used because the costly inversion operation can be omitted during scalar multiplication. Next to projective coordinate representation there exist several proposals to improve the performance and security of the scalar multiplication. One example is the Montgomery powering ladder [16] method that can be used with x-coordinate only group formulas (thus needing only intermediate registers for the projective X and Z coordinates) and additionally provides security against Simple Power Analysis (SPA).

3.2 The ECDSA Authentication Protocol

The following section describes tag authentication using ECDSA in a challenge-response protocol which is defined in the ISO 9798-3 [13] standard. Before starting the authentication process, the reader challenges the tag to get the public-key

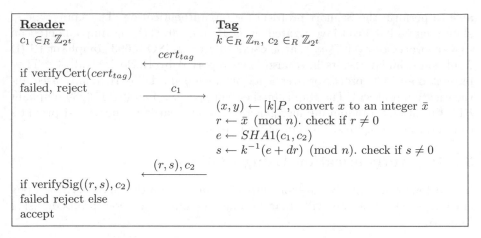

Fig. 1. Tag authentication protocol using ECDSA

certificate $cert_{tag}$. After validation of the certificate, the reader chooses a random number c_1 and sends it to the tag. After that, the tag digitally signs the challenge c_1 of the reader together with another random number c_2 using ECDSA. First, it performs a scalar multiplication using the ephemeral key k and a fixed point P on the elliptic curve. The result r is then multiplied with the private key d. Second, the hashed message e is added and the result is multiplied with the inverted ephemeral key k^{-1}. Finally, the intermediates r and s represent the digital signature which is sent together with the random value c_2 to the reader. The reader can then verify the signature and accept the tag authentication if succeeded.

4   System Architecture

The main components of the ECDSA processor are a microcontroller, a memory unit, and an arithmetic unit to perform elliptic-curve and SHA-1 operations. The reason why we have implemented a microcontroller instead of a dedicated finite state machine lies in the fact that we aimed a processor for RFID tags that is flexible and scalable in terms of different protocols and algorithm modifications. The processor should be rather modular to be re-used in different projects and already approved in practice. In fact, a microcontroller allows the writing of micro-code programs that can be easily modified and re-compiled if desired. In order to meet the performance requirements of ECC, we implemented several instruction-set extensions (ISE) that allow fast public-key arithmetic operations such as modular multiplication and inversion. In Figure 2, the architecture of an RFID tag including the proposed ECDSA processor is shown.

The ECDSA processor can be connected to an analog and digital front-end that transform analog signals into digital data. The analog front-end provides a circuit for voltage regulation, modulation, demodulation, clock extraction, communication signal pre-processing, as well as two antenna connections. The

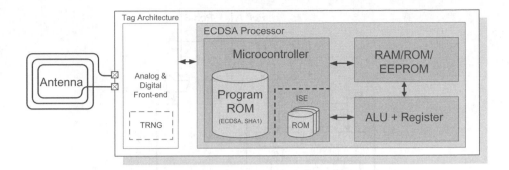

Fig. 2. Architecture of an RFID tag including the ECDSA processor

digital front-end implements the RFID protocol such as ISO 15693, ISO 14443, or ISO 18092. According to the ISO 7816-4 [14] standard, the ECDSA processor supports the INTERNAL AUTHENTICATE command that allows tag authentication using the protocol described in Section 3. A 16-byte challenge is sent from the reader that is signed by the tag. Next to that, the processor allows a direct access to the non-volatile memory to load and transmit the tag certificate, for instance. Random numbers are generated according to the FIPS 186-2 [23] standard. A random number generated from a TRNG has to be hashed using the SHA-1 algorithm and the result is used as a seed (XKEY seed) to produce any random number needed during ECDSA signature generation.

4.1 Memory Unit

The memory unit consists of a RAM, a ROM, and an EEPROM that can be accessed via a 16-bit dual-ported memory interface. One port (port A) is used to access the EEPROM, the other port (port B) is used to access the ROM table. The 128×16-bit RAM macro block can be accessed by both ports allowing the reading of data of two different addresses within one clock cycle. The first 192 bits, i.e. 12×16 bits, are reserved for the XKEY seed, 160 bits are used to store the hashed challenge, and 192 bits are needed for storing the ephemeral key. The remaining part of the RAM (7×192 bits) is used for ECDSA signing.

4.2 The 16-bit Datapath

The ECDSA datapath is shown in Figure 3 and consists of a 16×16-bit multiplier, two 40-bit adders, logic operations, several multiplexers, and one 40-bit accumulator register. According to the RAM organization, all operations are performed in words of 16 bits. The following 16-bit operations are supported: addition, subtraction, multiplication, NOT, AND, OR, and XOR. Furthermore, it allows to perform a 192-bit multiplication in a Multiply Accumulate (MAC) approach. The datapath supports only word-size operations, 192-bit finite-field operations are performed within the ISE architecture. Modular reduction has also been realized as an ISE.

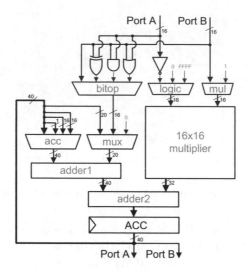

Fig. 3. The ECDSA datapath

5   The 8-bit Microcontroller

Controlling the ECDSA processor with a microcontroller provides much more flexibility than using a fixed state machine. We are using an 8-bit microcontroller with a Harvard architecture, *i.e.* program memory and data memory are separated. Such a design has the advantage that the program memory can have a different bit width than the data memory. The microcontroller is a Reduced Instruction Set Computer (RISC) supporting 32 instructions that have a width of 16 bits. The instructions are mainly divided into four groups: logical operations like XOR and OR, arithmetic operations like addition (ADD) and subtraction (SUB), control-flow operations like GOTO and CALL, and ISE operations.

Main components of the microcontroller are the ROM, the register file, the program counter, the instruction decode unit, and the ALU. The ROM contains the program memory and has a size of 600×16 bits. The register file is the data memory of the microcontroller and consists of 16 registers with a width of 8 bits each. Instructions are executed within a two-stage pipeline that consists of a fetch and a decode/execute step. In the first stage, the instruction that is addressed by the 11-bit program counter is loaded from the ROM into the instruction decode unit. In the second stage, the instruction is decoded by the instruction decode unit and executed by the ALU, followed by updating the program counter. The program counter contains a call stack that allows up to three recursive subroutine calls. All instructions are executed within a single clock cycle, except the control-flow operations and the ISE operations. Control-flow operations require two clock cycles. The number of clock cycles required for an ISE operation is not fixed and depends on the operation that is executed.

There are two types of registers in the register file of the microcontroller: special-purpose registers and general-purpose registers. The special-purpose registers involve an accumulator register for advanced data manipulation, a status register that gives information about the status of the ALU (e.g. carry bit after addition), and input/output (I/O) registers. The latter are used for accessing external devices like the memory unit or the ECDSA arithmetic unit via memory-mapped I/O. The I/O registers are also used for reacting on external events via busy waiting, since interrupts are not supported by the microcontroller. General-purpose registers are used for arbitrary data manipulations and temporarily storing data.

For implementing the microcontroller program, we have developed a self-written instruction-set simulator and assembler. Both programs are written in JAVA and allow a fast and easy way of program development. The simulator supports a single-step mode and gives access to the internal state of the microcontroller. This makes debugging and testing of the program very convenient. Moreover, optimizing the instruction set and adjusting parameters of the microcontroller like data bit width or call-stack size can be done much faster than in a direct hardware simulation.

In the following, the implemented ISE-microcode sequences are explained in a more detail and the program for ECDSA is described.

5.1   Instruction Set Extensions

The processor supports 55 instruction-set extensions for several ECDSA operations. The ISEs have been implemented in eight distinct microcode ROM tables that are able to address up to 128 microcode patterns. The partition has its reason in the fact that each table can possess a different data bit width which actually reduces the area footprint of the processor. In the following, we first describe the modular arithmetics such as addition, subtraction, multiplication, and Mersenne-like NIST prime reduction. The NIST recommended prime over $\mathbb{F}_{192}$ is $p_{192} = 2^{192} - 2^{64} - 1$. Second, we describe Montgomery-based operations such as multiplication and inversion that are mainly used for the general prime-field operations during the signing process. Third, we will focus on the ISE implementation of the message-digest calculation using SHA-1.

Modular Arithmetics. Modular addition has been realized as an ISE operation and works as follows. First, the microcontroller sets the needed address parameters to perform an addition. Second, an ISE-INST_ADD sequence is invoked using a MICRO instruction. The addition sequence needs 19 microcode patterns to add the 192-bit values a and b. Third, the microcontroller jumps to the NIST_RED subroutine which is also used for modular multiplication. Within the subroutine, another MICRO instruction is called to reduce the result. For modular reduction, we applied the fast NIST reduction method that needs 12 microcode patterns to reduce the result. The reduction sequence takes the carry ε of the addition result c and adds it to the result at bit position 0 and 63 (using the NIST prime we used the fact that 2^{192} is congruent to $2^{64} + 1$ (mod p)). If the carry is zero, a zero value is added accordingly. However, the performed reduction step guarantees that the result is still smaller than 2^{192} but

| **Algorithm 1.** Modular addition | **Listing 1.1.** Program for addition |

Algorithm 1. Modular addition

Require: Modulus p, and $a, b \in [0, p-1]$.
Ensure: $c = a + b \pmod{p}$, $\varepsilon \in [0, 1]$.
1: $(\varepsilon, C[0]) \leftarrow A[0] + B[0]$.
2: **for** i from 1 to 11 **do**
3:    $(\varepsilon, C[i]) \leftarrow A[i] + B[i] + \varepsilon$.
4: **end for**
5: $c \leftarrow c + (2^{64} + 1) * \varepsilon$. (NIST Red.)
6: **if** $(c \geq p)$ **then**
7:    $c \leftarrow c - p$.
8: **end if**
9: Return (c).

Listing 1.1. Program for addition

```
...
MovLF(ADDR1_REG, 0x4);
MICRO(INST_ADD, addr_par9, 19);
CALLR("NIST_RED");
...

LABEL("NIST_RED");
  MICRO(INST_RED1, addr_null, 4);
  MICRO(INST_RED2, addr_null, 8);
  BWS(STATUS, CU_NEXT_INSTR);
  BTC(STATUS, CU_CARRY);
  MICRO(INST_SUB, addr_par14, 19);
RET();
```

does not guarantee the case that $2^{192} - 2^{64} - 1 \leq c < 2^{192}$. To handle this case, a logical AND operation is performed on the higher eight words, i.e. the most 128 significant bits of the result. For this, we separated the sequence into the INST_RED1 and INST_RED2 instruction. The INST_RED1 instruction reduces the four least significant words of the result, the remaining eight words are handled by the INST_RED2 instruction. In particular, during the INST_RED2 instruction, an AND operation is performed on all words (i.e. 128 bits) and the resulting bit is stored in the MSB of the accumulator. If the MSB is one, the obtained result is greater than the modulus p and an extra-reduction step has to be performed, otherwise it is zero. The microcontroller tests if the MSB of the accumulator is set by reading a dedicated memory mapped I/O register bit (CU_CARRY) which is directly connected to the ECDSA datapath. A subtraction operation is called afterwards that reduces the result modulo p. Note that this extra reduction is performed in extremely rare cases since the probability of occurrence is $P(p \leq c) = \sum_{i=1}^{2^{64}} \frac{1}{2^{192}} = \frac{1}{2^{128}}$. Neglecting the execution of that extra reduction step, modular addition can be performed in $19 + 12 + 1 = 32$ clock cycles. The modular addition algorithm is shown in Algorithm 1. and the ISE invocations are shown within a code snippet of the ECDSA program in Listing 1.1.

Modular subtraction is performed similar. First, the ISE subtraction sequence is invoked by the microcontroller. It needs 19 patterns and clock cycles, respectively. Second, the microcontroller checks if there exists a borrow or not and adds the modulus p if necessary.

Modular multiplication is basically more complex than modular addition and subtraction and needs special attention in the design to obtain adequate performance. We implemented the multiplication in a Multiply Accumulate (MAC) architecture where every 16-bit word of the operands are multiplied and accumulated to the datapath register. The approach of adding partial products is similar to the method proposed by J. Grossschädl [9]. The multi-precision multiplication is done in a product scanning form (often referred as Comba multiplication method). On the algorithmic level, there exist mainly two loops to perform the multiplication. The inner loop performs a multiplication of two 16-bit words and the outer loop assigns the sum of the partial products to the accumulator register. In order to minimize the needed memory consumption (192*2=384 bits are naturally necessary to store the multiplication result), we reduced the result during multiplication within an interleaved reduction method. Thus, no additional register is needed to obtain the result. For reducing the higher part of the result, we again used the properties of the recommended NIST prime p by simply adding the modulus at the bit positions 63 and 0. This has to be done two times to reduce the entire 192-bit number. After that, the lower 192-bits of the multiplication are computed and added to the already reduced higher parts. Note that a final reduction is necessary afterwards to reduce the carry of the final addition. The entire modular multiplication including final reduction needs 204 clock cycles. Two ISE instructions (INST_MUL1 and INST_MUL2) have been implemented in two ROM tables. For the final reduction, we re-used the NIST_RED subroutine as it has been already used for modular addition.

Montgomery Inversion and Multiplication. In order to perform inversion of the ephemeral key k in ECDSA and also to convert the projective coordinates back into affine coordinates, we implemented the inversion algorithm proposed by P. Montgomery [22]. On the one hand, this has the advantage that not only the modular inversion but also the modular multiplication (for general primes) can be computed faster than with conventional methods. On the other hand, values have to be transformed into the so-called Montgomery representation, e.g. $x \mapsto \tilde{x} = xR \bmod p$, where $R > p$ represents the Montgomery constant. Due to that reason, we implemented the Montgomery inversion algorithm according to B. Kaliski [17]. It takes an input a and outputs the inverse of a in Montgomery representation, i.e. $a^{-1}R \pmod{p}$. Furthermore, we implemented the Montgomery modular multiplication operation according to G. Hachez and J. J. Quisquater [10]. It takes operands which are already transformed into the Montgomery domain. Thus, no Montgomery-domain transformations have to be performed online during the ECDSA-signature generation. For Montgomery inversion, we have implemented seven ISEs, for the Montgomery multiplication there exists five ISEs.

The SHA-1 Algorithm. Basically, the SHA-1 algorithm takes a 512-bit input-message block and performs several logic operations on 6 different state variables A,B,C,D,E, and F. After each round, the state is shifted to the right. In total, 80 rounds are performed to obtain the message digest of 160 bit. For the computation, we implemented 14 ISEs: two instructions are used to initialize the state by loading the ROM constants (h0..h4 and k0..k3) into RAM, nine ISEs are used within the 80 rounds (one ISE is executed only after loop index 16, and eight ISEs are individually executed before loop index 20, 40, 60, and 80), and three ISEs are used to produce the final hash value. Furthermore, we did not rotate the content of the state but simply shifted the addresses to reach the best performance. The loop index and branching conditions have been realized in the microcontroller. 3 639 clock cycles are needed to hash a 512-bit message.

5.2   The Program for ECDSA Signature Generation

In the following, we describe the ECDSA program for signature generation. The program needs about 600 lines of code and is stored in a dedicated program ROM that is accessed by the microcontroller. Note that the program can also contain the protocol execution according to the used RFID standard. This will only add costs in the program ROM but not in all other parts. The program can be separated into the following eight main parts.

1. **Power Up.** After power up of the tag, a generated TRNG seed is used for further random number generation.
2. **Random Number Generation (RNG).** After receiving a reader challenge, the tag first performs four SHA-1 computations to generate random numbers for the ephemeral key and the applied side-channel countermeasures. The RNG is done according to the FIPS 186-2 [23] standard.
3. **Randomized Projective Coordinates (RPC).** As a side-channel countermeasure, we randomized the projective coordinates of the base point P according to the proposal of S. Coron [5]. We multiplied the X coordinate of P with a random number λ and took λ as a Z coordinate.
4. **Double the Base Point.** Instead of doubling the base point P before scalar multiplication, we pre-computed it and stored the projective coordinates (X, Z) of $Dbl(P)$ in ROM needing 24×16 bits of memory. Note that the entire scalar multiplication is performed without projective Y coordinates as described in part 6.
5. **Common-Z Coordinates.** For better scalar-multiplication performance, we raised the projective coordinates of $P = (X_0, Z_0)$ and $Dbl(P) = (X_1, Z_1)$ to a common Z coordinate by performing $X_0 \leftarrow X_0 \cdot Z_1$, $X_1 \leftarrow X_1 \cdot Z_0$, and $Z \leftarrow Z_0 \cdot Z_1$. This has the advantage that only three coordinates have to be maintained in RAM during scalar multiplication which actually can be used to reduce the number of needed registers or to increase the computation performance [20,21].
6. **ECC Scalar Multiplication.** We applied the improved Montgomery ladder proposed by T. Izu, B. Möller, and T. Takagi [15]. First, the method provides security against SPA attacks by performing the same operations in every Montgomery-ladder iteration. Second, x-coordinate only formulas have been applied according to E. Brier and M. Joye [4]. This allows to perform all computations without y coordinates. Third, the doubling and addition operations are combined to one operation which helps to reduce the computation of intermediate values that are used in both group operations. Fourth, performing doubling and addition in common Z-coordinate representation allows fast formulas for our implementation needing 12 finite-field multiplications, 4 squarings (realized as multiplications), 9 additions, and 7 subtractions for one Montgomery-ladder iteration (including common Z-coordinate transformation). Three coordinates (X_0, X_1, and Z) and four intermediate values of 192 bits have to be stored in RAM. The resulting storage requirement for the point multiplication is therefore 7×192 bits. Fifth,

the Montgomery ladder holds the base point as invariant throughout the entire point multiplication. This fact can be used to provide fault-injection countermeasures by checking the invariant during and/or after scalar multiplication. The following curve-equation check incorporates the invariant to provide such a countermeasure.

7. **Check Curve Equation.** We check if the resulting point is still on the curve after scalar multiplication. We implemented the countermeasure according to N. Ebeid and R. Lambert [6] that checks the curve equation in projective coordinates without the need of inversions[1]. However, the countermeasure includes also the recovery of the projective Y coordinate which results in 22 multiplications, 12 additions, and 7 subtractions to perform the countermeasure in our implementation. The additional overhead for including the countermeasure is 2.36 % of total chip area and 0.82 % of execution time.

8. **Final Signing Process.** The last step in our ECDSA implementation is to perform the final signing process. For this, the projective X coordinate of the scalar multiplication is transformed into affine coordinates by a multiplication with the inverted Z coordinate. After that, all operations are performed modulo the general prime n. First, the ephemeral key k is inverted. Second, the value $\bar{x}$ is tested to be zero or greater than the modulus n (a subtraction of n is performed if necessary). Third, we calculated $s = k^{-1}e + (k^{-1}r)d$ instead of $s = k^{-1}(e + dr)$. This has its reason in the fact that the fixed private key d will be multiplied by a randomized intermediate value $k^{-1}r$ which avoids first-order Differential Power Analysis (DPA) attacks targeting the intermediate values of the private key multiplication [12]. The resulting digital signature is stored in RAM and consists of the tuple (r, s).

6 Synthesis Results

The proposed ECDSA processor has been synthesized using a $0.35\,\mu m$ CMOS technology (c35b4 AMS) with Cadence RTL compiler. The synthesis result includes the entire processor including microcontroller, program ROM, ISE ROM tables, address and instruction decoding, RAM macro, ROM (ECC constants), datapath (ALU + register), and an 16-bit AMBA interface. The synthesis results are shown in Figure 4.

The power consumption of the processor has been simulated using Synopsys NanoSim. For the $0.35\,\mu m$ CMOS technology, the simulated total mean current is $387\,\mu A$ at 3.3 volt and 847 kHz. The power consumption distribution of the circuit is shown in Figure 5. The highest power consumption is needed for the RAM macro followed by the datapath, clock tree, and ISE circuit. The program ROM, the ROM for ECC constants, and the microcontroller circuit need only around 3-4 % of the total power consumption.

Table 1 gives a comparison with related work. ECC implementations over 192-bit prime fields have been reported by F. Fürbass et al. [8], J. Wolkerstorfer [27], and A. Satoh et al. [25]. E. Öztürk et al. [24] reported a $\mathbb{F}_p$ coprocessor over

---

[1] The curve-equation formula at page 3 should be $Z(Y^2 - bZ^2) = X(X^2 + aZ^2)$.

Fig. 4. Synthesis results

Fig. 5. Power consumption chart

Component	GE
Microcontroller without program ROM	1 786
Program ROM (ECDSA, SHA1, RNG)	2 132
ISE control logic (ROM, decoder,...)	3 310
2048-bit RAM macro	8 727
ROM for ECC constants	789
Datapath (ALU+register)	2 371
Total Size	**19 115**

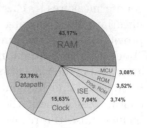

the field $(2^{167} + 1)/3$. Their implementations differ in the supported features but need between 23 000 GE and 30 000 GE of chip area. ECC implementations over binary fields have been reported by D. Hein [11], H. Bock [3], Y. K. Lee [19], S. Kumar [18], L. Batina [2], and R. Schroeppel [26].

Table 1. Comparison with Related Work

	Area [GE]	Time [Cycles]	Field	Features
This Work	**19 115**	**859 188**	$\mathbb{F}_{p192}$	**ECDSA, SHA1, RNG**
Fürbass07 [8]	23 656	502 000	$\mathbb{F}_{p192}$	ECDSA(no SHA1,no RNG)
Wolkerstorfer05 [27]	23 800	677 000	$\mathbb{F}_{p192}$	ECC
Öztürk04 [24]	30 333	545 440	$\mathbb{F}_{(2^{167}+1)/3}$	ECC
Satoh03 [25]	29 655	4 165 000	$\mathbb{F}_{p192}$	ECC
Hein08 [11]	11 904	296 000	$\mathbb{F}_{2^{163}}$	ECC
Bock08 [3]	12 876	80 000	$\mathbb{F}_{2^{163}}$	ECC, DH, RNG
Lee08 [19]	12 506	302 457	$\mathbb{F}_{2^{163}}$	ECC, Schnorr
Kumar06 [18]	19 048	527 284	$\mathbb{F}_{2^{193}}$	ECC
Batina06 [2]	8 104	353 000	$\mathbb{F}_{2^{131}}$	ECC, without memory
Schroeppel02 [26]	191 000	93 000	$\mathbb{F}_{2^{178}}$	ECC, ElGamal, PRNG

7 Conclusions

In this article, we present results of a low-resource ECDSA processor suitable for RFID applications. The processor allows digitally signing of challenges of a reader and offers a large scale of important cryptographic services such as entity and message authentication, non-repudiation, and data integrity. Furthermore, it allows applications to perform an electronic proof of origin of RFID tags in the field. To meet the low-area requirements, we based our design on a tiny microcontroller that implements several instruction-set extensions for public-key cryptography. The total size of the processor is 19 115 GE and needs 859 188 clock cycles to digitally sign a message. The chip will be fabricated as a prototyping sample in summer 2010.

Acknowledgements

The authors would like to thank Johannes Wolkerstorfer and Marcel Medwed for their valuable inputs and discussions. This work has been supported by the Austrian Government through the research program FIT-IT Trust in IT Systems (Project CRYPTA, Project Number 820843), and by the IAP Programme P6/26 BCRYPT of the Belgian State (Belgian Science Policy).

References

1. Batina, L., Guajardo, J., Kerins, T., Mentens, N., Tuyls, P., Verbauwhede, I.: Public-Key Cryptography for RFID-Tags. In: Workshop on RFID Security 2006 (RFIDSec 2006), Graz, Austria (July 12-14, 2006)
2. Batina, L., Mentens, N., Sakiyama, K., Preneel, B., Verbauwhede, I.: Low-Cost Elliptic Curve Cryptography for Wireless Sensor Networks. In: Buttyán, L., Gligor, V.D., Westhoff, D. (eds.) ESAS 2006. LNCS, vol. 4357, pp. 6–17. Springer, Heidelberg (2006)
3. Bock, H., Braun, M., Dichtl, M., Hess, E., Heyszl, J., Kargl, W., Koroschetz, H., Meyer, B., Seuschek, H.: A Milestone Towards RFID Products Offering Asymmetric Authentication Based on Elliptic Curve Cryptography. Invited talk at RFIDsec (July 2008)
4. Brier, E., Joye, M.: Weierstraß Elliptic Curves and Side-Channel Attacks. In: Naccache, D., Paillier, P. (eds.) PKC 2002. LNCS, vol. 2274, pp. 335–345. Springer, Heidelberg (2002)
5. Coron, J.-S.: Resistance against Differential Power Analysis for Elliptic Curve Cryptosystems. In: Koç, Ç.K., Paar, C. (eds.) CHES 1999. LNCS, vol. 1717, pp. 292–302. Springer, Heidelberg (1999)
6. Ebeid, N., Lambert, R.: Securing the Elliptic Curve Montgomery Ladder Against Fault Attacks. In: Proceedings of Workshop on Fault Diagnosis and Tolerance in Cryptography, FDTC 2009, Lausanne, Switzerland, pp. 46–50 (September 2009)
7. Feldhofer, M., Dominikus, S., Wolkerstorfer, J.: Strong Authentication for RFID Systems using the AES Algorithm. In: Joye, M., Quisquater, J.-J. (eds.) CHES 2004. LNCS, vol. 3156, pp. 357–370. Springer, Heidelberg (2004)
8. Fürbass, F., Wolkerstorfer, J.: ECC Processor with Low Die Size for RFID Applications. In: Proceedings of 2007 IEEE International Symposium on Circuits and Systems. IEEE, Los Alamitos (May 2007)
9. Großschädl, J., Savacs, E.: Instruction Set Extensions for Fast Arithmetic in Finite Fields GF(p) and GF(2^m). In: Joye, M., Quisquater, J.-J. (eds.) CHES 2004. LNCS, vol. 3156, pp. 133–147. Springer, Heidelberg (2004)
10. Hachez, G., Quisquater, J.-J.: Montgomery exponentiation with no final subtractions: Improved results. In: Koç, Ç.K., Paar, C. (eds.) CHES 2000. LNCS, vol. 1965, pp. 91–100. Springer, Heidelberg (2000)
11. Hein, D., Wolkerstorfer, J., Felber, N.: ECC is Ready for RFID A Proof in Silicon. In: Avanzi, R.M., Keliher, L., Sica, F. (eds.) SAC 2008. LNCS, vol. 5381, pp. 401–413. Springer, Heidelberg (2009)
12. Hutter, M., Medwed, M., Hein, D., Wolkerstorfer, J.: Attacking ECDSA-Enabled RFID Devices. In: Abdalla, M., Pointcheval, D., Fouque, P.-A., Vergnaud, D. (eds.) ACNS 2009, vol. 5536, pp. 519–534. Springer, Heidelberg (May 2009)

13. International Organisation for Standardization (ISO). Information Technology - Security Techniques - Entity authentication mechanisms - Part 3: Entity authentication using a public key algorithm (1993)
14. International Organisation for Standardization (ISO). ISO/IEC 7816-4: Information technology - Identification cards - Integrated circuit(s) cards with contacts - Part 4: Interindustry commands for interchange (1995), http://www.iso.org
15. Izu, T., Möller, B., Takagi, T.: Improved Elliptic Curve Multiplication Methods Resistant against Side Channel Attacks. In: Menezes, A., Sarkar, P. (eds.) INDOCRYPT 2002. LNCS, vol. 2551, pp. 296–313. Springer, Heidelberg (2002)
16. Joye, M., Yen, S.-M.: The Montgomery Powering Ladder. In: Kaliski Jr., B.S., Koç, Ç.K., Paar, C. (eds.) CHES 2002. LNCS, vol. 2523, pp. 291–302. Springer, Heidelberg (2003)
17. Kaliski, B.: The Montgomery Inverse and its Applications. IEEE Transactions on Computers 44(8), 1064–1065 (1995)
18. Kumar, S.S., Paar, C.: Are standards compliant Elliptic Curve Cryptosystems feasible on RFID? In: Workshop on RFID Security 2006 (RFIDSec 2006), Graz, Austria, July 12-14 (2006)
19. Lee, Y.K., Sakiyama, K., Batina, L., Verbauwhede, I.: Elliptic-Curve-Based Security Processor for RFID. IEEE Transactions on Computers 57(11), 1514–1527 (2008)
20. Lee, Y.K., Verbauwhede, I.: A Compact Architecture for Montgomery Elliptic Curve Scalar Multiplication Processor. In: Kim, S., Yung, M., Lee, H.-W. (eds.) WISA 2007. LNCS, vol. 4867, pp. 115–127. Springer, Heidelberg (2008)
21. Meloni, N.: Fast and Secure Elliptic Curve Scalar Multiplication Over Prime Fields Using Special Addition Chains. Cryptology ePrint Archive, Report 2006/216 (2006)
22. Montgomery, P.L.: Modular Multiplication without Trial Division. Mathematics of Computation 44, 519–521 (1985)
23. National Institute of Standards and Technology (NIST). FIPS-186-2: Digital Signature Standard (DSS) (January 2000), http://www.itl.nist.gov/fipspubs/
24. Öztürk, E., Sunar, B., Savas, E.: Low-Power Elliptic Curve Cryptography Using Scaled Modular Arithmetic. In: Joye, M., Quisquater, J.-J. (eds.) CHES 2004. LNCS, vol. 3156, pp. 92–106. Springer, Heidelberg (2004)
25. Satoh, A., Takano, K.: A Scalable Dual-Field Elliptic Curve Cryptographic Processor. IEEE Transactions on Computers 52(4), 449–460 (2003)
26. Schroeppel, R., Beaver, C., Gonzales, R., Miller, R., Draelos, T.: A Low-Power Design for an Elliptic Curve Digital Signature Chip. In: Kaliski Jr., B.S., Koç, Ç.K., Paar, C. (eds.) CHES 2002. LNCS, vol. 2523, pp. 366–380. Springer, Heidelberg (2003)
27. Wolkerstorfer, J.: Is Elliptic-Curve Cryptography Suitable for Small Devices? In: Workshop on RFID and Lightweight Crypto, Graz, Austria, July 13-15, pp. 78–91 (2005)

Towards a Practical Solution to the RFID Desynchronization Problem*

Gerhard de Koning Gans and Flavio D. Garcia

Institute for Computing and Information Sciences
Radboud University Nijmegen
P.O. Box 9010, 6500 GL
Nijmegen, The Netherlands
{gkoningg,flaviog}@cs.ru.nl

Abstract. Even though RFID technology has expanded enormously, this expansion has been hindered by privacy concerns. In order to prevent an adversary from tracking RFID tags and thus breaking location privacy, tags have to update their internal state with every authentication attempt. Although this technique solves the privacy problem, it has the side effect that tags and back office might desynchronize. This desynchronization can be caused by physical conditions or by adversarial intervention. If we look at consumer product identification, RFID labels and barcodes are bound to coexist for quite some time. In this paper we exploit this coexistence to reduce the workload at the reader/backoffice and allow re-synchronization. Concretely, we propose an authentication protocol that achieves correctness, forward-privacy under mild additional assumptions and synchronization in the random oracle model.

Keywords: RFID, barcodes, location privacy, forward-privacy, random oracle model.

1 Introduction

Over the last few years, the use of RFID technology has expanded enormously. It is currently deployed in electronic passports, tags for consumer goods, public transport ticketing systems, race timing, and countless other applications.

RFID technology have recently become popular as a replacement for traditional barcodes in the consumer supply chain. Even though RFID labels have indeed advantages over barcodes, they also have some drawbacks. On the one hand, RFID labels can be read faster than barcodes and have less restrictions on the physical positioning of the label. These advantages do not necessarily imply that barcodes will be replaced by RFID labels and are no longer needed. It is still useful to have some backup identification possibility. For

* Partially supported by the research program Sentinels (www.sentinels.nl), project PEARL (7639). Sentinels is being financed by Technology Foundation STW, the Netherlands Organization for Scientific Research (NWO), and the Dutch Ministry of Economic Affairs.

instance, when an RFID label breaks down it is still possible to switch to barcode identification. Barcodes are often printed right on the product (wrapping) and therefore are currently cheaper than an RFID label. Furthermore, the barcode system is deeply entrenched in many systems and complete replacement is not going to happen in the near future [WNLY06]. Actually, barcodes and RFID systems have to be used in parallel for many more years. On the other hand, the widespread use of RFID has raised various privacy concerns. Since most RFID tags will send a unique identifier to every reader that attempts to communicate with it, an adversary could build an "RFID profile" of an individual, i.e., the collection of unique identifiers of the RFID tags that the individual usually carries. This profile could be used to track this person, or to infer behavior such as spending or traveling patterns, jeopardizing this person's privacy.

If we focus on inexpensive EPC-like tags, think of the ones attached to a product in the supermarket, we observe that RFID tags are often used in parallel with barcodes, instead of replacing them. The combination of barcode and RFID label can be found on several products nowadays. Figure 1 shows an example of such a tag.

In this paper we exploit this duality by using a combination of barcode and RFID labels in order to get the best of each technology. On the one hand, flexible reading and unique identification, on the other hand the infeasibility for an adversary to track goods at will. We present a practical solution where both RFID label and barcode are combined in order to provide location privacy.

Many privacy notions have been discussed in the literature but the notion of forward privacy is generally considered satisfactory [Vau07, BBEG09]. This privacy notion requires that an adversary who has control over the communication media should not even be able to tell whether two protocol instances involve the same tag or not. Moreover, even when all secret information in the tag is revealed to the adversary, this should not be able to link this tag with previously recorded protocol runs. In order to achieve

Fig. 1. Barcode and RFID label

such a strong security notion, it is necessary that the tag updates its state (using a one-way function) with every authentication attempt. This continuous updating might lead to desynchronization between the back office and the tag. This desynchronization can be both, induced by an adversary or simply due to physical conditions like the distance between tag and reader.

Related Work. A large number of protocols have been proposed in the literature that aim to achieve location privacy [JW05, Tsu06, BdMM08] and concretely forward-privacy [OSK[+]03, Vau07, BBEG09]. Unfortunately, many of these proposals turn out to be either impractical due to the resource-constrained nature of RFID or suffer from desynchronization. Achieving forward privacy without using public key cryptography has shown to be a very challenging task. In fact, Vaudenay [Vau07] showed that having a forward private stateless RFID scheme implies key agreement, which is believed to be require public-key cryptography. Achieving forward-privacy with symmetric cryptography requires heavy workload on the reader side and these protocols often suffer from desynchronization. A distinguished example is due to Avoine [AO05], who proposed a scheme based on OSK [OSK $^+$03] that achieves forward-privacy. Unfortunately this protocol suffers from desynchronization which has impact on availability. The scheme of Dimitriou [Dim05] is reminiscent of the Hash-Locking scheme of Weis [WSR $^+$04] but it also suffers from desynchronization. For a complete survey of related work we refer the reader to [Jue06].

Our Contribution. This paper proposes a forward private RFID authentication protocol that incorporates a mechanism for re-synchronization. We exploit the coexistence of RFID and barcodes in the protocol design in order to achieve a more efficient search procedure on the reader side. The main idea of the protocol resembles that of OSK, except that we allow a limited and small number of failed authentication attempts. This reduces dramatically the search space on the reader side. Should this limit be exceeded, then the barcode allows the protocol to re-synchronize. This re-synchronization takes place within the authentication protocol itself so that it does not compromises privacy.

We propose a model for RFID privacy using provable security techniques, following the lines of [Avo05, Vau07, JW09, GvR10]. Within this model we define correctness, forward-privacy and synchronization. Finally, we show that our protocol satisfies all these security notions using the random oracle methodology.

Organization of the Paper. In Section 2 we briefly explain the desynchronization problem. Section 3 describes the system and adversarial models. Section 4 then provides definitions for security, (forward-)privacy, (strong-)correctness and desynchronization. Section 5 describes our protocol and Section 6 substantiates the security claims. Finally, Section 7 concludes the paper and discusses future work.

2   The Desynchronization Problem

Our goal is a practical RFID protocol that provides location privacy. The meaning of the adjective "practical" heavily depends on the resources and restrictions that are given. A good first attempt is the following protocol where a tag T sends the hash of its identity id concatenated with some random value r and r itself to a reader R.

$$T \rightarrow R : \ h(id, r), r$$

Assuming a perfect hash function and random number generator it is impossible for an eavesdropper to retrieve the identity id. This small protocol is more or less what was proposed as the Randomized Hash-Locking scheme by Weis et al.

in [WSR $^{+}$04]. The reader is connected to a back-end where a database is maintained with all tag identities. The big drawback in this solution is in the search procedure. To look up a tag every identity needs to be hashed in combination with the random r. This drastically reduces the applicability of this solution to small systems with a limited number of tags.

Another well-known RFID protocol from the literature is OSK [OSK $^{+}$03] where the tag identifiers are updated in every protocol run regardless whether it was a successful run or not. This is done by a hash chain where $h^i(x)$ means that x is successively hashed i times. In [CC08] it is shown that the OSK scheme is synchronizable since $D_\mathcal{R} = \infty$, $D_\mathcal{T} = 0$, $R_\mathcal{R} = \infty$ and $R_\mathcal{T} = 0$. This illustrates the fact that a resynchronizable protocol is not automatically efficient in its search procedure. For instance, a denial-of-service attack (DoS attack) might be induced by simply sending a random value to the reader.

Barcode Analogy. The protocol that is introduced in this paper can be best explained in analogy to the traditional and very successful barcode. RFID is used to automatically identify products and to process the gathered data. This can be used to track products along the supply chain in industry [Att07], the medical sector [WCO^{+}07], libraries [MW04] and many other situations where barcodes are already employed.

A well known daily example of barcodes can be found in a shop. The cashier scans the barcodes of products that the customer wants to buy. From time to time the scanner might not be able to read a barcode. In such cases the cashier enters the serial number by hand using a keypad. This backup procedure costs more time and effort, but at the end the checkout procedure is far more efficient than it would be when every product was entered manually at default.

The number of times that the cashier has to fall back to the manual input procedure is very low. If this was not the case, the use of barcodes would be questionable. Actually, we face the same problem in privacy friendly RFID. Here, the tag and reader need to stay synchronized in some way. To the best of our knowledge, all attempts to design a protocol that keeps up with these discrepancies try to achieve this without any human intervention. Many proposals try to prevent desynchronization purely by means of the wireless link. This becomes a very hard task when, at the same time, an adversary is allowed to exhaustively query a tag. In practice desynchronization is a problem that should be handled, merely because it may also occur due to physical problems in the reading process. Now, recall the same shop as mentioned before but let the products be equipped with RFID tags. When a tag is no longer synchronized with a genuine reader and the system fails to identify a tag, we fall back to the use of a *second channel* which provides the reader with the needed identity. This identity can then be read from a barcode or serial number which is physically printed on the RFID tag. A protocol run in which a *second channel* is used to synchronize the tag and reader state is called a *synchronization run*. Since a *synchronization run* involves additional actions apart from running the protocol it can be treated as a special instance of the protocol. In general, these special instances occur scarcely in practical settings. In this paper we further elaborate on a system like presented above.

3 System Model

Consider a scheme where readers have a secure communication channel with the back office. We assume that readers are single threaded, i.e., can only have one active protocol instance with a tag at a time. After running a protocol with a tag, the reader has an output that is typically the identity of the tag. New readers and tags can be added to the system at will. The formal definition follows.

Definition 1 (RFID scheme). *An* RFID scheme Π *consists of:*

- *a probabilistic polynomial-time algorithm* SetupSystem *that takes as input the security parameter* 1^η *and outputs the public key pair* (sk, pk) *of the system.*
- *a probabilistic polynomial-time algorithm* SetupReader *that takes as input the secret key of the system* sk *and outputs the initial state of the reader* s *and the reader's secret* k.
- *a probabilistic polynomial-time algorithm* SetupTag *that takes as input the secret key of the system* sk *and outputs the initial state of the tag* s *and the tag's secret* k.
- *a polynomial-time interactive protocol between a reader and a tag, where the reader returns* Output. *Output is typically the identity of the tag.*

An adversary is a probabilistic polynomial-time algorithm that interacts with the system by means of different oracles. The environment keeps track of the state of each element in the system and answers the oracle queries according to the protocol. Besides adding new tags and readers to the system and being able to communicate with them, an adversary can also corrupt tags. This models techniques like differential power analysis and chip slicing. By corrupting a tag an adversary retrieves its internal state.

Definition 2 (Adversary). *An* adversary *is a probabilistic polynomial-time algorithm that takes as input the system public key* pk *and has access to the following oracles:*

- CreateReader($\mathcal{R}$) *creates a new reader by calling* SetupReader(sk) *and updates the state of the back-office. This new reader is referenced as* $\mathcal{R}$.
- CreateTag($\mathcal{T}$) *creates a new tag* $\mathcal{T}$ *by calling* SetupTag(sk) *and updates the state of the back-office. This new tag is referenced as* $\mathcal{T}$.
- CorruptTag($\mathcal{T}$) *returns the internal state* s *of the tag* $\mathcal{T}$.
- Launch($\mathcal{R}$) *attempts to initiate a new protocol instance at reader* $\mathcal{R}$. *If* $\mathcal{R}$ *has already an active protocol instance then* Launch *fails and returns zero. Otherwise it starts a new protocol instance and returns one.*

- Send(m, A) *sends a message* m *to the entity* A *and returns its response* m'. *The entity* A *can either be a reader* $\mathcal{R}$ *or a tag* $\mathcal{T}$.
- Result$(\mathcal{R})$ *outputs whether or not the output of the last finished protocol instance at reader* $\mathcal{R}$ *is not* $\perp$, *i.e.,* Output $\neq \perp$.

Definition 3. *We denote by* $\mathcal{O}$ *the set of oracles* {CreateReader, CreateTag, CorruptTag, Launch, Send, Result}.

4   Security Definitions

This section elaborates on the security and privacy definitions from the literature, much of it is standard.

The main goal of an RFID system is security, which means that readers are able to authenticate legitimate tags. Throughout this paper we focus on privacy. For the sake of self containment, we include here the following security definition which is an adapted version of the security definition proposed in [Vau07].

Definition 4 (Security). *An RFID scheme is* secure *if for all adversaries* $\mathcal{A}$ *and for all readers* $\mathcal{R}$, *the probability that* $\mathcal{R}$ *outputs the identity of a legitimate tag while the last finished protocol instance at reader* $\mathcal{R}$ *and this tag did not have any matching conversation, is a negligible function of* η. *Matching conversation here means that* $\mathcal{R}$ *and the tag (successfully) executed the authentication protocol.*

Next we define privacy composing the definitions of Juels and Weis [JW09] and Vaudenay [Vau07] since each of them has its advantages: the former is indistinguishability based, which makes it more practical; the latter has the drawback of being simulation based but is stronger and allows for a variety of adversaries with custom capabilities. Privacy is defined in an IND-CCA like fashion where the adversary tries to win the privacy game. In this game, the environment creates system parameters by calling SetupSystem. Then it gives the public key of the system pk to the adversary $\mathcal{A}_0$. This adversary has access to the set of oracles $\mathcal{O}$. Eventually, $\mathcal{A}_0$ must output two uncorrupted challenge tags $\mathcal{T}_0^\star$ and $\mathcal{T}_1^\star$. Then, the environment chooses a random bit b and gives the adversary $\mathcal{A}_1$ access to $\mathcal{T}_b^\star$. At this point, the original references to $\mathcal{T}_0^\star$ and $\mathcal{T}_1^\star$ are no longer valid. Again, the adversary has access to all oracles $\mathcal{O}$. Finally, the adversary outputs a guess bit b'. The adversary wins the game if $b = b'$. The formal definition follows.

Definition 5 (Privacy game).

$$
\begin{array}{l}
\textbf{\textit{Priv-Game}}_{\Pi, \mathcal{A}}(\eta) : \\
\quad (sk, pk) \leftarrow \text{SetupSystem}(1^\eta) \\
\quad \mathcal{T}_0^\star, \mathcal{T}_1^\star \leftarrow \mathcal{A}_0^{\mathcal{O}}(pk) \\
\quad b \leftarrow \{0, 1\} \\
\quad b' \leftarrow \mathcal{A}_1^{\mathcal{O}}(\mathcal{T}_b^\star) \\
\quad \textbf{\textit{winif}}\ b = b'.
\end{array}
$$

The challenge tags $T_0^\star$ and $T_1^\star$ must be uncorrupted, which means that no CorruptTag($T_{\{0,1\}}^\star$) *query has been made. Adversaries implicitly pass state.*

In general, it is hard to define a realistic adversarial model as different applications have different requirements. Following the lines of Vaudenay [Vau07], we consider different classes of adversaries depending on their capabilities. The notions of forward, weak and narrow adversaries are due to Vaudenay. The notion of thin adversary is introduced in this paper to handle protocols that use a *second channel*. Intuitively, a *forward* adversary is an adversary that observes communication between tags and readers and later on acquires one of these tags and tries to link it with some of the past sessions, compromising its privacy. If the adversary succeeds to do so, with non-negligible probability, we say that is a *winning* adversary. A *weak* adversary is an adversary that is unable to corrupt tags. In real life scenarios it is often realistic to assume that an adversary can see the outcome of an authentication attempt. For instance, this is the case of transport ticketing systems where an adversary could observe whether the gate of the metro opens or not, for a specific tag. An adversary that is unable to do so is called *narrow*. In line with the *narrow* adversary we introduce the *thin* adversary. A *thin* adversary cannot see additional information that is provided to the reader. Think for example of additional identifying information to make the search procedure more efficient.

Definition 6 (Types of adversaries). *A* forward *adversary is an adversary that has access to all oracles $\mathcal{O}$. A* weak *adversary cannot perform any* CorruptTag *query at all. A* narrow *adversary does never query the* Result *oracle. Finally, we introduce the notion of* thin *adversary which, like the* narrow *adversary, does never query the* Result *oracle. Furthermore, a* thin *adversary cannot see synchronization runs and thus cannot see protocol runs where information is used that is obtained by the* second channel.

Remark 1. Note that this notion of forward adversary is stronger than the one proposed by Vaudenay and closer to the notion of Juels and Weis.

Definition 7 (Privacy). *Let C be a class of adversaries in {forward, weak, narrow, thin}. An RFID scheme is said to be C-private if for all probabilistic polynomial-time adversaries $\mathcal{A} = (\mathcal{A}_0, \mathcal{A}_1) \in C$*

$$\mathbb{P}[\boldsymbol{Priv\text{-}Game}_{\Pi,\mathcal{A}}(\eta)] - \frac{1}{2}$$

is a negligible function of η.

In our definition of *desynchronization* we follow [CC08]. Consider a valid tag which is referenced by id. Let its corresponding key k be denoted k_{id}. Every tag is initialized by SetupTag using the initial key k_{id}^0. Then, k_{id}^i denotes the tag key after i updates. Since both reader and tag keep track of their own instance of k_{id}, we write rk_{id} for the reader instance and tk_{id} for the tag instance of k_{id}. Usually, $rk_{id} = tk_{id} = k_{id}^*$, but when the tag and reader are no longer synchronized we have $tk_{id} = k_{id}^i$ and $rk_{id} = k_{id}^j$ where $i \neq j$. In order to allow reasoning about desynchronization, first *correctness* is defined, then the definition of a *strong correctness game* follows. In its turn this game is used to define *strong correctness*. Finally, it is defined when an RFID scheme can be subject to *desynchronization*.

Definition 8 (Correctness). *An RFID system is said to be correct when the reader outputs $\bot$ after an authentication protocol π with a non-legitimate tag and outputs the tag id after an authentication protocol π with a legitimate tag.*

The **Strong Correctness Game** is comparable to the **Privacy-Game** and its setup is also indistinguishability based. Again, the challenger generates system parameters by calling SetupSystem. Then, the public key pk is given to an adversary $\mathcal{A}$ which has access to the set of oracles $\mathcal{O}$. At some point $\mathcal{A}$ outputs an uncorrupted challenge tag $\mathcal{T}^\star$. Then, the environment runs the authentication protocol with $\mathcal{T}^\star$. This yields an output $\bot$ when the tag was not recognized as legitimate or an identifier id when a legitimate tag was found. Finally, the adversary wins if the reader outputs $\bot$ and cannot identify $\mathcal{T}^\star$.

Definition 9 (Strong Correctness Game).

$$
\begin{array}{|l|}
\hline
\textbf{\textit{Strong-Corr-Game}}_{\Pi,\mathcal{A}}(\eta) \;: \\
(sk, pk) \leftarrow \text{SetupSystem}(1^\eta) \\
\mathcal{T}^\star \leftarrow \mathcal{A}^{\mathcal{O}}(pk) \\
\text{Execute}(\mathcal{R}^\star, \mathcal{T}^\star) \\
b \leftarrow \text{Result}(\mathcal{R}^\star) \\
\textbf{\textit{win if}}\ b = 0. \\
\hline
\end{array}
$$

where $\text{Execute}(\mathcal{R}, \mathcal{T})$ *runs the authentication protocol between the reader $\mathcal{R}$ and the tag $\mathcal{T}$. The challenge tag $\mathcal{T}^\star$ must be uncorrupted, which means that no* $\text{CorruptTag}(\mathcal{T}^\star)$ *query has been made.*

Definition 10 (Strong Correctness). *Let C be a class of adversaries in $\{forward, weak, narrow, thin\}$. An RFID system is said to be C-strong correct if for all probabilistic polynomial-time adversaries $\mathcal{A} \in C$*

$$\mathbb{P}[\textbf{\textit{Strong-Corr-Game}}_{\Pi,\mathcal{A}}(\eta)] - \frac{1}{2}$$

is a negligible function of η.

Definition 11 (Key shifts). *A key shift in an RFID scheme is the increment of $|i - j|$ by 1 for an arbitrary tag $\mathcal{T}$ with tk_{id}^i and reader $\mathcal{R}$ with rk_{id}^j. The value $|i - j| \in \mathbb{N}$ is called* number of key shifts.

Remark 2. Note that our definition of *key shift* corresponds with the definition of *desynchronization* in [CC08]. We prefer to define *desynchronization* as the case where synchronization between a tag and reader is no longer possible.

The desynchronization value is a pair $(D_{\mathcal{R}}, D_{\mathcal{T}})$ where $D_{\mathcal{R}}$ is the maximum number of key shifts $j - i$ with $rk_{id}^i \neq tk_{id}^j$ and $i < j$, while $D_{\mathcal{T}}$ is the maximum number of key shifts $i - j$ with $rk^i_{id} \neq tk^j_{id}$ and $i > j$. Correspondingly, the resynchronization value is a pair $(R_\mathcal{R}, R_\mathcal{T})$ where $R_\mathcal{R}$ and $R_\mathcal{T}$ are the maximum number of possible key shifts after which the RFID system still is *strong correct*. An RFID scheme is said to be synchronizable when both $D_\mathcal{R} \leq R_\mathcal{R}$ and $D_\mathcal{T} \leq R_\mathcal{T}$.

Definition 12 (Desynchronization). *An RFID scheme is subject to* desynchronization *when* $D_\mathcal{R} > R_\mathcal{R}$ *or* $D_\mathcal{T} > R_\mathcal{T}$.

5 Protocol Description

This section introduces a protocol that exploits the use of a *second channel* to achieve *thin-forward* privacy. The protocol should not be subject to desynchronization. Even when a tag is queried an unbounded number of times, this should not result in a denial-of-service (DoS) or in identification failure. First, we briefly elaborate on the notion of *second channel* that we use, then we define the tag and reader state in this protocol, and finally we discuss the protocol itself.

Second Channel. The protocol uses a *second channel* which is a channel between the tag and reader that allows a tag to send its tag identity to the reader. This channel uses other physical means than the wireless link and is therefore out of the scope of a *narrow* adversary. Like *narrow* adversaries cannot perform the Result query [Vau07], i.e. cannot learn outgoing messages on channels other than the wireless link, they cannot learn incoming messages that are sent on channels other than the wireless link. An example of an outgoing message on a *second channel* is for instance a door that opens when a tag is successfully authenticated. An example of an incoming message is for instance a barcode scanner or keypad connected to an RFID reader that communicates the tag identity to the reader. Of course, this identity still needs to be verified by the reader using the wireless link. The *second channel* speeds up the search process at the reader side when the tag and reader keys are relatively shifted. It does not replace the wireless link.

Tag and Reader State. In order to keep track of all the state changes and achieve an RFID system that cannot be desynchronized, the state is managed as follows. First we introduce some notation.

Notation	Meaning
id	The tag identifier
k	The session key; this key is updated in every protocol run
$\tilde{k}$	The synchronization key; for tag-reader synchronization
$h^i(x)$	i times successively hashing of x

Every tag is identified by an identifier id, but this identifier is not part of the tag state. However, a reader needs to relate this tag state somehow to the identifier of the tag. The tag state consists of a session key k and a synchronization key $\tilde{k}$.

This pair of keys $(k, \tilde{k})$ uniquely identifies a tag and thus can be related to id. The session key is updated in every protocol run, while the synchronization key is only updated after an authenticated message from the reader. A tag always starts to execute an internal key update before it sends any message to the outer world. The purpose of $\tilde{k}$ is to allow synchronization between the tag and reader. Finally, it should be possible to extract the identity id from the tag using a *second channel*. For example, the identity id can be printed on the tag as a barcode, which allows a barcode scanner to send id over the *second channel*. The reader state contains, apart from k and $\tilde{k}$, also the tag identifier id. To distinguish the keys in the reader state from the keys in the tag state we write $rk_{id}, r\tilde{k}_{id}$ and $tk_{id}, t\tilde{k}_{id}$, respectively. There are two ways in which the reader identifies a tag.

- The reader pre-computes $h(h^i(rk_{id}), n_r)$ for all $i < N$, all tag ids, and some nonce n_r. Now, identification is a look-up in its pre-computed table (See Tables 1 and 2).
- The reader obtains the identity id by use of a *second channel*. Now, id allows the reader to look up the synchronization key $r\tilde{k}_{id}$, which in its turn is used to induce synchronization of the tag and reader state.

The first way solely uses the wireless link whereas the latter way also uses the *second channel*. The synchronization is needed when the tag's session key is beyond the scope N of the reader. It allows a reader to quickly frame which tag it is targeting.

The protocol design is such that after a synchronization attempt of the reader a tag could either update its synchronization key or not. Depending on the situation there are two tag states possible. Therefore, the reader keeps track of two states for each tag simultaneously. The next protocol run in which this particular tag participates resolves then which of the two states is valid. In Table 1 and 2 the two states are captured by the record status st, which can either be 'old' (**O**) or 'new' (**N**). This makes the reader state consist of at most two tuples $(id, st, k, \tilde{k})$ per tag.

Table 1. Reader Database

id	Status st	Key k	Sync Key $\tilde{k}$	Identifier 1	$\ldots$	Identifier i
id_1	**O**	k_1	$\tilde{k}_1$	$h(h^1(k_1), n_r)$	$\ldots$	$h(h^i(k_1), n_r)$
id_1	**N**	k'_1	$\tilde{k}'_1$	$h(h^1(k'_1), n_r)$	$\ldots$	$h(h^i(k'_1), n_r)$
id_2	**O**	k_2	$\tilde{k}_2$	$h(h^1(k_2), n_r)$	$\ldots$	$h(h^i(k_2), n_r)$
$\vdots$	$\vdots$	$\vdots$	$\vdots$	$\vdots$	$\ddots$	$\vdots$
id_n	**N**	k_n	$\tilde{k}_n$	$h(h^1(k_n), n_r)$	$\ldots$	$h(h^i(k_n), n_r)$

Table 2. Look-up

Identifier	id	st
$h(h^1(k_1), n_r)$	id_1	**O**
$h(h^1(k'_1), n_r)$	id_1	**N**
$h(h^2(k_1), n_r)$	id_1	**O**
$h(h^2(k'_1), n_r)$	id_1	**N**
$\vdots$	$\vdots$	$\vdots$
$h(h^i(k_1), n_r)$	id_1	**N**
$h(h^1(k_2), n_r)$	id_2	**O**
$h(h^2(k_2), n_r)$	id_2	**O**
$\vdots$	$\vdots$	$\vdots$
$h(h^i(k_2), n_r)$	id_2	**O**

Precomputation and State Resolution. Two important questions need to be answered. First, how can the reader construct a precomputed table for look-up while a random nonce n_r is used in the protocol of Figure 2. Second, how can the number of possible tag states be limited in such a way that state resolution is always possible.

The reader state is stored as shown in Table 1. For every tag the reader precomputes the identifiers $h(h^i(rk_{id}), n_r)$ for all $i < N$. In practice, $N = 3$ might already be a good choice to withstand desynchronizations that occur due to bad physical circumstances. Since the reader cannot know id in advance, all nonces n_r in the precomputed table need to be the same. During idle time the reader can precalculate several tables as shown in Table 1 for different values n_r. A different representation of Table 1 is given by Table 2.

When a *synchronization run* is needed, first the identifier id is obtained by using the *second channel*. Then, the reader executes a *synchronization run*, immediately followed by a normal run. This second run makes clear whether the key update on the tag side was successful or not. If it was successful the reader is able to lookup the tag identifier in the database. However, in case of a *failure run* it is unclear whether the update was successful but the second run failed, or if the update already failed in the first place. For both scenarios the reader keeps a record corresponding to id, namely **O** and **N**. In order to prevent desynchronization on this level, this specific tag can be labeled as 'suspicious' to indicate that something went wrong in the synchronization run. The tag needs then to be synchronized in a safe environment. Every other attempt of a reader to synchronize would potentially leak location information to an adversary and should therefore not be executed.

Success, Failure and Synchronization Run. This section discusses the *success*, *failure* and *synchronization run*. The authentication protocol is depicted in Figure 2. The *success run* is a protocol run in which a reader is able to successfully identify a tag and updates the identifiers in the database accordingly. This update might just concern the next identifier k, or update the synchronization key $\tilde{k}$ as well. Whenever a reader fails to identify a tag, the corresponding protocol run is called a *failure run*. After a failure run, the reader needs to be provided with the tag identifier id using a *second channel*. Now, id can be used to select the tag in the database and find the corresponding synchronization key $\tilde{k}$ which can be used to execute a *synchronization run* and update both k and $\tilde{k}$. The idea behind the different run types is that they look the same to an adversary.

A *success run* starts with a challenge nonce n_r. Under all circumstances, the tag computes the successive tag key $k \leftarrow h(k)$ before it sends any message. This key updating is done regardless of the number of requests that are made. After this phase, the identifier m_1 is sent, which directly depends on k as $m_1 \leftarrow h(k, n_r)$. Due to this dependence on k, the successive tag identifiers might run beyond the identifiable scope N of the reader. Since a reader cannot continue to search for an identifier forever, N determines the maximum number of key updates considered in a look-up attempt. In the success run we consider a lookup successful when it is of the form $\exists (id, k) \in T, i \leq N : h(h^i(k), n_r) = m_1$. The corresponding identity id, key k and resynchronization key $\tilde{k}$ of the tag are resolved, which completes the identification of the tag. For similarity reasons, the reader finishes by sending a random m_2 message.

The *failure run* starts like every run with a challenge n_r. In its turn, the tag first computes the next tag key $k \leftarrow h(k)$ before any message is sent. In contrast to a *success run*, the reader is unable to resolve the tag's identity from message m_1. Since m_2 can be a random message, the reader is still able to finish the protocol, as it is designed to show equal behavior in every run. However, identification was unsuccessful and thus the reader has to obtain the tag identifier id by using a second channel, e.g. the id could also be available as a barcode on the RFID label. Of course, the adversary can obtain id as well, but the tracking effort per tag is relatively large compared to the tracking of RFID labels with fixed identifier. Hence, this protocol reduces the problem of tracking RFID labels to the problem of tracking barcodes.

Finally, the *synchronization run* is used once the identifier id is obtained by the reader. The identifier id can be provided over the second channel and allows the lookup of k and $\tilde{k}$, which are used later on in this run. Again, the reader starts the protocol by sending a nonce n_r. The tag computes $m_1 \leftarrow h(k, n_r)$ and updates the tag key $k \leftarrow h(k)$, then it sends m_1 which is used as unpredictable input for the last message m_2. By m_2 the reader proves knowledge of the synchronization key $\tilde{k}$ to the tag. This time, m_2 is constructed from m_1 and $\tilde{k}$ as $m_2 \leftarrow h(m_1, \tilde{k})$. The tag knows $\tilde{k}$ and can therefore check the validity of m_2. If it is indeed a valid message, the tag updates the tag key $k \leftarrow h(\tilde{k}, m_1)$ and the synchronization key $\tilde{k} \leftarrow h(\tilde{k})$.

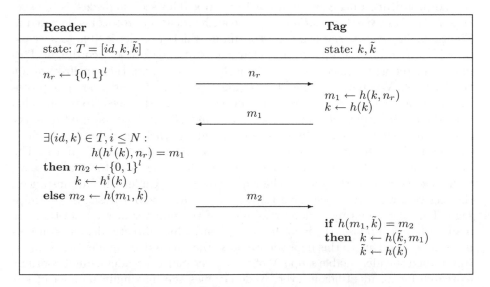

Fig. 2. The Protocol

6   Security Analysis

This section analyzes the security of the proposed protocol in the random oracle model. In the *resynchronization run* the last message m_2 of the protocol leaks location information. For this reason, and in general because forward privacy cannot be achieved for any type of synchronized symmetric protocol construction [NSMSN09], we use the slightly more restricted *thin* adversary. First, we show that our protocol is *thin-forward* private. Then we show that the protocol is not subject to desynchronization.

Theorem 1. *The protocol depicted in Figure 2 is thin-forward private in the random oracle model.*

The proof closely follows the *narrow-forward privacy* proof of modified OSK in [GvR10]. In short, it introduces a simulator S which keeps track of all oracle calls H and stores them as an entry of the form $\langle \text{IN}, \text{OUT} \rangle$ in a table T_H. Then, T_H is adapted such that the protocol messages and thus the resulting view of a particular adversary A_1 remain the same while the keys, and thus the tag identities, are swapped. This leads to a contradiction.

Proof (Sketch). Suppose there exists an adversary $A = (A_0, A_1)$ that wins the **Priv-Game**$_\Pi$ given in Definition 5 with non-negligible probability. Then, imagine a simulator S that first initializes the system and then runs the adversary A_0. Every oracle call of A_0 to the oracle H is simulated as usual by a table T_H which contains all previous queries with their corresponding answers. At some point A_0 finishes and chooses two tags T_0^* and T_1^*. Let $(k_0, \tilde{k}_0)$ be the key pair of T_0^* and $(k_1, \tilde{k}_1)$ be the key pair of T_1^* after they are returned by A_0. As in the game, S will draw a random bit b. Next, S runs $A_0^O(T_b^*)$ which at some point outputs a guess bit b'. By hypothesis we get that $b' = b$ with probability significantly higher than $\frac{1}{2}$. By † we identify the predecessor value of a key, so the predecessor of k_0 is $k_0^\dagger$. Now S swaps all occurrences of k_0 with k_1 in all entries of T_H. Note that either the entry $\langle h(\tilde{k}_0^\dagger, \_), k_0 \rangle$ or the entry $\langle h(k_0^\dagger), k_0 \rangle$ is present in T_H. The first one occurs when the last update of k was in a *synchronization run*. The latter one occurs when the last update of k was in a *non-synchronization protocol run*. The replacement of k_0 by k_1 and vice versa does not affect the protocol messages since k_0 and k_1 are not involved in any protocol messages after the oracle call entries defined above. Furthermore, $m_2 \leftarrow h(m_1, \tilde{k})$ is the only message that involves $\tilde{k}$ and only occurs in a *synchronization run*. Since A_1 is thin, it is clear that $\tilde{k}$ does not have any influence on the view of the adversary.

Now, S runs adversary $A_1^O(T_{1-b}^*)$ with the adjusted T_H. Again by hypothesis, we get that A_1 outputs $b' = 1 - b$ with probability significantly higher than $\frac{1}{2}$. Since A_1 is thin, its view is exactly the same as in the previous run, which leads to a contradiction.

Theorem 2. *The protocol depicted in Figure 2 is not subject to desynchronization in the random oracle model.*

Proof (Sketch). In order to show that desynchronization is impossible we have to show that both $D_\mathcal{R} \leq R_\mathcal{R}$ and $D_\mathcal{T} \leq R_\mathcal{T}$ hold. The tag state is the tuple $(k, \tilde{k})$. First, k is always updated, $\tilde{k}$ is only updated after a *synchronization run*. Therefore, we focus $\tilde{k}$ to induce key shifts since only then a desynchronization is possible. From the protocol definition we deduce that $D_\mathcal{R} = R_\mathcal{R} = 1$ since a reader only starts a synchronization run when it was able to look up $\tilde{k}$ in one of the two possible tag states. Furthermore, we know that $D_\mathcal{T} = 0$ from which follows that $D_\mathcal{T} \leq R_\mathcal{T}$ since $R_\mathcal{T}$ has to be positive. Suppose that either $D_\mathcal{R} > R_\mathcal{R}$ or $D_\mathcal{T} \leq R_\mathcal{T}$ is true, then there exists an adversary $\mathcal{A}$ that wins the **Strong-Corr-Game**$_\Pi$ given in Definition 9 with non-negligible probability. This means that $\mathcal{A}$ outputs a tag $\mathcal{T}^\star$ with key $\tilde{tk}^i$ while the reader has no matching key $\tilde{rk}^{j-1}$ or $\tilde{rk}^j$, since $i \neq j - 1$ and $i \neq j$ has to be true. There are two ways for the adversary to achieve this:

$i > j$:   The tag key is updated $(i - j)$-times more than the reader key. The only way to induce a key update on the tag side is to construct the message $m_2 = h(m_1, \tilde{k})$. Because of the one-wayness of h and since the adversary cannot call CorruptTag, the key $\tilde{k}$ is not known and it is impossible to construct m_2 for the adversary. Only the reader $\mathcal{R}$ is able to construct $m_2 = h(m_1, \tilde{k})$, but inherent to this generation of m_2 is the storage of the new reader keys $(rk^{j+1}, \tilde{rk}^{j+1})$ while at the same time the old keys $(rk^j, \tilde{rk}^j)$ are maintained. The last option would be a replay of m_2, but this is rendered impossible by the use of n_r in m_1, and thus in m_2, which introduces freshness in every protocol run. To conclude, it is not possible to obtain $i > j$.

$i < j - 1$:   The reader key is updated $(j - i)$-times more than the tag key. By hypothesis we know that $i < j - 1$ since $i \neq j$, $i \neq j - 1$ and $i \not> j$ as concluded in the previous case. Let $i = j$, the only way to update $\tilde{rk}^j$ to $\tilde{rk}^{j+1}$ comes with the generation of $m_2 = h(m_1, \tilde{k})$. If m_2 is received by the tag it will update its key from $\tilde{tk}^i$ to $\tilde{tk}^{i+1}$ and consequently $i = j$ again. Obviously, to prevent incrementation of i is to block or replace m_2 since then the tag does not update its key and as a result $i = j - 1$. Next, the adversary needs to go one step further since the reader is still able to identify the tag $(\tilde{tk}^i = \tilde{rk}^{j-1})$. To induce another reader key update, the reader has to be provided with the tag identifier *id* by using the *second channel*. When the last synchronization attempt turned out to be unsuccessful, which is stored in the reader state belonging to *id*, the reader just sends random data for m_2. In this situation resynchronization has to be done in a safe environment. The tag state either contains $\tilde{tk}^i$ when in the last synchronization attempt m_2 was blocked or the tag state contains $\tilde{tk}^{i+1}$ when the last synchronization run was successful. In the latter case the reader is able to identify the tag since it knows $\tilde{rk}^j$ which equals $\tilde{tk}^{i+1}$, respectively. To conclude, the adversary needs to induce a synchronization run, which can be done by first querying the tag more than N times. Then, before the reader starts a *synchronization run* it retrieves *id*. By looking up the correct entry using *id* the reader has enough information to decide on the execution of another *synchronization run*. If the last attempt was unsuccessful this indicates that something suspicious is going on and resynchronization should be done in a safe environment. If the last attempt was successful the reader is sure that $i = j$. So, $\max(|i - j|) = 1$ where $i < j$, which is not enough to satisfy $i < j - 1$.

Finally, from the two possible strategies to win the **Strong-Corr-Game**$_{II}$ we conclude that both $i > j$ and $i < j - 1$ cannot be satisfied, therefore contradicting the assumption that such an adversary $\mathcal{A}$ exists.

7   Conclusion

This paper presents a new approach to tackle the desynchronization problem. This desynchronization problem is actually an unwanted side effect of a solution to another problem: location privacy for RFID tags. Many solutions tend to solve this problem by introducing a stateful protocol. A main challenge of these protocols is to keep the tag and reader state synchronized while at the same time no information can be leaked that enables an adversary to track a specific tag. To the best of our knowledge there have been no attempts to seek the solution beyond the bounds of the wireless link. In line with the abilities of a *narrow* adversary, introduced by Vaudenay in [Vau07], in which an adversary is unable to see the result of a protocol run like a gate that opens, this paper proposes to use this information flow also in the opposite direction. This means that additional information is made available to the reader which it can use to identify and resynchronize with the tag. A *narrow* adversary does not have access to this information since it is not send on the wireless link but some other communication channel which is introduced in this paper as the *second channel*. This paper adds some mild restrictions to the *narrow* adversary and introduces this as the *thin* adversary which is needed to prove forward-privacy under mild additional assumptions. Suppose that barcode scanners are used as *second channel* and RFID tags are additionally equipped with barcodes. Additionally, assume a protocol P that uses the *second channel* such that it provides *thin-forward* privacy and is not subject to desynchronization. Then, tracking tags in this system has become as hard as tracking barcodes.

The *second channel* can be used in new protocol designs and relaxes the workload of the reader and/or database. It allows to solve the desynchronization problem in an elegant way and eliminates the need for restrictions on the number of key updates that can be induced by an adversary between two synchronizations. In order to show that such a protocol can be constructed we proposed a protocol that only uses hash functions. We have shown that it it provides *thin-forward* privacy in the random oracle model. Furthermore, we followed the desynchronization definition of [CC08] to show that the protocol is not subject to desynchronization.

We are currently working on the formalization of the security claims in Proverif, following the direction of [BCdH10]. This task turned out to be non-trivial due to the fact that our protocol is state-full.

Acknowledgments

We like to thank the anonymous reviewers of this paper for their valuable comments.

References

[AO05]   Avoine, G., Oechslin, P.: A scalable and provably secure hash based RFID protocol. In: International Workshop on Pervasive Computing and Communication Security, PerSec 2005, pp. 110–114 (2005)

[Att07]   Attaran, M.: RFID: an enabler of supply chain operations. Supply Chain Management: An International Journal 12(4), 249–257 (2007)

[Avo05]   Avoine, G.: Adversary Model for Radio Frequency Identification. Technical Report LASEC-REPORT-2005-001, Swiss Federal Institute of Technology (EPFL), Security and Cryptography Laboratory (LASEC), Lausanne, Switzerland (September 2005)

[BBEG09]   Berbain, C., Billet, O., Etrog, J., Gilbert, H.: An efficient forward private RFID protocol. In: Proceedings of the 16th ACM conference on Computer and communications security, CCS 2009, pp. 43–53. ACM Press, New York (2009)

[BCdH10]   Brusó, M., Chatzikokolakis, K., den Hartog, J.: Formal verification of privacy for RFID systems. In: Proceedings of the 23nd IEEE Computer Security Foundations Symposium (2010)

[BdMM08]   Burmester, M., de Medeiros, B., Motta, R.: Anonymous RFID authentication supporting constant-cost key-lookup against active adversaries. Journal of Applied Cryptography 1(2), 79–90 (2008)

[CC08]   Canard, S., Coisel, I.: Data synchronization in privacy-preserving RFID authentication schemes. In: Conference on RFID Security (2008)

[Dim05]   Dimitriou, T.: A lightweight RFID protocol to protect against traceability and cloning attacks. In: Security and Privacy for Emerging Areas in Communications Networks, SecureComm 2005, pp. 59–66 (2005)

[GvR10]   Garcia, F., van Rossum, P.: Modeling privacy for off-line RFID systems. In: Gollmann, D., Lanet, J.-L., Iguchi-Cartigny, J. (eds.) CARDIS 2010. LNCS, vol. 6035, pp. 194–208. Springer, Heidelberg (2010)

[Jue06]   Juels, A.: RFID security and privacy: A research survey. IEEE Journal on Selected Areas in Communications 24(2), 381–394 (2006)

[JW05]   Juels, A., Weis, S.: Authenticating Pervasive Devices with Human Protocols. In: Shoup, V. (ed.) CRYPTO 2005. LNCS, vol. 3621, pp. 293–308. Springer, Heidelberg (2005)

[JW09]   Juels, A., Weis, S.A.: Defining strong privacy for RFID. ACM Transactions on Information and System Security (TISSEC) 13(1), 1–23 (2009)

[MW04]   Molnar, D., Wagner, D.: Privacy and security in library RFID: Issues, practices, and architectures. In: Proceedings of the 11th ACM conference on Computer and Communications Security, pp. 210–219. ACM, New York (2004)

[NSMSN09]   Ng, C.Y., Susilo, W., Mu, Y., Safavi-Naini, R.: New Privacy Results on Synchronized RFID Authentication Protocols against Tag Tracing. In: Backes, M., Ning, P. (eds.) ESORICS 2009. LNCS, vol. 5789, p. 321. Springer, Heidelberg (2009)

[OSK⁺03]   Ohkubo, M., Suzuki, K., Kinoshita, S., et al.: Cryptographic approach to privacy-friendly tags. In: RFID Privacy Workshop, Citeseer, vol. 82 (2003)

[Tsu06]   Tsudik, G.: YA-TRAP: Yet Another Trivial RFID Authentication Protocol. In: International Conference on Pervasive Computing and Communications, PerCom 2006, Pisa, Italy. IEEE Computer Society Press, Los Alamitos (March 2006)

[Vau07]   Vaudenay, S.: On privacy models for RFID. In: Kurosawa, K. (ed.) ASIACRYPT 2007. LNCS, vol. 4833, pp. 68–87. Springer, Heidelberg (2007)

[WCO⁺07]   Wanga, S.W., Chenb, W.H., Onga, C.S., Liuc, L., Chuangb, Y.W.: RFID applications in hospitals: a case study on a demonstration RFID project in a Taiwan hospital. Hospitals 8, 33 (2007)

[WNLY06]   Wu, N.C., Nystrom, M.A., Lin, T.R., Yu, H.C.: Challenges to global RFID adoption. Technovation 26(12), 1317–1323 (2006)

[WSR⁺04]   Weis, S.A., Sarma, S.E., Rivest, R.L., Engels, D.W.: Security and privacy aspects of low-cost radio frequency identification systems. In: Hutter, D., Müller, G., Stephan, W., Ullmann, M. (eds.) Security in Pervasive Computing. LNCS, vol. 2802, pp. 201–212. Springer, Heidelberg (2004)

Optimal Security Limits of RFID Distance Bounding Protocols

Orhun Kara[1], Süleyman Kardaş[1,2],
Muhammed Ali Bingöl[1,3], and Gildas Avoine[4]

[1] TUBITAK UEKAE, Gebze, Kocaeli, Turkey
[2] Sabanci University, Istanbul, TR-34956, Turkey
[3] Istanbul Technical University,
Institute of Science and Technology, Istanbul, Turkey
[4] UCL, Information Security Group, Louvain-la-Neuve, Belgium

Abstract. In this paper, we classify the RFID distance bounding protocols having bitwise fast phases and no final signature. We also give the theoretical security bounds for two specific classes, leaving the security bounds for the general case as an open problem. As for the classification, we introduce the notion of *k-previous challenge dependent* (*k*-PCD) protocols where each response bit depends on the current and *k*-previous challenges and there is no final signature. We treat the case $k = 0$, which means each response bit depends only on the current challenge, as a special case and define such protocols as *current challenge dependent* (CCD) protocols. In general, we construct a trade-off curve between the security levels of mafia and distance frauds by introducing two generic attack algorithms. This leads to the conclusion that CCD protocols cannot attain the ideal security against distance fraud, i.e. $1/2$, for each challenge-response bit, without totally losing the security against mafia fraud. We extend the generic attacks to 1-PCD protocols and obtain a trade-off curve for 1-PCD protocols pointing out that 1-PCD protocols can provide better security than CCD protocols. Thereby, we propose a natural extension of a CCD protocol to a 1-PCD protocol in order to improve its security. As a study case, we give two natural extensions of Hancke and Kuhn protocol to show how to enhance the security against either mafia fraud or distance fraud without extra cost.

Keywords: RFID, distance bounding protocol, security, mafia fraud, distance fraud.

1 Introduction

Radio Frequency IDentification (RFID) is a technology pervasively used in many applications, from supply chain tracking systems to credit card payment systems. Security is a major concern in these applications and is definitely a critical point when tags are required to provide a proof of identity, which is the case in applications like payment, access control, ticketing, e-passport,... Such evolved

S.B. Ors Yalcin (Ed.): RFIDSec 2010, LNCS 6370, pp. 220–238, 2010.

applications can benefit from powerful tags that implement cryptographic algorithms, which are commonly block and stream ciphers. Standardized and well-
established authentication protocols can then be used, e.g., ISO/IEC 9798 or
ISO/IEC 11770.

The seminal work of Desmedt *et al.* [3,6,7] on *relay attacks* shows that *mafia
fraud* can defeat all the conventional authentication protocols. The mafia fraud,
in an RFID challenge-response authentication protocol, can be summarized as
follows (Fig. 1). The adversary, who aims to impersonate a legitimate prover
(tag), first gets the challenge from the verifier (reader) using a rogue tag, and
transmits it to the remote legitimate tag through a rogue reader. The adversary
then receives the corresponding response from the legitimate tag, and relays it
to the legitimate reader. It really makes sense in practice, especially when considering a payment system with point-of-sale credit card terminals, even though
the contactless credit cards are tamper resistant and certified. Feasibility and
practical considerations are addressed in [8,10].

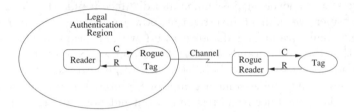

Fig. 1. A mafia fraud scenario

Similar to mafia fraud, there is also another attack called *distance fraud*
(Fig. 2). In this attack, a party having access to the secret key persuades a
verifier that she is within a certain distance whereas she is not. Home confine-
ment based on electronic monitoring with ankle bracelets is a typical example
where distance fraud is definitely relevant. This fraud would allow the person
under monitoring to temporary leave his residence without being detected.

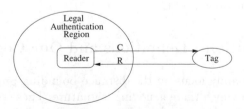

Fig. 2. A distance fraud scenario

Two main approaches have been adopted so far to prevent relay-like attacks.
One of them is based on measuring the radio signal strength (RSS), so that
the verifier learns whether the prover is close to it. However, this method has a

drawback that a capable adversary can regulate the signal strength to convince the verifier of her proximity [9]. The other important approach was introduced by Beth and Desmedt [3], called *distance bounding*, based on calculating the *round trip time* (RTT) of the response after a challenge is sent. The verifier checks the distance of a prover by measuring the RTT given that the speed of the radio signal can not exceed that of light.

Brands and Chaum proposed the first distance bounding protocol at Eurocrypt 93 [4]. This protocol is composed of three phases; *slow phase-I*, *fast phase*, and *slow phase-II*. The slow phases consist of the time-consuming operations such as random nonce generations, commitment and signature calculations. On the other hand, the fast phase includes non-time consuming response generations and rapid bit exchanges. Particularly during the *slow phase-II* the prover has to calculate a *final signature*.

Afterwards, Hancke and Kuhn proposed the first RFID-dedicated distance bounding protocol [9], which does not involve any final signature. Then, several distance bounding protocols based on those two protocols have been proposed to improve security levels against mafia and distance frauds [1, 2, 5, 11–18].

In this paper, we aim at investigating how to achieve the optimum security against mafia fraud and distance fraud without using a final signature. We show that these two frauds are correlated and we express the trade-off between the adversary success probabilities with respect to these frauds. In other words, we prove that, under some assumptions, protocols can be designed to enforce the mafia or distance fraud resistance, but not both at the same time. For that, we define and address Current Challenge-Dependent (CCD) protocols and k-Previous Challenge-Dependent (k-PCD) protocols.

The rest of the paper is organized as follows: In Section 2, we briefly give general definitions and summarize our contributions. Then, in Section 3, we describe two generic attacks for CCD protocols and state the security trade-off between mafia and distance frauds for these attacks. In Section 4, we consider 1-PCD protocols and also provide generic attacks and trade-off between mafia and distance frauds. In Section 5, we introduce the notion of natural extension on CCD protocols and apply two extensions on an existing CCD protocol to enhance the security. Lastly, in Section 6, we give a brief discussion and conclude the paper with some open problems.

2   General Notions, Definitions and Our Contributions

In this paper, we mainly focus on the distance bounding protocols appropriate to RFID systems in which there is no final signature. These protocols are generally composed of two phases: a slow phase and a fast phase. In the slow phase, both parties constitute the *session secrets* (for example, the session secret in the HK protocol presented in Appendix A consists of two registers) that are used to produce response bits during the fast phase. Throughout the fast phase, both parties use the same *response generating function* which produces a response by using the session secrets and given a challenge value.

In what follows we study on how to achieve the optimum security against mafia fraud and distance fraud. For that, we first define a class of protocols without a final signature and, in which each response bit depends on the current challenge. It is described below.

Definition 1 (Current Challenge-Dependent (CCD) Protocol). *Let* $f :$ $\mathbb{F}_2^{m+1} \to \mathbb{F}_2$ *be a Boolean function. A CCD protocol* $\mathcal{P}$ *is a distance bounding protocol that satisfies the following properties:*

- *During the fast phase, each response bit* r_i *is computed as* $r_i := f(c_i, y_0^i, \dots, y_{m-1}^i)$, *where* c_i *is the i-th challenge bit and* $(y_0^i, \dots, y_{m-1}^i)$ *is the i-th string of the session secret shared by both prover and verifier for* $i = 1, \dots, n$, *where* n *is the number of rapid bit exchanges.*
- *There is no final slow phase.*

The protocol $\mathcal{P}$ *is denoted as* $f(c_i, y_0^i, \dots, y_{m-1}^i) \to r_i$ *CCD protocol. The function* f *is called the response function of the protocol* $\mathcal{P}$.

One popular example of CCD protocols is Hancke and Kuhn (HK) protocol [9]. The protocol is explained in detail in Appendix A. The response function of the protocol can be described as the following Boolean function:

$$f(c_i, y_0^i, y_1^i) = c_i \cdot y_1^i \oplus (1 \oplus c_i) \cdot y_0^i = y_{c_i}^i \tag{1}$$

where $\oplus$ and $\cdot$ are the addition and the multiplication operations of the binary Galois Field respectively.

Let us denote P_{maf}^E the success probability of correctly guessing one bit response for mafia fraud of an attack E, and similarly P_{dis}^E for distance fraud of an attack E. The security levels of a given protocol $\mathcal{P}$ are defined as follows.

Definition 2. $P_{maf}(\mathcal{P}) = \max_E P_{maf}^E$ *and* $P_{dis}(\mathcal{P}) = \max_E P_{dis}^E$. *That is,* $P_{maf}(\mathcal{P})$ *is the maximum of* P_{maf}^E *over all the mafia fraud attacks* E *mounted on* $\mathcal{P}$, *and similarly* $P_{dis}(\mathcal{P})$ *is the maximum of* P_{dis}^E *over all the distance fraud attacks* E *mounted on* $\mathcal{P}$.

The security levels of HK protocol are given as 3/4 for both mafia and distance frauds for the attacks given in [9] and Appendix A, respectively. So $P_{maf}(HK) \geq 3/4$ and $P_{dis}(HK) \geq 3/4$. It has been an open question that these security levels are optimum for CCD protocols. Also, it is not known whether it is possible to improve the security level against mafia fraud without sacrificing the security level against the distance fraud and vice versa. In general, we have the following open questions for CCD protocols:

- What is the best security levels for both mafia fraud and distance fraud among all CCD protocols?
- What is the optimum achievable security level for mafia fraud of a CCD protocol?
- For a CCD protocol, what is the minimum value of P_{maf} if P_{dis} is ideal (i.e. $\frac{1}{2}$)?

The above-mentioned questions are answered in this paper. We first describe two generic attacks for mafia and distance frauds that can be mounted on all CCD protocols. Then, we show that there is a trade-off between mafia fraud and distance fraud, namely $P_{maf}(\mathcal{P}) + P_{dis}(\mathcal{P}) \geq 3/2$. We also prove that for any CCD protocol there is a security limit concerning the mafia fraud such that $P_{maf}(\mathcal{P}) \geq 3/4$ for any CCD protocol $\mathcal{P}$. As a consequence of this result we show that if $P_{dis}(\mathcal{P}) = 1/2$ then the protocol is completely vulnerable to mafia fraud (i.e., $P_{maf}(\mathcal{P}) = 1$).

In order to improve the security levels against these frauds without using a final signature, we introduce the notion of k-*Previous Challenge Dependent* (k-*PCD*) protocol, in which each response bit depends on the current and the k previous challenges during fast phase. We define k-PCD protocol as follows.

Definition 3 (k-Previous Challenge-Dependent (k-PCD) Protocol). *Let* $g : \mathbb{F}_2^{m+k+1} \to \mathbb{F}_2$ *be a Boolean function. A k-PCD protocol $\mathcal{P}$ is a distance bounding protocol that satisfies following properties*

- *During the fast phase, each response bit r_i is computed as $r_i := g(c_i, \ldots c_{i-k}, y_0^i, \ldots, y_{m-1}^i)$ where c_j is the j-th challenge bit and $(y_0^i, \ldots, y_{m-1}^i)$ is the i-th string of the session secret shared by both prover and verifier for $i = 1, \ldots, n$, where n is the number of rapid bit exchanges.*
- *There is no final slow phase.*

The protocol $\mathcal{P}$ is denoted as $g(c_i, \ldots, c_{i-k}, y_0^i, \ldots, y_{m-1}^i) \to r_i$ k-PCD protocol. The function g is called the response function of the protocol $\mathcal{P}$.

Remark 1. From Definitions (1) and (2), a CCD protocol is a k-PCD protocol for $k = 0$.

We provide security analysis of 1-PCD protocols. In order to analyze the security against mafia and distance frauds, we present two generic attacks which can be mounted against all 1-PCD protocols. We show that, there is also a trade-off between the security levels of mafia fraud and distance fraud such that $P_{maf}(\mathcal{P}) + P_{dis}(\mathcal{P}) \geq 5/4$ for any 1-PCD protocol $\mathcal{P}$. Let us remark that, this trade-off curve lies below that of CCD protocols. Therefore, we propose a natural extension concept in order to provide a 1-PCD protocol from a CCD protocol. We claim that, the security of existing CCD protocols can be improved by applying natural extension without using a computationally expensive phase (e.g. a final signature). Moreover, we illustrate two natural extensions on HK protocol to make the protocol more secure against all the known attacks. For the first version, we achieve $P_{dis}(HK') \geq 1/2$ and $P_{maf}(HK') \geq 3/4$, and for the second one $P_{dis}(HK'') \geq 5/8$ and $P_{maf}(HK'') \geq 5/8$, in which both versions are optimum among 1-PCD protocols. Finally, we conclude the paper with several conjectures and open problems related to k-PCD protocols.

3   Optimal Security Limits for CCD Protocols

In this section, we show the security trade-off between mafia and distance frauds for CCD protocols. In order to analyze the security against mafia and distance frauds, we consider the characteristics of the response function f used in a CCD protocol. We assume that all the challenges and the shared session secrets, which are used to compute response bits, are uniformly random. For a given response function f, let us define the sets:

$$\mathcal{A} = \{y = (y_0, y_1, \ldots, y_{m-1}) \in \mathbb{F}_2^m : f(0, y_0, \ldots, y_{m-1}) \neq f(1, y_0, \ldots, y_{m-1})\},$$

$$\mathcal{B} = \{y = (y_0, y_1, \ldots, y_{m-1}) \in \mathbb{F}_2^m : f(0, y_0, \ldots, y_{m-1}) = f(1, y_0, \ldots, y_{m-1})\}.$$

Let us denote a and b as the cardinalities of the sets $\mathcal{A}$ and $\mathcal{B}$, respectively. Then, $a + b = 2^m$. We describe a generic distance fraud attack which can be mounted on all CCD protocols given in Algorithm 3.1.

Algorithm 3.1. A GENERIC DISTANCE FRAUD ATTACK FOR CCD PROTOCOLS(n)

---

n: Number of rounds
for $i \leftarrow 1$ **to** n

$\quad$ **then** $\begin{cases} t \leftarrow f(0, y_0^i, \ldots, y_{m-1}^i) + f(1, y_0^i, \ldots, y_{m-1}^i) \\ \textbf{if } t = 0 \\ \quad \textbf{then } \text{Send } 0 \\ \\ \textbf{else if } t = 2 \\ \quad \textbf{then } \text{Send } 1 \\ \\ \textbf{else} \\ \quad \textbf{then } \text{Send a random bit} \end{cases}$

We also describe a generic mafia fraud attack that can be mounted on all the CCD protocols. During the slow phase, the adversary relays the messages (e.g nonces or commitments etc.) between the verifier and the prover. Then, during the fast phase she executes the attack described in Algorithm 3.2. We assume that, the protocol is public. So, a and b can be computed during the off-line phase.

Algorithm 3.2. A GENERIC MAFIA FRAUD ATTACK FOR CCD PROTOCOLS(n, a, b)

---

n: Number of rounds
flip: Deciding on flipping the response
if $b \leq a$
  then $flip \leftarrow 1$

  else $flip \leftarrow 0$
for $i \leftarrow 1$ **to** n
  do $\begin{cases} \text{Send a random challenge } c_i' \in \{0,1\} \text{ to the prover} \\ \text{Record the prover's response } r_i' \end{cases}$
/*Then, Mafia continues the protocol with the verifier*/
for $i \leftarrow 1$ **to** n

  do $\begin{cases} \text{record i-}th \text{ challenge of the verifier in } c_i \\ \textbf{if } c_i' = c_i \\ \quad \textbf{then} \text{ Send } r_i' \\[6pt] \quad \textbf{else} \text{ Send } r_i' \oplus flip \end{cases}$

    The following statement gives a trade-off between mafia fraud and distance fraud for CCD protocols.

Theorem 1. *Let* $\mathcal{P}$ *be a* $f(c_i, y_0^i, \ldots, y_{m-1}^i) \to r_i$ *CCD protocol. Assume that* c_i *and* $y_j^i s$ *used during the fast phase of* $\mathcal{P}$ *are uniformly random. Then, (i)* $P_{maf}(\mathcal{P}) \geq 3/4$*, and (ii)* $P_{maf}(\mathcal{P}) + P_{dis}(\mathcal{P}) \geq 3/2$*.*

Proof. Let us first consider the distance fraud attack described in Algorithm 3.1. For any challenge c_i, the adversary always produces a correct response if $y_0^i, y_1^i, \ldots, y_{m-1}^i$ are in the set $\mathcal{B}$. Otherwise, i.e., when they are in the set $\mathcal{A}$, she successfully predicts the response with a probability of $1/2$ because c_i, and y_j^i s are uniformly random. Thus, the success probability of P_{dis} for the attack given in Algorithm 3.1 is equal to $\dfrac{b}{2^m} \cdot 1 + \dfrac{a}{2^m} \cdot \dfrac{1}{2} = \dfrac{a + 2b}{2^{m+1}} = \dfrac{1}{2} + \dfrac{b}{2^{m+1}}$.

    Concerning the mafia fraud attack given in Algorithm 3.2, let the adversary receive the r_i' responses from the prover for her predicted challenges c_i'. Then, she executes the attack against the verifier. Since c_is are randomly produced by the verifier, there are two equally likely cases. (a) If $c_i = c_i'$ the adversary knows the answer then sends r_i'. (b) If $c_i \neq c_i'$ she has to predict the response bit r_i. The probability that r_i' and r_i are equal is $\dfrac{b}{2^m}$, and that are not equal is $\dfrac{a}{2^m}$. The adversary chooses the larger probability in order to decide whether she flips the response bit (i.e., $r_i' \oplus 1$). Then, we have $P_{maf} = \dfrac{1}{2} \cdot 1 + \dfrac{1}{2} \cdot \max\{\dfrac{a}{2^m}, \dfrac{b}{2^m}\}$. Since $a + b = 2^m$, $\max\{\dfrac{a}{2^m}, \dfrac{b}{2^m}\} \geq \dfrac{1}{2}$ and this implies that $P_{maf} \geq \dfrac{3}{4}$.

If $b \leq 2^{m-1}$ $(b \leq a)$, then, $P_{maf} = \dfrac{1}{2} + \dfrac{a}{2^{m+1}}$ for the attack. So, we have $P_{dis} + P_{maf} = \dfrac{3}{2}$. On the other hand, when $b \geq 2^{m-1}$ $(b \geq a)$, $P_{maf} = \dfrac{1}{2} + \dfrac{b}{2^{m+1}} \geq \dfrac{3}{4}$. Thus, $P_{dis}(\mathcal{P}) + P_{maf}(\mathcal{P}) \geq \dfrac{3}{2}$. $\qquad\square$

The first part of Theorem 1 indicates that there is a security limit for CCD protocols concerning the mafia fraud, and the second part attests the security trade-off between mafia and distance frauds. Figure 3 depicts the *trade-off curve* between the success probabilities of these frauds for any CCD protocol.

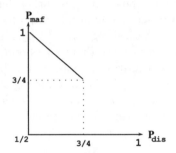

Fig. 3. The trade-off curve between distance and mafia frauds for CCD protocols

One interesting result of Theorem 1 is that CCD protocols cannot attain the ideal security level against the distance fraud without being vulnerable against mafia fraud. This is stated in Corollary 1.

Corollary 1. *For a CCD protocol $\mathcal{P}$, if the security level for the distance fraud is ideal (i.e. $P_{dis}(\mathcal{P}) = 1/2$) then, $P_{maf}(\mathcal{P})$ is 1.*

Proof. The probability $P_{dis}(\mathcal{P})$ satisfies the condition in Theorem 1, so $P_{maf}(\mathcal{P}) = 3/2 - 1/2 \geq 1$. $\qquad\square$

Remark 2. Recall that the security levels of the HK protocol against the mafia and distance frauds are both 3/4. Security levels of HK protocol lie on the trade-off curve.

4   Optimal Security Limits for k-PCD Protocols

In this section, we analyze the security of k-PCD protocols. We first describe the several neighborhood concept that is useful for the distance fraud analysis. Then, we introduce two generic attacks for the mafia and the distance frauds that can be mounted on all 1-PCD protocols.

While designing k-PCD distance bounding protocol, there are n-round one-bit challenge/response during fast phase. There is an exceptional case for the first round of this phase. In the first round, the verifier sends k initial challenges before sending c_1. For example, in the first round of a 1-PCD protocol, the verifier first sends c_0 and c_1 then waits for r_1.

4.1   Security Regions for Distance Fraud

Let us consider an adversary who tries to cheat on the distance against a verifier. While producing a response bit r_i, the adversary may use some of the received previous challenges in her attack. This can increase the success probability of the attack. However, receiving the challenges earlier depends on how far the adversary is away from the verifier. Therefore, in order to make the attack analysis simpler, we describe three spherical regions (Z_1, Z_2, Z_3) in which the adversary can communicate with the verifier (see Figure 4). Let d_1 be the maximum radius of Z_1 that is the legal authentication region, and t_1 be the elapsed time for a signal to travel the distance d_1. Z_2 is the annulus region between two concentric spheres with radius of d_1 and $d_1 + d_2$ where $d_2 \geq k \cdot d_1$, and $k = 0, 1, 2, \ldots$. Z_3 is the outside of Z_2. We assume that the speed of the signal is constant.

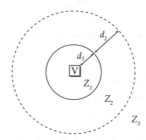

Fig. 4. Regions for distance fraud

When the adversary is in the region Z_1, she always accesses to all the challenges and produces valid responses on time. However, when the distance between the adversary and the verifier is $d_1 + \delta_d$ $(\delta_d > 0)$, any signal traveling this distance takes $t_1' > t_1$, i.e., $t_1' = t_1 + \delta_t$. In order to run her attack successfully, the adversary should send each current response (r_i), at least $2\delta_t$ before receiving the current challenge (c_i). When $\delta_t > k \cdot t_1$, she is in region Z_3, she should send the response r_i before receiving $c_i, c_{i-1}, \ldots, c_{i-k}$. However, when the adversary is in Z_2, she accesses some of the previous challenges to send r_i. This may increase the attacker's success probability. As a result, while analyzing the security of a k-PCD protocol against distance fraud, the region of the adversary should be considered.

In the next subsection, we focus on the security of k-PCD protocols against mafia and distance frauds when $k = 1$. To make the analysis easier for distance fraud, we assume that the adversary is in Z_3.

4.2   Security Trade-off for 1-PCD Protocols

Let g be the function that outputs the response bit r_i from the challenges c_{i-1}, c_i and the precomputed session secrets $y_0^i, y_1^i, \ldots, y_{m-1}^i$. The function g is executed n times to form the whole set of responses. For $y = (y_0, y_1, \ldots, y_{m-1}) \in \mathbb{F}_2^m$, let α_y be

$$\alpha_y = \sum_{\substack{c_i \in \{0,1\} \\ c_{i-1} \in \{0,1\}}} g(c_i, c_{i-1}, y) - 2.$$

Also, we define the following sets:

$$\mathcal{A} = \{y \in \mathbb{F}_2^m : |\alpha_y| = 2\},$$
$$\mathcal{B} = \{y \in \mathbb{F}_2^m : |\alpha_y| = 1\},$$
$$\mathcal{C} = \{y \in \mathbb{F}_2^m : \alpha_y = 0\},$$

where $|\cdot|$ denotes the absolute value.

Algorithm 4.1. A Generic Mafia Fraud Attack For 1-PCD Protocols(n, a, c)

---

n: Number of rounds
flip: Deciding on flipping the response
Send a random challenge $c_0' \in \{0, 1\}$ to the prover
if $c \geq 3a$
  then $flip \leftarrow 1$

  else $flip \leftarrow 0$
for $i \leftarrow 1$ **to** n
  do $\begin{cases} \text{Send a random challenge } c_i' \in \{0,1\} \text{ to the prover} \\ \text{Record the prover's response } r_i' \end{cases}$
/*Then, Mafia continues the protocol with the verifier*/
Record first challenge of the verifier c_p
for $i \leftarrow 1$ **to** n
  do $\begin{cases} \text{record i-}th \text{ challenge of the verifier in } c_i \\ \textbf{if } c_i' = c_i \textbf{ and } c_{i-1}' = c_p \\ \quad \textbf{then Send } r_i' \\ \\ \quad \textbf{else Send } r_i' \oplus flip \\ c_p \leftarrow c_i \end{cases}$

The set $\mathcal{A}$ includes the session secrets that produce the same response bit for any c_i and c_{i-1}. The set $\mathcal{B}$ consists the session secrets that produce the responses, majority of them are equal, for any c_i and c_{i-1}. The set $\mathcal{C}$ contains the session secrets that produce the responses, half of them are equal, for any c_i and c_{i-1}.

Let us denote a, b and c as the cardinalities of the sets $\mathcal{A}$, $\mathcal{B}$, and $\mathcal{C}$, respectively. Then we have $a + b + c = 2^m$. We assume that all the challenges and the precomputed session secret bits, which are used to compute response bits, are uniformly random.

Algorithm 4.2. A GENERIC DISTANCE FRAUD ATTACK FOR 1-PCD PROTOCOLS(n)

---

n: Number of rounds
$c_p \leftarrow \{0,1\}$
for $i \leftarrow 1$ **to** n

$\quad$ **then** $\left\{\begin{array}{l} \textbf{if } \alpha_{y^i} = 1 \\ \quad \textbf{then} \left\{\begin{array}{l} \text{Send } 1 \\ \textbf{if } g(0, c_p, y_0^i, \ldots, y_{m-1}^i) = 1 \\ \quad \textbf{then } c_p \leftarrow 0 \\ \\ \quad \textbf{else } c_p \leftarrow 1 \end{array}\right. \\ \textbf{else if } \alpha_{y^i} = -1 \\ \quad \textbf{then} \left\{\begin{array}{l} \text{Send } 0 \\ \textbf{if } g(0, c_p, y_0^i, \ldots, y_{m-1}^i) = 0 \\ \quad \textbf{then } c_p \leftarrow 0 \\ \\ \quad \textbf{else } c_p \leftarrow 1 \end{array}\right. \\ \textbf{else} \\ \quad \textbf{then} \left\{\begin{array}{l} \text{Send } g(0, c_p, y_0^i, \ldots, y_{m-1}^i) \\ c_p \leftarrow 0 \end{array}\right. \\ c_p \leftarrow c_i \end{array}\right.$

We introduce a generic mafia fraud attack and a generic distance fraud attack which can be mounted on all 1-PCD protocols. The mafia fraud attack and the distance fraud attack, given in Algorithm 4.1, Algorithm 4.2 are the extensions of the the attacks given in Algorithm 3.2 and Algorithm 3.1 to 1-PCD protocols, respectively. The values a, b, and c are computed during the off-line phase from the function g. Given a response generating function g, the cardinalities are computed as the expected number of elements in each set. In addition, during the slow phase the adversary relays the messages (e.g. nonces or commitments) between the verifier and the prover.

The following statement defines a security bound for mafia fraud in any rapid bit exchange round of the 1-PCD protocols and gives a trade-off between P_{dis} and P_{maf} for 1-PCD protocols. The statement is obtained by computing P_{maf} and P_{dis} of the Algorithm 4.1 and 4.2, respectively.

Theorem 2. *Let $\mathcal{P}$ be a $f(c_i, c_{i-1}y_0^i, \ldots, y_{m-1}^i) \rightarrow r_i$ 1-PCD protocol. Assume that c_is and y_j^is used in the fast phase of the protocol $\mathcal{P}$ are uniformly random. Then $P_{maf}(\mathcal{P}) \geq 5/8$, and $P_{maf}(\mathcal{P}) + P_{dis}(\mathcal{P}) \geq 5/4$.*

Proof. Considering distance fraud attack depicted in Algorithm 4.2, for any challenge value, the adversary can always guess a correct response if y^i is in the set $\mathcal{A}$. If it is in the set $\mathcal{B}$, she can predict the response with probability $3/4$. However, if it is in the set $\mathcal{C}$, she can predict the response with probability $1/2$. Therefore, the success probability P_{dis} for this attack is computed as follows:

$$
\begin{aligned}
P_{dis} &= \frac{a}{2^m} \cdot 1 + \frac{b}{2^m} \cdot \frac{3}{4} + \frac{c}{2^m} \cdot \frac{1}{2} \\
&= \frac{1}{2} + \frac{2a+b}{2^{m+2}}.
\end{aligned}
\tag{2}
$$

Considering the mafia fraud attack described in Algorithm 4.1, let an adversary first query the prover with predicted challenges c_i' and get the corresponding responses r_i'. Then, the adversary carries out the attack against the verifier. The adversary knows the correct response (i.e., $r_i' = r_i$) if $c_{i-1} = c_{i-1}'$ and $c_i = c_i'$. The probability of this event is $1/4$ since all the challenge bits are produced uniformly random. For the remaining cases, the adversary has to predict the corresponding response bit r_i.

The attacker has to predict the response bit r_i corresponding to a different pair of challenge bits (c_i, c_{i-1}). If the corresponding session secret y^i is in the set $\mathcal{A}$, then the probability that $r_i = r_i'$ is 1 by definition. This probability reduces to $1/2$ if y^i is in the set $\mathcal{B}$ since this happens only if both the input vectors (c_i, c_{i-1}, y^i) and (c_i', c_{i-1}', y^i) produce the same response even though the vectors are not equal. Similarly, the probability is $1/3$ if y^i is in the set $\mathcal{C}$. Then, the probabilities that $r_i \neq r_i'$ are deduced straightforward.

The attacker has two strategies for predicting a response value corresponding to a different pair of challenge bits.

(i) She sends the same response value received from the prover (r_i') and the success probability of mafia fraud ($P_{maf}^{no-flip}$) is computed as follows.

$$
\begin{aligned}
P_{maf}^{no-flip} &= \frac{1}{4} + \frac{3}{4} \cdot \left(\frac{a}{2^m} \cdot 1 + \frac{b}{2^m} \cdot \frac{1}{2} + \frac{c}{2^m} \cdot \frac{1}{3} \right) \\
&= \frac{1}{2} + \frac{4a+b}{2^{m+3}}.
\end{aligned}
\tag{3}
$$

(ii) She sends the complement of the response value and the success probability of mafia fraud with this strategy is computed as follows.

$$
\begin{aligned}
P_{maf}^{flip} &= \frac{1}{4} + \frac{3}{4} \cdot \left(\frac{a}{2^m} \cdot 0 + \frac{b}{2^m} \cdot \frac{1}{2} + \frac{c}{2^m} \cdot \frac{2}{3} \right) \\
&= \frac{1}{4} + \frac{3b+4c}{2^{m+3}}.
\end{aligned}
\tag{4}
$$

Both $P_{maf}^{no-flip}$ and P_{maf}^{flip} probabilities depend on the characteristic of function g. The adversary chooses the larger probability. Hence, we get

$$P_{maf} = \max(P_{maf}^{no-flip}, P_{maf}^{flip})$$
$$= \frac{1}{2} + \frac{b}{2^{m+3}} + \max(\frac{4a}{2^{m+3}}, \frac{2c-2a}{2^{m+3}}). \tag{5}$$

When $c \geq 3a$, we have $P_{maf}^{flip} \geq P_{maf}^{no-flip}$. So,

$$P_{maf} = \frac{1}{2} + \frac{b+2c-2a}{2^{m+3}}$$
$$= \frac{5}{8} + \frac{c-3a}{2^{m+3}}$$
$$\geq \frac{5}{8}. \tag{6}$$

Then we have $P_{dis} + P_{maf}^{flip} = 1 + \frac{2 \cdot (a+b+c)+b}{2^{m+3}} \geq \frac{5}{4}$ for the attacks in Algorithms (4.1) and (4.2). On the other hand, if $c \leq 3a$, then $P_{maf}^{no-flip} \geq P_{maf}^{flip}$. Hence,

$$P_{maf} = \frac{1}{2} + \frac{4a+b}{2^{m+3}}$$
$$= \frac{5}{8} + \frac{3a-c}{2^{m+3}}$$
$$\geq \frac{5}{8}. \tag{7}$$

In this case, we have $P_{dis} + P_{maf}^{no-flip} = 1 + \frac{8a+3b}{2^{m+3}} = \frac{5}{4} + \frac{b+2\cdot(3a-c)}{2^{m+3}} \geq \frac{5}{4}$. Hence, (6) and (7) yield that the success probability of mafia fraud cannot be less than 5/8. Thus, $P_{maf}(\mathcal{P}) + P_{dis}(\mathcal{P}) \geq \frac{5}{4}$. □

Figure 5 compares the trade-off curves for 1-PCD and CCD protocols, between the success probabilities of mafia and distance frauds. The figure shows that, the trade-off curve for 1-PCD is closer to the ideal security than the curve for CCD protocols. Another interesting result of the theorem is that 1-PCD protocols can attain the ideal security level against the distance fraud while $P_{maf} \geq 3/4$.

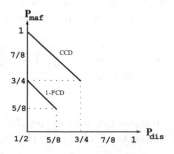

Fig. 5. Comparison of the trade-off curves for CCD and 1-PCD protocols

Corollary 2. *For a 1-PCD protocol* $\mathcal{P}$, *if the security level for the distance fraud is ideal (i.e* $P_{dis}(\mathcal{P}) = 1/2$) *then,* $P_{maf}(\mathcal{P}) \geq 3/4$.

Proof. The probability $P_{dis}(\mathcal{P})$ satisfies the condition in Theorem 2, so P_{maf} $(\mathcal{P}) \geq \dfrac{5}{4} - \dfrac{1}{2} = \dfrac{3}{4}$. $\square$

4.3   Simulation

We implement four different 1-PCD response generating functions on HK protocol structure. We simulate the attacks given in Algorithms 4.1 and 4.2 for each of them. The simulation for each protocol is repeated 2^{20} times with fresh nonces. We have shown that the experimental results, which are shown in Table 1, are in parallel with the results in Theorem 2.

Table 1. The simulation results for success probabilities of mafia fraud and distance fraud

a	b	c	P_{maf}	P_{dis}
1	0	3	0.6247	0.6249
2	1	1	0.7813	0.8124
0	0	4	0.7498	0.4996
0	4	0	0.6251	0.7500

5   Enhancing Security of CCD Protocols by Extending to 1-PCD

In the previous section, we have shown that 1-PCD protocols can provide better security than the CDD protocols. In this section, we aim to give a method to ameliorate the security of CCD protocols by extending them to 1-PCD protocols. We first introduce the notion of a natural extension. Then, we apply this extension on an existing protocol to show the security enhancement.

Let $\mathcal{P}$ be a CCD protocol with the response function $f(c_i, y_0^i, \ldots, y_{m-1}^i) \to r_i$ and $\mathcal{P}'$ be a 1-PCD protocol with the response function $g(c_i, c_{i-1}, y_0^i, \ldots, y_{m-1}^i)$ $\to r_i'$. We give the definition for a natural extension of a CCD protocol to provide a 1-PCD protocol as follows.

Definition 4 (Natural Extension for CCD to 1-PCD). $\mathcal{P}'$ *is called a natural extension of* $\mathcal{P}$ *if* $g(c_i, c_{i-1}, y_0^i, \ldots, y_{m-1}^i)$ *is a Boolean function of the variables* $f(Q(c_i, c_{i-1}), y_0^i, \ldots, y_{m-1}^i)$ *and* $T(c_i, c_{i-1})$, *where* Q *and* T *are Boolean functions of two variables.*

The objective of the natural extension is not to propose a new distance bounding protocol but enhancing the security level of a given protocol via extending its response function by using simple polynomial arithmetic. We want to show that the security level can be improved without using a computationally expensive final signature.

We study HK protocol as an example of CCD protocols which has the security levels as 3/4 against both mafia and distance frauds. We provide two natural extensions on this protocol: (i) The first version is to provide the ideal security level for distance fraud (i.e., 1/2), and (ii) The second one is to achieve the best security against mafia fraud (i.e. 5/8) among 1-PCD protocols.

5.1   A Natural Extension of HK Protocol for Improving Distance Fraud Resistance

In order to obtain the ideal security against distance fraud, we construct a response generating function such that $a = 0$, $b = 0$ and $c = 4$ (see Equation (2)). Therefore, we extend the response function of the original HK protocol (see Equation 1) by choosing $Q(c_{i-1}, c_i) = c_i$ and $T(c_{i-1}, c_i) = c_{i-1}$. We have the extended response function as follows.

$$
\begin{aligned}
g(c_i, c_{i-1}, y_0^i, y_1^i) &= f(c_i, y_0^i, y_1^i) \oplus c_{i-1} \\
&= c_i \cdot y_1^i \oplus ((1 \oplus c_i) \cdot y_0^i) \oplus c_{i-1} \\
&= y_{c_i}^i \oplus c_{i-1}
\end{aligned}
\tag{8}
$$

Equation (8) shows that, we obtain the natural extension by only XORing the original HK protocol's response function with c_{i-1}. In what follows, we analyse this extended version-1 to show the security enhancement of distance fraud.

Security analysis of extended version-1. As stated in Section 4, we apply the generic attacks for mafia fraud and distance fraud on extended protocol as follows.

Considering the mafia fraud attack described in Algorithm 4.1, the adversary uses the strategy of sending complement of the response received from the tag when she does not guess the challenges correctly since $c \geq 3a$. Therefore, by using Equation (4) the success probability of mafia is computed as $P_{maf} = \frac{1}{4} + \frac{3 \cdot 0 + 4 \cdot 2^m}{2^{m+3}} = \frac{3}{4}$.

While considering the distance fraud attack given in Algorithm 4.2 three regions should be taken into account as described in Section 4.

- In region Z_1, the prover can access all the challenges and there is no attack.
- In Z_2, the prover can access c_{i-1} challenge but she has no knowledge on c_i while sending r_i. She can compute two different r_i values using session secrets. In the first case, the adversary can always send a valid response r_i when $y_0^i = y_1^i$. In other case, she guesses r_i value with probability of 1/2 when $y_0^i \neq y_1^i$. Hence, the distance fraud probability for a single challenge-response is $1/2 \cdot 1 + 1/2 \cdot 1/2 = 3/4$. Therefore, it is concluded that when the prover is in Z_2 the security of the extended version is equivalent to the original HK protocol.
- In Z_3, the prover is not able to access both c_{i-1} and c_i challenges while computing the response r_i. Equation (2) yields $P_{dis} = 1/2$.

5.2   A Natural Extension of HK Protocol for Improving Mafia Fraud Resistance

We apply another natural extension for HK protocol to obtain an optimum security level for mafia fraud among 1-PCD protocols (i.e. $P_{maf} = \frac{5}{8}$). Considering the Equations (6) and (7), we construct a response function that satisfies $c = 3a$, also $a = 1$, $b = 0$ and $c = 3$. The natural extension on the response function is given below.

$$g(c_i, c_{i-1}, y_0^i, y_1^i) = f(c_i, y_0^i, y_1^i) \oplus f((1 \oplus c_{i-1}), y_0^i, y_1^i)$$
$$= y_{c_i}^i \oplus y_{\bar{c}_{i-1}}^i, \tag{9}$$

where $\bar{c}_{i-1}$ is the complement of c_{i-1} (i.e. $1 \oplus c_{i-1}$).

Security analysis of extended version-2. While analyzing the mafia fraud attack described in Algorithm 4.1, the adversary may use any of the strategies described in Section 4 since $c = 3a$. Therefore, both Equations (6) and (7) yields that, $P_{maf} = 5/8$.

Considering the distance fraud in region Z_2, the security level is same as the original HK protocol (i.e. 3/4) since the response function becomes same as in the HK protocol when the adversary receives c_{i-1}. In Z_3, the prover cannot access both c_{i-1} and c_i challenges while computing the response r_i. By using Equation (2), the success probability of distance fraud is calculated as $P_{dis} = 5/8$.

6   Discussion and Open Problems

In this paper, we have classified the low-cost RFID distance bounding protocols having no final signature and introduced the notion of CCD protocols and k-PCD protocols. We have shown that there is a trade-off between the security levels of mafia fraud and distance fraud for both CCD protocols and 1-PCD protocols. We have constructed trade-off curves by introducing generic attacks mounted on CCD protocols and 1-PCD protocols. On the other hand, there are several questions left open. The most natural questions may be the following ones:

- Are the attacks given in Algorithm 3.1 and Algorithm 3.2 the best generic attacks mounted on CCD protocols? In other words, is there a trade-off curve lying above the curve $P_{maf} + P_{dis} = 3/2$ for CCD protocols?
- Similar question for 1-PCD protocols can be given as: Is there a trade-off curve lying above the curve $P_{maf} + P_{dis} = 5/4$ for 1-PCD protocols?

We conjecture that the both curves deduced in the paper are the best trade-off curves. That is, the answer to the both questions above seems to be "no". Apart from the security analysis of CCD protocols and 1-PCD protocols, it is still an open question to construct trade-off curves for k-PCD protocols where $k > 1$. In general, we expect the security to be enhanced when k is increased. More formally, we have the following conjecture:

Conjecture 1. The best trade-off curve for k_1-PCD protocols lies above the best trade-off curve for k_2-PCD protocols where $k_1 < k_2$.

The most general question may be how far the security is enhanced when k is increased. Could we attain the ideal security when k is large enough? We have the following conjecture for this:

Conjecture 2. $P_{maf} + P_{dis}$ tends to 1 when k and n both tends to infinity.

In summary, we claim that the security levels approach the ideal security when k is increased. If it is really true, then the next question is how fast $P_{maf} + P_{dis}$ tends to 1? For practical purpose, it must be quite fast and we believe it is really fast.

Acknowledgment

This work has been partially funded by FP7-Project ICE under the grand agreement number 206546, and by the Walloon Region Marshall plan through the SPW DG06 Project TRASILUX. The authors wish to thank Mehmet Sabir Kiraz, Benjamin Martin, and Umut Uludag for their helpful comments.

References

1. Avoine, G., Floerkemeier, C., Martin, B.: RFID Distance Bounding Multistate Enhancement. In: Roy, B., Sendrier, N. (eds.) INDOCRYPT 2009. LNCS, vol. 5922, pp. 290–307. Springer, Heidelberg (2009)
2. Avoine, G., Tchamkerten, A.: An Efficient Distance Bounding RFID Authentication Protocol: Balancing False-acceptance Rate and Memory Requirement. In: Samarati, P., Yung, M., Martinelli, F., Ardagna, C.A. (eds.) ISC 2009. LNCS, vol. 5735, pp. 250–261. Springer, Heidelberg (2009)
3. Beth, T., Desmedt, Y.: Identification Tokens - or: Solving the Chess Grandmaster Problem. In: Menezes, A., Vanstone, S.A. (eds.) CRYPTO 1990. LNCS, vol. 537, pp. 169–177. Springer, Heidelberg (1991)
4. Brands, S., Chaum, D.: Distance-Bounding Protocols. In: Helleseth, T. (ed.) EUROCRYPT 1993. LNCS, vol. 765, pp. 344–359. Springer, Heidelberg (1994)
5. Capkun, S., Butty'an, L., Hubaux, J.-P.: SECTOR: Secure Tracking of Node Encounters in Multi-hop Wireless Networks. In: ACM Workshop on Security of Ad Hoc and Sensor Networks, SASN 2003, Fairfax, Virginia, USA, pp. 21–32. ACM Press, New York (October 2003)
6. Desmedt, Y.: Major security problems with the' Unforgeable' (Feige)-Fiat-Shamir proofs of identity and how to overcome them. In: SecuriCom 1988, pp. 15–17 (1988)
7. Desmedt, Y., Goutier, C., Bengio, S.: Special uses and abuses of the fiat-shamir passport protocol. In: Pomerance, C. (ed.) CRYPTO 1987. LNCS, vol. 293, pp. 21–39. Springer, Heidelberg (1988)
8. Hancke, G.: A Practical Relay Attack on ISO 14443 Proximity Cards. (February 2005) (manuscript)
9. Hancke, G., Kuhn, M.: An RFID Distance Bounding Protocol. In: Conference on Security and Privacy for Emerging Areas in Communication Networks, SecureComm 2005, Athens, Greece. IEEE Computer Society Press, Los Alamitos (September 2005)

10. Hancke, G., Mayes, K., Markantonakis, K.: Confidence in Smart Token Proximity: Relay Attacks Revisited. Elsevier Computers & Security (June 2009)
11. Kapoor, G., Zhou, W., Piramuthu, S.: Distance Bounding Protocol for Multiple RFID Tag Authentication. In: Proceedings of the 2008 IEEE/IFIP International Conference on Embedded and Ubiquitous Computing, EUC 2008, Shanghai, China, pp. 115–120. IEEE Computer Society Press, Los Alamitos (December 2008)
12. Kim, C.H., Avoine, G.: RFID distance bounding protocol with mixed challenges to prevent relay attacks. In: Garay, J.A., Miyaji, A., Otsuka, A. (eds.) CANS 2009. LNCS, vol. 5888, pp. 119–133. Springer, Heidelberg (2009)
13. Kim, C.H., Avoine, G., Koeune, F., Standaert, F.-X., Pereira, O.: The Swiss-Knife RFID Distance Bounding Protocol. In: Lee, P.J., Cheon, J.H. (eds.) ICISC 2008. LNCS, vol. 5461, pp. 98–115. Springer, Heidelberg (2009)
14. Munilla, J., Peinado, A.: Distance bounding protocols for RFID enhanced by using void-challenges and analysis in noisy channels. Wireless Communications and Mobile Computing 8(9), 1227–1232 (2008)
15. Nikov, V., Vauclair, M.: Yet Another Secure Distance-Bounding Protocol. Cryptology ePrint Archive, Report 2008/319 (2008)
16. Reid, J., Gonzalez Neito, J., Tang, T., Senadji, B.: Detecting relay attacks with timing based protocols. In: Bao, F., Miller, S. (eds.) Proceedings of the 2nd ACM Symposium on Information, Computer and Communications Security, ASIACCS 2007, Singapore, Republic of Singapore, pp. 204–213. ACM Press, New York (March 2007)
17. Singelée, D., Preneel, B.: Distance Bounding in Noisy Environments. In: Stajano, F., Meadows, C., Capkun, S., Moore, T. (eds.) ESAS 2007. LNCS, vol. 4572, pp. 101–115. Springer, Heidelberg (2007)
18. Tu, Y.-J., Piramuthu, S.: RFID Distance Bounding Protocols. In: First International EURASIP Workshop on RFID Technology, Vienna, Austria (September 2007)

A Hancke and Kuhn's Protocol

Hancke and Kuhn [9] proposed a simple and efficient distance bounding protocol that has been used as a key-reference in RFID context. Hancke and Kuhn's protocol consists of two phases: *Slow phase* and *fast phase* (or rapid bit exchange phase). As depicted in Figure 6 the protocol steps are as follows.

Slow phase – The prover and the verifier exchange randomly generated nonces. From these nonces and a shared secret x both party compute two $n-bit$ registers y_0 and y_1, using a pseudo-random function h. These registers are used as session secrets during the fast phase.

Fast phase – The verifier sends a random challenge c_i to the prover, then the later replies with r_i, by using the challenge and shared session secrets such that $f(c_i, y_0^i, y_1^i) = y_{c_i}^i$, where $i = 1, 2 \ldots n$. For each rapid bit exchange the verifier measures the round trip time Δt_i. After n rapid bit exchanges the verifier checks the correctness of r_i's and $\Delta t_i \leq t_{max}$ where n is the security parameter and t_{max} is the maximum allowed time delay for each rapid bit exchange.

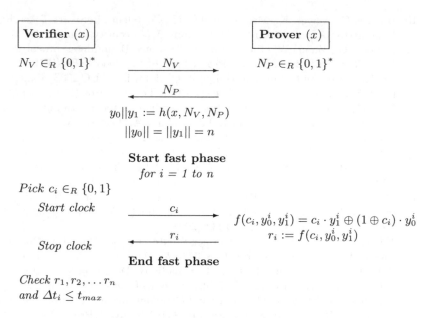

Fig. 6. Hancke and Kuhn's protocol

Distance Fraud Analysis. Let P be the prover who carries out the attack, and V be the verifier who wants to be sure that P is inside the authentication region. P can compute all session secrets (i.e. two $n - bit$ registers) as soon as they exchanged the nonces. During the rapid bit exchange, P should send a response r_i before receiving the challenge c_i in order to accomplish the attack. She computes two response r_i values using two registers. In half of the cases, they are the same and P always sends the correct r_i. In the remaining cases, they are not the same and P correctly predict r_i value with probability $1/2$. Hence, for any i, P sends a valid r_i corresponding to the challenge c_i with probability $\frac{1}{2} \cdot 1 + \frac{1}{2} \cdot \frac{1}{2} = \frac{3}{4}$. Since n rounds occurs during the fast phase, the success probability of the attack is $\left(\frac{3}{4}\right)^n$.

The Poulidor Distance-Bounding Protocol

Rolando Trujillo-Rasua[1], Benjamin Martin[2], and Gildas Avoine[2]

[1] Universitat Rovira i Virgili
Department of Computer Engineering and Mathematics
Catalonia, Spain
rolando.trujillo@urv.cat
[2] Université catholique de Louvain
Information Security Group
B-1348 Louvain-la-Neuve, Belgium
{benjamin.martin,gildas.avoine}@uclouvain.be

Abstract. RFID authentication protocols are susceptible to different types of relay attacks such as mafia and distance frauds. A countermeasure against these types of attacks are the well-known *distance-bounding protocols*. These protocols are usually designed to resist to only one of these frauds, though, behave poorly when both are considered. In this paper (i) we extend the analysis of mafia and distance frauds in recently released protocols. (ii) We introduce the concept of distance-bounding protocols based on graphs while previous proposals rely on linear registers or binary trees. (iii) We propose an instance of the graph-based protocol that resists to both mafia and distance frauds without sacrificing memory. To the best of our knowledge, this protocol achieves the best trade-off between these two frauds.

Keywords: RFID, authentication, distance-bounding protocol, mafia fraud, distance fraud, graph.

1 Introduction

Radio Frequency IDentification (RFID) is a contactless technology that is becoming the solution for everyday identification/authentication applications, such as access control, passport, public transportation, payment, ticketing, etc. The main purpose of RFID is to allow *readers* to communicate wirelessly with *tags* implanted into objects. While identification does not involve heavy computation capabilities for tags, authentication process, such as the ISO/IEC 9798 [2] or ISO/IEC 11770 [1] standards, requires more powerful tags performing strong cryptographic algorithms.

The most widespread and low-cost tags are *passive*, meaning that they do not have their own power source, and are supplied by the electromagnetic field of a reader. Although capacities of such tags are quite limited, some of them benefit from cryptographic building blocks and secure authentication protocols. They are typically used in the above-mentioned applications. Nevertheless, Desmedt, Goutier and Bengio [5] presented in 1987, an attack that defeated any

S.B. Ors Yalcin (Ed.): RFIDSec 2010, LNCS 6370, pp. 239–257, 2010.

authentication protocol. In this attack, called *Mafia Fraud*, the adversary passes through the authentication process by simply relaying the messages between a legitimate reader (the verifier) and a legitimate tag (the prover). Thus she does not need to modify or decrypt any exchanged data. Later in 1993, Brands and Chaum [4] proposed a countermeasure that prevents from such an attack by estimating the distance between the reader and the tag to authenticate: the *distance-bounding protocol*. They also introduced in [4] a new kind of attack, named *Distance Fraud*, where a dishonest prover claims to be closer to the verifier than it really is.

Since then, many distance-bounding protocols have been proposed to thwart these attacks. In 2005, Hancke and Kuhn [6] proposed the first distance-bounding protocol dedicated to RFID. It is split in two phases: a *slow phase*, in which reader and tag exchange two nonces, and carry on resource-consuming operations; followed by a *fast phase* divided into n rounds where, in each one, the reader measures the time taken by a single bit challenge/response. Based on these exchanges, the reader is able to bound the distance between itself and the tag. These communications also provide the identity proof of the tag. Unfortunately, the adversary success probability regarding mafia and distance frauds is $(3/4)^n$ while one may expect $(1/2)^n$. Therefore, others protocols [3,7,8,10,11,12] attempt to fix the Hancke and Kuhn's proposal.

There exist distance-bounding protocols structured differently than the one proposed by Hancke and Kuhn. For example, the protocols [4,8,9] perform a third additional phase in which the tag signs the exchanged bits. However, in practice this final phase represents an additional delay. As stated in [3], as the authentication entirely relies on this phase, if the latter is interrupted or not reached, then the whole process is lost. Therefore, protocols without this final slow phase are more flexible and faster. In the sequel we only focus on such protocols.

Kim and Avoine's protocol [7] and Avoine and Tchamkerten's protocol [3] are built in the same manner as Hancke and Kuhn's one. To the best of our knowledge, they have the best resistance considering only mafia fraud. However, Kim and Avoine's protocol [7] severely sacrifices the distance fraud security, whereas Avoine and Tchamkerten's one [3] requires an exponential amount of memory ($2^{n+1} - 2$ in its standard configuration) to achieve such a high mafia fraud resistance. Either Hancke and Kuhn nor the two latter protocols achieve a good balance between memory, mafia fraud resistance and distance fraud resistance.

The first contribution of this paper is the mafia and distance fraud detailed analysis of the protocols [3] and [7]. Then, we introduce the concept of distance-bounding protocols based on graphs, and we propose a new distance-bounding protocol based on a particular graph. Our goal is not to provide the best protocol in terms of mafia fraud or distance fraud, but to design a protocol that ensures a good trade-off between these concerns, while still using a linear memory. So, our protocol is never the best one when considering only one property, but is undeniably a good option when considering the three properties all together. That is why we name our protocol *Poulidor* as a famous French bicycle racer known as *The Eternal Second* : never the best in any race, but definitively the best in average.

The paper is organized as follows. In Section 2, we describe in detail Hancke and Kuhn's protocol [6], Kim and Avoine's protocol [7] and Avoine and Tchamkerten's protocol [3]. Section 3 presents our graph-based protocol. In Section 4, we formally define the adversary strategies for mafia and distance frauds, and give a security analysis of the graph-based protocol regarding these two strategies. We show in Section 5 that our protocol has the best trade-off between mafia fraud resistance, distance fraud resistance and memory consumption. Finally, Section 6 discusses the obtained results, and raises some open problems to the scientific community.

2   State of the Art

2.1   Hancke and Kuhn's Protocol

Hancke and Kuhn's protocol (HKP) [6], depicted in Figure 1, is a key-reference protocol in terms of distance bounding devoted to RFID systems. HKP is a simple and fast protocol, but it suffers from a high adversary success probability.

Initialization. The prover (P) and the verifier (V) share a secret x and agree on (i) a security parameter n, (ii) a public hash function H whose output size is $2n$, and (iii) a given timing bound $\Delta t_{\max}$.

Protocol. HKP consists of two phases: a slow one followed by a fast one. During the slow phase V generates a random nonce N_V and sends it to P. Reciprocally, P generates N_P and sends it to V. V and P then both compute $H^{2n} := H(x, N_P, N_V)$. In what follows, H_i $(1 \le i \le 2n)$ denotes the i-th bit of H^{2n}, and $H_i \ldots H_j$ $(1 \le i < j \le 2n)$ denotes the concatenation of the bits from

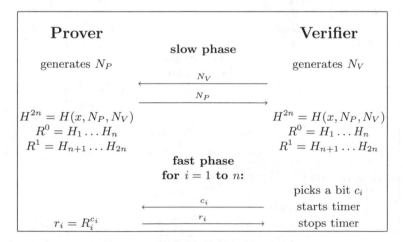

Fig. 1. Hancke and Kuhn's protocol

H_i to H_j. Then V and P split H^{2n} into two registers of length n: $R^0 := H_1 \ldots H_n$ and $R^1 := H_{n+1} \ldots H_{2n}$. The fast phase then consists of n rounds. In each of them, V picks a random bit c_i (the challenge) and sends it to P. The latter immediately answers $r_i := R_i^{c_i}$, the i-th bit of the register R^{c_i}.

Verification. At the end of the fast phase, the verifier checks that the answers received from the prover are correct and that $\Delta t_i \leq \Delta t_{\max}$ $(1 \leq i \leq n)$.

2.2   Kim and Avoine's Protocol

Kim and Avoine's protocol (KAP) [7], represented in Figure 2, basically relies on *predefined* challenges. Predefined challenges allow the prover to detect that an attack occurs as follows: the prover and the verifier agree on some predefined 1-bit challenges; if the adversary sends in advance a challenge to the prover that is different from the expected predefined challenge, then the prover detects the attack and until the end of the protocol execution, sends random responses to the adversary. The complete description of KAP protocol is provided below.

Initialization. The prover (P) and the verifier (V) share a secret x and agree on (i) a security parameter n, (ii) a public hash function H whose output size is $4n$, and (iii) a given timing bound $\Delta t_{\max}$.

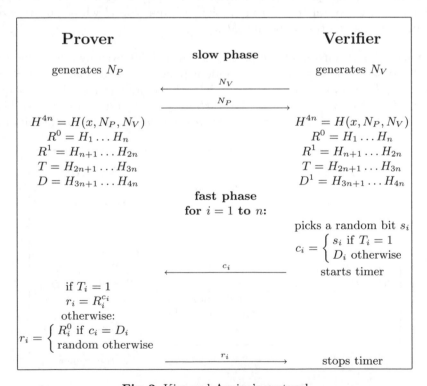

Fig. 2. Kim and Avoine's protocol

Protocol. As previously, V and P exchange nonces N_V and N_P. From these values they compute $H^{4n} = H(x, N_P, N_V)$, and split it in four registers. $R^0 := H_1 \ldots H_n$ and $R^1 := H_{n+1} \ldots H_{2n}$ are the potential responses. The register $D := H_{3n+1} \ldots H_{4n}$ constitutes the potential predefined challenges. Finally, the register $T := H_{2n+1} \ldots H_{3n}$ allows the verifier (resp. prover) to decide whether a predefined challenge should be sent (resp. received): in round i, if $T_i = 1$ then a random challenge is sent; if $T_i = 0$ then the predefined challenge D_i is sent instead of a random one.

Verification. At the end of the fast phase, the verifier checks that the answers received from the prover are correct and that $\Delta t_i \leq \Delta t_{\max}$ $(1 \leq i \leq n)$.

2.3 Avoine and Tchamkerten's Protocol

The Avoine and Tchamkerten's protocol (ATP) [3] is slightly different from the other existing distance bounding protocols. This protocol is also based on single bit challenge/response exchanges. However, the authors propose to use a decision tree to set up the fast phase. Figure 3 depicts the protocol detailed below.

Initialization. The prover and the verifier share a secret x, agree on (i) two security parameters $n = \alpha k$ and m, (ii) a pseudo-random function PRF whose output size is at least $m + \alpha(2^{k+1} - 2)$ bits, (iii) a timing bound $\Delta t_{\max}$.

Protocol. The prover P and the verifier V both generate a nonce, N_P for P and N_V for V. The verifier sends his nonce to P. Upon reception, the latter computes $PRF(x, N_P, N_V)$. He then sends $[PRF(x, N_P, N_V)]_1^m$, the first m bits of $PRF(x, N_P, N_V)$, and his nonce. These bits are used for the authentication.

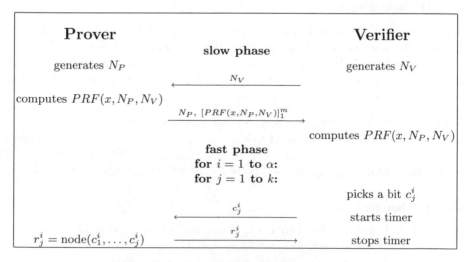

Fig. 3. Avoine and Tchamkerten protocol

P and V use the remaining $\alpha(2^{k+1} - 2)$ bits to label the nodes of α binary decision trees of depth k. Each node of the trees[1] is labeled by one bit from $[PRF(x, N_P, N_V)]_{m+1}^{m+\alpha(2^{k+1}-2)}$ (the remaining bits) in a one-to-one way. These labels represent the prover's responses during the fast phase. The challenges are symbolized by the edges of the trees, the left and right edges are labeled with 0 and 1 respectively.

Afterwards, the fast phase begins, for $1 \leq i \leq \alpha$, and $1 \leq j \leq k$, V picks a bit c_j^i at random, starts a timer and sends c_j^i to P. The latter immediately answers a bit $r_j^i = \text{node}(c_1^i, \ldots c_j^i)$, the value in the i-th tree of the node relied to the root by the edges labeled $c_1^i, \ldots, c_j^i$. Once V receives P's response, he stops his timer and computes Δt_j^i.

Verification. The verifier authenticates the prover if the m bits, sent during the slow phase, are those he expected. The prover succeeds the distance-bounding stage, if all his responses are correct and if for all $1 \leq i \leq \alpha$ and $1 \leq j \leq k$, $\Delta t_j^i \leq \Delta t_{\max}$.

3   Graph-Based Distance-Bounding Protocol

The ATP protocol [3] in its standard configuration ($\alpha = 1$) relies on a binary tree. The amount of memory needed to build this binary tree is exponential regarding to the number of rounds. Although the authors in [3] proposed to split the binary tree in order to reduce the memory requirements, they point out that this leads to a significant decrease in the security level of the protocol. We intend to go a step forward by proposing protocols based on graphs rather than trees. The graph-based protocols, as presented below, provide a greater design flexibility, a high security level and a low memory consumption.

3.1   Initialization

Parameters. The prover P and the verifier V agree on four public parameters: (i) a security parameter n that represents the number of rounds in the protocol, (ii) a timing bound $\Delta t_{\max}$, (iii) a pseudo random function PRF whose output size is $4n$ bits, and (iv) a directed graph G whose characteristics are discussed below. They also agree on a shared secret x.

Graph. To achieve n rounds, the proposed graph requires $2n$ nodes $\{q_0, q_1, \ldots, q_{2n-1}\}$, and $4n$ edges $\{s_0, s_1, \cdots, s_{2n-1}, \ell_0, \ell_1, \cdots, \ell_{2n-1}\}$ such that, s_i ($0 \leq i \leq 2n - 1$) is an edge from q_i to $q_{(i+1) \mod 2n}$, and ℓ_i ($0 \leq i \leq 2n - 1$) is an edge from q_i to $q_{(i+2) \mod 2n}$. Figure 4 depicts the graph when $n = 4$.

3.2   Exchanges

As described below, the protocol is divided in two phases, a slow phase followed by a fast one. Figure 5 summarizes the protocol.

---

[1] Except the roots.

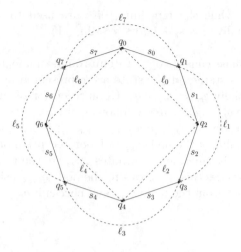

Fig. 4. Graph when $n = 4$

Slow phase – P and V generate nonces N_P and N_V respectively, and exchange them. From these values and the secret x, they compute $H_1||\ldots||H_{4n} = PRF(x, N_P, N_V)$ where H_i denotes the i-th bit of the output of $PRF(x, N_P, N_V)$. The bits $H_1, \ldots, H_{4n}$ set up the graph G as follows: the first $2n$ bits are used

Prover		**Verifier**
	slow phase	
generates N_P		generates N_V
	$\xleftarrow{N_V}$	
	$\xrightarrow{N_P}$	
$H_1 \ldots H_{4n} = PRF(x, N_P, N_V)$		$H_1 \ldots H_{4n} = PRF(x, N_P, N_V)$
fills the graph:		fills the graph:
for $i = 0$ to $2n - 1$:		for $i = 0$ to $2n - 1$:
$\begin{cases} \ell_i = \overline{H_{i+2n+1}} \\ s_i = H_{i+2n+1} \\ q_i = H_{i+1} \end{cases}$		$\begin{cases} \ell_i = \overline{H_{i+2n+1}} \\ s_i = H_{i+2n+1} \\ q_i = H_{i+1} \end{cases}$
	fast phase	
	for $i = 0$ to $n - 1$:	
		picks a bit c_i
	$\xleftarrow{c_i}$	starts timer
moves from q_{p_i} to $q_{p_{i+1}}$		
$r_i = q_{p_{i+1}}$	$\xrightarrow{r_i}$	stops timer
		moves from q_{v_i} to $q_{v_{i+1}}$
		checks if $r_i = q_{v_{i+1}}$

Fig. 5. Our proposal

to value the nodes while the remaining bits are used to value the edges s_i $(0 \leq i \leq 2n - 1)$, finally $\ell_i = s_i \oplus 1$ $(0 \leq i \leq 2n - 1)$.

Fast phase – This phase consists of n stateful rounds numbered from 0 to $n - 1$. In the i-th round P's state and V's state are represented by the nodes q_{p_i} and q_{v_i} respectively: initially $q_{p_0} = q_{v_0} = q_0$. Upon reception of the i-th challenge c_i, P moves to the node q_{p_i} to $q_{p_{i+1}}$ in the following way: $q_{p_{i+1}} = q_{(p_i+1) \mod 2n}$ if s_i is labeled with c_i, otherwise $q_{p_{i+1}} = q_{(p_i+2) \mod 2n}$. Finally, the prover sends as response r_i the bit-value of the node $q_{p_{i+1}}$. Upon reception of the prover answer r_i, the verifier stops his timer, and computes Δt_i, i.e. the round trip time spent for this exchange. Besides this, V moves to the node $q_{v_{i+1}}$ using the challenge c_i (as the prover did but from the node q_{v_i}) and checks if $q_{v_{i+1}} = r_i$.

3.3 Verification

The authentication succeeds if all the responses are correct, and each round is completed within the time bound $\Delta t_{\max}$.

4 Security Analysis of the Graph-Based Protocol

As stated in the introduction, mafia fraud and distance fraud are the two main security concerns when considering distance bounding protocols. We analyze in this section the graph-based protocol with respect to these frauds.

4.1 Mafia Fraud

To analyze the mafia fraud we consider the adversary abilities complying with the models provided in [3], [6] and [7]. Below, we define the *head node* and rephrase the well-known pre-ask strategy (see for example [9]) with our terminology.

Definition 1 (Head node). *Given a sequence of challenges* $\{c_1, c_2, \cdots, c_i\}$ *($1 \leq i \leq n$), the head node is the node that should be use by the prover to sends the response to the verifier according to this sequence of challenges. The head node is denoted as* $\Omega(c_1, c_2, \cdots, c_i)$.

Definition 2 (Pre-ask strategy). *The pre-ask strategy begins at the end of the slow-phase and before the beginning of the fast phase. First, the adversary sends a sequence of challenges* $\{\tilde{c}_1, \tilde{c}_2, \cdots, \tilde{c}_n\}$ *to the prover and receives a sequence of responses* $\{\Omega(\tilde{c}_1), \Omega(\tilde{c}_1, \tilde{c}_2), \cdots, \Omega(\tilde{c}_1, \tilde{c}_2, \cdots, \tilde{c}_n)\}$.

Later, during the fast phase, the adversary tries to use the information obtained from the prover in the best way. Let consider $\{c_1, c_2, \cdots c_i\}$ *the challenges sent by the verifier until the i-th round during the fast phase. If* $\forall j$ *s.t.* $1 \leq j \leq i$, *we have* $c_j = \tilde{c}_j$ *then the adversary sends as response* $\Omega(\tilde{c}_1, \tilde{c}_2, \cdots, \tilde{c}_i)$. *Otherwise she sends as response the value* $\Omega(\tilde{c}_1, \tilde{c}_2, \cdots, \tilde{c}_j)$ *where j is selected according to some rule that will be defined later.*

Remark 1. Sending a combination of two or more values as response is completely useless for the adversary because the nodes' values in the graph are independent from each other. Furthermore in the graph-based protocol, one node is never used twice to send a response. Therefore, the adversary can neither obtain nor infer more information than the one obtained from the prover. Finally, note that in the security analysis of previous protocols [3], [6] and [7], the best adversary strategy is to pick $j = i$ for every round, i.e. the adversary sends exactly what she received from the prover in the i-th round. However, as we explain below, in the graph-based protocol it makes sense to send a value received in a different round.

While the challenges sent by the adversary match with the challenges sent by the verifier, then the adversary is able to send the correct response. However, after the first *incorrect* adversary challenge, she can no longer be convinced about the correctness of her response. Consequently, we analyze below the adversary success probability when the adversary sends at least an *incorrect* challenge to the prover during the pre-ask strategy.

Theorem 1. *Let $(c_1, c_2, \cdots, c_i)$ be the sequence of verifier challenges until the i-th round, and let $(\tilde{c}_1, \tilde{c}_2, \cdots, \tilde{c}_n)$ be the sequence of adversary challenges in the pre-ask strategy. Let F be the random variable representing the first round in which $c_t \neq \tilde{c}_t$ $(1 \leq t \leq n)$. Given, $\Omega(\tilde{c}_1, \tilde{c}_2, \cdots, \tilde{c}_j)$, the adversary response in the i-th round for some $(1 \leq j \leq n)$, we have:*

$$\Pr(\Omega(\tilde{c}_1, \tilde{c}_2, \cdots, \tilde{c}_j) = \Omega(c_1, c_2, \cdots, c_i)|F = t) = \begin{cases} 1 & \text{if } i < t \text{ and } i = j, \\ \frac{1}{2} & \text{if } i < t \text{ and } i \neq j, \\ \frac{1}{2} & \text{if } i \geq t \text{ and } j < t, \\ p(t) & \text{if } i \geq t \text{ and } j \geq t, \end{cases}$$

where $p(t) = \frac{1}{2} + \frac{1}{2^{i+j-2t+2}} \sum_{k=0}^{k=2n-1} \left(A^{i-t}[1, k] A^{j-t}[2, k] + A^{i-t}[2, k] A^{j-t}[1, k] \right)$, and A is the adjacency matrix of the graph which represents the graph-based protocol.

Proof. We analyze the problem by cases:

Case 1 ($i < t$ and $i = j$). As $i < t$ then $\forall 1 \leq k \leq i$, $\tilde{c}_k = c_k$, therefore $\Omega(\tilde{c}_1, \tilde{c}_2, \cdots, \tilde{c}_j) = \Omega(c_1, c_2, \cdots, c_i)$.

Case 2 ($i < t$ and $i \neq j$). As $i < t$ then $\Omega(\tilde{c}_1, \tilde{c}_2, \cdots, \tilde{c}_i) = q_{v_i} = \Omega(c_1, c_2, \cdots, c_i)$. On the other hand, as $i \neq j$ then q_{v_i} and $\Omega(\tilde{c}_1, \tilde{c}_2, \cdots, \tilde{c}_j)$ are not the same node in the graph. As the node values in the graph are independent, we conclude that, $\Pr(\Omega(\tilde{c}_1, \tilde{c}_2, \cdots, \tilde{c}_j) = \Omega(c_1, c_2, \cdots, c_i)) = \frac{1}{2}$.

Case 3 ($i \geq t$ and $j < t$). This case is analog to Case 2.

Case 4 ($i \geq t$ and $j \geq t$). Let be $q_{v_i} = \Omega(c_1, c_2, \cdots, c_i)$ and $q_{a_j} = \Omega(\tilde{c}_1, \tilde{c}_2, \cdots, \tilde{c}_j)$, so:

$$\Pr(\Omega(\tilde{c}_1, \tilde{c}_2, \cdots, \tilde{c}_j) = \Omega(c_1, c_2, \cdots, c_i)) = \Pr(q_{v_i} = q_{a_j}). \tag{1}$$

Now, $\Pr(q_{v_i} = q_{a_j}) = \Pr(q_{v_i} = q_{a_j}|v_i = a_j)\Pr(v_i = a_j) + \Pr(q_{v_i} = q_{a_j}|v_i \neq a_j)\Pr(v_i \neq a_j)$ where $\Pr(q_{v_i} = q_{a_j}|v_i = a_j) = 1$ by definition of the graph-based protocol. On the other hand, $\Pr(q_{v_i} = q_{a_j}|v_i \neq a_j) = \frac{1}{2}$ because the node values are selected at random in the protocol, then:

$$\Pr(q_{v_i} = q_{a_j}) = \frac{1}{2} + \frac{\Pr(v_i = a_j)}{2} . \tag{2}$$

As $0 \leq v_i, a_j \leq 2n - 1$ then:

$$\Pr(v_i = a_j) = \sum_{k=0}^{k=2n-1} \Pr(v_i = k)\Pr(a_j = k) . \tag{3}$$

As $c_t \neq \tilde{c}_t$ for the first time, then two equally probable cases occur: 1) $\Omega(c_1, \cdots, c_t) = q_x$ and $\Omega(\tilde{c}_1, \cdots, \tilde{c}_t) = q_{x+1}$, 2) $\Omega(c_1, \cdots, c_t) = q_{x+1}$ and $\Omega(\tilde{c}_1, \cdots, \tilde{c}_t) = q_x$, where $(0 \leq x \leq 2n - 1)$ and $\forall x$, $x + 1 = (x + 1) \mod 2n$. Using these two events in the equation 3 we obtain:

$$\Pr(v_i = a_j) = \frac{1}{2} \left(\sum_{k=0}^{k=2n-1} \Pr(v_i = k|\Omega(c_1, \cdots, c_t) = q_x)\Pr(a_j = k|\Omega(c_1, \cdots, c_t) = q_x) \right.$$

$$\left. + \sum_{k=0}^{k=2n-1} \Pr(v_i = k|\Omega(c_1, \cdots, c_t) = q_{x+1})\Pr(a_j = k|\Omega(c_1, \cdots, c_t) = q_{x+1}) \right) . \tag{4}$$

As $A^y[x, k]$ represents the number of walks of size y between the nodes x and k, then $\Pr(v_i = k|\Omega(c_1, \cdots, c_t) = q_x) = \frac{A^{i-t}[x,k]}{2^{i-t}}$ and $\Pr(v_i = k|\Omega(c_1, \cdots, c_t) = q_{x+1}) = \frac{A^{i-t}[x+1,k]}{2^{i-t}}$, in the same way $\Pr(a_j = k|\Omega(c_1, \cdots, c_t) = q_x) = \frac{A^{j-t}[x,k]}{2^{j-t}}$ and $\Pr(a_j = k|\Omega(c_1, \cdots, c_t) = q_{x+1}) = \frac{A^{j-t}[x+1,k]}{2^{j-t}}$. Then using Equation 4:

$$\Pr(v_i = a_j) = \frac{1}{2^{i+j-2t+2}} \sum_{k=0}^{k=2n-1} \left(A^{i-t}[x, k]A^{j-t}[x + 1, k] + A^{i-t}[x + 1, k]A^{j-t}[x, k] \right) . \tag{5}$$

Given the graph characteristics, we have $A^y[x, k] = A^y[(x - z) \mod 2n, (k - z) \mod 2n]$ for any $z \in \mathbb{N}$. Therefore, $A^{i-t}[x, k] = A^{i-t}[1, (k - x + 1) \mod 2n]$ and $A^{i-t}[x + 1, k] = A^{i-t}[2, (k - x + 1) \mod 2n]$, in the same way, $A^{j-t}[x, k] = A^{j-t}[1, (k - x + 1) \mod 2n]$ and $A^{j-t}[x + 1, k] = A^{j-t}[2, (k - x + 1) \mod 2n]$. So:

$$\sum_{k=0}^{2n-1} \left(A^{i-t}[x, k]A^{j-t}[x + 1, k] + A^{i-t}[x + 1, k]A^{j-1}[x, k] \right) =$$

$$\sum_{k=0}^{2n-1} \left(A^{i-t}[1, k]A^{j-t}[2, k] + A^{i-t}[2, k]A^{j-t}[1, k] \right) . \tag{6}$$

Equations 1, 2, 5, and 6 yield the expected result.   □

Remark 2. Using Theorem 1, assuming $c_1 \neq \tilde{c}_1$, then for $i = 1$ we obtain that $\Pr(\Omega(\tilde{c}_1, \tilde{c}_2) = \Omega(c_1)) = \frac{5}{8} > \Pr(\Omega(\tilde{c}_1, \tilde{c}_2, \cdots, \tilde{c}_j) = \Omega(c_1))$ for every $j \neq 2$. It means that in this case it is better for the adversary to send the second response of the prover $(\Omega(\tilde{c}_1, \tilde{c}_2))$. These results only reinforce the ideas expressed in the Remark 1, that is the best adversary strategy is not always to pick $j = i$ in the graph-based protocol.

Corollary 1. *Given* $r_i = \Omega(\tilde{c}_1, \tilde{c}_2, \cdots, \tilde{c}_i)$ *and* $c'_i = \Omega(c_1, c_2, \cdots, c_i)$ *for every* $1 \leq i \leq n$, *the best adversary success probability in the mafia fraud is:*

$$\sum_{t=1}^{t=n} \frac{1}{2^t} \left(\prod_{i=t}^{i=n} \max(\Pr(r_1 = c'_i|F = t), \cdots, \Pr(r_n = c'_i|F = t)) \right) + \frac{1}{2^n}$$

where $\Pr(r_j = c'_i|F = t)$ *is defined in Theorem 1.*

Proof. The adversary success probability in the mafia fraud is:

$$\sum_{t=1}^{t=n} (\Pr(\text{success}|F = t) \Pr(F = t)) + \Pr(c_1 = \tilde{c}_1, c_2 = \tilde{c}_2, \cdots, c_n = \tilde{c}_n) . \quad (7)$$

As the challenges are selected at random, then:

$$\begin{aligned} \Pr(F = t) &= \tfrac{1}{2^t} . \\ \Pr(c_1 = \tilde{c}_1, c_2 = \tilde{c}_2, \cdots, c_n = \tilde{c}_n) &= \tfrac{1}{2^n} . \end{aligned} \quad (8)$$

Considering the pre-ask attack strategy in Definition 2:

$$\Pr(\text{success}|F = t) = \prod_{i=t}^{i=n} \max(\Pr(r_1 = c'_i|F = t), \cdots, \Pr(r_n = c'_i|F = t)) . \quad (9)$$

Equations 7, 8, and 9 yield the expected result. □

4.2   Distance Fraud

The distance fraud analysis for most of the distance-bounding protocols is not a hard task. However, for the ATP [3] protocol, to the best of our knowledge, nobody has found the distance fraud success probability. Unfortunately, in the graph-based protocol which has some similarities with the ATP protocol, distance fraud analysis is also not trivial. Then, in this paper we provide an upper bound of the distance fraud for a sub-family of the distance-bounding protocols, which will be useful for the ATP protocol, and of course, for the graph-based protocol too.

Definition 3 (Distance-bounding protocol sub-family). *Let consider* $\mathcal{P}$, *a distance bounding protocol.* $\mathcal{P}$ *belongs to the distance-bounding protocol sub-family if it fulfills the following requirements:*

- *During the fast phase, in each round the verifier sends a bit as challenge and the prover answers with a bit alike.*
- *There is no final phase.*
- *After the slow-phase, it should be possible to build a function $f : \{0,1\}^n \to \{0,1\}^n$ such that, given any sequence of challenge $\{c_1, c_2, \cdots, c_n\}$, then $f(c_1, c_2, \cdots, c_n)$ is the correct response sequence for the verifier. Since now on, we are going to call this function as "prover function".*

Definition 4 (Prover function pre-image). *For a sequence $y \in \{0,1\}^n$ and a prover function f, the prover function pre-image is the set $I_y = \{x \in \{0,1\}^n | f(x) = y\}$.*

We now define the adversary capability in the distance fraud:

Definition 5 (Adversary capability in the distance fraud). *The adversary capability in the distance fraud is twofold:*

1. *The adversary has access to the prover function.*
2. *The adversary can send in advance a sequence $y \in \{0,1\}^n$ to the verifier, trying to maximize $\Pr(f(c_1, c_2, \cdots, c_n) = y)$ where $\{c_1, c_2, \cdots, c_n\}$ is a random sequence of challenges.*

Proposition 1. *Let y be the sequence sent by the adversary in advance, then the success probability in the distance fraud is $\frac{|I_y|}{2^n}$.*

So, the adversary strategy is pretty clear, she must find and send a sequence $y \in \{0,1\}^n$, such that for any sequence $x \in \{0,1\}^n$ it holds that $|I_y| \geq |I_x|$.

Theorem 2. *Given $x, y \in \{0,1\}^n$ two random sequences, and a prover function f, then, for any sequence $z \in \{0,1\}^n$ such that $I_z \neq \emptyset$ we have:*

$$\Pr(x \in I_z) \leq \frac{\frac{1}{2^n} + \sqrt{\frac{1}{2^{2n}} - \frac{4}{2^n} + 4\Pr(f(x) = f(y))}}{2}$$

Proof. Given that $I_z \neq \emptyset$, we have:

$$\Pr(f(x) = f(y)) = \Pr(f(x) = f(y)|y \in I_z) \Pr(y \in I_z)$$
$$+ \Pr(f(x) = f(y)|y \notin I_z) \Pr(y \notin I_z) \quad (10)$$

But, $\Pr(f(x) = f(y)|y \in I_z) = \Pr(x \in I_z) = \Pr(y \in I_z)$ because x and y are random sequences. On the other hand, $\Pr(f(x) = f(y)|y \notin I_z) \geq \frac{1}{2^n}$ because of the "prover function" definition. Therefore, using these results in Equation 10:

$$\Pr(f(x) = f(y)) \geq \Pr(x \in I_z)^2 + \frac{1}{2^n}(1 - \Pr(x \in I_z)) . \quad (11)$$

Calculating the discriminant of this quadratic inequality, and obtaining its solutions, we conclude the proof. Note that, this quadratic inequality has real solutions because $\Pr(f(x) = f(y)) \geq \frac{1}{2^n}$, and in this case, the discriminant value is always positive. $\qquad \square$

Corollary 2. *For every distance-bounding protocol that complies with Definition 3, the adversary success probability in the distance fraud is upper bounded by:*

$$\frac{\frac{1}{2^n} + \sqrt{\frac{1}{2^{2n}} - \frac{4}{2^n} + 4\Pr(f(x) = f(y))}}{2}.$$

With this last result, we are giving a way to compute an upper bound of a sub-family of the distance-bounding protocols. We show below how it is possible to apply this result to the graph-based protocol, and later we apply the same result for the ATP protocol.

Theorem 3. *The distance fraud success probability for the graph-based protocol is upper bounded by:*

$$\frac{\frac{1}{2^n} + \sqrt{\frac{1}{2^{2n}} - \frac{4}{2^n} + 4p}}{2}.$$

where

$$p = \prod_{i=1}^{i=n} \left(\frac{1}{2} + \frac{1}{2^{2i+1}} \sum_{k=0}^{k=2n-1} (A^i[0,k])^2 \right).$$

Proof. Let considered two random sequences $x = \{x_1, x_2, \cdots, x_n\}$ and $y = \{y_1, y_2, \cdots, y_n\}$, then by the definition of the graph-based protocol and the definition of "Prover Function":

$$\Pr(f(x) = f(y)) = \prod_{i=1}^{i=n} \Pr(\Omega(x_1, \cdots, x_i) = \Omega(y_1, \cdots, y_i)). \tag{12}$$

Let be $q_{x_i} = \Omega(x_1, \cdots, x_i)$ and $q_{y_i} = \Omega(y_1, \cdots, y_i)$, then, like in Theorem1, we can obtain that:

$$\Pr(q_{x_i} = q_{y_i}) = \frac{1}{2} + \frac{\Pr(x_i = y_i)}{2}. \tag{13}$$

and

$$\Pr(x_i = y_i) = \sum_{k=0}^{k=2n-1} \Pr(x_i = k)\Pr(y_i = k). \tag{14}$$

Once again, as $A^i[j,k]$ represents the number of walks of size i between the nodes j and k, where A is the adjacency matrix of the graph, then $\Pr(x_i = k) = \frac{A^i[0,k]}{2^i} = \Pr(y_i = k)$. Therefore, using Equation 14:

$$\Pr(x_i = y_i) = \sum_{k=0}^{k=2n-1} \left(\frac{A^i[0,k]}{2^i} \right)^2. \tag{15}$$

Equations 12, 13, and 15, yield to:

$$\Pr(f(x) = f(y)) = \prod_{i=1}^{i=n} \left(\frac{1}{2} + \frac{1}{2^{2i+1}} \sum_{k=0}^{k=2n-1} (A^i[0,k])^2 \right). \tag{16}$$

Applying Equation 16 to Corollary 2, considering that $p = \Pr(f(x) = f(y))$, we conclude the proof of this theorem.   □

5   Comparison

In this paper we are analyzing three parameters: mafia fraud, distance fraud and memory consumption. Therefore, we need these values for each of the previous considered protocols. Unfortunately, the computation of the mafia fraud success probability for KAP protocol [7] is not correct, but in Appendix A we provide a correct calculation. On the other hand, as we previously said, ATP distance fraud success probability was not presented in [3], nevertheless, in Appendix B we give a distance fraud upper bound for this protocol exactly as we did with the graph-based protocol.

Table 1. This table depicts the values of the three parameters (memory, mafia fraud success probability and distance fraud success probability), for the HKP protocol, the KAP protocol, the ATP protocols (ATP and ATP3), and the graph-based protocol (GRAPH)

	Memory	Mafia Fraud	Distance Fraud
HKP	$2n$ [6]	$\left(\frac{3}{4}\right)^n$ [6]	$\left(\frac{3}{4}\right)^n$ [2]
KAP	$4n$ [7]	Appendix A	$\left(\frac{3}{4} + \frac{p_d}{4}\right)^n$ [7]
ATP	$2^{n+1} - 2$ [3]	$\left(\frac{1}{2}\right)^n \left(\frac{n}{2} + 1\right)$ [3]	Appendix B
ATP3	$\frac{14n}{3}$ [3]	$\left(\frac{1}{2}\right)^n \left(\frac{5}{2}\right)^{\frac{n}{3}}$ [3]	$(0.3999)^{\frac{n}{3}}$ [3]
GRAPH	$4n$	Corollary 1	Theorem 3

Since we consider memory consumption as a main concern in distance-bounding protocols, we relax the ATP protocol, as its authors propose, to fit with linear memory. Nevertheless, reducing the memory in ATP protocol, increases the adversary success probability for both type of fraud. Hence, we pick $\alpha = \frac{n}{3}$ in which case the memory consumption equals to $\frac{14n}{3} \approx 5n$ whereas the security is still ensured. Note that this memory consumption is in the range of the other studied protocol. This instance of the ATP protocol is named "ATP3".

Table 1 depicts the values of the three parameters for each protocols that we are considering. In terms of memory the Hancke and Kuhn protocol is, undoubtedly, the best protocol. As can be seen in Figure 6, when considering only mafia fraud resistance KAP and ATP protocols are the best ones. And only in terms of distance fraud, the lowest adversary success probability is reached by the ATP protocol (see Figure 7).

---

[2] The distance fraud probability for the HKP protocol is computed using the distance fraud probability in the KAP protocol. Note that, the KAP protocol with $p_d = 0$ and the HKP protocol are the same.

[3] The distance fraud probability for the ATP3 protocol is the accurate value and not an upper bound like in ATP or GRAPH protocols. It was computed by brute force, i.e. for a given instance, we computed the adversary success probability. Then, considering all the possible instance we deduce the probability in the average case.

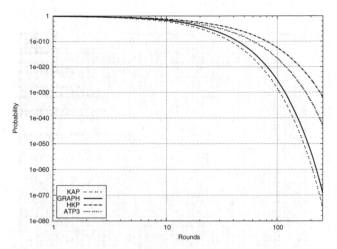

Fig. 6. In this figure we show the mafia fraud probability achieved by the GRAPH protocol, HKP protocol , and ATP3 protocol. The ATP protocol in its standard configuration is not presented in this chart because it has the same mafia fraud probability than the KAP protocol.

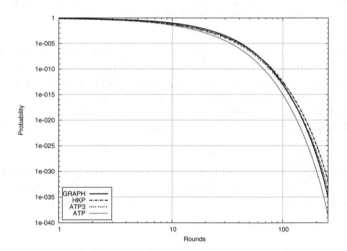

Fig. 7. In this figure we show the distance fraud probability achieved by the GRAPH protocol, HKP protocol, and the ATP protocols (ATP and ATP3). The KAP protocol was not presented in this chart because in the best case has the same distance fraud probability than the HKP protocol.

However, our interest is finding the best protocol given a security level in terms of mafia fraud and distance fraud. Therefore, Figure 8 depicts for each configuration (mafia and distance), the protocol needing a lower number of rounds to reach these security values. As it can be seen in Figure 8, the graph-based protocol is, in general, the best protocol when considering memory consumption, distance, and mafia fraud at the same time. In particular, if one requires low success probabilities

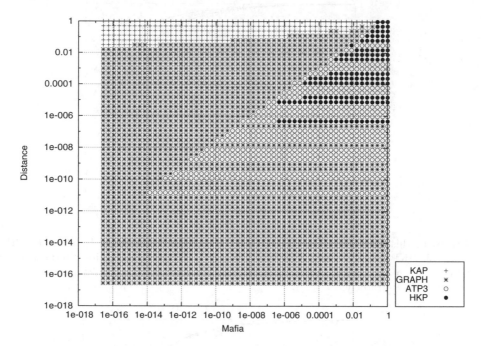

Fig. 8. In this figure we show the best protocol in terms of number of rounds given different values of mafia fraud probability and distance fraud probability. The considered protocols are: the graph-based protocol (GRAPH), the Hancke and Kuhn's protocol (HKP), the Kim and Avoine's protocol (KAP), and the Avoine and Tchamkerten's protocol (ATP3). The ATP protocol in its standard configuration is not considered in this chart because we are comparing only protocols with linear memory consumption.

for both mafia and distance fraud, we stress out the particularly good behavior of the graph-based protocol. Note that in some cases more than one protocol is optimal in terms of number of rounds, in this case the best in terms of memory is chosen.

6   Conclusions and Remarks

In this paper we take a step forward in the parameters (mafia fraud, distance fraud, and memory) for the distance-bounding protocols. In particular, we provide a way to compute an upper bound on the distance-fraud probability, which is useful for analyzing previous protocols and designing future ones. In addition, we propose a new distance-bounding protocol, and we show that the achieved security level is better than all previously published papers when considering the three parameters at the same time.

This paper do not only provide a simple, fast, and flexible protocol, but it also introduces the graph-based protocol concept and new open questions along with.

First of all, an interesting question is to know if there are graph-based protocols that behave still better than the one presented here. In particular, if the number of rounds is not a critical parameter, prover and verifier may be allowed to increase the number of rounds while keeping a 2n-node graph. This means that some nodes may be used twice. In such a case, the security analysis provided in this paper must be refined. On the other hand, although a bound on the distance fraud success probability is provided, calculating the exact probability of success is still cumbersome.

Acknowledgments. This work is partially funded by the Spanish Government through projects TSI2007-65406-C03-01 "E-AEGIS" and CONSOLIDER INGE-NIO 2010 CSD2007-00004 "ARES", by the Government of Catalonia under grant 2009 SGR 1135, and by the Walloon Region Marshall plan through the SPW DG06 Project TRASILUX.

The authors thank to Chong Hee Kim for his support in the computation of the adversary mafia fraud probability for the Kim and Avoine's protocol [7], Tania Martin for her precious help, Pierre François and Juan A. Rodríguez for the interesting discussions about graphs.

References

1. ISO/IEC 11770: Information technology – security techniques – key management
2. ISO/IEC 9798: Information technology – security techniques – entity authentication
3. Avoine, G., Tchamkerten, A.: An efficient distance bounding RFID authentication protocol: balancing false-acceptance rate and memory requirement. In: Samarati, P., Yung, M., Martinelli, F., Ardagna, C.A. (eds.) ISC 2009. LNCS, vol. 5735, pp. 250–261. Springer, Heidelberg (2009)
4. Brands, S., Chaum, D.: Distance-bounding protocols. In: Helleseth, T. (ed.) EUROCRYPT 1993. LNCS, vol. 765, pp. 344–359. Springer, Heidelberg (1994)
5. Desmedt, Y., Goutier, C., Bengio, S.: Special uses and abuses of the fiat-shamir passport protocol. In: Pomerance, C. (ed.) CRYPTO 1987. LNCS, vol. 293, pp. 21–39. Springer, Heidelberg (1988)
6. Hancke, G., Kuhn, M.: An RFID Distance Bounding Protocol. In: Conference on Security and Privacy for Emerging Areas in Communication Networks, SecureComm 2005, Athens, Greece, pp. 67–73. IEEE Computer Society Press, Los Alamitos (September 2005)
7. Kim, C.H., Avoine, G.: RFID Distance Bounding Protocol with Mixed Challenges to Prevent Relay Attacks. In: Garay, J.A., Miyaji, A., Otsuka, A. (eds.) CANS 2009. LNCS, vol. 5888, pp. 119–133. Springer, Heidelberg (2009)
8. Kim, C.H., Avoine, G., Koeune, F., Standaert, F.-X., Pereira, O.: The Swiss-Knife RFID Distance Bounding Protocol. In: Lee, P.J., Cheon, J.H. (eds.) ICISC 2008. LNCS, vol. 5461, pp. 98–115. Springer, Heidelberg (2009)
9. Munilla, J., Ortiz, A., Peinado, A.: Distance Bounding Protocols with Void-Challenges for RFID. In: Workshop on RFID Security, RFIDSec 2006, Graz, Austria (July 2006) Ecrypt
10. Munilla, J., Peinado, A.: Security Analysis of Tu and Piramuthu's Protocol. In: New Technologies, Mobility and Security, NTMS 2008, Tangier, Morocco, pp. 1–5. IEEE Computer Society Press, Los Alamitos (November 2008)

11. Reid, J., Neito, J.G., Tang, T., Senadji, B.: Detecting relay attacks with timing based protocols. In: Bao, F., Miller, S. (eds.) Proceedings of the 2nd ACM Symposium on Information, Computer and Communications Security, ASIACCS 2007, Singapore, Republic of Singapore, pp. 204–213. ACM Press, New York (March 2007)
12. Tu, Y.-J., Piramuthu, S.: RFID Distance Bounding Protocols. In: First International EURASIP Workshop on RFID Technology, Vienna, Austria (September 2007)

Appendix

A   Mafia Fraud Success Probability for KAP [7]

In the Kim and Avoine protocol the adversary success probability in the mafia fraud depends on the predefined challenges probability (p_d). Let:

- L_i be the event that the adversary win the i-th round.
- D_i be the event that the adversary is detected in the i-th round by the tag for the first time.
- N_i be the event that the adversary is detected by the tag in the i-th round, and N the event that the adversary is never detected.

Remark 3. The notation $\bar{A}$ represents the complement of the event A.

By the law of total probability:

$$P(\text{success}) = \sum_{i=1}^{i=n} \Pr(\text{success}|D_i)\Pr(D_i) + \Pr(\text{success}|N)\Pr(N) . \qquad (17)$$

As $\Pr(N_i) = \frac{p_d}{2}$, then:

$$\Pr(N) = (1 - \frac{p_d}{2})^n . \qquad (18)$$

The probability of being detected in the i-th round for the first time is:

$$\Pr(D_i) = \prod_{j=1}^{j=i-1} \Pr(\bar{N}_j)\Pr(N_i) = \left(\frac{2 - p_d}{2}\right)^{i-1}\left(\frac{p_d}{2}\right) . \qquad (19)$$

On the other hand:

$$\Pr(\text{success}|D_i) = \prod_{j=1}^{j=i-1} \Pr(L_j|\bar{N}_j)\prod_{j=i}^{j=n} \Pr(L_j|N_j) \qquad (20)$$

where $\Pr(L_j|N_j) = \frac{1}{2}$ and:

$$\Pr(L_j|\bar{N}_j) = \frac{\Pr(L_j \cap \bar{N}_j)}{\Pr(\bar{N}_j)} . \qquad (21)$$

where $\Pr(L_j \cap \bar{N}_j) = \Pr(L_j \cap \bar{N}_j|p_d)p_d + \Pr(L_j \cap \bar{N}_j|p_r)p_r$. But, $\Pr(L_j \cap \bar{N}_j|p_d) = \frac{1}{2}$ because the adversary must send the correct challenges c_j in this round. And,

$\Pr(L_j \cap \bar{N}_j | p_r) = \frac{3}{4}$ because this is the same case as in Hancke and Kuhn protocol. Therefore, $\Pr(L_j \cap \bar{N}_j) = \frac{1}{2}p_d + \frac{3}{4}p_r = \frac{3-p_d}{4}$. Using this result in Equation 21:

$$\Pr(L_j | \bar{N}_j) = \frac{3 - p_d}{4 - 2p_d} . \tag{22}$$

using Equation 20, and 22:

$$\Pr(\text{success} | D_i) = \left(\frac{3 - p_d}{4 - 2p_d} \right)^{i-1} \left(\frac{1}{2} \right)^{n-i+1}, \tag{23}$$

and

$$\Pr(\text{success} | N) = \left(\frac{3 - p_d}{4 - 2p_d} \right)^{n} . \tag{24}$$

Using the equations 17, 18, 19, 23 and 24 we obtain the adversary success probability for the mafia fraud in the Kim and Avoine protocol:

$$P(\text{success}) = \frac{p_d}{2} \sum_{i=1}^{i=n} \left(\frac{3 - p_d}{4} \right)^{i-1} \left(\frac{1}{2} \right)^{n-i+1} + \left(\frac{3 - p_d}{4} \right)^{n} . \tag{25}$$

B   Distance Fraud Success Probability for ATP [3]

To find an upper bound of the adversary success probability in the distance fraud for the ATP protocol, we use the result of the Theorem 3. Indeed, this protocol has the same behavior than the graph-based protocol. The only difference between them is that the ATP protocol create a full tree as graph. Therefore, in ATP protocol the distance fraud success probability is upper bounded by:

$$\frac{\frac{1}{2^n} + \sqrt{\frac{1}{2^{2n}} - \frac{4}{2^n} + 4p}}{2},$$

where

$$p = \prod_{i=1}^{i=n} \left(\frac{1}{2} + \frac{1}{2^{2i+1}} \sum_{k=0}^{k=2n-1} (A^i[0,k])^2 \right).$$

To give a complete equation, we define $A^i[0, k]$ for a tree. For this purpose, we consider that the nodes in the tree are labeled between 0 and $2^n - 1$ using a breadth-first algorithm, then:

$$A^i[0, k] = \begin{cases} 1 & \text{if } 2^i - 1 \leq k < 2^{i+1} - 1, \\ 0 & \text{otherwise.} \end{cases}$$

Finally we obtain:

$$p = \prod_{i=1}^{i=n} \left(\frac{1}{2} + \frac{1}{2^{i+1}} \right).$$

A Lightweight Implementation of Keccak Hash Function for Radio-Frequency Identification Applications

Elif Bilge Kavun and Tolga Yalcin

Department of Cryptography
Institute of Applied Mathematics, METU
Ankara, Turkey
{e168522,tyalcin}@metu.edu.tr

Abstract. In this paper, we present a lightweight implementation of the permutation *Keccak-f*[200] and *Keccak-f*[400] of the SHA-3 candidate hash function Keccak. Our design is well suited for radio-frequency identification (RFID) applications that have limited resources and demand lightweight cryptographic hardware. Besides its low-area and low-power, our design gives a decent throughput. To the best of our knowledge, it is also the first lightweight implementation of a sponge function, which differentiates it from the previous works. By implementing the new hash algorithm Keccak, we have utilized unique advantages of the sponge construction. Although the implementation is targeted for Application Specific Integrated Circuit (ASIC) platforms, it is also suitable for Field Programmable Gate Arrays (FPGA). To obtain a compact design, serialized data processing principles are exploited together with algorithm-specific optimizations. The design requires only 2.52K gates with a throughput of 8 Kbps at 100 KHz system clock based on 0.13-µm CMOS standard cell library.

Keywords: RFID, Keccak, SHA-3, sponge function, serialized processing, low-area, low-power, high throughput.

1 Introduction

In recent years, the developments on digital wireless technology have improved many areas such as the mobile systems. Mobile and embedded devices will be everywhere in times to come, making it possible to use communication services and other applications anytime and anywhere. Among these mobile devices, radio-frequency identification (RFID) tags offer low-cost, long battery life and unprecedented mobility [1-2]. Today, we see RFID tags everywhere, in electronic toll collection systems, product tracking systems, libraries, passports, etc. Due to this rise in the usage of RFID tags in the past few years, research activities were started in RFID security area and security challenges have been identified.

However, security of the RFID tags is a main concern. The autonomously interacting capability of these digital devices makes them inherently unsecure. The authentication of devices and privacy are among the major critical problems. As a result, new cryptographic protocols have been proposed to preserve user privacy,

S.B. Ors Yalcin (Ed.): RFIDSec 2010, LNCS 6370, pp. 258–269, 2010.
© Springer-Verlag Berlin Heidelberg 2010

authenticate the RFID tag communication and make it anonymous. Many works have been made on this subject, and most of them use symmetric cryptography because of the severe constraints for hardware implementations of RFID tags. In applications that demand low-cost and low-power such as RFID, the use of cryptographic functions requires the low gate count. To provide a low gate count in RFID tags, the researches have focused on block ciphers and hash functions. In [3] and [4], the use of block ciphers is discussed in more detail.

The compact realization of hash functions for RFID applications is still a major research subject. In [5], a lightweight implementation of the standard SHA-1 hash function is presented, while in [7] the hash function MAME, which is specifically designed for lightweight applications, was implemented at a very low gate count for protecting RFID tags. Our implementation differs from both via its unusual sponge construction, which offers a better gate count with a decent throughput value. We used two different permutations of SHA-3 candidate hash function Keccak - *Keccak-f*[200] and *Keccak-f*[400]. Keccak is based on sponge functions that use the sponge construction, and exploit all its advantages such as permutation-based structure, variable-length output, flexibility, functionality and security against generic attacks [6].

The paper is organized as follows: Section 2 and 3 briefly describe the sponge functions and Keccak, respectively. In Section 4, we present our serialized compact Keccak architecture and implementations of *Keccak-f*[200] and *Keccak-f*[400] for RFID applications. Section 5 summarizes the performance results for our implementations as well as comparison with straightforward parallel implementations. Section 6 is the conclusion.

2   Sponge Functions

Sponge functions can be used to generalize cryptographic hash functions to more general functions with arbitrary output lengths. They are based on the sponge construction, where the finite memory is modeled in a very simple way.

To specify the difference between the sponge functions and the sponge construction, we use the term sponge construction to define a fixed-length permutation for building a function that maps inputs of any length to arbitrary-length outputs and the term sponge functions for functions that are built using this sponge construction [8]. In section 2.1, the sponge construction will be explained.

2.1   The Sponge Construction

The sponge construction is a repetitive construction to build a function F with variable-length input and arbitrary-length output based on a fixed-length permutation f operating on a fixed number of b-bit, which is called the width. The sponge construction operates on a state of $b=r+c$ bits. r is called the bit rate and c is called the capacity. In the first step, the bits of the state are all initialized to zero. Then, the input message is padded and cut into blocks of r-bit. The construction consists of two phases, namely the absorbing phase and the squeezing phase.

In the absorbing phase, the r-bit input message blocks are XORed with the first r-bit of the state, then interleaved with the function f. After processing all of the message blocks, the squeezing phase begins.

In the squeezing phase, the first r-bit of the state is returned as output blocks, and then interleaved with the function f. The number of output blocks is chosen by the user. The block diagram of the sponge construction is shown in Figure 1.

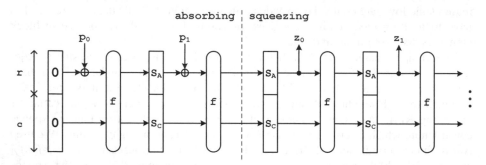

Fig. 1. The sponge construction: The sponge construction operates on a state of $b=r+c$ bits. The value r is called the *bitrate* and the value c the *capacity*.

The least significant c-bit of the state is never directly affected by the input blocks and never output during the squeezing phase. The capacity c determines the attainable security level of the construction. In sponge functions, indifferentiability framework [9] is used to assess the security of the construction. In [10], the expected complexity resistance level was approximated by the expression $2^{c/2}$. This value is independent of the output length. For example, the collisions of a random sponge which has output length shorter than c-bit, has the same expected complexity as a random source.

The sponge construction provides many advantages with its permutation-based structure, variable-length output and security against generic attacks. In addition, it has flexibility to choose the adequate bit rate/capacity values while using the same permutation and it is functional because it can also be used as a stream cipher, deterministic pseudorandom bit generator or mask generating function with its long output and proven security bounds to generic attacks properties.

3 Keccak

Keccak [11] is a cryptographic hash function submitted to the NIST SHA-3 hash function competition by Guido Bertoni, Joan Daemen, Michaël Peeters and Gilles Van Assche. Keccak is a family of hash functions that are based on the sponge construction and used as a building block of a permutation from a set of seven permutations. The basic component is the *Keccak-f* permutation, which consists of a number of simple rounds with logical operations and bit permutations.

3.1 The Structure of Keccak

The fundamental function of Keccak is a permutation chosen from a set of seven *Keccak-f* permutations, denoted by *Keccak-f[b]*, where $b \in \{25,50,100,200,400, 800,1600\}$ is the width of the permutation. The width b of the permutation is also the width of the state in the sponge construction. The state is organized as an array of 5×5 lanes, each of length w-bits, where $w \in \{1,2,4,8,16,32,64\}$, ($b=25w$). The $Keccak[r,c,d]$ sponge function can be obtained by applying the sponge construction to $Keccak\text{-}f[r+c]$ with the parameters capacity c, bit rate r and diversifier d and also padding the message input specifically. The pseudo-code of $Keccak\text{-}f$ is given in Algorithm 1. The number of rounds n_r depends on the permutation width which is calculated by $n_r = 12+2 \times l$, where $2^l = w$. This yields 12, 14, 16, 18, 20, 22, 24 rounds for $Keccak\text{-}f[25]$, $Keccak\text{-}f[50]$, $Keccak\text{-}f[100]$, $Keccak\text{-}f[200]$, $Keccak\text{-}f[400]$, $Keccak\text{-}f[800]$, $Keccak\text{-}f[1600]$, respectively.

Algorithm 1. Pseudo-code of $Keccak\text{-}f$

$Keccak - f[b](A)\{$

$for\ i\ in\ 0\ \dots\ n_r - 1$

  $A = Round[b](A, RC[i])$

$return\ A$

$\}$

$Round[b](A, RC)\ \{$

$\theta\ step:$

  $C[x]\quad = A[x,0] \oplus A[x,1] \oplus A[x,2] \oplus A[x,3] \oplus A[x,4],\quad \forall x\ in\ 0\dots4$

  $D[x]\quad = C[x-1] \oplus ROT(C[x+1],1),\qquad\qquad\quad \forall x\ in\ 0\dots4$

  $A[x,y] = A[x,y] \oplus D[x],\qquad\qquad\qquad\qquad\quad \forall(x,y)\ in\ (0\dots4,0\dots4)$

$\rho\ and\ \pi\ steps:$

  $B[y,2x+3y] = ROT(A[x,y],r[x,y]),\qquad\qquad\quad \forall(x,y)\ in\ (0\dots4,0\dots4)$

$\chi\ step:$

  $A[x,y] = B[x,y] \oplus ((NOT\ B[x+1,y])\ AND\ B[x+2,y]),\quad \forall(x,y)\ in\ (0\dots4,0\dots4)$

$\iota\ step:$

  $A[0,0] = A[0,0] \oplus RC$

$return\ A$

$\}$

In Algorithm 1, all of the operations on the indices are done in modulo 5. A denotes the complete permutation state array, and $A[x,y]$ denotes a particular lane in that state. $B[x,y]$, $C[x]$, $D[x]$ are intermediate variables, the constants $r[x,y]$ are the rotation offsets and $RC[i]$ are the round constants. $rot(w,r)$ is the bitwise cyclic shift operation which moves the bit from position i into position $i+r$, in the modulo lane size.

The pseudo-code of the sponge function $Keccak[r,c,d]$ is given in Algorithm 2, again with parameters capacity c, bit rate r and diversifier d. This description is restricted to the case of messages that span a whole number of bytes. For messages with a number of bits not dividable by 8, the details are given in [12]. In the algorithm, S denotes the state as an array of lanes. The padded message P is organized as an array of blocks P_i. The operator $\parallel$ denotes the byte string concatenation.

Algorithm 2. Pseudo-code of the sponge function $Keccak[r,c,d]$

$Keccak[r,c,d](M)\{$

    Initialization and padding:

        $S[x, y] = 0,$ $\forall(x, y)$ in $(0...4, 0...4)$

        $P = M \parallel 0x01 \parallel byte(d) \parallel byte(r / 8) \parallel 0x01 \parallel 0x00 \parallel ... \parallel 0x00$

    Absorbing phase:

        $\forall$ block P_i in P

            $S[x, y] = S[x, y] \oplus P[x+5y],$ $\forall(x, y)$ such that $(x+5y) < (r / w)$

            $S = Keccak - f[r+c](S)$

    Squeezing phase:

        $Z = empty\ string$

        while output is requested

            $Z = Z \parallel S[x, y],$ $\forall(x, y)$ such that $(x+5y) < (r / w)$

            $S = Keccak - f[r+c](S)$

    return Z

$\}$

---

4 Lightweight Keccak

Fast and parallel implementations of the Keccak have already been reported [13-14]. The main components in these implementations are the *Keccak-f* round function module and the state register. Sizes of both modules depend on the choice of width, b, of the *Keccak-f[b]* permutation. In the official SHA-3 proposal, this width is chosen to be 1600 [11]. In a fully parallel implementation, this corresponds to a minimum gate count of 1600 flip-flops, 1600 inverters, 1600 AND gates, and 4864 XOR gates. Table 1 lists the equivalent gate counts for fully parallel implementations of *Keccak-f[1600]* and a few other SHA-3 candidates. Only the ones with the lowest gate counts are listed for convenience. As seen from the table, the gate count for a fully parallel implementation of Keccak is beyond the acceptable numbers for a lightweight implementation [15].

    The gate count can be lowered by a serialized implementation, where the internal state is kept in a RAM based memory instead of registers, and a single datapath serves as the *Keccak-f* round function module, processing one lane at a time. However, such an approach is not really applicable to the Keccak round function. Both θ and χ steps require data from 3 lanes on the x-axis to compute a single lane data, whereas π transposes lanes on the y-axis to x-axis after shuffling their locations. Each of these operations will require several temporary storage registers in addition to the state

RAM. It would also be practical to replace the *Keccak-f* datapath with a simple arithmetic-logic unit, resulting in a micro-processor rather than a dedicated hardware. The number of cycles required to complete the processing of all lanes will be rather large.

Table 1. Area comparison for parallel (fast) implementation of SHA-3 candidates

Function	Area (KGE)
BLAKE-32	45.64
CubeHash16/32-h	58.87
Fugue-256	46.25
Grøstl-256	58.40
Hamsi-256	58.66
JH-256	58.83
Keccak-256	**56.32**
Luffa-224/256	44.97
Shabal-256	54.19
SHAvite-3	57.39
Skein-256-256	58.61

The RAM can be replaced with flip-flop based registers, making it possible to reach more than a single lane at a time. However, this time register cost will be equal to that of a parallel implementation, since the internal state size is independent of implementation strategy.

Variable permutation width characteristic of Keccak, together with the low data rate requirements of lightweight hash functions, presents us with an alternative solution to deal with the large internal state size. We can choose a Keccak permutation with a lower data width, without altering the overall structure of the *Keccak-f*[b] permutation.

4.1 Serialized *Keccak* Architecture

We propose the serialized architecture given in Figure 2 for our lightweight Keccak implementations. The architecture utilizes area advantages of serialized processing to the full extend. Data is processed in lanes (1/25 of the whole state). The state (circled) registers numbered 24-0 are used to store the internal state, while the four summation registers (rightmost registers numbered 4-0) store the row sums. The operational blocks which implement step of a Keccak round are the θ, ρ, π, χ and ι-modules. All of these modules, except for the π-module, operate on a single lane, reducing the combinational gate count drastically. π-step is executed in parallel on all 25 lanes. However, since it is just a fixed permutation operation, its only area cost comes from the additional multiplexers and routing. There is an additional area cost caused by the sum registers, required for the θ-step, and the two temporary registers, required for the χ-step. These extra registers are well compensated by the huge area saving caused by the serialized processing and the resulting single lane combinational blocks.

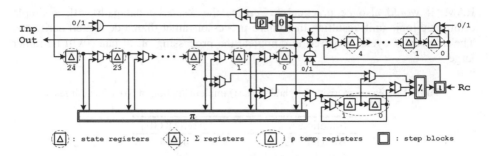

Fig. 2. Serialized Keccak architecture

In the first phase of each Keccak round, data is written in lanes into the state registers column by column while each row sum is accumulated in the sum registers in parallel. The first incoming lane is *lane*(0,0) and shifted into *state_register*[24] while *sum_register*[4] is initialized to the same value. The next incoming data is *lane* (1,0); it is shifted into *state_register*[24], *state_register*[24] into *state_register*[23]. At the same time, *sum_register*[4] is shifted into *sum_register*[3], and *sum_register*[4] is re-initialized with *lane*(1,0). At the end of the first 5 cycles, the first 5 lanes of data are in *state_registers*[24] to [20], while *sum_registers*[4] to [0] have the first column lanes of each corresponding column. In the following cycles, incoming lane data are added on to sum registers and shifted into the state registers, so that at the end of the first 25 cycles, state registers contain the full state and sum registers contain the row sums.

Starting with the next cycle, θ and ρ operations are run in parallel on each lane starting with *lane*(0,0), continuing with *lane*(1,0), *lane*(2,0), …, all the way to *lane*(4,4), covering the whole state. This phase is completed in 25 cycles. It is followed by another 25 cycles, where π, χ and ι operations are performed. π can only be executed on the whole state, therefore done in parallel with the calculation of χ for the very first lane. ι operation (round constant addition) is also done in the same cycle. In the following 24 cycles, χ operation are performed on the remaining lanes, completing the first round. We name each of these 25 cycles as "half rounds".

As an additional optimization, the row summations for the following round are also performed in parallel with π, χ and ι operations of the current round. In average, a full round takes 50 cycles to complete. The very first half round (half round "0") is used for the "absorption" of the first input block, while the following input block absorptions can be done during the second half round of each last round. The final half round (following the last input block) is used for "squeezing" of the message digest. This scheme is illustrated in Figure 3.

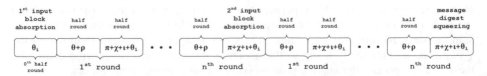

Fig. 3. Serialized Keccak data processing rounds

The whole data processing in each half round is explained by a tweaked version of Keccak, where there are 3×3 lanes in Figures 4 and 5. In our implementation, we apply the same timing to the actual 5×5 lanes configuration.

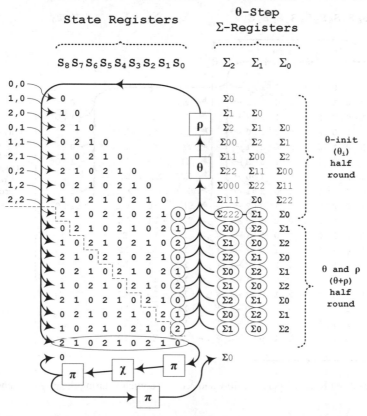

Fig. 4. Serialized Keccak operation flow and register contents during the θ-init and θ+ρ half cycles

4.2 *Keccak-f[200]* and *Keccak-f[400]* Implementations

Our first lightweight candidate is *Keccak-f[200]*. In this configuration, the lane width is chosen as 8-bits (2^l, where $l=3$) in accordance with the definition of Keccak [11]. The target message digest size is 64-bits. This corresponds to a capacity, c, value of 128-bits, limiting the highest achievable data rate, r, to 72-bits (200-128).

Our second candidate is *Keccak-f[400]*, where the lane width is chosen as 16-bits ($l=4$). The target message digest size is 128-bits, resulting in a capacity value of 256-bits and data rate of 144-bits (400-256).

We have implemented both candidates using the serialized architecture presented in section 4.1, as well as using a fully parallel straightforward approach for a fair comparison. In addition, we have also implemented the original Keccak configuration (*Keccak-f[1600]*) using both the serialized and fully parallel architectures in order to demonstrate the compactness of our architecture. The comparison results and performance figures are presented in section 5.

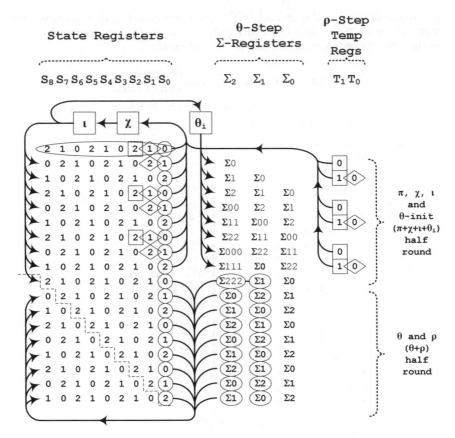

Fig. 5. Serialized Keccak operation flow and register contents during the $\pi+\chi+\iota+\theta_i$ and $\theta+\rho$ half cycles

In addition to their lane widths, the two implementations also differ in the total number of rounds. According to the Keccak specification, the total number of rounds is specified as $12+2l$, corresponding to 18 and 20 rounds for *Keccak-f*[200] and *Keccak-f*[400], respectively.

The sponge construction of Keccak hash function makes it possible to use *Keccak-f*[200] for message digests longer than 72-bits via consecutive squeezes. However, such a usage will add extra rounds to the overall hashing operation, which may be effective especially for short message lengths. Instead, we fix our functions and their respective message digest sizes, resulting in *Keccak-f*[200]-64 and *Keccak-f*[400]-128 lightweight hash functions.

We rely on our own statistical analyses as well as the security claims in the Keccak proposal for the security of these two hash function implementations. Furthermore, we assume that 64 and 128-bit message digest sizes are sufficient for RFID applications making our proposed variations and serialized architecture ideal lightweight hash functions.

5 Implementation and Performance Results

We have realized both straightforward parallel implementations and serialized implementations (using our proposed architecture) of Keccak for lane widths of 8-bits ($l=3$), 16-bits ($l=4$) and 64-bits ($l=6$), corresponding to Keccak-f[200], Keccak-f[400] and Keccak-f[1600], respectively, on a standard 0.13μm digital CMOS technology. The corresponding gate counts, throughput values and power consumptions are listed in Table 2. Additionally, we compare our lightweight candidates with MAME [7], a hash function specifically designed for lightweight applications, and a compact SHA-1 [5] implementation in Table 3.

Table 2. Performance comparison for parallel and serialized Keccak implementations

	Hash output size	Data path size	Input data size	Cycles per block	T/put at 100 KHz (Kbps)	Area (KGE)	Efficiency (bps/GE)	Power cons. (μW/MHz)
Parallel Keccak-f[1600]	256	64	1088	24	4533	47.63	95.40	315.1
Parallel Keccak-f[400]	128	16	144	20	720	10.56	68.18	78.1
Parallel Keccak-f[200]	64	8	72	18	400	4.9	81.63	27.6
Serial Keccak-f[1600]	**256**	**64**	**1088**	**1200**	**90.66**	**20.79**	**4.36**	**44.9**
Serial Keccak-f[800] (estimate)	**128**	**32**	**544**	**1100**	**49.45**	**13.00**	**3.80**	**28.2**
Serial Keccak-f[400]	**128**	**16**	**144**	**1000**	**14.4**	**5.09**	**2.83**	**11.5**
Serial Keccak-f[200]	**64**	**8**	**72**	**900**	**8**	**2.52**	**3.17**	**5.6**

Table 3. Performance comparison for lightweight Keccak implementation against MAME and SHA-1

	Hash output size	T/put at 100 KHz (Kbps)	Area (KGE)	Efficiency (bps/GE)
SHA-1 [5]	160	148.8	5.53	26.91
MAME [7]	256	146.7	8.1	18.10
Serialized Keccak-f[400]	**128**	**14.4**	**5.09**	**2.83**
Serialized Keccak-f[200]	**64**	**8**	**2.52**	**3.17**

The figures depict both the throughput and area drop in the serialized architecture. The throughput drop is much more drastic due to the extra cycles coming from the serialization. However, it should be noted that we are more interested in lower areas in lightweight applications, which only demand acceptable figures for throughput [16]. In that respect, even our more secure lightweight candidate Keccak-f[400]-128 offers a throughput of 14.4 Kbps at 100 KHz system clock, which is deemed acceptable for RFID applications, while occupying only 5.09KGE. In case, higher throughput is targeted at the expense of area, it is also possible to implement Keccak-f[800] using our serialized architecture, which gives an estimated throughput of 49.45 Kbps occupying 13KGE.

6 Conclusion

In this study, we have presented a pipelined serialized architecture for the SHA-3 candidate Keccak, which offers very low area and power consumption with acceptable throughput. Our architecture is especially attractive for lightweight applications when implemented with compact versions of Keccak. With its flexible structure, our architecture is very easy to modify for faster versions, at the expense of increased area. Lane-based processing can easily be turned into row or column based processing, raising the throughput by a factor of 5, while the estimated area increase is only about 50 percent. We have also shown that even straightforward parallel implementations of compact versions of Keccak offer acceptable areas (4.9KGE for parallel *Keccak-f*[200]) with very high data rates (400 Kbps at 100 KHz system clock).

References

1. European Commission, Draft Recommendation on the Implementation of Privacy, Data Protection and Information Security Principles in Applications Supported by Radio Frequency Identification (RFID),
   http://ec.europa.eu/yourvoice/ipm/forms/dispatch?form=RFIDRec
2. Finkenzeller, K.: RFID Handbook. John Wiley, Chichester (2003)
3. Feldhofer, M., Dominikus, S., Wolkerstorfer, J.: Strong Authentication for RFID Systems using the AES Algorithm. In: Joye, M., Quisquater, J.-J. (eds.) CHES 2004. LNCS, vol. 3156, pp. 357–370. Springer, Heidelberg (2004)
4. Rolfes, C., Poschmann, A., Leander, G., Paar, C.: Ultra-Lightweight Implementations for Smart Devices - Security for 1000 Gate Equivalents. In: Grimaud, G., Standaert, F.-X. (eds.) CARDIS 2008. LNCS, vol. 5189, pp. 89–103. Springer, Heidelberg (2008)
5. O'Neill, M.: Low-Cost SHA-1 Hash Function Architecture for RFID Tags. In: Proceedings of RFIDSec (2008)
6. The KECCAK sponge function family, http://keccak.noekeon.org
7. Yoshida, H., Watanabe, D., Okeya, K., Kitahara, J., Wu, H., Kucuk, O., Preneel, B.: MAME: A compression function with reduced hardware requirements. In: Paillier, P., Verbauwhede, I. (eds.) CHES 2007. LNCS, vol. 4727, pp. 148–165. Springer, Heidelberg (2007)
8. Bertoni, G., Daemen, J., Peeters, M., Van Assche, G.: ponge Functions. In: Ecrypt Hash Workshop (2007)
9. Maurer, U., Renner, R., Holenstein, C.: Indifferentiability, impossibility results on reductions, and applications to the random oracle methodology. In: Naor, M. (ed.) TCC 2004. LNCS, vol. 2951, pp. 21–39. Springer, Heidelberg (2004)
10. Bertoni, G., Daemen, J., Peeters, M., Van Assche, G.: On the Indifferentiability of the Sponge Construction. In: Smart, N.P. (ed.) EUROCRYPT 2008. LNCS, vol. 4965, pp. 181–197. Springer, Heidelberg (2008)
11. Bertoni, G., Daemen, J., Peeters, M., Van Assche, G.: Keccak sponge function family main document. NIST (2009) (submission to)
12. Bertoni, G., Daemen, J., Peeters, M., Van Assche, G.: Keccak specifications, version 2, NIST (2009) (submission to)

13. Tillich, S., et al.: High-Speed Hardware Implementations of BLAKE, BMW, CubeHash, ECHO, Fugue, Grostl, Hamsi, JH, Keccak, Luffa, Shabal, SHAvite-3, SIMD, and Skein. In: Cryptography ePrint (November 2009)

14. Namin, A.H., Hasan, M.A.: Hardware Implementation of the Compression Function for Selected SHA-3 Candidates, CACR 2009-28 (July 2009)

15. Feldhofer, M., Rechberger, C.: A Case Against Currently Used Hash Functions in RFID Protocols. In: Meersman, R., Tari, Z., Herrero, P. (eds.) OTM 2006 Workshops. LNCS, vol. 4277, pp. 372–381. Springer, Heidelberg (2006)

16. Bogdanov, A., Leander, G., Paar, C., Poschmann, A., Robshaw, M.J.B., Seurin, Y.: Hash Functions and RFID Tags: Mind The Gap. In: Oswald, E., Rohatgi, P. (eds.) CHES 2008. LNCS, vol. 5154, pp. 283–299. Springer, Heidelberg (2008)

Author Index

Printing: Mercedes-Druck, Berlin
Binding: Stein+Lehmann, Berlin